THE GLORIOUS DEAD

THE GLORIOUS DEAD

❊

FIGURATIVE SCULPTURE
OF
BRITISH FIRST WORLD WAR
MEMORIALS

Geoff Archer

MMIX

FRONTIER PUBLISHING

First Published 2009
Frontier Publishing
Kirstead
Norfolk NR15 1EG

Copyright © Geoff Archer 2009
All Rights Reserved

British Library Cataloguing in Publication Data
Archer, Geoff.
The glorious dead : figurative sculpture of British First
World War memorials.
1. World War, 1914-1918--Monuments--Great Britain.
2. Soldiers' monuments--Great Britain. 3. Public sculpture-
- Great Britain. 4. Figure sculpture--20th century. 5. War
memorials--Great Britain.
I. Title
731.7'6'0941-dc22

ISBN-13: 978 1 872914 38 1

Design frontier
www.frontierpublishing.co.uk

PRINTED IN GREAT BRITAIN
by MPG Biddles of Kings Lynn

CONTENTS

Pl.1.
Macclesfield.
John Millard,
1921

Introduction

Of the estimated tens of thousands of war memorials produced in Britain in the wake of the First World War literally hundreds featured figurative sculpture. Many were by relatively unknown, or entirely anonymous sculptors, others the work of the most reputable practitioners of the time. The memorial at Macclesfield in Cheshire was designed by John Millard, a sculptor not widely known in his lifetime and long since forgotten. It consists of three bronze figures arranged on an elaborate structure of Portland stone pedestal and plinth and is located in a small 'Garden of Remembrance', an essential and integral part of the scheme. This monument, 'In honour of Macclesfield men who gave their lives for King and Empire in the Great War 1914-1918',[1] was unveiled on 21 September 1921, less than three years after a war which had seen around three quarters of a million British men killed, with many more severely wounded. Some seven hundred of the dead, whose names are included on the monument, were from the Borough of Macclesfield.

It is appropriate that I start this study with reference to the Macclesfield memorial. I have lived in the town for over thirty years and the war memorial is within walking distance of my home. Although it is the only substantial example of public sculpture in the town, and certainly the most impressive, for many years I had paid it relatively little attention. But it was my growing interest in this monument and others like it which eventually led to a more detailed investigation, and ultimately to the wider study of memorial sculpture presented here.

It is only in recent years that the figurative sculpture of war memorials has received serious consideration in art historical discourse. But when art historians *have* discussed this subject it has often been with some disparagement. It is not unusual to read for example that 'the great demand for [First World War] memorials ... set back the cause of modern sculpture in this century for over a decade'.[2] This summary dismissal of what amounted to an unprecedented programme of public sculpture is clearly inadequate. Indeed, to echo the comments of Sarah Crellin, one art historian who *has* shown a sympathetic awareness of the sculpture of war memorials, to distinguish between 'modern' and memorial sculpture is to distort the definition of modern. Memorialisation was not merely an unavoidable employment opportunity which deferred the real business of sculptors; on the contrary, it represented, in the early 1920s, the most vital work to be done at that time. 'If the success of the avant-garde was delayed by the war', as Crellin puts it, 'it was of small consequence'.[3]

That war memorial sculpture was essentially traditional in style is undeniable. As became increasingly clear, the need to help mediate the grief of the bereaved rather than simply to commemorate victory and the sacrifice of the troops was of paramount importance. Whilst modernism could express the anger and despair of individuals, it could not easily provide appropriate ways of remembering which would enable the bereaved to come to terms with their losses. Modernism was seen, with some justification, as hostile to those traditional values in whose name the war had been waged, an acknowledgement of which fact was quite literally carved in stone on numerous memorials. Having been construed both before and during the war as positively Germanic, modernism seemed entirely inappropriate.[4]

For those critics impatient to have done with traditionalism and to condemn the work of artists born in the nineteenth century *to* the nineteenth century, there was little interest in an art which, by its very nature, involved a backward look. Furthermore, as Alan Borg, the former Director General of the Imperial War Museum, has acknowledged, 'Public art no longer seemed in tune with the spirit of the modern world, almost as if people could no longer believe that states which were responsible for producing such carnage could also produce genuine public reactions to war'.[5] However, as he goes on to say, and as I hope to show, 'There is much genuine feeling and much genuine artistic integrity in our war memorials, and many can stand comparison with the official art of the past'.[6]

Memorials to the battlefield dead, and sometimes also to those who fought and survived or who contributed in other ways at home and abroad, were erected by almost every town, village and parish in the country and by a wide range of institutions within these communities. The vast majority of memorials took the form of wall plaques with minimal decoration. Many more were in the form of obelisks or crosses.[7] Memorials can be found not only in public places erected by civic or military authorities but in private places of worship, work, recreation and sport, sometimes to a half dozen or fewer of citizens, parishioners, workers or club members (or indeed individuals) but often to hundreds whose names are most usually, and most importantly, listed there.

Intrinsic to the rituals of remembrance which took place around war memorials was an idealisation of the dead, frequently endorsed by figurative imagery which often appeared to ignore or contradict the realities of a war which had thrown into question the attitudes and

8

precepts of the Edwardian era which had inspired men to go to war and women to encourage them to do so. This idealisation was encouraged by the needs of the bereaved to symbolically replace absent bodies and a longing for a return to 'normality' which the years preceding the war were seen to represent. The unprecedented numbers of dead and the severity of injuries had placed considerable strains on the expected responses of men under fire. Furthermore, the changing roles of women, with their assimilation of what had until then been considered masculine attributes and their annexation of previously prohibited spheres, had created an additional destabilisation of traditional attitudes.

The representation and reinforcement of gender difference and the restoration of iconography and rhetoric of pre-war patriotism in many memorial statues seem to provide clear evidence of a post-war rehabilitation of pre-war ideals. However, memorial sculpture has been used throughout this book to illustrate not only pre-war constructs and their subsequent reinstatement, but the wartime destabilisation of those constructs. The figurative sculpture of memorials was overwhelmingly traditional but there was also, in many cases, some acknowledgement of the destabilising

Pl.2.
Macclesfield.
John Millard,
1921

effects and realities of modern warfare and it is this candour which distinguishes First World War memorials from those of earlier conflicts and which adds considerably to their potential to continue to impress.

The building of war memorials after the First World War represents the greatest single project of public art the country has ever seen.[8] Although many of the works discussed in the following pages are by sculptors such as George Frampton, Albert Toft or Goscombe John, already with well established reputations, there were others, such as Charles Sargeant Jagger or Gilbert Ledward, whose reputations were first formed by their work on war memorials. In addition, such was the volume of commissions in the decade after the end of the war that numerous memorials were designed and created by sculptors who, like John Millard at Macclesfield, are generally known, if at all, by name alone and largely, or solely, by their commemorative work produced at this time. Many more were produced by local monumental masons who adapted their usual practices in producing funerary monuments and who usually had no pretension to artistic fame or success.

Most of us are aware of such monuments and some continue to use them as they were originally intended to be used, but how and why and by whom they were produced are questions which deserve answers. It is the aim of this book to help to provide the answers.

I

Pro Patria

There are many fine examples of British First World War memorials which depict the enthusiasm of newly enlisted men marching off to war. On occasion accompanied by a sorrowful wife with babe in arms, and sometimes still in civilian clothes as the soldier leaves for initial training rather than for the front, he is invariably shown as the willing volunteer, eager to 'do his duty for King and Country'.

Imagery such as this served the dual purpose of acknowledging selfless patriotism in the country's 'hour of need' while providing a poignant reminder of the reality that many men who marched away failed to return, their deaths the very reason the memorial existed. Significantly

Pl. 3
Birmingham
Hall of Memory.
William Bloye,
1925

the depiction of an optimistic response to the outbreak of war was often placed within a broader narrative scheme, with other images recording the reality of warfare or its tragic aftermath.

In the immediate post-war period (and even while the war still raged) throughout the country communities were planning memorials to the dead. The main purpose of the war memorial was not to celebrate victory, nor even simply to acknowledge the debt owed to those who had died in the service of their country. More importantly the memorial provided a focus for the grief of the bereaved. But in so doing it was necessary also to provide a context which conferred honour on those who had fought and died. Imagery which reflected the country's gratitude for the enthusiastic response to 'the call to arms' and which stressed the validity of pre-war, patriotic attitudes is therefore frequently featured.

Whilst there were many reasons for the 'rush to the colours' which accompanied the declaration of war in August 1914, an appeal to manhood played an important part in encouraging enlistment. In his appeal to the men of Manchester to join what was to become one of the first of the Pals battalions (for clerks and warehousemen) the city's Lord Mayor suggested, 'It would be an indelible disgrace to our manhood if we, who are spared so many of the worst horrors of war, hesitate to bear our full share with our gallant allies in this great fight for honour and liberty'.[1]

The response was immediate. Thousands clamoured to enlist with the authorities overwhelmed and unable to cope. As soon as the appeal had been published in the local press hundreds of would-be recruits gathered outside Artillery headquarters. Inside, with only two doctors in attendance, they struggled to deal with the unexpectedly large numbers and fewer than one hundred men were enlisted that day. However, following demonstrations outside Manchester Town Hall, the nearby Free Trade Hall and Albert Hall were annexed to alleviate the pressures. Extra medical and clerical staff were drafted in and over the next fortnight enough battalions were raised to create the first of Manchester's two brigades. On 3 September 1914, 2,151 men enlisted in Manchester, second only to the 3,521 who had joined the colours in London that day.[2] Nation-wide, over three-quarters of a million men volunteered within the first two months of war.[3]

By no means all who ultimately chose to enlist approached the war with unbounded enthusiasm or a sense of adventure, nor did they necessarily see it as Manchester's Lord Mayor did as 'a great fight for honour and liberty'. For many working class men who lived in extreme poverty in appalling conditions and who were used to difficult and often dangerous work, if not actually unemployed, the army could be seen as an improvement in their situation. The facts of their unhealthy lifestyles are attested by the large numbers who had to be rejected as unfit for duty. The widely held view that the war would very soon be over also encouraged some who might otherwise have held back.

Ironically, for many middle class men who might have been expected to show greater patriotic enthusiasm (and generally did) there was sometimes some reluctance to enlist alongside the working classes whose background and assumed character was seen as a concern. It was precisely for this reason that the Clerks' and Warehousemen's Pals Battalion, aimed as it was at the city's middle class men, had been proposed.[4] However, the willingness to 'do one's duty', to fight and possibly die for one's country and to demonstrate bravery in the face of danger would have been accepted by most men in the early years of the century as reasonable expectations of appropriate masculine behaviour. Many men would no doubt have been aware of their own shortcomings in at least some of these respects, but it was these expectations which helped shape the response to the call to arms.

Physical violence in a good cause was very much a part of the discourse of masculinity in the second half of the 19th century, at least for the middle and upper classes; for the more unruly members of the working class the good cause was no doubt optional. This was particularly apparent in the cult of 'muscular Christianity' (or 'Christian manliness') which has been defined as 'an association between physical strength, religious certainty, and the ability to shape and control the world around oneself".[5] It was to find frequent expression in books by such writers as Charles Kingsley, Thomas Hughes and G.A Henty.

The success of these writers' books is echoed by the popularity of a range of magazines for boys published from mid-century onwards, best known of which was *The Boys' Own Paper*. The predominently middle and upper class readership of both the magazines and books is reflected in the many stories with public school settings, most famously *Tom Brown's Schooldays* by Thomas Hughes, published in 1856. In it the author had written that 'from the cradle to the grave, fighting, rightly understood, is ... the real, highest, honestest business, of every sort of man'.[6] In the preface to the sequel, *Tom Brown at Oxford*, he expounded his views.

> The least of the muscular Christians has hold of the old chivalrous
> and Christian belief, that a man's body is given him to be trained
> and brought into subjection and then used for the protection of the
> weak, the advancement of all righteous causes, and the subduing of
> the earth which God has given to the children of men.[7]

Specifically concerned with the training of bodies were the rifle corps established during the 1860s in many public schools.[8] By 1914 more than one hundred cadet groups had been created.[9] The rifle corps reflected and ran parallel to adult Volunteer forces, an important adjunct to the Regular Army. They were predicated on the ideology of a Christian militarism which also gave rise at this time to the Salvation Army (founded in the 1870s) and to militaristic hymns such as *Onward Christian Soldiers, Fight The Good Fight* or *The Son Of God Goes Forth To War*, all of which were to remain popular for many years.

In the early 1900s the rifle corps were replaced by Officer Training Corps (the OTC) at a time when war in the not too distant future was considered highly likely. Boys in the OTC were consequently trained to a high standard. With the reorganisation of the Regular Army in 1906-1907, which included the replacement of Militia, Yeomanry and Volunteer forces by the Territorials, the OTC, now divided into senior branches in the Universities and junior branches in the schools, was actively supported by the War Office. It became, in effect, an official junior training force. When war broke out in 1914, this training enabled and encouraged many ex-public schoolboys to apply for commissions in the armed forces. Memorial plaques in numerous schools provide evidence of the high cost paid for such enthusiasm.

In emulation of the rifle corps other militaristic clubs, mainly intended to appeal to working class boys in large cities, became common from the 1880s onwards, most notably the Boys' Brigade and the Church Lads' Brigade. Popular mainly through their emphasis on pseudo-militaristic activities, they were seen by their founders as a form of social control of the potentially unruly and as a means of inculcating a moral ethos.[10] This was particularly the case with the Boy Scouts, a similar, if less militaristic organisation, founded in 1909 by Robert Baden-Powell.

It has been suggested that as many as 41% of adolescent boys may have belonged to one organisation or another by 1914.[11] In the post-war years, members of boys' clubs frequently played a prominent role in the unveiling ceremonies for war memorials. At Farnsworth in Manchester a Boy Scouts' troupe marched to the memorial at the unveiling ceremony in November 1924 with the two leading boys wearing the medals of their dead fathers.

Significantly, boys' clubs members are depicted on a number of First World War memorials. Numerous memorials exist to those older members of boys' clubs who fought and died in the war, mostly in the form of unadorned plaques but occasionally in more elaborate form, including figurative statues. Scouts and other boys' club members are also sometimes shown on the memorials of local communities and here, taking their place alongside soldiers and sailors, they are presented as the signifiers of a

Pl.4
Nelson
Scout
Memorial.
J Davies,
1919

14

continuing moral and militaristic attitude amongst the young who, if subsequently called upon, would, as the Boy Scouts' famous motto suggests, 'be prepared'.

Although the Scouts had limited appeal for working class boys whose parents could ill afford to pay for the uniform or the subscription fees, Baden-Powell maintained that they were specifically intended to counteract a perceived moral and physical deterioration in the youth of the time and to train them to become positive and 'characterful' contributors to society.[12] Indeed, the Scouts specifically mimicked the public school ethos. As one scoutmaster wrote of wartime scouting, 'I was chiefly concerned with putting into them ... something of what we call the public school spirit, which makes a boy play up and play the game for his side'.[13]

The quotation of a line - 'Play up! play up! and play the game!' - from Henry Newbolt's popular poem *Vitai Lampada*, published in 1892, underlines the importance attached to team games in the process of character building.[14] Indeed, by the end of the nineteenth century, the dominant paradigm of manliness was the athlete whose muscular form was seen to embody the changing ideal of a masculinity in which physical strength and strength of will, the most important elements in the formation of 'character', were intrinsically linked.[15]

The Young Men's Christian Association (the YMCA), which had been founded in London in 1844 and soon had branches around Britain and indeed around the world, was at the forefront of the encouragement of physical training, opening a large gymnasium in London in the 1880s, soon to be followed by more facilities in other cities. As Charles Kingsley saw it,

> In the playing field boys acquire virtues which no books can give them, not merely daring and endurance, but, better still temper, self-restraint, fairness, honour, unenvious approbation of another's success, and all that 'give and take' of life which stands a man in good stead when he goes forth into the world, and without which, indeed, his success is always maimed and partial.[16]

The discovery of large numbers of unfit men during recruitment campaigns for the Crimean War, and later for the Boer Wars, had led to concerns about the nation's physical degeneracy. The healthy body served therefore as a signifier for the well-ordered society.

The popularity of game-playing, with its emphasis on co-operation, sportsmanship and, if necessary, personal self-sacrifice for the common

Pl.5
Bury (detail)
Hermon Cawthra,
1920

good was of particular significance. The analogy between game playing and warfare was often made explicit, not least in Newbolt's *Vitai Lampada* where the cricket match of the first verse - with 'ten to make and the match to win' - is compared to a scene of battle in the second where 'the voice of a schoolboy rallies the ranks: "Play up! play up! and play the game!"' As one ex-soldier recalled, 'War, to my mind, was a kind of super sport. We were used to hard knocks in football and rugby, and healthy competition in cricket and running ... and war was just an extension of this manliness'.[17]

Certainly the idea of war as a game and the battlefield as the field of play was a popular aspect of the discourse of militarism in the early months of the war, as an anonymous poem printed in *The Times* in November 1914 suggests:

> Come, leave the lure of the football field
> With its fame so lightly won,
> And take your place in a greater game
> Where worthier deeds are done.
> No game is this where thousands watch
> The play of a chosen few;
> But rally all! if you're men at all,
> There's room in the team for you. [18]

The sporting analogy was even a part of the official military rhetoric: a weapons training manual noted that 'the sporting spirit and desire to play for his side, or team, or regiment is inherent in every individual of the British race. This should be fostered and made use of by the instructor'.[19]

Such rhetoric was literally enacted by some on the field of battle. At the Battle of the Somme, the most bloody battle of the war, one officer, a Captain Wilfred Nevill of the 8th East Surreys, offered a prize to the first platoon to dribble a football as far as the German trenches. He signalled the advance by kicking a ball towards the enemy lines.

Nevill may well have been inspired by the actions of Rifleman Frank Edwards of the London Irish Rifles who the previous year at the Battle of Loos, in which the 8th East Surreys had also been involved, had similarly provided a ball to be dribbled across no-man's land. Little was made of the earlier incident, though Lady Butler produced a water-colour of the event, now in the regimental museum along with the rescued football. Nevill's exploits on the other hand were widely reported and well received by the British press - though understandably derided by the Germans - and the event was depicted in the *Illustrated London News* in July 1916. Whilst Frank Edwards, though badly wounded, survived both the battle and the war, Captain Nevill along with many of his men died in the attack.[20]

16

If his class and assumed qualities of leadership confirmed the public schoolboy as officer material his similarly assumed sense of sportsmanship (of 'playing the game') was equally to be valued. The analogy between sport and war emphasised the idea of 'fair play' on both the sporting field and the field of battle. In 1915 Sir Arthur Conan Doyle compared unfavourably what he saw as the 'military spirit' of the Germans with the 'sporting spirit' of the English claiming that the latter was 'England's invention, and the chief characteristic of Englishmen'.[21] The occasional iconography of sporting equipment on war memorials clearly reflects this ideology.

At Llandaff, a young recruit, with rifle over his shoulder, wears shorts, shirt and football boots while at Burnley a cricket bat is one of a number of items lying at a mother's feet, indicative of her memories, in this case of childhood, which the monument attempts to illustrate. At Port Sunlight a series of relief panels supplementing the main memorial each depict two or three children and here, on a panel which shows two young boys holding wreaths, the cricket bat which the younger boy is also holding is intended to be seen as a reference to the sporting attitudes which formed, and it is implied continued to form, the foundations for moral certitude.

Pl.6
Llandaff
Sir William
Goscombe John,
1924

Whilst the realisation that war was not a game quickly became all too apparent to those who found themselves on the field of battle, Rifleman Edwards and Captain Nevill excepted, the potential for an almost mythic heroism was emphasised by many at the start of the war. As H.G Wells wrote in September 1914: 'This is the heroic age, suddenly come again. No legendary feats of the past, no battle with dragons or monstrous beasts, no quest or feat that man has hitherto attempted can compare with this adventure, in terror, danger and splendour'.[22]

Pl.7
Port Sunlight
Sir William
Goscombe John,
1924

The potential for the depiction of acts of bravery on the battlefield was signalled on numerous memorials to those who had died in the last major war in South Africa. In Manchester, a typical example could be seen in St Anne's Square, close to the scene of the later clamour to enlist.

Sir William Hamo Thornycroft's Boer War memorial to the men of the Manchester Regiment illustrated a famous incident at Caesar's Camp near Ladysmith. One soldier, head and rifle both held high, resolutely protects his injured comrade who, in obvious pain and with half-closed eyes and bandaged head, hands him more ammunition to continue the fight.

Such a scheme of heroism in the thick of battle, often seen elsewhere on Boer War memorials, was, for both realistic and ideological reasons, less easy to replicate on memorials of the Great War. That said, L.F Roslyn's 1924 memorial to the men of Haslingden in Lancashire is

remarkably similar to Thornycroft's monument and was, we might assume, directly influenced by it. (The same scheme was also used at nearby Oswaldtwistle and at Maesteg in Wales, though it was initially devised for a monument at Port of Spain in Trinidad, unveiled in 1920).

The Edinburgh sculptor William Birnie Rhind produced a number of Boer War memorials for Scottish towns and regiments and at Alloa he too made use of this format of one soldier protecting another. But for his First World War memorial to the old boys of the Fettes School in Edinburgh, unveiled in 1921, he presents the fallen soldier, a kilted officer, alone. Barely able to support himself, he raises his right arm to wave his men on. At the base of the plinth are the words 'Carry On', a reference not only to the officer's encouragement to his troops but equally suggestive of a military tradition and patriotic response to be continued by future generations of scholars. A similar gesture, though this time by a standing officer, was used by Henry Poole for his memorial at Nottingham School for Boys. Here the soldier looks over his shoulder to the men he is encouraging and, significantly, to the school itself.

Despite the relative scarcity of such overtly heroizing schemes on First World War memorials, commemorative inscriptions and allegorical imagery provided widely used alternative ways to acknowledge the heroic ideal, with acts of courage deflected onto medieval or mythological icons of honourable action. Probably unique in its choice of subject, though entirely typical in its intended message, was the memorial at the Victoria

Pl.8 *left*
Manchester
Regiment.
Sir William
Hamo
Thornycroft,
1908

Pl.9 *right*
Haslingden.
L.F Roslyn,
1924

18

College in Jersey. Here Alfred Turner's monument to the 636 Old Victorians who enlisted in the Great War, a quarter of whom died, takes the form of a life-size statue of that apotheosis of knightly chivalry, Sir Galahad.

If the depiction of Sir Galahad was rare, images of St George were predictably popular, the adoption of England's heroic patron saint as a symbol of the nation's victorious exploits being entirely apt. The analogous implications of good defeating evil, and usually being seen in graphic detail to do so, reinforced its perceived appropriateness. C.F Kernot, writing in 1927 of Alfred Drury's figure of the saint for another public school memorial, at Malvern College, suggested that 'as the patron saint of Chivalry, and representing England, it is the symbol of the best qualities in the character of English manhood and those most worth while striving for'.[23] Furthermore, St George was frequently shown on horseback and the mounted warrior had long provided a powerful paradigm for courageous action.

In the 'pecking order' of regiments the cavalry remained the elite and, despite the anachronism, cavalier attacks were regularly depicted in the popular press during the war. In fact, at the start of the war there were thirty-one cavalry regiments in the British Army, each consisting of over five hundred men and more than six hundred horses.[24] Following the onset of trench warfare however these cavalry divisions necessarily remained underemployed.

The impressive memorial to the Cavalry regiments in Hyde Park predictably depicts a victorious, equestrian St George. It was designed by Adrian Jones. Born in Shropshire in 1845, Jones had studied at the Royal Veterinary College, qualifying as a surgeon in 1866. The following year he joined the army where he served in the Royal Horse Artillery until 1890, by which time he had achieved the rank of Captain. On retirement from the army, he became a full-time artist. Despite a lack of formal training he had, during the 1880s, been encouraged and instructed by the eminent sculptor Charles Bell Birch and had already exhibited works at the Royal Academy, to some acclaim. Specialising in equine subjects, and with his military and veterinary background, he was an obvious and apposite choice for the cavalry commission.

The memorial, cast from guns captured by the Cavalry, depicts the victorious St George in medieval armour with his sword held high above

Pl.10
Fettes School, Edinburgh. William Birnie Rhind, 1921

19

his head. The slain dragon lies dead beneath his horse's hooves. An interesting detail of the dragon's head are horn-like protuberances either side of his nose, seen by some as a sly reference to Kaiser Wilhelm's famous facial hair. Around the base of the monument is a continuous frieze of mounted soldiers from the various dominions of the Empire trotting, we may assume, towards the front lines. This was echoed at the unveiling ceremony, where a company of Cavalrymen was formed, with representatives from each of the thirty-seven Cavalry regiments in the British Empire.

Significantly perhaps, there is no suggestion in the Cavalry memorial of the sort of heroic action familiar from popular illustrations. *The Times*, in its review of the sculpture on the occasion of its unveiling, suggested that it presented 'an entirely fresh conception of St. George. It departs from the conventional representation of the saint, which usually dismounts him and shows him in the act of killing the dragon'.[25] Mounted figures of St George can hardly be considered unusual but the fact that the saint is shown not in the act of killing but merely celebrating the dragon's death might be seen as a significant though surely unintentional indication of the Cavalry regiments' relative impotence in modern trench warfare.

In contrast, Charles Hartwell's memorial at Marylebone shows the saint thrusting his lance into the dragon's open jaws. Hartwell's sculpture had originally been created in 1923 for the war memorial at Newcastle-upon-Tyne where it is placed on a much taller and more imposing Portland stone pedestal. Unfortunately the monument is somewhat over-embellished with less impressive bronze reliefs of 'Justice' and 'Peace' at either end and, on the front, a carved lion in high relief. Newcastle-upon-Tyne Council agreed to a second cast being made for Marylebone's memorial at the request of an anonymous donor - in fact the artist and local resident, Sigismund Goetze. (Somewhat bizarrely, the memorial was intended by Goetze to additionally commemorate his silver wedding). It was unveiled in 1936.

Newcastle's monument is large, as befits such a city's major memorial, but elsewhere for smaller monuments, with the exception of relief panels, St George is more often shown without his horse, occasionally in the act of slaying the dragon but commonly in iconic pose with the slain beast, or sometimes just the head, at his feet. Though the absence of the horse in most of these cases can be explained by the more modest scale and budgets allowed by local communities it may well have been felt more appropriate, given the grim realities and largely static nature of the recent conflict, to depict the patron saint as non-cavalier (in both senses of the word).

John Reid's memorial to the 6th Northumberland Fusiliers stands outside St Thomas' Church in Newcastle and was erected in 1924, the year

Pl.11 (facing page)
Cavalry Division
Memorial. London
Adrian Jones, 1924

after Hartwell's monument. It shows a calmly confident figure of St George with the severed head of the dragon at his feet, like David with the head of Goliath. The sheathing of his sword is clearly intended to be seen as symbolic of the end of hostilities. Elsewhere, even this modest action is avoided, the saint seeming closer to the contemporary soldier so often depicted on war memorials, with the reversed rifle replaced by the rested sword, more a figure of mourning than of celebration. The influence of Donatello's more pensive and pacific fifteenth century figure for Orsanmichele in Florence can also be seen in such depictions and indeed close copies of the original were sometimes used in memorial statuary.[26]

The figure of St George had been a popular subject for sculptors in the late nineteenth century and older practitioners employed on First World War memorial projects could quite easily adapt pre-war pieces to the new needs of commemoration. The work of Henry Charles Fehr provides more than one example. Fehr was born in London in 1867 and, after studying at the Royal Academy Schools, had become a studio assistant to Thomas Brock. From 1887 onwards he exhibited regularly at the Royal Academy, up until his death in 1940. His *Perseus Rescuing Andromeda*, purchased by the Chantrey Bequest for the Tate in 1894, still stands outside the gallery at Millbank.

Pl.12
St Mary-le-bone.
Charles Hartwell,
1936

22

Fehr was a minor member of the New Sculpture, a movement first identified in the 1890s by the art critic Edmund Gosse.[27] Their work was marked by a freedom of modelling and an adventurous and expressive use of materials. The main practitioners included George Frampton, Alfred Drury, Frederick Pomeroy, Albert Toft, William Goscombe John, William Hamo Thornycroft and, pre-eminently, Alfred Gilbert.

Thornycroft, who died in 1925, produced just two First World War public monuments, a somewhat subdued, and now badly weathered carved figure of a soldier at Moulton in Cheshire and a more impressive and animated bronze figure of 'Courage' for Luton.[28] However, the younger artists of the movement, Frampton, Pomeroy, Goscombe John, Toft and Drury, were each to produce a range of notable war memorials. Although Alfred Gilbert continued to produce work throughout the 1920s and into the thirties, until his death in 1834 at the age of eighty, he was unfortunately never commissioned to produce a First World War memorial. (The one Boer War memorial he worked on, for the city of Leicester, he was unable to complete in time, consequently losing the commission).

Like other members of the New Sculpture, Henry Fehr was much influenced by Gilbert. His figure of St George for memorials at Colchester

Pl.13 *left*
Sandwich. Charles Hartwell, 1922

Pl.14 *right*
6th Northumberland Fusiliers Memorial. Newcastle-upon-Tyne John Reid, 1924

and Burton-upon-Trent was clearly inspired by Gilbert's own figure of the saint intended for the *Tomb of the Duke of Clarence*. Unlike the St George for the Cavalry memorial, which Adrian Jones had based on close studies of Medieval armour, Gilbert's approach was highly imaginative. 'There is not the slightest resemblance to anything we know of Gothic work' was his comment on the armour of his St George and Fehr adopts a similar approach.[29] Although Fehr's figure is rather less androgynously effete, the fin-de-siécle shell shapes and leafy forms in the detail of the armour are closely modelled on the older artist's work.

Gilbert's figure had been exhibited at the Royal Academy in 1896. Two years later, at the same venue, Fehr had exhibited his own St George, again Gilbert-inspired. Ideological constructions of gender difference in the juxtaposition of the armour-clad knight and naked woman and the contingent ambiguities of threat and vulnerability serve to relegate the slain dragon to a subsidiary and indeed literally supporting role. In adapting this image for his 1922 war memorial at Leeds the naked female predictably disappears. The upraised arm which previously supported her now holds only a shield whilst the dragon-slaying, with its implications of 'good triumphant over evil', assumes far greater importance.

Of all the members of the New Sculpture, George Frampton was perhaps the most intimately involved in memorialisation, having an additional advisory role as a member of the Executive Committee on War Memorials which had been established by the Royal Academy in 1918 to assist and advise local communities on the design of their monuments. Born in London in 1860, Frampton, the son of a journeyman stonemason, had initially been apprenticed to a firm of architectural stone carvers. Like many others from a similar background, including Frederick Pomeroy, Harry Bates and Goscombe John, all of whom started their careers as architectural carvers, he attended modelling classes at the South London Technical Art School before going on to study at the Royal Academy Schools (between 1881 and 1887).

In 1887 Frampton won the Royal Academy Gold Medal and Travelling Scholarship (like Bates and Pomeroy before him and Goscombe John two years later) which took him to Paris, where he became a pupil of Antonin Mercié. Elected ARA in 1894 and RA in 1902, he was knighted in 1908. Preferring the term 'art worker' to that of sculptor, Frampton was

Pl.15
Burton-upon-Trent.
H.C Fehr, 1922

24

closely involved with the Arts and Crafts movement and the Art Workers'
Guild and in 1894 he became joint head, with W.R Lethaby, of the newly
established Central School of Arts and Crafts.

    An exhibitor at the first Vienna Secession exhibition and a
regular exhibitor at the Royal Academy, Frampton was heavily influenced
both by the sculpture of Alfred Gilbert and the paintings of Edward
Burne-Jones. Frampton is now perhaps best known for his statue of *Peter
Pan* in Regent's Park but his symbolist influenced, low relief panels and
half-length busts, with their use of polychrome and multiple materials, are
also much admired and arguably represent his greatest achievements.

    Frampton was to retain a prominent position for many years
within the sculptural establishment. Indeed, with his contributions to the

Pl.16
Leeds.
H.C Fehr, 1922

Pl.17
St George.
H.C Fehr,
exhibited 1898

Pl.18
Maidstone.
Sir G Frampton,
1922

process of memorialisation after the war, he was to remain a significant presence well into the 1920s. In addition to his advisory role Frampton also received a number of his own commissions for war memorials, showing in these works a predilection for the figure of St George for which he was able to draw on pre-war prototypes, a reflection of a waning originality perhaps, but also of the continuing popularity of such imagery.

His 1922 memorial at Maidstone is typical. Grasping the top of a scallop-shaped shield with his left hand and with his lance in his right, St George stands proudly over the conquered beast, his raised left leg resting on the dragon's neck. This imagery had its origins in a Boer War memorial produced for Radley College in 1903. It was also used at this time on monuments to Queen Victoria at St Helens and Winnipeg and later on a monument in Northampton to King Edward VII. In 1921, Frampton revived the theme for memorials to the dead of the Great War, one for the staff of the Pearl Assurance company, others at Fordham in Cambridgeshire and Hove in Sussex where, on memorials designed in collaboration with Sir Edwin Lutyens, the saint stands on top of a tall column. (See Pls. 222 & 223).

These post-war versions are somewhat less flamboyant than his earlier depictions of St George, with the sword held less triumphantly. Their altered function as memorials to the war dead is signified on the Pearl Assurance memorial by a wreath added to the sword, an implied analogy with the cross consequently being made explicit. The same basic cast would appear to have been used again the following year for the Maidstone figure, with relatively minor alterations, most notably the sword replaced by a lance and the Cross of St George transferred from shield to flag.

Born in the 1860s, both Fehr and Frampton were too old to have served in the war. It is therefore unsurprising that such men should have recourse to the well-tried iconography of the mythic hero rather than attempt to present, in realistic form, a response to the horrors of modern warfare of which they lacked any direct personal experience. Their proposals, and those of many like-minded sculptors, clearly met with some approval however, not only from war memorial selection committees who would no doubt have been of a similar generation, but a general public whose opinions were often sought during the selection process. Indeed, such imagery, though seen predominantly in the work of an older generation of sculptors, was by no means exclusive to them and many younger men provided examples of statues or reliefs of St George for First World War memorials.

The mythic and realistic were in fact sometimes combined. At Witham in Essex, Gilbert Ledward's relief at the base of the memorial cross depicts a soldier of the Great War kneeling on a rocky outcrop, waving the regimental colours. In the background, backing him both literally and metaphorically, is an equestrian St George. And at Trumpington in Cambridgeshire, Eric Gill's memorial, a tall cross at the base of which are four relief carvings, combines the mythic and contemporary in the single image of St George. The saint is shown wearing a First World War tin helmet thereby emphasising his presence as a surrogate for the soldier. His heroism is underlined by his semi-naked vulnerability with only a short spear to defend the nation, personified by the helpless maiden bound to a tree. The juxtaposition of the saint's bare leg with the visciously clawed foot of the dragon which snaps at the man's head emphasises the considerable danger he faces. The hand of God above his head confirms the moral validity of his actions.

Many other sculptors were to produce their own variations of the nation's patron saint and literally dozens can be seen on memorials in all parts of the country including, surprisingly perhaps, Scotland and Wales. St George was not merely a symbol of heroism, he was of course a representative of the country itself. Given that a dragon was the symbol of Wales, it might be expected that depictions of the creature being put to the sword - by the patron saint of England no less - would have been considered particularly contentious, and depictions of St George and the Dragon in Wales, though existing, are admittedly rare.[30] But imagery such as this very much resonated with popular wartime propaganda and George and the Dragon was seen as having symbolic significance for all Britons. Ironically however this was an iconography shared by both sides of the conflict and, with the saint's long-standing popularity in Germany as well as England, his image appeared in both British and German propaganda.

The symbolic significance of images of St George in post-war memorialisation was often stressed by memorial committees and in commemorative booklets on the occasion of the unveiling of monuments.

Pl.19
Trumpington.
Eric Gill, 1921

At Colchester for example, attendants at the unveiling of the war memorial were reminded that the saint was 'symbolical of the chivalry and the manhood of England'. In addition it was stressed:

> He is not only the Patron Saint of England, he is the Patron Saint of the Scouts. And on every St. George's Day it would be well for the Scouts of Colchester to visit the monument, think of what the manhood of England accomplished in the Great War, and pray that in their turn they may be able to follow the example set them ... may the figure in our monument inspire them to try and live up to the ideal of the great Knight who was, 'without fear and without approach'.[31]

The Patriotic fervour underlying such heroizing iconography had been fomenting for many years. Whilst an acknowledgement of bravery featured in the inscriptions of many memorials, the patriotic incentive was even more commonly highlighted. 'Pro Patria', 'For King and Country', 'In Defence of their Country's Rights', 'They Loved Their Land More Than They Loved Their Lives', such grand pronouncements were more normally present than absent on First World War memorials. The rhetoric was greatly exaggerated perhaps, and undoubtedly untrue for many, but the assumption of patriotism nonetheless clearly had real validity.

The Yorkshire Observer, in its 15 August 1914 edition reporting events at a recruitment meeting at Bradford's aptly named St George's Hall, commented:

> The vast audience simply breathed patriotic fervour, which was heightened to an indescribable intensity as the national songs followed one on another. Again and again the audience rose and cheered, and even the pressmen for once in a way threw custom aside and forgot their traditional impassivity.[32]

Even those who had experienced years of ferocious fighting could still reiterate the patriotic incentive. 2nd Lieutenant George Barber, a Macclesfield scoutmaster and teacher in civilian life, writing to his parents in October 1916 a few days before his death on the battlefields of the Somme, reassured them that, 'If I don't come through you'll know that I don't wish for anything better than to give my life for my country'.[33]

Patriotism, in the sense of a readiness to sacrifice oneself for one's country or community, has a lengthy lineage, though more as an expression of individual loyalty than of collective action. If patriotism was seen in the late nineteenth century as being very much in concert with governmental and national concerns, a century earlier it had been more commonly associated with radicalism. Opposition to the perceived corruption of government, and a concern with the restoration of 'ancient liberties', was frequently couched in terms of patriotism.

Increasingly during the nineteenth century however, the patriotic incentive became linked to national interests. This was particularly so in times of war and, more specifically, of threatened invasion. As the historian, Linda Colley, has said of the British nation, it was 'an invention forged above all by war. Time and again, war with France brought Britons ... into confrontation with an obviously hostile Other and encouraged them to define themselves collectively against it'.[34]

Patriotic rhetoric and nationalistic imagery became increasingly popular from the mid-eighteenth century onwards with such familiar icons as John Bull, the National Anthem, and *Rule Britannia* all dating from this time. It was also in the late eighteenth and early nineteenth centuries that the image of Britannia, which had been rescued in the seventeenth century from its classical origins as a symbol of a defeated nation, took on a more militaristic shade. Reappearing on coins of the realm in the 1660s, by the end of the eighteenth century Britannia, by now a symbol of a united kingdom, had been given a trident to signify naval mastery and, in the 1820s, a military helmet. Her association not merely with the nation but with militaristic interests was therefore firmly established well before her appearance in this form in the memorial statuary of the Great War.[35]

Pl.20
Liverpool
Newsroom
Joseph Phillips,
1924

Pl.21
'The Freeman's
Oath',
William Nelson
Gardiner,
1803.National
Army Museum

Two figures of
Britannia by
Walter Gilbert

left
Pl.22
Morley, 1927

right
Pl.23
Troon, 1924

Britannia is depicted on numerous memorials. Three variations of a figure by Walter Gilbert are to be found at Crewe in Cheshire, Morley near Leeds and Troon in Scotland. Born in Rugby in 1872, Walter Gilbert, second cousin of Sir Alfred Gilbert, had studied his craft initially at the Birmingham Municipal Art School before going on to the Royal College of Art in London. After further studies abroad, in France, Belgium and Germany, he taught art at Rugby, Harrow and the Bromsgrove School of Art and in 1890 founded the Bromsgrove Guild, a company which manufactured architectural accoutrements in a wide range of media including metal, wood, plaster, tapestry and glass.

At the end of the war Gilbert left the Guild to become assistant manager at one of the Bromsgrove Guild's major competitors, H.H Martyn and Co. of Cheltenham, which, as one of the country's leading foundries, were to cast numerous war memorial sculptures. (At the beginning of the century, the company employed some two hundred men; by 1920 the number was around one thousand).[36] In addition, H.H Martyn, which produced amongst other things funerary monuments, both carved and cast, were happy to expand their business to incorporate the new demand for war memorials, offering 'off-the-peg' designs in brochures distributed from showrooms throughout the country.[37]

Often working with his fellow sculptor Louis Weingartner, with whom he collaborated on numerous war memorials, Gilbert's specialism

30

was large scale ornamental metal work such as doors and gates and in this capacity he contributed to projects at Buckingham Palace (with the Bromsgrove Guild) and Liverpool's Anglican Cathedral (with H.H Martyn). At the latter venue he also designed the war memorial to the 55th West Lancashire Division, again in collaboration with Weingartner. Although rarely acknowledged as being their work, Gilbert and Weingartner's best known sculpture (for the Bromsgrove Guild) can also be found in Liverpool: the famous liver birds, symbol of the city, perched proudly on top of the Liver Building.

The reuse of a figure for more than one town's memorial was common practice. No doubt often offered by artists for sound commercial reasons, it was also sometimes specifically requested by memorial committees, impressed perhaps by a nearby figure and keen to obtain a replica for their own monument.

The methods used for casting bronze, where the finished figure would most usually be built up from a number of separate pieces co-joined, allowed not only for repetition but for variation of details, and in Gilbert's work at Crewe, Morley and Troon we see a perfect illustration of this in practice.[38] The draped figure of Britannia at each of these locations is virtually the same, the identical cast clearly being used for the body but with alterations to the positions of the lower arms, to details of the helmet and to the particular combination of attributes she holds.

The victorious gesture seen in these memorials, holding aloft a palm leaf or trident, was frequently used by other sculptors in their depiction of Britannia. Quite often it is a sword which is held aloft, in much the same manner as with many images of St George. The sword is of course the Sword of Justice, emphasising the validity of the nation's cause. The figure of Justice, invariably with her sword, was frequently depicted in wartime propaganda. A well-known poster from 1915 showed an angry Justice, with clenched fist and sword held high, a propaganda image which drew on the outrage felt at the sinking of the passenger ship the 'Lusitania' by German U-Boats. Justice walks on waves, beneath which the ship slowly sinks and her passengers drown. The title of the poster entreats us to 'Take Up The Sword of Justice'.[39]

Post-war memorial imagery was usually less dramatic. C.S Jagger's figure at Brimington in Derbyshire, in the Parish Church of St Michael's and All Angels, holds her shield and sword in front of her and bows her head. Jagger referred to the figure as a Victory, the attitude of mourning intended to represent 'victory through suffering'. Other features, he explained, had specific significance: 'the helmet for Britannia (or the Navy),

Pl.24
Brimington
C.S Jagger, 1921

31

the sword and shield for the Army, and the wings (on the helmet) for the Royal Air Force'.[40] Nonetheless, with familiar attributes, including the Sword of Justice, he has presented an image we naturally identify simply as Britannia.

In memorial sculpture elsewhere the Sword of Justice is often combined with a laurel wreath to stress the correspondence of sacrifice and justice, as in Derwent Wood's finely carved figure for his home town of Keswick, a figure which has also been identified as Victory though surely intended as Britannia. In another depiction of Britannia at Hanley, by Harold Brownsword, we see the laurel entwined around the short sword which has unmistakable and intentional echoes of the cross with its inherent implications of self-sacrifice. Brownsword was a local man who had studied at Hanley School of Art before going down to London where he became a student at the Royal College of Art. (His fellow students included C.S Jagger and Gilbert Ledward). He later became Headmaster of the Regent Street Polytechnic. As with the Brimington figure, Britannia's head at Hanley is significantly bowed as she gazes down, as though in acknowledgement of those beneath her placing wreaths at the foot of the memorial.

The explicit linkage of Britannia with the soldier's sacrifice, both in war memorial sculpture and elsewhere, firmly grounds his acts of heroism in the discourse of patriotism.[41] This correspondence is of course always implied by her very presence on memorials to the war dead but sometimes the connection is overtly stressed. The figure of Britannia in John Millard's monument at Macclesfield is more active than most as she leans over the effigy of a prostrate soldier to place a laurel wreath upon his head. The soldier has clearly died in the service of his country, the gas mask he has failed to use indicative of the cause of death. Britannia, representing the nation and holding the

Pl.25
Keswick
F Derwent Wood.
1922

32

national flag, acknowledges the country's debt to such men.

At Macclesfield, Britannia's movement is contrasted with the stillness of the dead soldier. Although all attention is rightly focused on the soldier, directing *our* attention and thoughts to the serviceman's sacrifice in our name, Britannia remains the dominant figure. As we approach the memorial from the front it is her helmeted head and crouching body that we initially see, the dark bronze silhouetted against the white stone pedestal.

We are not encouraged to dwell on the reality of death. Indeed, following criticisms of the harrowing nature of the depiction of the soldier in Millard's original model the sculptor made appropriate alterations to the final piece to make it less so. Rather we are encouraged to think of the implications of his death. Because of the soldier's ultimate sacrifice the country, we are reminded, survives. Britannia's animation, in contrast to the soldier's inert state, can be seen as a literal illustration of the commonly recited mantra frequently inscribed on monuments, 'They died that we might live'.[42]

A similarly impressive memorial which symbiotically combines the figure of Britannia with those of contemporary soldiers can be found in Liverpool. The News Room War Memorial, in remembrance of all members of the Liverpool Exchange news room and members' sons who served in the Great War, was originally located in Derby House and was unveiled by Lord Derby on 18 July 1924. When the old Exchange building was subsequently demolished the monument was relocated to its present position in a semicircular niche outside the new building in Exchange Flags.

Pl.26
Hanley.
Harold
Brownsword,
1922.

Designed by the Liverpool sculptor Joseph Phillips, Britannia is shown here at the apex of a pyramidal arrangement of figures. Wearing the traditional helmet, fish-scale breastplate and billowing cloak, decorated around the edges with dolphins, sea shells and sea-horses, not only for the country's seafaring achievements but for Merseyside's specific maritime connections, she has a formidable presence. On other memorials where Britannia is shown in isolation, the attributes she holds - palm leaves, wreaths, or miniature Victories - indicate the martial nature of the monument. At Liverpool the accompanying servicemen serve this purpose and she is therefore shown only with the more conventional trident. Like a 'Madonna Misericordia' (Madonna of Mercy) her voluminous cloak enfolds and protects a small girl who gazes up at her and on whose shoulder her hand protectively rests.

The five figures below are shown as though in the thick of battle with a captain in jodhpurs and laced-up knee-length boots slightly crouched with pistol in hand and flanked on one side by a kneeling soldier, his rifle held at the ready, and on the other a sailor who scans the horizon from behind his ship's gun. Designed to be viewed, not in the round but against a wall within the news room, all of these figures look outwards, lined up as though protecting a bulwark against an advancing army, or of course more symbolically, protecting the country, as represented by Britannia, from the threat of attack. The serviceman who

Pl.27
'The Shrine of
Honour'
John Bernard
Partridge,
Punch
10 November 1920

Pl.28
Macclesfield.
J Millard, 1921

scours the horizon has been seen elsewhere as representing a search for lost comrades - at Dornoch or Keighley for example - and as such, a poignant reminder of those missing in action, but here we see him merely as watching expectantly for the unseen enemy.[43]

Despite these naturalistic details this is obviously not a battlefield scene; the inclusion of a wounded man tended by a nurse and the juxtaposition of soldiers and sailor makes this clear. Instead these are representative figures who, like the little girl, are equally included in the protective embrace of this secular Madonna by the unnatural extension of her cloak which creates the somewhat forced triangular composition. These are all Britannia's citizens, proudly presented, representatives of the thousands who willingly fought in her name and who would be ready and

Pl.29
Liverpool
Newsroom.
Joseph Phillips,
1924

willing to fight again if the need arose to protect her future generations, here represented by the little girl.

At Macclesfield we are shown a proud but sorrowful Britannia who expresses gratitude to her dead soldier (and by implication to all of the dead); at Liverpool the emphasis is on the peace and victory the soldiers and sailors achieved on our behalf, though again only at the expense of injury (depicted) and death (not shown but named). In other memorials featuring the figure of Britannia, such as Stockport's, with its semi-naked figure of a 'warrior', the victory achieved, and its cost, is similarly expressed, though at Stockport in an entirely allegorical form.

Gilbert Ledward's Stockport figure is draped in the union flag and with the Sword of Justice in one hand, laurel wreath in the other, she towers above the naked man who kneels at her feet. The warrior, an apparent survivor, but 'symbolic of the men who fell in the war' and whose 'great sacrifice is signified by the broken sword' he holds in his hand, raises his head to gaze up at Britannia as if for acclamation of his actions.[44] As in numerous other memorials, beneath his feet the symbolic serpent he has slain lies dead.

Britannia can be seen as an anglicised version of Athena, the Greek goddess of war, one of whose constant companions was Nike, bringer of victory. Consequently this winged figure is also frequently shown with Britannia. Walter Gilbert's memorials at Morley and Troon, and another for the Birmingham Gas Department, all featured the hand-held Nike. Similarly, on Southport's war memorial, in a particularly fine carving of Britannia by George Herbert Tyson Smith, the recently achieved victory is signified by the tiny Nike she holds in her left hand. Here Britannia's shield remains strapped to her arm but her spear and sword, no longer needed, rest against the framing architecture.. A matching relief shows Britannia in mourning, laying a garland onto a Greek helmet.

Elsewhere, on another memorial by Tyson Smith, this time to the Post Office workers of Liverpool, the figure of Victory is depicted on Britannia's shield. Smith's starkly Archaic Greek style of carving, typical of the sculptor, creates a degree of ambiguity as to the seated figure's intended identity. Although acknowledged as representing 'Britain mourning her

Pls.30
Southport.
GH Tyson Smith,
1927.

Pl.31 (opposite)
Stockport.
Gilbert Ledward,
1925

36

HAT TH   ARE N

1945

VY & ROYAL MARINES

HAZELDINE L.T.
HIBBERT S.
HILL J.
HULME H.
HULME T.S.
HURLEY J.B.
KENNY J.
KIRBY F.
KITCHEN H.H.
LAND T.S.
LAVELLE T.
LEAH S.
LEWIS J.E.C.
LOWE H.B.
MADDOCKS F.
MILLER J.
MILLS E.
MOLYNEAUX C.
MORAN W.
MURPHY A.E.
NUTTALL F.
O'CONNOR C.H.
O'DONNELL T.O.
ORME J.W.
PAKEMAN L.
PEARSON A.V.
PERRIN J.S.
POLLITT S.
POLLITT W.T.
RATHBONE A.

RIDGWAY C.
RIGBY W.
ROBERTS F.
ROSE L.E.
ROYLE F.
ROYLE K.
SAXON W.H.
SCHOFIELD T.
SELBY S.
SHAW W.
SMITH R.S.
SMITH T.
SMITH W.
TURNER H.B.
TWIGG A.E.
WADE E.H.
WARD E.H.
WEBSTER R.D.
WHALLEY G.E.
WHITTAKER R.A.
WILLIAMS C.
WILLIAMS F.
WILSON A.
WILSON B.
WOODHEAD T.N.
YATES T.
BOLLINGTON W.
LINDLEY A.M.
MACHIN E.
MARTIN J.P.

AIR FORCE

FYTTON R.W.
GALE E.
GARNER D.W.
GARSIDE R.
GREENHALGH C.
GRIFFIN J.
GUTERSOHN G.C.W.
HAMILTON C.S.R.
HAMMAN G.A.
HAMPSON E.
HEDGCOX W.
HICKSON E.
HOWARD D.J.
HOWARD P.N.
HUGHES L.L.
HOGG E.
HOLDEN D.
HUNT T.B.
HUTCHINSON J.E.
INGHAM J.R.
JACKSON C.
JACKSON S.
JARMAN T.H.
JONES R.R.
KILDUFF H.
LANDAU H.
LEE E.M.
LODGE R.
LUND J.W.
MALLON J.L.
MARTIN J.H.
MATTHEWS G.
MAYERS D.H.
MILLER F.
MITCHELL N.H.
MORRIS W.
MOTTERSHEAD G.H.
MULLANY J.T.
MURRAY A.

NEILD E.J.
NEWCOMBE F.P.
NORRIS R.
NOWELL D.C.
O'BRIEN V.W.
PARKER C.
PELL H.K.
PHILLIPS J.D.
POLAND D.A.
POLAND P.E.
POLLARD B.S.
ROBERTS J.
ROTHWELL H.J.
RUDGE E.A.
SHANN A.
SHAW J.A.
STEPHENS G.A.
SUMMERS H.
TAYLOR J.W.
TAYLOR R.
THRELFALL A.H.
TONER R.
TROWER-FOYAN J.R.
TURNER P.E.
TUSTAIN G.T.
WADILOWE G.
WALKER E.A.
WALLACE A.
WARD R.R.
WARREN W.
WHITLEY R.
WILDE R.
WILLIAMS G.M.
WILSON S.
WOOLEY S.
WOOLSTON R.E.
WYATT J.
YOUNG C.C.
BOWKER A.
BREEZE D.J.
BRYANT T.

dead', she was also referred to at the time as a personification of Grief.[45] However, with her distinctive helmet on her lap and seated as she is with shield beside her in a pose familiar from coins of the realm, there can be no doubt that the sculptor intended her as the personification of the nation, grieving for her lost sons.

In many respects, St George and Britannia, as representatives of the country, can be seen as interchangeable and are occasionally paired. The saint is presented as a personification of active patriotism. He denotes the armed forces who, on behalf of the country, achieved victory. Britannia most often represents the wider population, grateful for the victory achieved or in mourning for the dead. In either case however, in locating military victory in relation to the symbolic figures of Britannia or St George, it is the serviceman's sacrifice for 'King and Country' which is overtly stressed. The implication is that patriotism was the prime motivation. It is an assumption which may not have been universally true but which, as we have seen, was justified by widely held pre-war attitudes towards masculinity and militarism and the correlation of the two.

As suggested by the inscription on Gilbert's memorials at Crewe, Troon and Morley, identical in each case except for the substitution of the appropriate town's name, these statues were 'placed to commemorate the men of [the town] who, seeking the welfare of their country gave their lives in so doing and are now resting in and beyond the seas.' At Macclesfield the inscription simply states, 'They gave their lives for their King and Empire'. Many of those who died and many of those who mourned would have seen it in precisely this way.

II

Men Who March Away [1]

If a sense of nationhood was closely linked to the threat or actuality of war, it is hardly surprising that during the nineteenth century the reputation of common soldiers which had long been poor - the Duke of Wellington famously describing them as 'the scum of the earth' - began to change. Throughout the eighteenth century Britain had relied on a mix of press-ganged men and mercenaries to fight her wars and soldiers continued for many years to be seen as a decidedly dangerous rabble. As late as the end of the nineteenth century the Secretary of State for War could write that 'no tradition is more deeply rooted in the minds of the poorer classes ... than that which represents enlistment as the last step in the downward career of a young man'.[2]

Nonetheless, the soldier's reputation had begun to improve as early as the beginning of the nineteenth century. During the Napoleonic wars, with the added incentive of threatened invasion, large numbers of men had been encouraged to join the army. From 1789 to 1814 the British army had expanded from 40,000 to 250,000 men, and the navy from around 16,000 to over 140,000 over a similar period. In addition, by 1804, there were almost half a million men in part-time volunteer units intended for the defence of the home front.[3]

With this large-scale mobilisation of British working men came a necessary if slow adjustment of attitudes, both of potential recruits to a career in the armed forces and of the general public to these men. As this chapter will show, sympathetic representations of the common soldier (and sailor and airman) were to be central to the process of memorialisation after the First World War, reflecting the very different attitude to fighting and to those who fought, manifested in the response to the 'call to arms' of 1914.

Regardless of such changes of attitude, the potential for heroism had remained for some time exclusive to the officer classes. It wasn't until the war in the Crimea that the rank and file were cast in an heroic mould - the 'thin red streak topped with a line of steel'. This famous though often

Pl.33
Royal Welch
Fusiliers.
Wrexham.
Sir William
Goscombe John,
1924

misquoted line was written by W.H Russell, war correspondent of *The Times,* who, like other correspondents, was highly critical of the leadership of the Crimean campaign but lavished praise on the courage of the men.

The heroism of the common soldier in the Crimean War was to remain a potent image, not least in the increasing number of battle paintings exhibited in the last quarter of the century and the many popular reproductions they spawned. Foremost amongst the artists who made their reputations with battle paintings was Lady Elizabeth Butler whose *The Roll Call (Calling the Roll after an Engagement, Crimea)* was the sensation of the 1874 Royal Academy's annual exhibition. Significantly *The Roll Call,* and Lady Butler's paintings in general, concentrated on the experiences of the common soldier. Her work, and the work of followers and rivals such as Richard Caton Woodville, clearly chimed with public opinion. Popular papers such as *The Illustrated London News* and *The Graphic* also employed artists, including Caton Woodville, to follow and chronicle the British Army with suitably dramatic imagery.

The introduction of the Victoria Cross in 1856 in the immediate aftermath of the Crimean War - 'for Valour, regardless of rank' - was a further indication of the rising status of the ordinary soldier and similarly reflected the public's increasingly favourable attitude to the ordinary members of its armed forces. Campaign medals had been presented to the rank and file soldier in earlier wars but rewards for bravery had remained exclusive to officers. The introduction in December 1854 of a Distinguished Conduct Medal for gallantry for sergeants and lower ranks and, shortly after, the Conspicuous Gallantry Medal for naval petty officers and seamen was the result of a popular demand fired by newspaper correspondents' reports of the war. But the demand for a medal for gallantry regardless of rank remained until the Victoria Cross was introduced two years later.

By the time that First World War memorials were being planned and built it was certainly possible to present soldiers from all periods of British history as heroic figures and the contemporary soldier is linked, in a number of memorials, to what is seen as a continuing tradition of heroism on the field of battle by the juxtaposition of historical and

40

contemporary figures. Sir William Goscombe John's 1924 monument to the Royal Welch Fusiliers at Wrexham links an eighteenth century Fusilier with a modern soldier. The Fusilier holds the regimental flag around the top of which a wreath is looped. Both literally and metaphorically he stands behind his modern compatriot who appears lost in thought, as though recalling his regiment's glorious history, to which his recent exploits have added.

The combination of contemporary and historical figures was a favourite approach of Goscombe John and both here and elsewhere the uniform of the historical figure relates to the date of the regiment's formation, thereby suggesting a continuation of the regiment's honourable traditions from inception to the present day.[4] John Tweed's memorial to the Rifle Brigade in London's Grosvenor Square is similarly conceived. Here a Twentieth century soldier who represents the 11,575 officers and men of the Rifle Brigade who died in the Great War is flanked at a lower level by an officer and a soldier, both from the early 19th century. Although formed in 1800, it was only after distinguished service in the Peninsula War and at Waterloo that in 1816, on the recommendation of the Duke of Wellington, the regiment was named 'The Rifle Brigade' and it is in the uniform of this period that the historical figures are shown.

In these cases, it is regimental history which is referenced. Arguably more impressive, both in concept and composition, with a broader allusion to British military history, is a small roadside memorial at Royston in Hertfordshire by Benjamin Clemens. Clemens was a tutor at the Royal College of Art, his students including Gilbert Ledward and Charles Sargeant Jagger. His memorial at Royston features a finely modelled bronze figure of a soldier of the Great War who stands against a carved marble backdrop depicting six military men, from an archer at Agincourt to a nineteenth century infantryman. Behind them is a seventh figure, Thomas Cartwright, the founder of Presbyterianism in England and Royston's most famous son. (The detail of the bird at the soldier's feet is a reference to a local legend linking the crow with the town).[5] The contrast between the dark bronze of the contemporary soldier and the white marble of his historical forebears suggests the latter as ghosts of the past,

Pl.34
Royston.
Benjamin
Clemens, 1922

reminders of an heroic tradition of the defence of the realm which, it is implied, is a tradition continued into the present.

Rather different in mood and on a far grander scale, though with similar intentions, is Alice Meredith-Williams' 1924 Paisley memorial. Here a tall, imposing, twenty-five feet high square pillar by Sir Robert Lorimer is surmounted by an impressive, larger than life-size medieval knight on horseback who is surrounded by four British 'Tommies'. Alice Meredith-Williams (who was wrongly identified as a man in press reports) was commissioned after winning a competition which attracted 195 entries and which was judged by the architect, Sir Reginald Blomfield. (Nicholas Babb came second and Meredith-Williams, with a second entry, came third). The soldiers' thick coats and cloaks, bent heads but determined strides, suggest stoic resistance against both the elements and the enemy, rather than glorious victory. The juxtaposition of a crusader and contemporary soldiers is clearly intended to imply not only shared qualities of chivalry, as Lorimer suggested, but that in both cases God was on 'our side'.

Despite the undoubted popularity with memorial committees of allegorical figures of Victory or Britannia or the dragon-slaying St George, by far the most common image on municipal and regimental First World War memorials was that of the common soldier.[6] From the often crude carvings of local, anonymous stone masons to the finely cast bronzes of the most proficient and prestigious practitioners of the day we see a range of studies of the common soldier. He was predominantly presented as a dignified and resolute figure, as at Paisley, rather than glorifying in the victory he had helped to achieve. Certainly there are celebratory figures but

Pl.35
Paisley.
Alice Meredith
Williams,
1924

Pl.36
facing page
Strathspey

these can just as easily be seen as celebrating peace rather than victory, or simply greeting loved ones on their return home.[7]

Occasionally we see the soldier apparently on the field of battle shown confidently striding forwards, his head held high, as in Philip Lindsey Clark's figure at Southwark. Here he might almost be 'going over the top' were it not for his rifle slung over his shoulder rather than held ready for action. Clark explained his choice. 'A British soldier, portrayed in an attitude characteristic of the battlefield ... I have attempted ... to express the same dogged determination and unconquerable spirit displayed by all branches of our forces on land, on seas, and in the air'.[8]

'Going over the top' would, by 1922 when the memorial was unveiled, be recognised of course as all too often the soldier's final act and it may have been felt insensitive to emphasise this fact. Nonetheless, in other locations he occasionally seems to be shown this way, as for example at the Strathspey and District memorial at Grantown in Scotland where the kilted soldier, his rifle at the ready, would certainly appear to be clambering out of a trench to face the enemy. Courageous acts on the field of battle were only infrequently shown, though admittedly when depicted as if in battle the soldier is often placed, in contrast to the realities of trench warfare, in confident command of the space around him, as in Albert Toft's figure at Holborn for the Royal Fusiliers.

A leading member of the New Sculpture, Albert Toft had begun to establish a reputation as an artist in the 1880s. Born on the outskirts of Birmingham in 1862 he had initially served an apprenticeship in the ceramics industry around Stoke. His father was the principal modeller at the Birmingham silversmiths, Elkington and Co. and then later at Wedgwood and it was here that Toft began his employment. At the same time he attended evening classes at art schools in Hanley and Newcastle-under-Lyme.

After winning a scholarship in 1881 Toft moved to London where, at the National Art Training School, he studied modelling under Edouard Lantéri. Known for both his portrait sculpture and his ideal nudes, regularly exhibited from 1885 onwards at the Royal Academy, Toft soon received commissions for public monuments. These included memorials to Queen Victoria at Leamington Spa, Nottingham and South Shields and to Edward VII, also at Leamington. Boer War memorials were also produced, most notably for the Welsh National Memorial in Cardiff but additionally at Ipswich and Birmingham, the latter a location where he was later to produce particularly impressive figures for a memorial to the dead of the First World War.

Toft's soldier at Holborn stands upright, his right leg raised on a stoney mound which suggests that this is the field of battle. His left fist is clenched while his right hand holds his rifle at arm's length. The rifle, with bayonet attached, is held parallel to the ground and both his angled leg and his gun seem to point the way forward. His upper body however is half turned away and he looks back to where he has come from as if to encourage those behind him, or perhaps to await, impatiently, the order to advance. The clenched fist suggests determination and the relaxed, unhurried pose exudes confidence. When this figure was reused by Toft for his much larger memorial at Oldham he is shown at the apex of a group struggling to the top of a rocky outcrop and the sense of a confident command of surroundings becomes more indicative of ultimate success after considerable effort, both for the individual and, metaphorically, for the nation (see Pl.244).[9]

Heroic stature is more subtly implied at Hale. Here the seven feet tall, grim-faced soldier, described at the time as 'not of the parade ground, but of the battlefield',[10] his legs wrapped in sacking to protect against the cold and mud, adopts a pose which, though reversed, is strongly reminiscent of Michelangelo's statue of *David*, the right arm holding, in place of the sling, the strap of his rifle. This impression is reinforced by the soldier's bare left arm, his sleeve torn away to bind a wound. In his left hand is a German helmet. Such 'trophies of war' were often shown in

Pl.37
Royal Fusiliers
Memorial,
Holborn,
London.
Albert Toft,
1924

memorial sculpture and where the helmet lies at the foot of the soldier - as in Arthur Walker's memorial to the Gordon Highlanders at Keith in Scotland, C.S Jagger's soldier at Hoylake or Frederick Pomeroy's at Larne - it invariably invites comparison with the familiar head of Goliath at the foot of David.

The Hale memorial was by the Liverpool-born sculptor, Frederick Wilcoxson, a tutor at the Royal College of Art and studio assistant of Francis Derwent Wood. Unlike the older Toft, Wilcoxson had served in the trenches and it is perhaps significant that his figure suggests a heroism not so much of aggressive action but of stoicism and self-sacrifice. In dedicating the memorial, which was unveiled on 11 March 1922, the Bishop of Chester suggested that it represented 'the grim reality of war'.[11]

The suggestion of a battlefield scene is more easily achieved by the combination of two or more figures and with Roslyn's monuments at Oswaldtwistle and Haslingden, or Toft's memorial at Oldham, the intention is clearly to depict a scene of fighting or its immediate aftermath. Elsewhere, the grouping of figures may be more iconic than realistic. This is apparent with those monuments which show combinations of soldiers and sailors, as seen in the Liverpool News Room memorial where the additional figures of nurse and wounded sergeant made more explicit the unreality of the depiction.

Birnie Rhind's monument at Buckie in Scotland, a variant of earlier Boer War memorials by the same artist, might at first sight be assumed to depict a battle scene, with two figures, one kneeling, the other standing. The latter, with his rifle slung over his shoulder and his helmet at his waist, holds aloft a regimental flag. The convincing modelling, realistic detail and animation of the figures help to create a dynamic composition which further adds to the effect of action. However, as at Liverpool, the juxtaposition of soldier and sailor, not to mention the anachronistic raising of the regimental colours, a practice abandoned in the 1880s, is clearly unrealistic. Another Birnie Rhind sculpture at Wallasey, overlooking the estuary of the River Mersey, where the soldier and sailor are joined by a colonial soldier, is more static and consequently more obviously iconic, as indeed are other memorials, such as Kellock Brown's very similar monument for Largs in Ayrshire.

The pairing of soldier and sailor was a much-used

Pl.39
Buckie.
William Birnie Rhind, 1925

Pl.40
Twickenham.
Mortimer Brown, 1921

feature of First World War memorials, usually on either side of a central column or cenotaph or as figures flanking a list of names on wall plaques where the servicemen are most often shown in mourning pose. Airmen are less frequently shown, particularly in the round, but interesting images feature on the relief plaques of a number of memorials, including ones at Hastings, Twickenham and Dartford. At Hastings, in a memorial by Margaret Winser, an airman is shown in close-up in the cockpit of his plane; at Twickenham three smiling pilots shake hands before setting off; and at Dartford a bi-plane is readied for action.

At Bootle, in a memorial by Hermon Cawthra, figures in the round representing all three services are arranged around a central pedestal, on top of which is a mother and child, symbolic of the homeland they fought to protect. Often a fourth figure is included in this type of arrangement, perhaps of a nurse or an allegory of Victory or Peace. At Wolverhampton the fourth figure is St George, whilst in a memorial in the little village of East Brent in Somerset the fourth figure represents the merchant navy whose vital contribution to the war effort and considerable loss of life is surprisingly underrepresented elsewhere.[12] (The merchant navy is most conspicuously recognised in a major, largely architectural, national memorial by Sir Edwin Lutyens, built by the side of the Thames at Tower Bridge).

Fine figures of sailors can be found on numerous memorials in all parts of the country, both as reliefs and figures in the round. Londonderry provides a particularly dynamic example, the barefoot sailor shown in the act of hauling on his coat, as though responding to an emergency on deck. Sailors are also shown of course on those reliefs which feature a range of representative figures, such as Hermon Cawthra's impressive panels for the Bury memorial, one sailor, again barefoot, shown here with a coil of rope, alongside others marching with rifles on their shoulders.

With the exception of memorials to individuals, it is extremely unusual to find effigies of sailors in isolation. Indeed, I am aware of only one example, at Earsdon in Northumberland, where the sailor is shown in a mourning pose. At the seaside resort of Bridlington, in a memorial by Stanley Nicholson Babb, a sailor rather than a soldier is given the more prominent role in the imagery of their memorial. Here the sailor, with gun in hand and dead comrade at his feet, is paired, on opposite sides of the cenotaph, with a winged Victory. Soldiers are relegated to subsidiary roles, slumped at the feet of the figure of Victory. As for airmen, again with the exception of memorials to individuals, I know of no equivalent to the Earsdon memorial.

The emphasis on soldiering is of course understandable: those enlisting in the army far outnumbered those for the other services. In total, over 5,200,000 men served in the army between 1914 and 1918, whilst 'only' 640,000 served in the navy and just under 300,000 in the Royal Flying Corps and Royal Air Force.[13] Even at important naval bases such as Portsmouth, many men naturally enlisted in the other services as well, the town's war memorial reflecting this fact by the inclusion of figures of both a soldier and a sailor. Casualties were also proportionally greater in the army: almost 13% of those who served were killed but less than 7% in the navy and only 2% in the airforce.[14] At Earsdon, despite the emphasis of its imagery, only 2 of the 24 men from the town who died were sailors and at Bridlington, of 320 men killed, only 26 served at sea, with 10 in the airforce and the rest in the army.

If, by the beginning of the century, the reputation of the soldier had greatly improved, an important factor was his status as volunteer. The tradition of volunteer armies had arisen during the Napoleonic wars. In addition to normal recruitment, 'gentlemen' were encouraged to form their

Pl.41
Londonderry.
Vernon March
1927

47

own private volunteer forces of infantry or cavalry to protect the country in the event of an invasion. When the threat passed, such groups were disbanded. In 1858, rising tensions between the British and the French led to renewed fears of invasion which in turn led to the re-emergence of volunteers. This time they were officially authorised as part of the reorganisation of the armed forces in the wake of the Crimean War. They were to remain a popular and important aspect of military organisation until the early years of the twentieth century when they were replaced by the Territorials.

Earlier volunteer corps had been largely for the prosperous rather than the labouring classes but during the 1860s they were transformed into a mass movement with forces established in most regions, still with a predominance of middle class participants but with an audience drawn from all sections of British society. The historian, Hugh Cunnigham, goes so far as to suggest that volunteering could be considered the principal spectator sport of mid-Victorian Britain.[15] Hundreds of thousands participated as spectators or competitors in mock fights, rifle-shooting contests, and military reviews. At a review in 1860 at Knowsley in Lancashire it was estimated that between 150,000 and 200,000 'holiday-makers' watched 11,000 Volunteers parading and competing.[16] As with First World War recruitment, women played their part in encouraging men to join and by 1903, 2.7% of all British men between the ages of 15 and 49 were in the Volunteer Force.[17]

For General Wolseley, writing in 1878, volunteerism was undoubtedly responsible for the improving image of the common soldier.

> The stigma formerly attached to the man who enlisted is quickly disappearing, and must disappear altogether if the Volunteer movement goes on prospering as it has hitherto done. When you have the large proportion of our male population, which is now either in the Volunteer ranks or has passed through them, all taught to look up to the Regular Soldier as their model of excellence, and who ... have learnt to appreciate the many good sides of the British soldier's character ... it is quite certain that the old prejudice against the soldier must soon die out altogether.[18]

Whether all who had been taught to 'look up to the Regular Soldier' necessarily did so was of course open to some doubt. With the declaration of war in 1914 and the sudden need for large numbers of recruits to supplement the relatively few regulars and Territorials there were many who demanded the introduction of conscription to meet the crisis. There was however considerable resistance to this. The subsequent response to the call to arms more than vindicated the views of those who maintained that with a strong tradition of volunteering and a widespread belief in patriotic duty, compulsion would prove unnecessary. In the first eighteen months of the war some 2.4 million men joined the army voluntarily and in all, over 24% of men of eligible age in England and Wales, and almost 27% in Scotland, joined of their own volition. In Ireland, the take-up, understandably given the political instability in the country at the time, was somewhat less, at around 11%.[19]

The fact that so many of those who had sacrificed their lives in the First World War had been volunteers undoubtedly helped shape the forms and extent of commemoration after the war. There was a widely felt need for an acknowledgement of the response of so many men, not professional soldiers but 'ordinary' citizens who had answered the call. Indeed, it is significant that British war memorials frequently acknowledge not only those who died but also, more generally, those who fought, including survivors. Furthermore, unlike earlier memorials where the military figure is frequently an officer, depictions of officers on First World War memorials were relatively rare whilst the listing of names often took no account of the hierarchy of rank. This was in contrast to Boer War memorials where officers and NCOs are invariably listed ahead of 'the men'. This emphasis on equality in death parallels the contemporary treatment of graves in the cemeteries of the Imperial War Graves Commission where arguments for personalised gravestones were rejected in favour of a standardised approach which emphasised the common sacrifice made by all ranks.[20]

The response to the 'call to arms' of 1914 is significantly acknowledged on a number of war memorials. Outside Llandaff Cathedral in Cardiff, the memorial to the men and boys of the parish and the Cathedral School was designed by Sir William Goscombe John, a native of the city. It shows the figure of St Llandaff bestowing her blessing on 'her own sons' who answered the call, represented by the man and boy who stand on either side of her. The boy, in shorts and football boots, and the man, in civilian clothes, both hold rifles. They are in this way clearly identified as volunteers rather than professional soldiers, as ordinary townspeople ready and willing to fight for their country.[21]

Soldiers are shown marching off to war, often with a smile or looking back with a cheery wave, in reliefs at Hastings, Newlyn, Eccleston, Portsmouth,

Colwyn Bay and Birmingham amongst others. At Rockcliffe in Cumbria, a single soldier is shown walking away with a rifle over his shoulder. As the art historian Catherine Moriarty has pointed out, there was some poignancy in the image of the man marching off to war as this represented the last sighting of the man who would not return.[22]

That last sighting was often on the station platform and memorial plaques were frequently placed in these evocative locations. A plaque at Victoria Station in Manchester can be found at what was known as the 'fishdock', a goods platform used in peace time for the unloading of fish but during the war as a departure point for troop trains. The inscription records that it is 'To the memory of the many thousands of men who passed through this door to the Great War, 1914-1919, and of those who did not return'.

A most unusual memorial, which records not only the enlistment and departure of ordinary working men but also their military experiences, is to be found in the Yorkshire village of Sledmere. Designed by Sir Mark Sykes, landowner and MP for Central Hull, and later commander of the 5th Yorkshires, the memorial commemorates, as the inscription explains, 'The gallant services rendered in the Great War 1914-1919 by the Waggoners' Reserve, a corps of 1,000 drivers raised by him'. Concerned about an impending conflict and aware of the vital contribution that drivers of horse-drawn vehicles could make (and of the time it would take to train them from scratch), the reserve was raised from the local farmers of the Yorkshire Wolds by Sir Mark some two years before the outbreak of war.

The memorial was erected after Sir Mark's death in 1919 when designs by him were discovered in Sledmere House. Built by the Sykes' estate mason and carved by the London-based sculptor Carlo Magnoni, it was somewhat generously described by Nicholas Pevsner as 'curiously homely'.[23] What it may lack in aesthetic appeal, in its overall design and naive figuration, is however more than made up for by the fascination of the detail and the narrative flow. Continuous reliefs on three tiers around a squat drum show farm labourers at work in the fields, receiving their call-up papers and going to enlist. As soldiers, they are shown disembarking and working behind the lines and engaged in hand to hand combat. There are also scenes of German 'atrocities' and of ultimate defeat, with German soldiers shown confronted by and subsequently fleeing from a single advancing 'Waggoner'. The naivety of style seems to confirm the volunteers as unsophisticated innocents, responding to all demands with serious patriotic concern, from the delivery of 'call-up' papers to the advance of snarling German troops.

Pls.43 & 44 (detail) 'Waggoners Memorial'. Sledmere. Sir Mark Sykes and Carlo Magnoni, 1919

At Liverpool, in that city's rather more conventional memorial, the departure of newly trained troops becomes a major focus and an important aspect of the meaning of the monument. A thirty-one feet long bronze panel on one side of the great, tomblike slab depicts the massed ranks marching off to war. The stylised anonymity of the troops as they march, in step and four deep, a united and depersonalised fighting force, was interpreted at the time as intending 'to indicate a vast sustained movement'.[24] It is in marked contrast to the panel on the other side of the memorial depicting, in realistic detail, the individual reactions of the bereaved in mourning the dead. Again it emphasises the fact that many of those seen marching off had not marched back.

Liverpool's memorial was unveiled on Armistice Day 1930, considerably later than had first been envisaged. Like most civic memorials the intention was that it be funded by public subscription. However, the original scheme was postponed in 1920 in view of the city's considerable levels of unemployment which seriously restricted the potential for raising sufficient money for a suitable monument. It was not until five years later that a decision was made by the City Council to revive the scheme and to fund it with Corporation money. The present monument therefore had its origins in an open competition announced in June 1926 which attracted 257 competitors from France and Canada as well as all parts of the United Kingdom. Between them they submitted 767 drawings and 39 models.

The competition was won by the Liverpool architect Lionel Budden whose long, low, tomblike scheme was 'designed to harmonise in shape and material with the main lines and fabric' of St George's Hall in front of which it was intended to stand. His plans included the relief panels on either side described above.[25] These were the work of a local sculptor, George Herbert Tyson Smith, who had previously worked with

Budden on Birkenhead's war memorial and who may therefore have been involved in the scheme from the start. There are however significant differences between Budden's original sketches and Tyson Smith's final designs, not least in the depiction of the marching soldiers. Budden's naturalistically grouped soldiers are replaced by the stylised, massed ranks and it seems probable that the sculptor intended this to emphasise a sense of regrettable necessity rather than an acknowledgement of enthusiastic patriotism which, by the late 1920s, may no longer have seemed entirely appropriate. The emphasis on the other side of the memorial on the inevitable grief that war creates underlines the point.

This bracketing of the beginning and end of war - the initial response and ultimate sorrow - is a device repeated in various forms on other memorials. At Bolton it is shown as 'Struggle' and 'Sacrifice'. On one side of the memorial a female figure representing 'Peace' restrains a semi-naked youth, clearly anxious to be released; on the opposite side the same two figures form a pietá. The mother's gesture is familiar from religious art, Giotto's Bardi chapel to Caravaggio's Entombment, whilst the dead man's posture echoes Michaelangelo's unfinished Pietá in the Duomo in Florence. The meaning of the former group was explained at the time in the unveiling ceremony booklet:

Pl.45
Liverpool.
G.H Tyson
Smith, 1930

The figure of 'Peace' is seated on a raised platform or plinth, and with restraining hand she holds Youth' characteristic of the best manhood of our Town - clean and fit, with unbounded energy - prepared to give all for its Country ... Anxiety and sadness are plainly discernable [sic] in her features and she is loath to release her hold until honour demands that the issue can only be decided by War ... not until all else fail will she relax her hold. We believe them to be typical of the attitude of our Country in those critical days of 1914.[26]

Again the memorial had been initially planned in 1920 and again, through concerns about unemployment, but also in this case opposition from some, including the Bolton Trades Council, the scheme was put on hold. At a meeting in April 1921 the mayor told the council that 'many influential persons' as he put it were opposed to a municipal monument on the grounds that, with so many memorials in schools and churches already built, the necessity for a monument no longer existed.[27] The opening of a fund to raise money was consequently postponed. The scheme was eventually revived in 1924 and the design for a proposed monument (by A.J Hope, a local architect) was accepted. It was not until 1927, however, that a competition was finally held to find an appropriate artist for the sculptural group which Hope's design envisaged.

Of three sculptors short-listed, Walter Marsden was chosen. Born in nearby Church near Accrington in 1882, the son of a blacksmith, Marsden

Pls.46 and 47
Bolton.
Walter Marsden,
1932

began his working life in the terracotta department of the Accrington Brick and Tile Company. Between 1907 and 1911 he was a student at the Manchester Municipal School of Art, where he was taught by John Millard, before going on to study at the Royal College of Art in London. Although the memorial was unveiled in 1928, Marsden's sculptures were not completed in time and were only finally installed in 1932 when they were unveiled as part of that year's Armistice Day ceremony.

An allegorical approach was considered preferable at Bolton to the depiction of soldiers in modern uniforms which, the war memorial committee felt, would 'be considered by future generations [as] a relic, rather than a permanent memorial for all time'.[28] Although generally well received it is worth noting that Marsden's figures were scathingly criticised by Walter Gilbert who had been one of the unsuccessful competitors. He condemned them as superficial and failing to 'go deep enough into the fibre of our being', suggesting that, in depicting a mother reluctant to release her son for war, they were 'an incentive to cowardice [and] a justification of the outlook of the conscientious objector who reared his head in the last war'.[29]

Pls.48
'The Call'.
Scottish American
Memorial,
Edinburgh.
Robert Tait
McKenzie, 1927

Marsden however, unlike Gilbert, had fought in the war, serving as a junior officer in the Bolton 5th Loyal Lancashire Regiment, and had twice been decorated for bravery, winning the MC and Bar. In November 1917 he was taken prisoner at Cambrai and was to serve out the rest of the war in a prisoner of war camp in Germany. As his comments elsewhere indicate he had little enthusiasm for glorifying war or for underplaying its tragic consequences and his work at Bolton clearly reflected his views.

On monuments elsewhere the theme of a more enthusiastic response to war forms the central focus of the memorial. Robert Tait McKenzie's Scottish-American Memorial in the gardens below Princes

Street in Edinburgh - a 'tribute from men and women of Scottish blood and sympathies in the United States of America to Scotland' - is entitled *The Call, 1914.*[30] The idea for the memorial was at the suggestion, in 1923, of John Gordon Gray, a former President of the St Andrews Society of Philadelphia.

The Canadian born sculptor Tait McKenzie was an obvious choice for this commission. A resident of Philadelphia as Professor of Physical Education at the University of Pennsylvania, McKenzie was also a successful artist of Scottish descent who had previously produced war memorials in England, Canada and the USA. In addition he had himself been a former President of the St Andrews Society. Once the decision for the memorial had been confirmed and a site obtained, McKenzie was asked to submit a design. In the Spring of 1926 working models were sent to Edinburgh where the work was completed. The memorial was unveiled the following year.

In front of a fifty feet long wall, seated on a pedestal, is the figure of a young kilted soldier, his rifle across his knees. Gazing into the far distance he appears to be about to rise, indicating his eagerness to join the distant battle. In the twenty-five feet by four feet high bronze relief on the wall behind, a pipe band leads a recruitment party, followed by a representative group of recruits: miners, farmers, shepherds, fishermen and clerks. As at Liverpool, the men march four deep, but here there is considerably more life and vigour in the depiction of individual characters, based in fact on a series of relief studies made by the artist of members of the King's Own Scottish Borderers. Unlike at Liverpool, where the serried ranks are shown in stylised form, at Edinburgh a central, single-point perspective scheme is used to depict the marching men. This serves not only to increase the realism of the scene but also to emphasise the disciplined unity of the central group of recruiting sergeant and soldiers where only the end figures of each column are clearly visible, in contrast to the relative confusion of potential recruits and pipe band seen obliquely at either end.

Where the single seated figure at Edinburgh records the moment of response of the trained soldier, the frieze behind depicts the process of transformation, from eager civilians, accompanied by animals and children, to a disciplined and regimented fighting force. In this it closely echoes recruitment posters from the early years of the war. The fishermen and farmers on the extreme left in their oilskins and overcoats, sou'westers and flat caps, gradually begin to march in step and assume a more military guise. One man reaches down to support a small boy who, with his dog, runs to keep up. The miners behind the recruiting party mimic the soldiers by resting their picks, like rifles, on their shoulders.

Sir William Goscombe John's monument commemorating the raising of the Northumberland Fusilier battalions by the Newcastle and Gateshead Chambers of Commerce is in many ways similar. It was commissioned and paid for by Sir George Renwick, a local ship owner and Member of Parliament for Morpeth, and was intended to commemorate three things: first and foremost the safe return of Renwick's five sons from the war; secondly his attainment, by 1916, of fifty years of commercial life on Newcastle's quayside; thirdly the raising of the battalions by the Chambers of Commerce.

The 'Commercials', as they were known, were an example of what came to be referred to as 'Pals' units. The idea of forming battalions of men all drawn from the same community or workplace, on the assumption that they might more readily enlist if promised that they could serve with friends, neighbours or work mates, was not in fact new. Volunteer and Territorial forces had earlier been based on this very concept. These units however had been for home defence, not active service abroad, and had anyway been organised on an entirely different scale.

Although Lord Derby has often been given the credit, the idea for Pals units in the First World War seems to have originated in the War Office, the first of such units, popularly known as the Stockbrokers' Battalion, being raised in the City of London in late August 1914.[31] Within days similar schemes were

STEP INTO YOUR PLACE

being organised across the country but it was in the towns and cities of the industrial north where the idea had the greatest appeal. It was here that Lord Derby, former MP and Lord Mayor of Liverpool and subsequently Director-General of Recruiting for the British Expeditionary Force, was instrumental in organising recruitment, initially in Liverpool but later elsewhere.

Some Pals battalions such as the Stockbrokers' Battalion and those for a number of public schools, were composed of upper middle class men. Others were more or less exclusively composed of the working classes. The Salford Pals were drawn largely from the working class slums around the docks and cotton mills of the city whilst the North Eastern Railway Pioneers in Northumberland, like many others, arose out of a common workplace. In Manchester, the Clerks' and Warehousemen's Battalions, previously referred to, were specifically aimed to appeal to the middle classes who might have been reluctant to enlist alongside working class men.

Pl.51
'The Commercials'
War Memorial.
Newcastle.
Sir William
Goscombe John,
1923

Like the later erection of monuments to the dead, civic pride and a determination to be no less patriotic than one's neighbours became a powerful motivating force in the formation of Pals units and by the end of September fifty battalions had been created in towns across the British Isles. The Newcastle Commercials were formed in early September, the

required numbers being secured within eight days with two more battalions being raised before Christmas.

Goscombe John entitled his memorial to the Commercials, *The Response, 1914*. Set on a rusticated plinth against a granite wall, the bronze group depicts a large gathering of marching soldiers and would-be recruits led by two drummer boys. Intermingled with the men are women and children who bid them farewell. Leading the group is a trumpet-blowing angel floating above the heads of the front figures, adding considerable momentum to the group. This incongruously allegorical note was no doubt intentionally reminiscent of François Rude's carving of *The Departure* (of volunteers to the front) on the Arc de Triomphe in Paris where the winged, allegorical figure of France leading her people similarly rises above them. There is no echo however, in Goscombe John's vision, of Rude's furious aggression and violent passions, but rather a suggestion of grim determination mixed with sorrow at the unavoidable separation from loved ones.

Where Tait Mckenzie in his Edinburgh memorial illustrates by his selection and organisation of 'types' the metamorphosis of civilian into soldier - into the anonymous fighting force as depicted on the Liverpool frieze - Goscombe John's work at Newcastle conveys the impression of recently enlisted, newly uniformed men mingling with those yet to be kitted out or yet to be officially signed up. They are united not so much by

Pl.52
(detail)
'The
Commercials'
War Memorial.
Newcastle.
Sir William
Goscombe John,
1923

Pl.53
'The Departure'.
Arc de Triomphe,
Paris.
François Rude,
1833-36

a soon to be imposed military discipline, clearly lacking in the present cluttered mass, but by a shared sense of duty and the belief in a just cause.

It has been suggested that the scene the memorial depicts was based on descriptions of the massing of the 5th Northumberland Fusiliers in April 1915 when they marched from their camp in Gosforth Park, along the Great North Road, through the Haymarket and on to the Central Station to board the trains which would take them to the front, their route lined by cheering and weeping well-wishers and relatives.[32]

The reluctant departure from wives and children, which we see not only here but on many other memorials of the Great War, suggests a personal sacrifice on the part of women which hints at the far greater 'ultimate sacrifice' of so many men. It also reveals a tenderness and overt emotionalism which is in marked contrast to much of the heroizing of wartime propaganda. In a memorial at St Anne's-on-Sea, which contrasts the confident and enthusiastic departure of troops with their weary return, Walter Marsden qualifies the former by adding a scene of separation with the distressed wife comforted by her uniformed husband while their bewildered daughter looks on.

Pl.54
Workington.
Alexander
Carrick, 1928

One of Alexander Carrick's relief panels for the memorial at Workington, designed by the Scottish architect, Sir Robert Lorimer, shows a similar family group, the husband and wife here with touching heads and clasped hands. The woman's arm, reaching up to grasp her husband's hand, seems to form an unintended barrier between them. Her other hand reaches down to her son, holding his arm. He in turn reaches up to his father, but this unifying circularity is broken by the gap between the child's and the father's hands, symbolic perhaps of the Great War's shattering of family ties. Instead of his son's hand, the soldier significantly holds his rifle and the son can only grasp at the hem of his father's coat.

A similarly subtle suggestion of a separation which all too often became permanent is achieved in a detail from Hermon Cawthra's sculptural relief for Bury's war memorial, in a panel depicting the roles of women on the home front. Alongside the munitions, factory and farm workers is a woman carrying a small child in her arms. The mother

tenderly kisses her baby's forehead. In her left hand is an envelope and letter which we are clearly meant to understand to have been received from her husband, away fighting the enemy. The panel at Bury is an acknowledgement of the various contributions to the war effort of men and women on the home front. This detail acknowledges the sacrifices that women also made when encouraging their menfolk to go to war and we are reminded of the all too common letters and telegrams informing women of their husbands' deaths.

At Newcastle, Goscombe John shows a number of farewells. At the memorials' far end we see a new recruit kissing the baby his wife holds up to him. An older child clings to her mother, only half aware of the reasons for the turmoil around her. Nearby another man turns to his admiring son who carries his kit bag. Most conspicuously, particular attention is concentrated on a third young soldier's tender embrace of his daughter by placing this group centre stage. As the man pauses and turns to the girl one last time, his son, holding his father's rifle over his shoulder, impatiently beckons him on. His gesture is echoed by another, younger boy to the right of the girl, encouraging his own, not yet uniformed father. The tools of his trade the man carries in his hand suggest he has yet to answer the call; his presence in the mass of moving bodies intimates however that he is about to do so, though Goscombe John may also have intended this figure to be an acknowledgement of the contribution to the war effort of those men from 'reserved' occupations.

The inclusion of so many children is unusual but significant. For

Goscombe John, both here and in memorial sculpture elsewhere, young boys are shown, both literally and metaphorically, following in their fathers' footsteps, the fighting force of the future. Girls, like their mothers, stand passively by, watching and grieving.

Pl.58
(detail) 'The Commercials'
Newcastle.
Sir W Goscombe John, 1923

III

Women of Britain Say "Go!"

Fighting wars was seen as 'men's business'; the woman's role was merely supportive. Underlying this idea was the belief that men were naturally aggressive. An article entitled 'Woman's Attitude to War' published in *The Graphic* less than three weeks after war had been declared suggested that 'The primeval woman is opposed to war because her mission in the eternal scheme of things is to produce life, not to destroy it, ... She is the everlasting mother defending her young ... The Creative, constructive side of life is the "eternally feminine" ... The Destructive is the male'.[1]

Geddes and Thomson in *The Evolution of the Sexes*, first published in 1889, claimed that masculine aggression arose from 'the male tendency to dissipate energy' whilst 'female passivity [flowed] from the complementary tendency to conserve resources'.[2] The theory was an elaboration of Herbert Spencer's influential account of sex differences which, he suggested, revealed 'a somewhat earlier arrest of individual evolution in women than in men, necessitated by the reservation of vital power to meet the cost of reproduction'.[3] In other words female energy expended in reproduction was not available for intellectual growth but the male's contribution to the process, being restricted to mere fertilisation, meant less inhibition on his development. Man was consequently seen as more highly evolved than woman, with the inferior (or at least different) position of women claimed as having a biological basis.

Constructions of gender according to sexual difference were socially realised in the theory of 'separate spheres'. The definition of femininity which evolved during the nineteenth century produced a list of qualities which were the antitheses of those deemed essential to participation in the public sphere. The capacity for reasoning, decision making and action and an aggressive self-interest were seen as male attributes whilst women were claimed to be emotional, passive, submissive and dependent. The man's sphere was consequently seen as being that of industry and commerce, politics and law and, of course, the armed forces; in other words public life. Woman's place was in the home.

Such ideas were not universally accepted, either by women or men. Both the concept of separate spheres and the constructions of gender upon which they were based were vociferously contested, in particular by women's suffrage groups in the years leading up to the war. A petition for women's suffrage had first been presented to the House of Commons in the 1830s but it was not until 1897 and the formation of the National Union of Women's Suffrage Societies (the NUWSS) led by Millicent Garrett Fawcett that a concerted campaign to obtain votes for women was mounted. The campaign was soon intensified by the founding, in 1903 in Manchester, of the more militant Women's Social and Political Union (the WSPU). It was the vociferous and at times violent actions of the WSPU, led by Emmeline Pankhurst and her two daughters, Christabel and Sylvia, which gave rise to the term 'suffragettes', coined in 1906 by the *Daily Mail*. In addition to the regular rallies, marches and speech making, suffragette activities included window smashing, arson attacks and the damaging of works of art, most famously the slashing of Velasquez's *Rokeby Venus*. Many women were imprisoned and many went on hunger strikes.

Many suffragists were also pacifists and, with the outbreak of war, some resolved both to continue the campaign for votes and to support a peaceful settlement. However, both major organisations in support of women's suffrage, the NUWSS on the advice of its members and the WSPU on the advice of the Pankhursts, ceased campaigning and turned their energies, like those of the majority of women nation-wide, towards the war effort. Both Fawcett and Emmeline Pankhurst encouraged and supported the recruitment drive for the armed forces with Pankhurst's active participation and agreement to suspend all militant activity leading, in August 1914, to all imprisoned suffragettes being released.

Primarily, the role of women at the start of the war was the encouragement of men's enlistment and an acceptance of their own separate supportive sphere of action as wives and mothers. Posters encouraging women to encourage men to enlist were common. Many women were of course horrified at the prospect of their husbands leaving to fight, or dismayed to learn that sons had rushed to 'join the colours', but it is clear that large numbers of women did actively support enlistment.

Women were encouraged, in a campaign initiated by an elderly retired admiral, Penrose Fitzgerald, to hand out white feathers, a symbol of cowardice, to young men not in uniform. Inevitably, those on leave, in

Pl.59
Wartime Poster.
'Women of
Britain say 'Go!'
E.V Kealey, 1915

reserved occupations or simply underage were also targeted and many ex-soldiers have recalled being given white feathers under such circumstances. Norman Demuth was one, though he also recalled how girls would treat men not in uniform with utter contempt which, he suggested, was at least as hurtful as receiving white feathers.[4] Demuth was in fact given white feathers on more than one occasion, when on leave and out of uniform but the first time only weeks after leaving school at the age of sixteen. Encouraged by this to believe he looked older than his years he immediately enlisted in the London Rifle Brigade. Like many young men at the time he lied about his age.

The lower age limit for the armed services was supposed to be eighteen. It has been estimated however that as many as a quarter of a million soldiers were underage when they enlisted, some as young as fourteen, and many memorial statues of soldiers significantly emphasise the obvious youth of their models.[5] Despite his youth, Norman Demuth was apparently encouraged by his mother whom he felt was proud of him, claiming that 'when the mothers were seeing us off at Waterloo you could see an enormous sense of pride on their faces'.[6]

Post-war memorial sculpture frequently highlighted the role of wife and mother. Some, as we have seen, shown at the moment of separation from their uniformed husbands, reflect the mixed emotions expressed in the lyrics of one popular song of the day: 'We don't want to lose you, but we think you ought to go'.[7] Although the imagery of memorials at times seems to echo the iconography of wartime recruitment posters, by the end of the war the recognition of the grief and suffering of innumerable women who had lost husbands and sons tended to discourage, or at least temper, any overt representation of the pride which many women had undoubtedly felt in their menfolk's willingness to fight. John Cassidy's memorial at Clayton-le-Moors in Lancashire presents an interestingly ambiguous pair of figures.

The youthful figure of a soldier, which Cassidy was to reuse for memorials at Heaton Moor in Stockport and Colwyn Bay in North Wales, stands impassively, staring straight ahead, with both hands lightly holding the end of the barrel of his rifle, the butt of which rests on the ground. By his side, raised slightly above him on a rocky mound, is a barefoot female

Pl.60
Clayton-le-Moors.
John Cassidy,
1920

Pl.61
'Go! It's Your
Duty Lad'.
Poster, 1915

figure in a long, flowing classical robe and with a laurel wreath on her head. Her right arm is around the man, lightly touching his right shoulder. Her left arm is outstretched, pointing into the distance as if to indicate the direction in which he must go.

Despite the obvious comparison which might be made with the propaganda image of a mother indicating to her son where his duty lay, the allegorical nature of the female figure serves to distance her from such a specific interpretation. More generally, there seems to be an implication that, having accepted the call to enlist, he has done his duty to King and Country and that those who encouraged him had right on their side.

As in many other locations the original bronze plaques on Clayton's memorial were replaced and updated after the Second World War to add reference to that conflict. The inscription however is retained: 'Pass not in sorrow but in lowly pride, and strive to live as nobly as they died'. Its implications of the moral validity of the soldiers' and the Country's actions, and its specific reference to death, point to the possible origins and intended meaning of the iconography. A small statuette by William Goscombe John entitled *Old Man and Angel*, or *The Guardian Angel*, most probably derived from of a work entitled *The Reaper* exhibited at the Royal Academy in 1888, reveals a remarkably similar scenario. In this sculpture

66

the figure of a winged angel of death points the way ahead to his dying companion. This theme, of 'Mors Janua Vitae' ('Death as the gateway to everlasting life'), was a popular one in late Victorian painting and sculpture and was a sentiment frequently applied to the soldier's self-sacrifice by an encouraging clergy, with the Latin dictum occasionally inscribed on First World War memorials.

That said, the iconography of the Clayton memorial is also remarkably similar to the imagery of popular cards produced during the war for wives, girlfriends and mothers to send to their loved ones serving overseas. One such card shows an identically posed soldier, again accompanied by an allegorical female figure in long flowing robes. Her arms are also outstretched, though in this case to present to the soldier a vision of home, represented by the snow-covered rooftops of the half-timbered houses clustered around the village church. The accompanying caption, 'We'll keep the home fires burning and the church bells ringing till our lads come home', clearly implies the expectation of the soldier's survival. Despite what could be seen as the martyr's palm held in her hand, no doubt intended here in its original form as a symbol of victory, the female's identity is presumably that of guardian angel rather than angel of death.

Pl.62
Wartime Christmas card

Pl.63
'The Guardian Angel'.
William Goscombe John,
c1888

Whether the statue at Clayton would have been interpreted in this way, particularly given the sculpture's role in representing the 'absent dead', is however open to some doubt. A remarkably similar approach to Cassidy's monument at Clayton was used by Henry Poole for his memorial in Nottingham to the flying ace, Captain Albert Ball. Like Cassidy's soldier, the airman is shown with an allegorical female figure behind him, balancing in bare feet on billowing clouds. Her arm is similarly outstretched but she points, in this case, appropriately to the heavens. If we see this as indicating the serviceman's fate, as in Goscombe John's *Old Man and Angel,* we can read the gesture as having a double meaning, pointing to the heavens in which he operated, but also to the Heaven to which it is suggested he is bound.

By their encouragement, the very constructions of gender which had previously been opposed by suffragists were inevitably reinforced. Women now required men to act out the role of warrior in their defence, a role not necessarily in accord with their nature and imposed upon them by virtue of their sex. Indeed, for some women the ferocity of the war seemed to confirm what they had previously argued against, that gender was naturally rather than socially constructed and that masculinity was essentially characterised by violence and brutality.

The reality of course, for most men in war, was at best an ambivalent attitude towards aggression mixed with uncertainty and fear. Such feelings were not confined to understandable concerns for self preservation. Lyn McDonald quotes the initial reactions of one man to killing: "I felt, unaccountably, physically sick. I had a distinct fear of the consequences of breaking one of the most solemn laws of civilisation".[8] Another recalled killing a German in 1915. The man's head had appeared in his sights but he found it impossible to press the trigger, feeling that "to shoot such a 'sitter' so deliberately in cold blood required more moral courage than I possessed".[9] The next time his head appeared however he was shot. "I felt funny for days and the shooting of another German at 'stand-to' the next morning did nothing to remove those horrid feelings I had".[10]

Some men of course reacted quite differently, and in a manner more in keeping with stereotypical ideas of masculinity. Educated at Eton and Balliol College Oxford, Julian Grenfell, whose poem *Into Battle* is one of the most anthologised of the First World War, wrote about the pleasures of killing Germans, keeping a tally of how many he had killed. In a letter to his mother on 24 October 1914 just before the start of the Battle of Ypres, Grenfell exclaimed 'I've never been so fit or nearly so happy in my life before, I adore the fighting'.[11] A week earlier he had written 'It is all the most *wonderful* fun; better fun than one could ever imagine. I hope it goes on for a nice long time; but pig-sticking will be the only tolerable pursuit after this one or one will die of sheer ennui'.[12] In fact, he died of his wounds in April 1915. A memorial to Julian and his younger brother Gerald, kiled two months earlier, can be seen at Taplow Court in Buckinghamshire, the former family home. Carved by Bertram MacKennal, it features a suitably flamboyant image of a naked Apollo in his horse drawn chariot.

Such attitudes were by no means the norm, but equally and despite an understandable reluctance by many men to admit to it, these were not isolated views.[13] As Joanna Bourke says at the start of her exhaustive analysis of 20th century warfare, *An Intimate History of Killing,* 'The characteristic act of men at war is not dying, it is killing', but this was not something which post-war memorials were inclined to stress.[14]

The illustration of aggressive acts in memorial sculpture was certainly rare, a careful line needing to be drawn it was felt between the construction of positive images of resoluteness and strength, both physical and moral, and suggestions of bellicosity. Criticism could arise when it was believed that this line had been crossed. Bradford's war memorial, unveiled on 1 July 1922, the sixth anniversary of the first day of the Battle of the Somme where the Bradford Pals Battalion of the West Yorkshire Regiment had suffered very heavy losses, consists of a rather squat cenotaph in Victoria Square. The front of the cenotaph culminates in a solid, carved cross and on either side, facing the front, are representative figures of a soldier and a sailor.

The memorial had been produced by H.H Martyn Ltd. Their head sculptor was Robert Lindsey Clark who may well have been responsible for these figures. Both men are shown in aggressive poses with rifles and fixed bayonets. The soldier in particular appears to be lunging forwards, the downward tilt of his rifle suggesting his violent intentions. However, an ex-serviceman writing to the local press in response to some criticism of this image explained that the soldier was simply shown advancing 'in the position of short point: he is therefore ready for peace or war'.[15] The alderman who unveiled the memorial, similarly conscious of criticism, also insisted that it was 'not a glorifying image of militarism, but a monument to the self-sacrifice of Bradford men'.[16]

Nonetheless it was felt by many, including the Lord Mayor of Bradford, that the figures were 'altogether too ferocious, too aggressive'. They did not, he suggested, 'strike the right note' and were 'apparently too ready for restarting business immediately'.[17] A local Baptist minister added the comment that 'the idea of the fixed bayonet was not the motive which led some of our best to lay down their lives'.[18]

Pl.64
Bradford.
H.H Martyn Ltd,
1922

Pl.65
below
Londonderry.
Vernon March,
1927

Pl.66
opposite
Dingwall.
James Alexander
Stevenson, 1922

In contrast, at nearby Keighley on a memorial unveiled two years later, Henry Fehr's more static, undemonstrative figures of servicemen were praised for giving 'an impression of alertness and vigour, yet without any hint of aggressive force'.[19] Figures elsewhere, advancing or 'on guard' with bayonets fixed, were more often shown as neutral or defensive: L.F Roslyn's figure used at both Portstewart and Dromore in Northern Ireland provides one example. This soldier was also used by Roslyn on monuments at Haslingden, Oswaldtwistle and Maesteg, though in each of these locations the soldier is shown with a wounded comrade, further emphasising his defensive role.

At Shildon in County Durham, the soldier is shown kneeling down. James Stevenson's kilted soldier at Dingwall in Scotland is leaning back and seems ready to repel an attack rather than instigate violent

action whilst other similar, if less impressive Scottish examples include defensive figures at Ellon and Minto, the sculptors here remaining unidentified.

The monument at Londonderry in Northern Ireland however presents an even more aggressive image than at Bradford, the angle of the soldier's rifle leaving no doubt of his violent intentions. The local paper described the figure as 'an interesting reminder of the desperarate fighting through which the infantry had to pass before victory was won.[20] The sculptor of this monument, Vernon March, as we shall see with other works, was never reserved in his approach. His winged Victories, one of which is placed on top of the tall pillar against which the soldier and his equally animated maritime companion stand, can now appear inappropriately celebratory and the soldier's forceful gesture here certainly seems shockingly belligerent.

However, Londonderry's monument was very much an exception and it is clear that in the post-war years generally, and in the production of war memorials specifically, there was normally a reluctance to acknowledge the reality that men had been engaged in killing other men, with the widespread encouragement of women. To reiterate Joanna Bourke's comments on the tendency of military historians to 'gloss over' the facts of killing, readers 'might be excused for believing that combatants found in war zones were really there to *be* killed, rather than to kill'.[21]

The war memorial however, whilst acknowledging and sometimes celebrating military victory, had as its primary function the acknowledge-

ment of the combatant's death - of men seen as victims rather than as the perpetrators of violence - with the bereaved as its primary audience. It is therefore understandable that the imagery of overt aggression was seen as contentious or inappropriate. As Walter Gilbert commented of his memorial at Burnley, he had ' endeavoured to conceive a memorial that shall breathe nothing of slaughter but only of duty fulfilled'. It was an aim clearly shared by others.[22]

As on many other memorials, the bayonets at Bradford no longer remain having been removed since being deliberately bent and twisted in 1969. The meaning of the servicemen's gestures, however, is clear, emphasised by the handles of the bayonets, still fixed to the rifles. At Londonderry, the local political situation has unquestionably been a significant additional aspect of the vandalism of this monument, though here the bayonets remain intact.

When placed in a more obviously narrative context, violence, perceived to be in a just cause, became more acceptable. One of the few memorials to depict the heat of battle was Philip Lindsey Clark's monument in Glasgow to the Scottish Rifles, popularly known as the 'Cameronians'. As one man clambers up and towards the enemy lines from a mound of mud, he is supported on his left by a machine-gunner. To his right a comrade lies dead.

Clark was born in London in 1889, the son of a successful sculptor, Robert Lindsey Clark, head sculptor and art director at H.H Martyn and Co. His art training was interrupted by the war: from 1910 to 1914 he studied at the South London Technical Art School and between 1919 and 1921 at the Royal Academy Schools. In between he had served with some distinction as a Captain in the army. Edmund Blunden, in his book, *Undertones of War*, commented on his bravery: 'He took charge of all the fighting, apparently, and despite being blown off his feet by shells, and struck about the helmet with shrapnel, and otherwise physically harassed, he was ubiquitous and invincible'.[23]

Lindsey Clark's firsthand knowledge of combat clearly helped. The Glasgow figure of the standing soldier leading his troops is similar to the same sculptor's soldier at Southwark, previously discussed, though at Glasgow he is clearly in the thick of the action. Clark presents an image, not merely of grit and determination, as at Southwark, but of bravery and resolution in the face of enemy fire. In the unveiling ceremony booklet this figure was seen as symbolising Victory whilst the dead soldier was said to represent Sacrifice. The third figure, the machine-gunner, was intended to typify the 'dogged determination to succeed and of "sticking it" for which our men were so remarkable'.[24] As we shall see, narrative often played an important role in the construction of meaning in war memorials

Pl.67
Cameronians
War Memorial,
Glasgow.
Philip Lindsey
Clark, 1924

73

Pl.68
'The Recruit Who
took To It Kindly'.
H.M Bateman.
Punch, 17th Jan 1917

Pl.69
opposite
The Waggoners
memorial.(detail)
Sledmere.Sir Mark
Sykes and Carlo
Magnoni, 1919

and here the explicit depiction of death in battle provides justification for the aggression of the troops who are consequently seen as literally fighting for their lives and, by implication, for ours too.

Whether the possessors of innate aggression or not, new recruits were certainly encouraged to act in an aggressive manner on the field of battle. As a wartime cartoon in *Punch* suggests, bayonet practice suitably served this purpose. Its military importance was minimal - only 0.03% of war wounds were actually inflicted by the bayonet - but its symbolic value was considerable.[25] Even the Navy taught men to use the bayonet. In his book *A Brass-Hat in No-Man's Land*, published in 1930, Brigadier-General F.P Crozier explained the rationale..

> The German atrocities (many of which I doubt in secret), the employment of gas in action, the violation of French women, and the 'official murder' of Nurse Cavell all help to bring out the brute-like bestiality which is so necessary for victory ... In order that he [the British soldier] shall enter into the true spirit of the show however, the fun of the fair as we may call it, it is necessary to corrode his mentality with bittersweet vice and to keep him up to the vicious scratch on all occasions.[26]

Such legitimisation of murderous aggression was clearly ideologically problematic but was justified by an emphasis, not only on Freedom, Honour and Justice - 'all those capitalised nouns of the high tradition', to use Samuel Hynes' expression - but also, more specifically, on the defence of women and children.[27] Much of the official propaganda in the early months of the war centred on Germany's invasion of Belgium and on the claimed atrocities committed there. In particular, it was stressed, outrages were committed against women and children.

The accusations of the sexual violation of women echoed the claims that the country had been brutally 'raped' by the invading barbarians. Such allegations were commonly reported in the press as fact and were supported by the publication of the Bryce Report in May 1915 following a government appointed investigation into 'Alleged German Outrages' led by Lord Bryce, a well-respected professor of jurisprudence and former Ambassador to the United States. The report, which concluded that atrocities *had* taken place, reproduced, in an extensive appendix, numerous unquestioned and unverified 'eyewitness reports'. It had a considerable and intentional impact on public opinion, not least in the United States.

The publication of the Bryce Report coincided with reports about the sinking by German U-boats of the passenger ship, the 'Lusitania', also in May 1915, and the first use of poison gas by the Germans in April. These were followed, later in the year, by reports of the execution of Nurse Edith Cavell. All of these incidents were successfully used for propaganda purposes.

Ironically, the German press had similarly claimed the perpetration of atrocities committed by Belgian citizens against *their* troops. In fact it was a nervousness about what the Germans saw as 'illegal' guerilla attacks on its invading troops which consequently led to a number of massacres of Belgian civilians. In one incident in August 1914 the Germans entered the Belgian town of Dinant and in retaliation for coming under what they wrongly assumed was civilian attack, over 600 civilians, including women and children, were massacred.[28] That said,

many of the other stories of German atrocities, despite Lord Bryce's claims, were at the very least exaggerated.

One artistic response to such atrocities was Francis Derwent Wood's 1918 sculpture of an alleged incident from 1915. Entitled *Canada's Golgotha*, the three feet high bronze relief showed the 'crucifixion' by German soldiers of a Canadian sergeant, whose limbs and body were pinned to the wall of a barn by bayonets. Included in an exhibition of war art in London in 1919, the sculpture caused tremendous controversy and was eventually withdrawn following protests by the German government who demanded proof, which could not be provided, of the veracity of the event.

Pl.70
below
Renfrew
J. Young, 1922

Pl.71
opposite
Kingston-upon-Thames.
Richard Goulden, 1923

Such acts were rarely depicted on war memorials but one exception to this was the 'Waggoners' memorial at Sledmere in Yorkshire. Here, one of the numerous scenes of the Waggoners' wartime experiences shows a leering German soldier setting fire to a church while his colleague, with sword raised, grasps a helpless woman by her hair. In 1938 the German government objected to these scenes of what they considered crude propaganda. The German Embassy in London demanded their removal, though obviously, and fortunately, without success. (As if to stress the contrast between German atrocities and British 'fair play', a relief panel on a memorial at Brierley Hill depicts British sailors rescuing Germans from the sea after the sinking of their ship).

The defence of 'poor little Belgium' became a major rallying call for those encouraging enlistment and the frequent gendering of propaganda for this purpose exploited the acceptance of men as protectors of women and children. This was sometimes literally featured in memorial sculpture, as at Warlingham in Surrey where the sculptor J.E Taylerson has shown a soldier with rifle at the ready protecting a mother and child who are collapsed at his feet. The soldier appears calm, in contrast to the distressed and exhausted mother and child.

A carved relief on a monument at Renfrew in Scotland similarly shows an alert Scottish soldier, his rifle with bayonet fixed, on some imaginary field of battle. The carving is quite badly weathered but we can still make out a biplane, in low relief above the soldier's head, and to his left, in front of a church, a field gun. The soldier has a look of grim determination on his face as he protects a mother and small child; the child's gesture of reaching up to his mother for comfort, is echoed by her half-hidden

gesture towards the soldier. A second woman is just visible, cowering to the right, behind the protective soldier. Both here and at Warlingham, we are perhaps meant to read these scenes metaphorically, the women and children behind the soldiers intended as representing the homeland for which they fight. The risks the soldier faced are emphasised on the reverse of the monument at Renfrew. Here a relief shows an angel placing a wreath onto a battlefield cross in a variation of the 'before and after' in memorials at Bolton and Liverpool.

At Alfreton in Derbyshire the theme is simply expressed in William Aumonier's figures of a soldier and a girl, the man's arms protectively around the young child's shoulder. The naturalism of the grouping is emphasised in the relaxed poses and in the detail; one of the girl's socks has slipped down around her ankles and her hands stretch up to embrace the soldier's comforting arm. But the wider significance of military action on her behalf and their tragic consequences are also stressed: barely visible, she holds in her hands the laurel wreath of victory and honour, so often used in mourning.

Elsewhere this protective theme is expressed in more allegorical form. This seems to have been the preferred approach of Richard Goulden. Goulden was born in Dover in 1877. After studying at Dover School of Art he won a scholarship to the Royal College. During the war he served as a Captain with the Royal Engineers in France before being invalided out in 1916. His memorial for his home town shows a semi-naked youth holding a cross high above his head, his feet symbolically entwined by thorns. Dover's memorial was unveiled in 1924, by which time Goulden had produced memorial sculptures for towns around the country including Brightlingsea, Gateshead, Crompton, Kingston-upon-Thames, Malvern and Reigate.

One of his first commissions however had been for the Bank of England. Here the memorial depicts St Christopher with the Christ child on his shoulder. This unusual, seemingly incongruous theme, inspired by the fact that the garden in which the memorial was originally placed had once been the churchyard of St Christopher-le-Stocks, was proposed by Goulden after his initial idea for a different allegorical group had been rejected. The inscription on the pedestal provides an explanation of the imagery's significance. The memorial is dedicated 'to the comrades who at Duty's Call crossed the dark waters to the further shore'. Goulden

Pl.72 *above*
Alfreton.
W. Aumonier, 1927

Pl.73 *opposite*
St Michael's church, Cornhill, London.
Richard Goulden, 1920

explained his thinking in similar, if slightly more obscure terms: 'My interpretation ... depicts youth in full vigour joyfully bearing his precious burden onward triumphant to the end, and at the moment of exultation and realisation of victory, finding its reward - the Cross of Sacrifice'.[29]

The theme was developed in a secular form two years later in Goulden's memorials for Reigate and Kingston-upon-Thames (both unveiled in 1923). At Kingston a striding figure, with a small child standing by his side gazing up at him, is shown holding aloft a flaming torch. And at Reigate we again see the athletic, semi-naked male, this time cradling a small child in one arm while the other raises the torch high above his head.

The upturned or extinguished torch had been used for centuries in funerary monuments as a symbol of death,. The flaming torch deployed in war memorial statuary was, in contrast, seen as the inextinguishable flame of justice and a symbol of continuing struggle. At Reigate it is referred to as 'the torch of self-sacrifice', the monument being described as representing 'the triumphant struggle of mankind against difficulties that beset the path of life. Shielding and bearing onward the child, the figure holds aloft the torch of self-sacrifice, to light the way .... The torch, used as a symbol, is a cross, enveloped in flames, which, though able to consume the body, cannot harm the spirit'.[30] The 'difficulties that beset the path of life' had been literally interpreted at Dover as thorns encircling the figure's feet and here it

is the thick vines which entwine the man's legs, snaking up around his waist and towards his neck.

Goulden's first use of an allegorical 'warrior' in a monument to the war dead was however at Cornhill in the City of London. Placed against a buttress on the porch of George Gilbert Scott's Church of St Michael, the thirteen feet high monument was unveiled in November 1920 and is dedicated to the 2,130 men from the offices in the parish who volunteered for the armed services, including at least 170 who 'gave their lives for the freedom of the world'.[31] It is perhaps his most impressive memorial. (In 1927, a replica of this memorial was unveiled at Neuve Chapelle in north-west France and a variation in relief form was also produced for the City of London Regiment in St John's Church in Hackney).

Pl.74 Crompton. Richard Goulden, 1923

The slim, youthful figure of the Archangel Michael, standing on a narrow, bronze plinth, his sword held rigidly above his head, creates a strong vertical thrust, accentuated by the upward spread of his wings. In counterbalance to this, arranged in a swirl around the plinth and the archangel's legs, are what *The Builder* described at the time as, 'quarrelling beasts which typify 'war' ... sliding slowly, but surely, from their previously paramount position'.[32] A group of four small children clamber away from this receding threat for the shelter of the winged protector.

A more aggressive reuse was made of this theme in another memorial by Goulden unveiled a few years later at Crompton in Lancashire. This time we see the warrior leaning forward to thrust his sword into the open jaws of one of two snarling beasts below. Small children huddle around his legs for protection. The children, quite clearly, are meant to represent the future generations whose safe-keeping has been secured. Significantly, in all of his war memorials, Goulden shows only the protection of children rather than of mother and child.

The suggestion was sometimes made, as at Bolton, that an allegorical approach might be considered preferable to the depiction of soldiers in modern uniforms on the grounds that the latter might more quickly become dated and the former remain timeless. Sir George Frampton, who had recommended Goulden for the Bank of England memorial, commented on this in 1919:

There seems to be a strong feeling for the soldier figure in khaki ...
but my own feeling is that finer results are generally obtained by
the use of symbolic figures or at least by combining them with the
portrait study. For it is difficult to make a portrait more than a
type, whereas an allegorical group may embody a whole ideal.[33]

Though Goulden's allegorical approach may now seem extrava-
gantly melodramatic, clearly there was some demand in the 1920s, not only
for Goulden's work but also for that of other like-minded artists. George
Henry Paulin's memorial at Kirkcudbright in Scotland was, for example,
similarly conceived, with a powerfully muscled, bare-chested swordsman
protecting a vulnerably naked sleeping child. Such imagery would no
doubt have been encouraged by memorial committees who preferred the
symbolic to the realistic. At Crompton the memorial committee made it

Pl.75
Kirkcudbright.
George Henry
Paulin, 1921

clear that they considered that depictions of soldiers, battle scenes and 'engines of war' failed to express adequately the 'splendid effort and self-sacrifice' of Crompton men 'to prevent the will of a great and aggressive nation being brutally forced upon us' and that their preference was therefore for the allegorical.[34]

Whilst sculptors such as Goulden may have been happy to conform and may well have been chosen precisely because of their propensity for the allegorical, others such as Charles Sargeant Jagger hinted at frustration with the choices made by memorial committees.

> Some elderly members of a memorial committee came to my studio to look at a figure of a soldier. It did not please them. They thought the puttees were done up too untidily, that the tin hat was too much on one side, and that altogether the Tommy wasn't respectable or smart enough for their memorial. In the end they decided not to have the soldier but a pretty symbolical figure of Victory instead.[35]

The 'pretty symbolical figure' was presumably not by Jagger, but despite the tone of his comments here, he was not averse to providing such work, witness the figures he produced at Brimington (of Britannia) and Bedford (of Justice). Indeed, at Hoylake and West Kirby, an allegorical figure of Humanity was chosen by Jagger against pressure for an effigy of a contemporary sailor. In discussing his figure of Britannia at Brimington Jagger enthusiastically explained his thinking. The symbolism, he hoped, would ensure that 'the passer-by in days to come may read in the quiet, calm resignation of the figure the great ideals for which it stands, and for which his ancestors died'.[36]

The use of allegory certainly allowed for more overt images of aggression. Semi-naked or armour-clad warriors thrusting sword or lance into the throat of the dragon or mythological beast were seen to symbolically stress the struggle of good against evil. Defending the usually unseen but always implied 'maiden in distress' (and by analogy, the country) in images of St George, or cowering children (and by analogy, future generations) in the work of Goulden or Paulin, the vanquished enemy could be clearly and expressively illustrated. In contrast, the contemporary soldier, seen as more directly representative of every mother's son and widow's husband, was to be shown in defensive pose. When shown as fighting, it is typically against the odds, with the visible repercussions of death and injury. If not, then as at Bradford, such depiction was open to criticism.

Sir William Goscombe John's monument at Port Sunlight, one of the most elaborate and impressive of all First World War memorials, again presents the theme of the soldier as the protector of women and children. Here the soldiers, one of whom is seriously wounded, slumped at the feet of his comrade, are typically shown as defensive rather than aggressive, waiting to repel a fresh attack from an unseen enemy.

William John was born in Cardiff in 1860. (The Goscombe, from his mother's side of the family, was added some years later). William was the son of a wood carver, Thomas John, whose workshop he entered at the age of fourteen before moving to London to become a pupil-assistant in the studio of Thomas Nicholls. Like George Frampton, born in the same year as John, he took modelling classes at the South London Technical Art School prior to enrolling at the Royal Academy Schools where the tutors included Hamo Thornycroft and Thomas Brock. Again like Frampton, he won the RA Gold Medal and Travelling Scholarship. As a result, he was able to visit France, Italy, Sicily, North Africa and Spain before settling in Paris where he became acquainted with and influenced by Auguste Rodin.

Goscombe John's reputation gradually grew during the 1890s and after he was elected an Associate of the Royal Academy in 1899 he began to receive prestigious commissions for public monuments. These included a

Pl.76
Port Sunlight.
Sir William
Goscombe John,
1921

statue of King Edward VII for Cape Town and an equestrian monument to Viscount Tredegar in Cardiff. In 1909 he became an RA and in the same year was knighted.

Goscombe John's monument at Port Sunlight is a conventional stone cross, but clustered around this are men, women and children, as though in defence of a village cross or, paradoxically, of the village war memorial. The whole arrangement is encircled by a stone wall with eight bronze panels flanking openings in the wall, each one depicting boys and girls holding wreaths or palm leaves. Leading up to these openings are four broad flights of steps. Further panels, in high relief, of the different branches of the armed services in action are placed between each pair of children's panels.

Port Sunlight Village was built by Lord Leverhulme, owner of the soap manufacturers Lever Brothers. (William Hesketh Lever had started in his father's wholesale grocery business, packaging and marketing soap under the brand name 'Sunlight' before successfully manufacturing his own products). A philanthropist who believed in providing his workers with decent living conditions, in the late 1880s Lever began to build a 'model village' on a plot of land he had purchased on the banks of the Mersey. Within a year, a factory and twenty-eight cottages were ready for occupation and by 1909, in addition to the then seven hundred houses, the village had a theatre, concert hall, library, gymnasium, church and school.

The war memorial is effectively a roundabout at the junction of two avenues in the centre of the village. It commemorates the 481 dead out of some 4,000 employees of the Lever Brothers companies throughout the world who went to war. (In England, the employees became members of a Lever Brothers Pals Battalion). The memorial was unveiled, as an inscription records, on 3 December 1921 by ex-Sergeant T.G Eames, a former employee blinded at the Battle of the Somme, assisted by ex-Private R.E Cruikshank who had been awarded the Victoria Cross in 1918. Despite the strong narrative and realistic detail of the work there is an air of fantasy, of some imagined invasion which never came, which gives the tableau a melodramatic quality. The cross, both a symbol of the Christian faith and, in its guise as village cross, a symbol of the local community, becomes a prop which the soldiers and their civilian companions stand ready to defend against the implied threat of an advancing enemy.

William Goscombe John had been approached as early as 1916 to plan a memorial to the Lever Brothers workers. Lord Leverhulme was conscious that at the end of the war there would be a considerable demand for memorialists and he was anxious to engage the services of a man he considered to be amongst the best. Goscombe John was an obvious choice. Having already, in 1912, produced a bust of Lady Lever and, three years later, a recumbent effigy for her tomb in the village church (later to be joined by one of Lord Leverhulme himself), he had become a friend of the industrialist and was also well known on Merseyside for other, earlier monumental sculptures.[37]

As in his Newcastle 'Commercials' memorial, at Port Sunlight Goscombe John makes significant distinctions in his depictions of males and females. On one side of the memorial an anxious looking woman draws two distressed children and a small baby protectively towards her. Her head is raised as if listening to the sound of an advancing enemy and her children twist round in terrified anticipation of their impending arrival. The woman and children are sheltering behind the cross with soldiers standing guard.

At Warlingham and Renfrew the mother and child were present merely as signifiers of the soldier's role as protector, and, initially at least, this would appear to be the case at Port Sunlight. However, the numerous depictions of mother and child on war memorials, both with and without accompanying servicemen, frequently indicate, as here, a wider range of meanings. At Newcastle, Workington and St Anne's-on-Sea, women shown kissing their husbands good-bye represent the soldier's sacrifice in going off to war and their own sacrifice, through their encouragement, in having to bear the all too often fatal consequences. The depiction of the moment of separation makes this explicit but elsewhere, when mother and child are portrayed in isolation, the mother's sacrifice and suffering is nonetheless clearly implied. The figure in mourning on Macclesfield's memorial, for example, was described by the local paper as representing 'the silent heroism of the women who were left at home', her act of mourning clearly indicating that her man had failed to return.[38]

Pl.77
Croydon.
Paul Montford,
1921

The war memorial at Croydon is a small pylon surmounted by a casket, representing the absent dead. On opposite sides of the cenotaph are two figures, one a wounded soldier of the East Surrey Regiment, the other a mother who holds her small daughter in her left hand and reaches out with her right towards the soldier on the other side. They are the work of

85

the sculptor, Paul Montford. Montford was born in London in 1868 but, concerned that his age and his non-combatant status would hamper his chances of employment on memorials in Britain, he emigrated to Australia in 1923, just two years after Croydon's memorial was unveiled. His work on the National War Memorial of Victoria in Melbourne was to ensure his subsequent success as a sculptor in his adopted country.

The physical separation of the Croydon figures on either side of the monument symbolises their physical separation in wartime. The mother's gesture, in reaching out to her husband, seems to suggest an attempt to reach him, even to proffer her assistance in the binding of his wounds. At first sight she appears to be offering a cloth or bandage for this purpose, but this is in fact a letter which we may assume she has received from the front lines. Her gesture, accentuated by her closed eyes, suggests not a physical connection but a mental or spiritual bond between them. We may also read this as signifying the ultimate separation of husband and wife through death on the field of battle, the letter being, in this case, the official confirmation of her husband's death.

Elsewhere the mother with her child is presented as a more stoic figure, her stoicism again implying sacrifice or loss. In the booklet produced for the unveiling ceremony at St Anne's-on-Sea, the mother and

child featured here were grimly interpreted as showing, 'the agony of mind caused to Womanhood by the tragedies of the war'. The mother, it suggested, 'sits in anguish and sorrowful reverie, quite unconscious that her babe is looking to her for a mother's love. She looks, as it were, into the unknown future, realizing what her sacrifice means, and wondering why'.[39]

At Derby, the local newspaper quoted Arthur Walker, the sculptor of their memorial, on his intentions in depicting a mother holding her happily squirming baby. 'Typifying the widowed mother' she was, he said, 'grief-stricken but proud and courageous, holding her fatherless boy'.[40] The opening ceremony booklet placed a slightly different emphasis on the figures, seeing the woman as 'a typical English mother, bowed with her sorrow but not broken-hearted, for she is not alone in her grief, she is but one of a countless number of similar sufferers and she is thrilled with the glory of the great sacrifice of her son'.[41]

On other memorials the figures of mother and child play a more positive role. At Merthyr Tydfil, in a memorial designed by L.S Merrifield, a pupil of Goscombe John, the mother with her baby wrapped protectively in her shawl appears to be presented in a conventional and familiar light, but as one of two figures standing either side of a central Madonna-like figure (the other being a miner) she plays an important role as a surrogate for the mourners for whom the memorial is intended. Her gesture indicates the symbolic laying of wreaths at the base of the monument.

The memorial at Rawtenstall in Lancashire is by L.F Roslyn. Here the mother, holding an older child by her hand, is included in a bronze frieze in high relief which runs continuously around all four sides of a seventeen feet high obelisk. She is one of a number representing women's contributions to the war effort. At each of the four corners of the relief stands a member of the armed forces - infantryman, gunner, sailor and airman - and in the narrow spaces betwen each figure are male and female workers. Each of the women's roles are identified by their attributes, like saints in a Renaissance altarpiece, a farm worker by her fork and hoe, a factory worker by the box she carries, a Red Cross nurse by her uniform with its prominent symbol and the mother by her child. Although the mother is no more active in this memorial than those at St Anne's or Derby, by her association with such positive role models as the other female workers, she seems to take on a greater heroic dimension. Even the fact that her daughter is older than is usually depicted, and is literally 'standing on her own two feet', seems significant of independence, perseverance and survival, the slight smile on the child's face suggesting optimism rather than grief.(See Pl.100)

Similarly at Port Sunlight, the mother with her children takes a more active role in the meaning of the monument. In the narrative context of this memorial the woman is not only representative of

the protective role of the man, she too is shown as a protector of her own children. If the men, by their sacrifices on the field of battle, have provided for their children's futures, the women who encouraged their men to fight have also effectively assisted future generations.

Children at Port Sunlight feature to an unusual extent. Most obviously, eight panels on the surrounding wall are specifically allotted to them, but in addition they have a part to play in the narrative scheme. To the left of the mother protecting her young children, an older boy and a girl edge cautiously around the base of the cross looking out towards the imagined enemy, the boy protectively guarding the hesitant female. On the other side of the cross, a woman leans over to a wounded soldier as if to help him. The soldier is one of three, two of whom, with fixed bayonets, stand ready to repel an attack and the inclusion of the wounded man, suggests that battle has already commenced. The dominant, standing figure might at first glance be taken for a civilian. Bareheaded and without his jacket he is shown as vulnerable but defiant, defensive rather than aggressive and determined above all to protect his family and homeland. He is accompanied by a small boy whose clenched fist and determined look echo both that of the younger boy who protects his older sister, and the soldier (his father?) who protects him.

The scenario presented here was clearly not a reflection of the facts of the war. This was not trench warfare, nor did the presence of women and children in the midst of fighting make realistic sense. However in 1916, when the memorial was planned, there were real fears of an invasion of Britain; the defence of the homeland was therefore seen as an appropriate motif.

Pls.80 and 81
Port Sunlight.
Sir William
Goscombe John,
1921

Nonetheless, despite the apparent realism and narrative context, the figures have an obvious, additional symbolic significance. The children represent the country's future. The boys, appropriately in the uniform of the Boy Scouts, are the inheritors of the role of protectors and potential warriors. The girls represent future motherhood, an idea reinforced by the relief panels of children placed on the enclosing wall, where we see again the boys in the uniform of the Scouts and young girls with babes in arms.

90

IV

Strong, Sensible and Fit [1]

The woman who leans cautiously towards the wounded soldier on the Port Sunlight memorial, anxious to assist, hints at the more positive contributions women were to make during the war. On 6 August 1914 Vera Brittain recorded in her diary, 'Today I started the only work it seems possible as yet for women to do - the making of garments for the soldiers. I started knitting sleeping helmets'.[2] Anxious to play her part, and frustrated by the limited opportunities to contribute, she had complained in a letter to her friend and soon to be fiancé Roland Leighton, 'Women get all the dreariness of war, and none of the exhilaration'.[3]

Leighton was negotiating to obtain a commission in the army and Brittain very much approved of his attempts to enlist, just as she had encouraged her brother Edward and had argued for him and against her father who was strongly opposed to his son becoming a soldier.[4] Her diary entry for 2 September noted how, 'after dinner we all discussed again Daddy's refusal to let Edward go into the Army, and the unmanliness of it'.[5]

In her letter to Roland, Brittain had explained her feelings:

> The raging of these elemental forces fascinates me, horribly but powerfully, as it does you. I find beauty in it too; certainly war seems to bring out all that is noble in human nature, but against that you can say that it brings out all the barbarous too. But whether it is noble or barbarous I am quite sure that had I been a boy, I should have gone off to take part in it long ago; indeed I have wasted many moments regretting that I am a girl.[6]

Soon however, she was to offer her services in the local hospital and, after initial training and menial work in the Devonshire Hospital in her home town of Buxton, she eventually found her way to the front, working initially in Malta and then later at Étaples in France.[7]

Vera Brittain was not alone: thousands of women looked for ways to contribute to the war effort both on the home front and on the fields of battle. In so doing, as this chapter will show, they were to challenge long-held assumptions about their capabilities and their role in society, changes reflected in the imagery of numerous war memorials.

In anticipation of the eventuality of war, the War Office in 1909 had issued a Scheme for the Organisation of Voluntary Aid whereby the British Red Cross Society was given the role of providing, in the event of hostilities, supplementary aid to the existing Territorial Forces Medical Service. Regional branches of the Red Cross organised units which were named VADs (Voluntary Aid Detachments) whose members, both men and women, were trained in first aid and nursing. Their role was essentially supportive, assisting qualified staff to help keep hospitals and ambulance services running. Within twelve months there were over 6,000 trained members and when war did eventually break out in 1914 their numbers swelled considerably.

At this point the Red Cross joined forces with the Order of St John of Jerusalem to form the Joint War Committee to administer wartime relief work. Auxiliary hospitals and convalescent homes were established in most large towns in Britain and these were staffed by qualified nurses aided by VADs. In addition to nursing, the volunteers performed clerical, cleaning and kitchen duties. By the summer of 1914 there were some 2,500 detachments in Britain, served by around 74,000 individuals, three quarters of them women.[8]

With the declaration of war, attempts were also made by a number of women doctors to provide additional medical assistance, though there was some resistance to this from the male establishment. In August 1914, one Scottish doctor, Elsie Inglis, had asked the War Office what she could do to help and had received the reply, 'My good lady, go home and sit still'.[9] Ignoring this, Dr Inglis, a member of the Edinburgh branch of the NUWSS, formed the Scottish Women's Hospital Units to provide medical facilities in the war zones and eventually fourteen units were established in France, Serbia, Corsica, Salonika, Romania, Russia and Malta.[10]

Other women doctors who offered help were also discouraged. At the outbreak of war Dr Louisa Garrett Anderson (the daughter of Elizabeth Garrett Anderson, Britain's first female doctor) and Dr Flora Murray had formed the Women's Hospital Corps but they too were refused permission to work as surgeons at the front. Instead they were forced to work with the French Red Cross. Eventually however the War Office did give them permission to establish the Women's Military Hospital in Endell Street in London where Louisa became Chief Surgeon.[11]

The contribution of women in the medical services is recognised on a number of First World War memorials in Britain and one of the best-known and most prominently positioned monuments in England is a memorial to a nurse killed in the war. Edith Cavell's memorial stands

Pl.84
opposite
Cavell Monument.
London.
Sir George Frampton,
1920

outside the National Portrait Gallery close to Trafalgar Square. As a memorial to an individual this monument might be considered as falling outside of the scope of this study and closer to the tradition of the public celebration of prominent citizens. Edith Cavell, however, was clearly a casualty of war, and one whose story was presented, and came to be seen, as a signifier of the justice of the Allied case for war and of the bravery and self-sacrifice of all who fought against perceived injustice.

The London memorial, one of a number erected across the country, emphasises this broader significance by incorporating a somewhat severe and understated portrait statue of the nurse into an elaborate, forty feet high monument topped by a stylised cruciform emblem of Humanity.[12] This takes the form of a seated woman who protects with one hand an infant cradled in her lap while raising her other hand in a sign of benediction. On her skirt is carved, in low relief, a cross which echoes the larger form of the ensemble. This is not to identify the couple as Virgin and Child, who they otherwise resemble, but is in reference to the organisation to which Cavell belonged and is intended to suggest a conflation of the protective and caring roles of nurse and mother.

Edith Cavell's story is well known. Working as a nurse in Brussels, she was shot by a German firing squad in 1915. At the outbreak of war, the clinic where she had worked since 1907 became a Red Cross hospital treating both German and Belgian soldiers but when Brussels fell to the Germans it was commandeered by them solely for their own wounded. Most of the English nurses were sent home but Cavell and her chief assistant remained. When two stranded British soldiers found their way to the hospital in the Autumn of 1914 they were secretly sheltered for two weeks and then helped across the border into nearby neutral Holland. Others soon followed and eventually some two hundred Allied soldiers were helped to escape from the German-held territory. When the scheme was subsequently discovered, Edith Cavell was amongst those arrested. She admitted her part in the scheme and on 12 October 1915 she faced a firing squad and was buried at the site of her execution.

Although she was fully aware of the likely consequences of her actions and had clearly compromised her position as a Red Cross nurse protected by the Geneva

Convention, her death was immediately seized upon by the Allies for propaganda purposes, Cavell naturally being presented as a martyr. Recruiting was said to have doubled for some weeks following the news of her execution.

After the war Cavell's body was returned to England where, following a service at Westminster Abbey, she was taken back to her home town and re-interred beside Norwich Cathedral where a memorial to her already existed. This memorial, designed by Henry Pegram, had been unveiled in October 1918, one month before the end of the war. It consists of a bronze bust of Cavell placed on top of a small stone column on the front of which is carved a soldier who reaches up to grasp one of two carved laurel wreaths placed beneath the bust. This is an appropriate reversal of the more usual female figure mourning the dead soldier in similar fashion such as we see on a number of war memorials.[13] At the base of the monument at Norwich is carved the simple message, 'Edith Cavell, Nurse, Patriot and Martyr'.

The memorial in London was erected in 1920 and was designed by Sir George Frampton. The move to erect a monument in her memory had been initiated in 1915, less than two weeks after her death, when the *Daily Telegraph* published a letter which detailed Frampton's offer to design and complete a monument free of charge, proposing a public subscription to pay for materials. It was a scheme which the newspaper was happy to organise and promote. A week later the City of Westminster offered a site for the monument. Other memorial funds were simultaneously organised, many with the intention of providing some form of utilitarian rather than monumental commemoration. Within a fortnight the *Daily Telegraph* had received over £2,000 whilst a *Daily Mirror* Cavell Memorial Fund had, by the beginning of November, reached £4,800. (The money raised here was to go to an Edith Cavell Home for Nurses).

94

The considerable size and prominent placing of the monument indicate its importance in attempting to represent public outrage, much of it stoked during the war by the publication of lurid imagery for propaganda purposes. Two years after the end of the war there was still great sympathy for Edith Cavell but, despite this, the monument was somewhat coolly received. *The British Journal of Nursing* felt that the figure of Cavell was 'a beautiful conception, finely executed' but complained that 'it is overshadowed and dwarfed by the great mass of granite which forms the background, and the squat figure representing

Humanity, surmounting it, is as unpleasing as it is curious'.[14] Others felt that the portrait of Cavell was unimpressive, 'like an advertisement for a complete nurse's outfit,' according to Arthur Clutton-Brock in the *New Statesman*.[15] Ironically, although modernists and implacable opponents of Frampton such as Jacob Epstein and Eric Kennington were unsurprisingly disparaging, the figures were seen by some as overly modernistic.

It had been the original intention to cast the figure of Cavell in bronze which might have produced a less austere effect, but the cool white marble against light grey granite and the statue's stylistic severity effectively conveys a sense of Nurse Cavell's steely moral courage. In presenting a positive image of a resolute and courageous woman, Frampton's work can be seen as contradicting gendered stereotypes of a passive and dependent femininity precisely at a time when the reassertion of such stereotypes was seen as important to counter the disruption of the war years.

Indeed there were those who had advocated the depiction of a tragic Cavell with a German officer standing over the slain nurse. Images such as these had been produced during the war as propaganda and were based on allegations that she had fainted and been shot while lying prostrate. They invariably depicted the nurse as a much younger, more 'feminine' and, it is implied, more vulnerable woman. In contrast, Frampton has shown her as the self-assured fifty year old she actually was. And to reinforce the suggestion of moral strength the reverse of the monument features a 'British' lion trampling a serpent on stoney ground.

Pl.85 *opposite*
Nurse Cavell.
London.
Sir George
Frampton, 1920

Pl.86
'Remember'.
Post card, c1915

Carved out of the granite face of the pedestal, it is a symbolic emphasis in materials and imagery of the memorial's message.

At the base of Frampton's full length statue, below the simple identification, 'Edith Cavell, Brussels, Dawn, October 12th 1915', is an inscription of the words Cavell is said to have spoken before her execution: "I realise that patriotism is not enough, I must have no hatred or bitterness towards anyone". These words, which seem to contradict the prominently inscribed 'For King and Country', were not originally included on the memorial. They were added in 1924 after a sustained campaign for their inclusion, initiated by the National Council for Women. The campaign drew widespread support, including that of the Cavell family.

Pl.87
Exeter.
John Angel,
1923

The implication of her actual words, as revealed in a statement issued by the British Chaplain, the Reverend Stirling Graham, who met Cavell the night before her execution, was that whilst willing to 'die for England' she accepted her guilt and did not blame her executioners. The inclusion of only the final part of her comments suggests a willingness to help anyone regardless of nationality or circumstances but leaves ambiguous her attitude to her executioners.[16]

Although inscriptions sometimes give equal recognition to the role of nurses, relatively few are depicted on First World War memorials. The post-war glorification of male heroism, involving as it did the subordination of female contributions to the needs of the men returning from war, may be the major reason for this. The more dependent image of mother and child, or allegorical figures of mourning or Victory, Justice or Peace, no doubt seemed more acceptable options for representing women. The muted reception of the positive, unemotional image of Edith Cavell seems to confirm an antipathy towards depictions of assured and confident women.

Needless to say the war memorial primarily remembered those who had given their lives in the Great War and thankfully relatively few nurses died. Nonetheless, numerous memorials also acknowledged all who had served, both men and women, and, given the vital and outstanding job performed by these women and the acknowledgement of so many ex-soldiers of the importance of nurses, not only to their physical but also their spiritual well-being, it is surprising and disappointing that more were not portrayed.

Where nurses *are* shown on memorials they are usually young and most often passive, even meek, frequently depicted as one of three or four representative figures, the others usually being a soldier and sailor and perhaps an airman. At Exeter, the nurse, in a memorial by local artist John Angel, is particularly impressive and unusually prominent and is here accompanied by soldier, sailor and prisoner of war. (An interesting detail is the barely noticeable shell and sheaf of wheat at the nurse's feet, indicative of women's additional contributions in munitions and on the land). Where elsewhere nurses are similarly shown in the round it is usually on Eleanor or lantern crosses where they are consequently small, high up and hard to see.

An unusual example of this type of memorial is at Knowlton near Canterbury. Consisting of a medieval lantern cross with the four small carved figures in the lantern at the top, it was unveiled in 1919 but originally planned in 1914. As the inscription explains, the cross was erected 'in honour of those twelve men of Knowlton, out of a total population of thirty-nine, who enlisted prior to March 1915 and by their patriotic action won *The Weekly Dispatch* Bravest Village Competition'. The competition was for the village which had sent in the highest percentage of its population to the war and was clearly intended as an encouragement for others to enlist. As such, the monument, and similar ones in other counties, [17] is closer in concept to the concurrent rolls of honour or later street shrines which were erected in acknowledgement of a willing response to the call to arms. [18]

Most depictions of nurses on war memorials are in the form of subsidiary figures on reliefs around the base of the monument on which, more often than not, stands a figure in the round of soldier or Victory. Louis Frederick Roslyn provided more than one such example. Roslyn, who had changed his name from the Germanic sounding Louis Fritz Roselieb in 1916, was one of the most prolific of memorial sculptors.[19] Born in London in 1878, the son of a German sculptor who had emigrated to England in the mid-1870s, Roslyn studied at the South London Technical Art School and the Royal Academy Schools and during the war served in the Royal Flying Corps. His first war memorial was for Tonbridge parish church in Kent in 1904 to commemorate the Boer War but throughout the 1920s he was to produce some two dozen First World War memorials in all parts of the United Kingdom.

A particularly impressive memorial by Roslyn is the one at Rawtenstall in Lancashire, already referred to in relation to its image of a mother and child. As with all the other figures, the nurse is shown in iconic pose, identifiable by her uniform with its prominent cross. The slight smile on her face and relaxed pose suggest a confident and reassuring manner and we see this again in another splendid relief by Roslyn on his memorial at nearby Darwen. The monument here is more conventional with winged victory (the same cast as was used at Oswaldtwistle) on a squat pedestal on three sides of which are bronze reliefs of a soldier, a sailor and a nurse. The nurse is shown here as a working woman in a hospital ward, with sleeves pushed up above her elbows and her tunic slightly crumpled. In one hand she holds a small bowl and in the other a water bottle and to her side is a small bedside cabinet. Though typically undemonstrative, Roslyn's Darwen figure presents a more positive image than we tend to see elsewhere. At Mountain Ash in South Wales for example, the nurse is shown with hands clasped demurely in front of her and at Blackpool she is shown as a figure of mourning. (See Pl.179)

Pl.88
Rawtenstall.
Louis Frederick
Roslyn, 1929

98

HUMANITY

Red Cross
Christmas
Roll Call
Dec. 16-23rd

The
GREATEST MOTHER
in the WORLD

Whilst nursing certainly enabled women to present the positive (and 'unfeminine') face of skilful efficiency and composure under stress, it equally prompted a more acceptable image of the 'surrogate mother' administering to the infantalized and enfeebled male, as at least one well known poster at the time suggested.[20] The blatant appeal of the poster to a mothering instinct, in presenting the wounded soldier as a miniaturised child substitute, is unsurprisingly absent in memorial sculpture, though in those memorials where the nurse is shown assisting the wounded or treating their wounds it may be implied. This is most obvious in the Liverpool News Room memorial, where the nurse and kilted soldier, the man's head turned to look trustingly up at the nurse who gently tends his wounds, most conspicuously conform to the pietà-like imagery of *The Greatest Mother* poster. Elsewhere the nurse is more likely to be shown in a more matter-of-fact way, either supporting the soldier hobbling on crutches or bandaging a wounded wrist.

If nursing could be seen as an appropriate role for women in war, a potential destabilisation of stereotypical femininity was more obviously revealed in the adoption of other, more traditionally 'masculine'

Pl. 89 *left*
Rawtenstall (detail)
L.F Roslyn, 1929

Pl.90 *centre*
Darwen.
L.F Roslyn, 1921

Pl.91
'The Greatest Mother in the World'.
Alonzo Earl Foringer.
Poster, 1918

occupations. Despite initial opposition, particularly from the unions, jobs vacated by men bound for the front were increasingly filled by women. Between July 1914 and November 1918 the number of women at work increased by more than a million and a half.[21] The unions' concerns that men's jobs were being taken over by women were only placated following a 'Women's Right to Serve' march through London in July 1915 led by Emmeline Pankhurst. A compromise, known as 'dilution', was then agreed: the replacement by female labour of the work of skilled males would be for the duration of the war only.

Of course for suffragists the employment of women was an opportunity for them to prove their worth. For many women who accepted new, previously unimagined challenges, whether in voluntary or paid work, the experience was a revelation which changed not only men's views of their capabilities but their own views of themselves and their position in society. Paradoxically this could be seen to be at the expense of feminist principles. Vera Brittain for example considered herself a feminist before the war but, as her encouragement of her brother's and her fiancé's enlistment reveals, arguing as she did against the 'unmanliness' of not enlisting, her attitudes at the outbreak of war was marked by a retrograde step towards a more stereotypical view of gender. Her career also necessarily suffered as she abandoned her studies at Oxford to become a VAD nurse. Nonetheless, by becoming a nurse, and determinedly sticking with it throughout the war, she experienced the sort of arduous and physically demanding labour which someone of her privileged, middle-class background could not previously have imagined, which was to have a profound and lasting effect on her views of society.

Although frequently treated in the pages of the popular press as a mildly amusing novelty, the spectacle of women doing 'men's work' also received serious attention and admiring comment and was the subject of a number of popular propaganda films.[22] In May 1916 *The Times* noted that 'Even now one hears complaints which suggest that woman should keep to her separate sphere. She has no separate sphere in wartime. The more she branches out in new directions, the better.'[23] A few months later the same paper commented on 'the capacity of women to do work which they have not previously attempted' noting their precision, judgement and manual dexterity and adding, patronisingly, 'there is good reason to believe that women are capable of becoming thorough mechanics and undertaking very responsible work'.[24]

In similar vein, a book on munitions work entitled *The Woman's Part*, written in December 1917 and published in 1918, commented:

Pl.92
(detail)
Bury.
Hermon
Cawthra, 1920

They are also undertaking operations dependent on physical
strength, which in pre-war days would have been regarded as
wholly unsuitable to female capacity. War necessity has, however,
killed old-time prejudice and has proved how readily women adapt
themselves to any task within their physical powers.[25]

The author, L.K Yates, continued, 'One of the most surprising revelations
of the war in this country has, indeed, been the capacity of women for
engineering work, and to none has the discovery been more surprising and
more exhilarating than to the women themselves'.[26]

The wide range of responsible work that women undertook was
summed up by Jessie Pope in her poem *War Girls*, where she notes the
girls who work as butchers, deliver milk, clip tickets on trains, hail taxis
and drive vans. The list continues and is summed up with pride:

> Strong, sensible and fit,
> They're out to show their grit,
> And tackle jobs with energy and knack.
> No longer caged and penned up,
> They're going to keep their end up
> Till the khaki soldier boys come marching back.[27]

The type of work that women performed during the war was to a
large extent conditioned by their class. Voluntary work, including nursing,
was inevitably limited to those who didn't need to earn a living. Typical of
such women were those who joined the First Aid Nursing Yeomanry (the
FANY) which had been founded in 1907 by an ex-cavalryman who,
recalling the battles of the previous century, saw a role for equestrian
women, galloping in their scarlet uniforms onto the field of battle to tend
to the wounded and transport them quickly back to field hospitals.

In addition to training in first aid, signalling and stretcher-
bearing, the women also received cavalry drill and training in horse-drawn
ambulance driving.[28] Naturally the women who were most attracted to this,
and who could afford the considerable expenses - they were expected to
provide their own uniforms, and having their own horse helped - were
existing horse riders and horse owners, in other words the affluent middle
and upper classes.

The FANY was just one of a number of military-styled voluntary
organisations for women which included the Women's Emergency Corps,
the Women's Auxiliary Force and Women's Forage Corps, all founded
between 1914 and 1915. It was not until 1917, however, that the Women's
Army Auxiliary Corps (the WAAC) was formed. The WAAC, which was
renamed Queen Mary's Army Auxiliary Corps in April 1918, was created to

relieve men of what were referred to as 'soft' jobs, such as clerks, telephonists or cooks, to enable them to fight at the front. Although they wore a khaki uniform of cap, jacket and skirt, they were not given full military status.

Women in the WAAC worked in camps in both England and France. Working side by side with the men aroused largely unfounded suspicions of promiscuity and pregnancies, rumours supported by regular stories in the popular press of hundreds of women having to be dismissed or sent home because of this. Olive Taylor, who had joined the WAAC after previously working in munitions, recalled a first visit from camp to the local town.

> Some of us looked forward to going into Woolwich and perhaps
> enjoying egg and chips, but we were subject to such insults in
> Woolwich that we never tried again. Here we learned for the first
> time that we were regarded as scum and that we had been enlisted
> for the sexual satisfaction of soldiers. This, after we had worked
> ever so hard, and put up with so much deprivation for our country's
> sake, was absolutely terrible.[29]

Such was the gossip that an official investigation was held. The report concluded that the WAAC were 'a healthy, cheerful, self-respecting body of hardworking women, conscious of their position as links in the great chain of the nation's purpose, and zealous in its service'.[30] Indeed, although members of the WAAC were not involved in combat, those in France were nonetheless subject to heavy artillery fire and bombing raids, with some inevitable casualties.

The army was not the first of the services to recruit women: the Women's Royal Naval Service (the WRNS) had been formed in 1916. Unlike the WAAC, the WRNS did not serve abroad. This would have meant serving on board ship which the Navy would certainly not have allowed. They again performed the vital job of freeing men to fight by taking over as cooks, clerks, wireless telegraphists or electricians. The success of the enterprise led to the formation of the Women's Auxiliary Army Corps the following year and, in April 1918, the Women's Royal Air Force, which was created at the same time as the (men's) Royal Air Force when the existing Royal Naval Air Service and the Royal Flying Corps were amalgamated. By the end of the war over 100,000 women had enrolled in one or other of these branches of the women's services.[31]

As with nurses - indeed, even more so - it is hard to find examples of figurative sculptures of the Women's Services on war memorials. Whether this reflects a hangover from the wartime gossip about alleged promiscuity is hard to say. Many members of the women's armed services were certainly aware of feelings of disquiet about their abandonment of traditional roles. As one former member of the WAAC commented at the end of the war: "We weren't looked upon with favour by the people at home. We had done something that was outrageous for women to do. We had gone to France and left our homes".[32]

Perhaps the absence of representation again simply reflects the fact that the war memorial primarily acknowledged those who had died and, although nationally many women were killed in the Great War, in any one community the numbers were thankfully small or non-existent. Naturally, if the memorial had only one figure to represent the armed services it would be that of the soldier. However, that does not explain why, when there are a number of representative figures, or when supplementary reliefs are included, members of the Women's Services are very rarely shown. Certainly there are remarkably few examples.

The precise identity of figures representing the Women's Services on war memorials is complicated by the ad-hoc arrangements which applied to their employment. Many women supplied their own uniforms or retained those from membership of previous organisations, so when depicted the exact nature of the organisation to which they are meant to belong is not always clear. At Twickenham, the memorial on the banks of the Thames, designed by Mortimer Brown, features a bronze figure of a soldier on a stone plinth. Three bronze reliefs on the sides of the plinth show scenes representing the Navy, Air Force and the Women's Services, in this case possibly a member of the WRAF, though given the motor vehicle in the background and the nurse she accompanies, it is equally likely that the uniformed figure is intended to represent a VAD ambulance driver. Memorials at Bury and Rawtenstall also provide excellent, realistic images of members of the Women's Services, though in both locations these women are half-hidden, in contrast to the images of farmhands, munitions workers or nurses.

At Birmingham, a more allegorical figure, completing a quartet of effigies, was identified as representing the Women's Services. Birmingham's 'Hall of Memory', its £60,000 cost paid for entirely by public subscription, is a large, octagonal, classical structure with a domed roof. On each of four alternate sides are side chapels and a portico and against the remaining walls are granite pedestals, on which are crouched impressive, larger than life-size bronze figures, the work of Albert Toft.

The male figures, representing the Army, Navy and Air Force, are clothed only in a loose cloth wrapped around the waist and lower body and are identified by the appropriate attributes they hold: the sailor has a

Pl.93
Twickenham.
Mortimer
Brown, 1921

ship's wheel, the airman an aircraft propellor and the soldier a machine gun. The female figure for the Women's Services is clearly more difficult to characterise, in part because she represents a number of separate organisations and in part because there was no single role within them. The wreath she holds suggests, however, a figure of mourning rather than of active service and were she not so identified at the time, it would be difficult to recognise this figure as representing the positive and practical contribution of the Women's Services. In fact virtually the same figure, identical except for being more fully clothed, was used again by the sculptor on a First World War memorial for Benenden in Kent and had in fact been originally used on the Welsh National Boer War memorial in Cardiff. At both Benenden and Cardiff, without the qualifying presence of other representative figures, the female was identified as 'Grief'.

One location where members of the Women's Services *are* figuratively represented is in the Scottish National War Memorial. Opened on 14 July 1927, the memorial is located on Edinburgh's Castle Rock and was the culmination of proposals originating ten years previously when the Secretary of State for Scotland appointed a committee to report on the idea of a national memorial for Scotland. The building which forms the memorial was designed by the Scottish architect Sir Robert Lorimer in a traditional style intended to harmonise with the Castle, in whose grounds it stands.

In plan it forms a long narrow oblong, known as the 'Hall of Honour', with individual regimental memorials lining the walls. At each

Pl.94
facing page
Birmingham.
Albert Toft, 1925.

Pl.95
Birmingham Hall of Memory. Architects S. Cooke & W Twist. Sculpture by Albert Toft, 1925.

end of the Hall are side chapels containing, amongst others, memorials to nurses and members of the women's services. Directly opposite the central entrance to the Hall is 'The Shrine' and here, beneath stained glass windows, is a bronze frieze of figures representing servicemen and women, including nurses, a VAD ambulance driver, an officer of the WRNS and a member of the WRAF. The frieze was designed by Morris Meredith-Williams and modelled by his wife, Alice, who was also responsible for separate memorials to the Women's and Nursing Services.

Both middle and working class women were attracted to the Women's Services, though working class women who already worked in factories and mills or in domestic service might be more inclined to take on some of the familiar jobs listed by Jessie Pope. Numerous posters were produced to encourage them to do so. One major area of employment not referred to in Jessie Pope's poem was on the land. The Women's Land Army was established in 1916 (after Pope's poem had been written) and by the following year more than 260,000 women were working as farm labourers or in the Women's Forestry Corps.[33] This was exceptionally hard and badly paid work and tended to attract more middle class women who probably didn't realise what they were letting themselves in for. They were doubtless encouraged by articles in the popular press:

> The long-standing prejudice against farming work for women, as work essentially rough, vulgar and coarsening, is breaking down. This is in no doubt partly due to the fact that large numbers of girls of education and standing have taken up work on the land during the duration of the war.[34]

Perhaps the greatest impact made by women at this time was as munitions workers, previously an almost exclusively male preserve. At Woolwich Arsenal the female staff before the war numbered just 125; by 1917 there were some 25,000 women working there. New munitions factories had also been established across the country. In May 1915 a Ministry of Munitions had been created and by 1918 the three existing factories had become 150.[35] A further 5,000 establishments were involved in supplementary activities, making shrapnel, fuses, optical instruments and so on.

Making explosives, filling shells and working with heavy machinery was hard and dangerous work and resulted in injuries and deaths. The very first of the new munitions factories, eventually employing 17,000, all but 1,000 of them women, was built at Barnbow near Leeds where, on 5 December 1915, an explosion killed 35 women and injured many more. At Silvertown in the East End of London, in a similar disaster, 69 were reported killed and a further 400 injured, though the actual numbers were rumoured to be much higher. A number of memorials were erected to those killed at Silvertown and at other munitions factories.[36]

Even without such disasters, many women were poisoned by the toxic materials they worked with, or injured by heavy machinery. In risking, and in some cases sacrificing their lives, women could be seen to be sharing the dangers experienced by men. Furthermore they were directly contributing to the military effort (and indirectly killing Germans). Certainly the *Daily Chronicle* went so far as to claim that 'The nation's debt to these heroic women ... is so great that it may even be likened to the debt which the nation owes to its soldiers and seamen'.[37] Despite such wartime affirmations, and the fact that women's contribution to the war effort continued to be celebrated in the press in the immediate aftermath of the war, acknowledgement in the form of figurative imagery on war memorials is hard to find.

However, as with the Women's Services, it was apparent that some resentment of women workers existed. It had been by no means unusual to read letters in the popular press during the war protesting at the sight and behaviour of young women prominently garbed in paramilitary uniform and acting with what was seen as unsuitably 'masculine' manners. One 'female patriot', writing to the *Morning Post* about the women lorry drivers recently seen by her, complained that they 'should have blushed to be seen wearing a parody of the uniform which ... thousands ... have made a symbol of honour and glory'. If they felt a need to be involved they should, she argued, become nurses or 'make hay or pick fruit or make jam'.[38] Munitions workers in particular came in for criticism. As one ex-worker recalled,

Pl.96
Women's Memorial.
Scottish National
War Memorial,
Edinburgh.
Alice Meredith
Williams,
1927

Munitions workers were just about the lowest form of life in the eyes of the general public. We were supposed to make a great deal of money, and as other people didn't make so much they called us all sorts of things, even shouted things after us'.[39]

For those who had witnessed firsthand the horrors of trench warfare, resentment of any at home who could be seen to have benefited from the war could be bitter. In *Realities of War*, written in 1919 and published in the following year, Philip Gibbs recalled his experiences as a war correspondent. Early in his book he noted his hatred of those who could not seem to understand what the men had been through. He was particularly damning of 'the munition workers who were getting good wages out of the war' and 'the working women who were buying gramophones and furs while their men were in the stinking trenches'.[40] At the end of the book he reiterated his views: 'millions of girls were in some kind of fancy dress with buttons and shoulder straps, breeches and puttees, and they seemed to be making a game of the war and enjoying it thoroughly'.[41]

Whether such feelings led to some reluctance to depict women workers on war memorials is again difficult to assess. Indeed the resentment expressed above, or at least the level of resentment, may well have been the exception rather than the rule. In spite of such views, munitions workers are recognised on the inscriptions of a number of memorials, not only those specifically erected to acknowledge their deaths in factory explosions, but also, on occasion, elsewhere.[42]

One location where women's contributions to the war effort and their self-sacrifice during the conflict is positively acknowledged is in York Minster, where a memorial was erected to all 'The women of the Empire who gave their lives in the European War of 1914-1918'.[43] This consists of a large wooden screen, or reredos, with twelve doors which, when opened, reveal the names of 1,400 women who died in the various services - the Scottish Women's Hospitals, Nursing Corps, Women's Forage Corps, Women's Legion Motor Transport, Women's Emergency Canteens, Mercantile Marine Stewardesses and many more, including of course the more familiar organisations and occupations. The memorial lacks any figurative imagery but its installation was accompanied by the restoration of a stained glass window in the Minster (the so-called 'Five Sisters window'), to which was added an inscription noting that it was 'Sacred to the Memory of the Women of the Empire who gave their Lives in the European War of 1914-1918'.

For the most prominent images of women workers we must yet again turn to Bury and Rawtenstall. At Bury, the town's main memorial is located outside the parish church and consists of a 'Cross of Sacrifice' flanked by curving walls with bronze friezes by Hermon Cawthra.[44] These

108

panels, in effect, present a continuous procession from right to left with, on one side of the central cross the armed services, and on the other civilians. Unlike Tait McKenzie's frieze at Edinburgh, this is not an illustration of enlistment and the transformation of civilian into soldier, but rather the identification of vital contributions, at home and abroad, by both men and women. Consequently the left hand panel features a front line nurse and a member of Queen Mary's Army Auxiliary amongst the armed personnel, whilst the right-hand panel features, amongst the miners, fishermen, shipbuilders and engineers, women at work on the land and in the factories.

Pl.97
(detail)
Bury.
Hermon
Cawthra,
1920

On the left side of the 'civilian' panel, behind two miners with their lamps and an engineer with oily rag in hand, is a woman in overalls carrying a wicker basket, her headgear suggesting perhaps a fishmonger or market worker. Behind her is a smartly uniformed woman in skirt and buttoned-up boots who is probably a bus or tram conductor. Factory and farm workers are more easily identifiable. In the centre, one woman is shown working a lathe, making shells, while behind her another female factory worker carries a pile of boxes or parcels. Two members of the Women's Land Army are shown on the right-hand side of the relief, one carrying a lamb, suggesting a nurturing role, the other, in contrast, turning to look back and with a pitchfork held at the ready like a weapon. Both are dressed in the familiar 'uniform' of the land Army, with soft linen hats, knee-length belted calico coats, trousers and boots with leather gaiters.

Very similar figures can be seen at nearby Rawtenstall in L.F Roslyn's highly impressive memorial. Between the representative figures of the armed forces at each of the four corners of the continuous bronze relief around the obelisk are male and female workers, some of whom have already been described. The corner figures of servicemen are in the highest relief and face outwards in contrast to the left to right movement of the workers. They are seen, in their separateness, as the protectors and defenders of a way of life. Yet in their similar scale and partial integration with the other figures they are seen also as being part of that life, as 'ordinary men' whose contribution to the war was to fight.

What is remarkable about the Rawtenstall memorial is not only that the representations of workers considerably outnumber those of

servicemen, but also that men and women are equally represented. In
addition to the nurse and mother and child are images of a farmhand and
a factory worker, and behind them, other less easily identifiable members
of various women's organisations, including the armed services. As at
Bury, the farmhand is recognisable not only from the agricultural
implements she carries over her shoulder but from the familiar uniform.
On a second side of the monument is another woman in overalls, possibly a
munitions worker, similar in appearance to the factory worker at Bury but
clearly carrying a heavier load as she leans back to support the weight.

The contribution of women was also sometimes acknowledged in
speeches by those, usually male, who unveiled memorials. At Merthyr
Tydfil, Field-Marshal Allenby unveiled the memorial. It depicted, either
side of a Madonna-like central figure, a miner and a mother and child
(See Pl.246). The inscription, echoing the imagery of the memorial, made
reference to the 'men and women of Merthyr Tydfil who died and suffered
in the Great War'. In his speech Allenby noted:

> Not only the men, the daughters of your country came forward, at
> the call, as bravely as their husbands, brothers and sons ... Others,

at home, gave as great proof of endurance and patient bravery - in hospitals, munitions factories and war work. The strain suffered by the woman who had to work and wait, in torturing suspense, apart from him she held most dear ... cannot be even faintly imagined by us. Such courage was of even a finer type than the heroism so splendid in the clamour and clash of battle. Your Memorial has rightly recognised the share of women as well as men, in the war, and of children, too - for they also suffered.[45]

Where at Bury the monument is dedicated simply to 'The men of Bury who gave their lives in the Great War', at both Rawtenstall and Merthyr the inscription reinforces the visual message. At Rawtenstall it states: 'A tribute of honour to the men who made the supreme sacrifice, to the men who came back, and to those who worked at home to win safety for the Empire'. Appropriately perhaps, the memorial here was unveiled by a woman, Miss Carrie Whitehead, a local councillor and JP.

The inscription and imagery of Rawtenstall, like Allenby's speech at Merthyr, also drew attention to the fact that it was not only men who went off to war who made a contribution to the war effort, but others who stayed at home. Certain jobs were considered of such vital importance that employees in these 'reserved' occupations were excused from conscription when this was introduced in 1916, though very many had already enlisted by this time and others no doubt continued to do so. Comments were sometimes made about the contributions of such men, if not in the speeches at unveiling ceremonies then certainly in newspaper reports of the events.[46] This was particularly the case in those places where reserved occupations predominated, such as coal mining or shipbuilding areas.

Where figurative imagery is featured on company memorials, specifically intended to commemorate the workers in particular industries, not surprisingly it often included relevant scenes of industrial activity. For example, the memorial at Wallsend to the workers in the Swan Hunter

shipyards had, in addition to reliefs of soldier, sailor and battleships, a scene of shipbuilding in the company's own yard. And at Nantlle in North Wales, on a memorial for the Penyrtorsedd Slate Quarry, a scene of battle is added to one of quarrying.

On municipal memorials too, the imagery sometimes makes reference to vital, local industries and the workers who maintained them, as with the miner at Merthyr Tydfil. At Workington, the main sculptural elements of Sir Robert Lorimer's cenotaph are relief panels by Alexander Carrick. One depicts a soldier taking leave of his wife and child. The other shows another soldier, or the same man now at the Front, assisting a wounded comrade. In addition there are two smaller, circular panels, one

Pls. 100 and 101
Rawtenstall.
L.F Roslyn, 1929

Pl.102
Workington.
Alexander
Carrick, 1928

showing men working heavy machinery, either steel workers or ship
builders, the other depicting men at work in the mines.

Alexander Carrick had served in the army. L.F Roslyn, the
sculptor of the Rawtenstall memorial, had served in the Royal Flying
Corps. The sculptor of the Bury reliefs, Hermon Cawthra, had, however,
been rejected as unfit for military service. Born in 1886 of working class
parents in Baildon near Bradford, Cawthra had attended art schools at
Shipley and Leeds and then, between 1909 and 1911, the Royal College of
Art, and from 1912-16, the Royal Academy Schools. The half dozen war
memorials designed by Cawthra feature a range of imagery, from a
medieval knight, used at both Monifieth in Scotland and Hackney in
London, to contemporary servicemen at Bootle. One might suspect however
that his depiction at Bury of workers on the home front gave him the
greatest pleasure. Like the figures he represented, Cawthra too had
contributed to the war effort on the home front having been employed
carving wooden propellors for the Royal Flying Corps.

V

Under Fire

The young women who worked in the munitions factories frequently had to move away from family and home and live in hostels or lodgings provided by the ministry, again suggesting parallels with the situation of the troops. They wore 'masculine' clothing and enjoyed greater freedom and increased spending power. Other work too required more 'masculine' outfits: as we have seen, factory workers wore overalls, the farmhands of the Women's Land Army wore breeches and many more occupations required a uniform. However, whilst such work may have challenged gender stereotypes, affecting society's view of women's capabilities, at least throughout the duration of the war, it did not necessarily affect these women's views of men, nor did it necessarily lessen gender differences. If women were being permitted to do work which had previously been regarded as essentially masculine, even more extreme forms of masculinity were being demanded of men on the field of battle. As a consequence, expectations of appropriate behaviour were placed increasingly under stress.

This chapter considers some of the ways in which pre-war attitudes to masculinity were undermined during the war and, in particular, how images of battle and the repercussions of war were presented, both at the time and in subsequent memorial sculpture. The injuring of the serviceman, both physically and mentally, and the constant threat of an appalling death on the field of battle seriously questioned conventional attitudes. Mutilation and mental breakdown not only provided alternative constructs of the male body but challenged traditional expectations of 'manly' behaviour, which needed to be addressed by post-war memorialists.

The impact of modern weapons had particularly devastating effects and it was in the role of nurse, and specifically of front line nurse, that women most often noted in men's responses to injury an undermining of stereotypical attitudes towards manliness. The appalling injuries which had to be tended led many to see the very seriously wounded as something less than men. As Vera Brittain commented, 'After the Somme I had seen men without faces, without eyes, without limbs, men almost disembowelled, men with hideous, truncated stumps of bodies'.[1] Mary Borden, who worked as a nurse attached to the French army, exclaimed:

> There are heads and knees and mangled testicles; there are chests with holes as big as your fist, and pulpy thighs, shapeless; and stumps where legs once were fastened. There are eyes - eyes of sick dogs, sick cats, blind eyes, eyes of delirium; and mouths that cannot articulate; and parts of faces - the nose gone, or the jaw. There are these things but no men.[2]

To Enid Bagnold, visiting a man whose nose had been blown off, he is 'like an ape, he has only his bumpy forehead and his protruding lips - the nose, the left eye gone'.[3]

Whilst such appalling extremes of physical mutilation seemed beyond human classification, lesser disabilities elicited more compassionate descriptions, of 'whimpering men'[4] or men 'with the unquestioning faith of children,'[5] which contradicted constructions of a masculinity of aggression and potential brutality.

The descriptions of men by women at the front were frequently in marked contrast to those by women at home whose views were shaped by propaganda, censorship and the reticence of those on leave to speak openly about their experiences. Vera Brittain, who had earlier written of the nobility of war and of finding beauty in it, now saw things rather differently:

> I wish those people who write so glibly about this being a holy war ... could see a case - to say nothing of 10 cases - of mustard gas in its early stages - could see the poor things burnt and blistered all over with great mustard-coloured suppurating blisters, with blinded eyes ... all sticky and stuck together, and always fighting for breath.[6]

As Joanna Bourke has pointed out in her book, *Dismembering the Male*, the most significant fact about the male body in the Great War was that it was the intentional target of mutilation.[7] Over 41,000 British men had limbs amputated; a further 272,000 suffered less severe though still serious injuries to the arms and legs; 60,500 received head wounds and 89,000 were seriously injured in other parts of the body. Many were blinded. In all, 31% of those who served in the army were wounded, though figures for the navy and airforce were admittedly much lower.[8]

It is hardly surprising then that the male body during the war was the focus of considerable concern. Disablement was highly visible, not only in the field hospital but back in Britain and in particular in those towns

116

where servicemen were sent to recuperate. Bourke has detailed the impact that this confrontation with the realities of war had on attitudes to the disabilities of both civilians and servicemen.[9] Economic and emotional resources were shifted from the civilian disabled to those rendered disabled in war. The state, it was conceded, owed a debt to these men but, like the even greater sacrifice of lives, the mutilation of the serviceman, a visible reminder of British manhood's willingness to place himself at risk 'in the cause of freedom', was turned to advantage. Depictions in the wartime press showed cheerful and 'privileged' sufferers, with 'maimed soldiers' entertained by royalty and smiling amputees attended by attractive young women (to take just two examples from the pages of *The Graphic* in 1916).[10]

When the wounded were ferried back home in numbers, people would gather outside the railway stations and on the nearby streets to show support, greeting the men with concern and pity, but also with pride and admiration. Such concerned sympathy and regard was, however, to turn, before the war was over, to feelings of horror and disgust at the scale of the mutilation. With post-war programmes of remembrance, including the erection of memorials, the disabled enjoyed a further wave of sympathy. Disabled ex-servicemen were to play an important role at the unveiling ceremonies of many war memorials, as at Macclesfield where two ex-servicemen, one blind, the other crippled, placed the first wreaths on the newly unveiled monument, or at Port Sunlight where the memorial was unveiled by a man blinded at the Battle of the Somme.

But any sympathy was soon to be dissipated by the desire to forget both the war and its effects. Before long disabled ex-servicemen had become identified with the passivity and helplessness of disabled children who needed lifetime care, an association which ultimately denied any claim to special status. As Joanna Bourke has convincingly demonstrated, increasing concerns in the post-war years with physical fitness and training to develop the male body, in part to compensate for the loss during the war of what was perceived as 'the cream' of British manhood, had a further dissipating effect on sympathy for the disabled ex-serviceman.

Injury and suffering was sometimes shown on war memorials though it is rare to find representations of obviously permanent disability. There were good reasons for this: certainly society's wish to forget the horrors of war and move on, but more particularly a concern for the sensibilities of the bereaved for whom the memorials were primarily intended. Such sensibilities were of course also present during the war when the gruesome reality of so many deaths was understandably avoided in newspaper reports and illustrations. So too in communications to the

bereaved of the fact of their loved one's demise, whether in official notices or in the more personal communications of colleagues in letters or in person. As Vera Brittain commented, 'the number of officers who were instantaneously and painlessly shot through the head or the heart passed far beyond the bounds of probability'.[11]

For the returning soldier who knew the realities of trench warfare, a post-war reluctance on the part of the civilian population to admit the appalling horrors of the Great War must have been the cause of considerable bitterness, as must the appearance of what would have been seen in many cases as particularly inappropriate memorials. As one soldier commented on seeing the aftermath of an explosion, with bodies 'cut in two, some in three parts, legs and arms ... strewn all over the place ... all my romantic ideals of war completely vanished'.[12] The apparent reinstatement of such ideals in post-war memorialisation would be hard to accept. Indeed for some, what Vera Brittain described as 'our post-war frenzy for memorials - as though we could somehow compensate the dead by remembering them regardless of expense', the very existence of memorials might have been questioned.[13]

Even during the war, when on leave, soldiers were all too conscious of the inability, reluctance or refusal of those at home to try to understand what conditions for the front line servicemen were really like. Many ex-soldiers have commented on the gulf which existed between those at the front and those back home, with the soldier unable or unwilling to talk about his experiences, and the relatives and friends at home seemingly uninterested or unsympathetic. And when people tried to understand, communication was often impossible. Vera Brittain was dismayed at the changes she observed in her brother's demeanour:

> He was an unfamiliar, frightening Edward, who never smiled nor spoke except about trivial things, who seemed to have nothing to say to me and indeed hardly seemed to notice my return ... Silent, uncommunicative, thrust in upon himself, he sat all day at the piano.[14]

118

When injury was shown on war memorials it was rarely in the context of battle, though a relief panel on a memorial at Brierley Hill near Birmingham, now unfortunately badly weathered, does show members of the Royal Army Medical Corps tending the wounded on what appears to be the field of battle. Elsewhere, a calm and resolute binding of wounds usually sufficed, whether by the soldier himself as at Croydon, or more commonly by a nurse - at St Anne's-on-Sea and Colwyn Bay, for examples. In either case this signified a stoic resistance to pain rather than emasculation. At Croydon there is no sign of suffering on the face of the soldier as he concentrates his efforts on the difficult task of single-handedly bandaging his injured arm, while at both St Anne's and Colwyn Bay, from the expressions on the faces of soldier and nurse, the serviceman seems to have little more than a scratch or a sprain. Such imagery exactly reflects much of the wartime propaganda which similarly underplayed the appalling realities of injury.

Pl. 104
'Well Done The New Army'.
F.H Townsend, Punch, July 1916

In addition to the nurse and soldier, the memorial at St Anne's included a relief of weary troops and walking wounded returning from the battlefield, including those blinded by gas and one barely able to walk, even with his comrades' assistance. A more seriously wounded soldier is carried on a stretcher. Around the corner of the panel another man is carried on his friend's back. Although relatively unusual, the stretcher-born soldier is an image occasionally seen elsewhere, for example on memorial plaques for the Royal College of Art, for the Nursing Services in the Scottish National Memorial at Edinburgh, and on Hermon Cawthra's memorial at Bury.

The depiction of victims of a gas attack is also unusual. John Singer Sargent's painting, *Gassed*, for the British War Memorial Committees' intended 'Hall of Remembrance', showing blindfolded men leading each other hesitantly forwards is well known. So too is William Roberts' painting of *The First German Gas Attack at Ypres* (for the

Canadian equivalent of the British scheme) but in sculpture such depictions are rare. At Macclesfield, however, the dead soldier is shown grasping his gas mask, the implication being that he has succumbed to the poison gas before being able to protect himself. Typically his death appears to have been peaceful; there is no anguish on his face and no hint here of Wilfred Owen's 'blood come gargling from froth corrupted lungs' - of the awful truth, in other words, of this appalling form of death.[15]

In fact the depiction of injury, whilst acknowledging a reality of war, allowed an emphasis of the 'comradeship of the trenches' and of the qualities of compassion and concern and of (literal) support, providing a metaphor for a more general defence of the weak and needy which had been claimed as an original motivation for the country's declaration of war in 1914.

One rare example of a rather more bitter depiction of permanent mutilation can be found at Birmingham in the city's 'Hall of Memory'. Inside are a series of relief panels by William Bloye which depict the departure, the fighting, and the return of the troops. Bloye, who had studied at Birmingham School of Art before the war had also spent time studying with Eric Gill whose influence can be detected in his stylised

Pl. 105
Port Sunlight.
William
Goscombe
John, 1921

Pl. 106
Birmingham.
William Bloye,
1925

reliefs for this memorial. As an inscription records, 'of 150,000 who answered the call to arms 12,320 fell: 35,000 came home disabled'. The panel depicting the return shows, at the head of the procession which passes row upon row of crosses in front of a stylised, shattered landscape, a man whose right leg has been amputated. The woman who waits to greet them establishes this panel as a counterpoint to the relief depicting enlistment where the woman bids her husband farewell.

Pl. 107
St Anne's-on-
Sea.
Walter
Marsden, 1924

Whilst the illustration of men's compassionate assistance of injured comrades provided a softening of more stereotypical constructs of aggressive manliness, depictions of the endurance of physical suffering reinforced the image of stoicism and bravery which was part of that stereotype. Mental disability was however more problematic, for here there was an apparent failure to 'act like men' at all and suppress 'unmanly' emotions in the face of stress which led to 'men who had "done their bit in France" crying like children'.[16]

An all too typical response to mental breakdown was the tendency, as one commentator at the time noted, of referring to '*detecting* instead of *diagnosing* hysteria'.[17] Such attitudes were, however, being questioned as early as 1915: a series of articles in *The Times* that year discussed the phenomenon of what was referred to as 'the wounded mind'.[18] Certainly by the end of the war it was no longer possible to unquestioningly maintain pre-war attitudes and on 28 April 1920 Lord Southborough proposed a motion in the House of Lords to establish a committee to investigate the nature and treatment of what was now generally referred to as shell shock.

The term 'shell shock' had first been used by Charles Samuel Myers, a psychologist and neurologist and Cambridge academic, in an article in *The Lancet* in February 1915 where he discussed cases of soldiers he had treated when working in France in the early months of the war. As a result, Dr Myers was attached to a unit investigating neurological problems. His duties included not only supervising and assisting in the treatment of sufferers but advising in cases of suspected malingering and giving evidence in courts martial for desertion.

The symptoms of shell shock varied widely but included loss or impairment of hearing, speech or vision, insomnia, memory loss, nightmares and hallucinations, pains, apparent 'fits', violent convulsions, and uncontrollable muscle spasms or muscle contractions such as fists remaining clenched for months or a back bent at right-angles to the lower limbs.

G. Elliot Smith and T.H Pear, writing on 'Shell Shock and Its Lessons' in 1917, commented:

> A common way of describing the condition of a man sent back with 'shock' is to say that he has 'lost his reason' or 'lost his senses'. As a rule, this is a singularly inapt description of such a condition. Whatever may be the state of mind of the patient immediately after the mine explosion, the burial in the dugout, the sight and sound of his lacerated comrades, or other appalling experiences which finally incapacitate him for service in the firing line, it is true to say that by the time of his arrival in a hospital in England his reason and his senses are usually not lost but functioning with painful efficiency.[19]

As they explain, the shell-shocked victim is all too aware of the reasons for his condition and, except in the cases of temporary loss of particular senses, all too often hypersensitive to sensory stimulation such as sudden loud noises or flashes of light. It is not, they suggest, in the intellectual but in the emotional sphere that we must look for terms to describe these conditions.[20]

Eighteen months after the war had ended some 65,000 ex-servicemen still drew disability pensions for neurasthenia and over 9,000 remained hospitalised. In his address to the House, Lord Southborough commented:

> All would desire to ... bury our recollections of the horrible disorder, and to keep on the surface nothing but the cherished memory of those who were the victims of this malignity. But, my Lords, we cannot do this, because a great number of cases of those who suffer from shell-shock and its allied disorders are still upon our hands and they deserve our sympathy and care.[21]

Investigations into the nature and handling of shell shock had broad implications, throwing into question the very concepts of bravery and cowardice and of realistic expectations of behaviour under fire. The acceptance of the need for debate and for an enquiry was itself indicative of a considerable change in attitudes towards mental or psychological injury. In the early years of the war the very existence of shell shock was questioned by many, including some charged with helping to cure the sufferers, and indeed, throughout the committee's enquiries, the relationship between shell shock and cowardice and the implication that they might be one and the same remained a major theme. There were still those who felt that shell shock 'gave fear a respectable name' or who claimed that shell shock 'must be looked upon as a form of disgrace to the soldier'.[22]

Even those prepared to accept the devastating mental as well as physical effects of the close proximity of exploding shells were sometimes inclined to react differently to the 80% of shell shock victims who were 'merely' affected by the general conditions in the trenches. 'No man who has simply broken down mentally should be given a wound stripe, but the man with an obvious commotional shock, who has been buried or blown up, deserved one'.[23]

Such views were countered however by the clear evidence that under the most severe conditions even the bravest of men could fall victim to shell shock. Bravery did not require the absence of fear. On the contrary, the presence of fear, and its suppression, was essential: what constituted the act of bravery were actions taken despite fear. But, as Smith and Pear noted in 1917, the suppression of fear for very long periods of time 'accounts for the collapse of men who have shown themselves repeatedly to be brave and trustworthy'.[24]

Charles Myers in his capacity as consultant psychologist to the British Army in France had considerable experience of treating shell shock victims. Myers identified different categories of shock, in particular making distinctions between neurasthenia, a breakdown due, as he put it, to 'persistent wear and tear', and hysteria, the physical manifestation of emotional states characterised by a sudden 'snap'.[25] Officers, he claimed, were predominantly susceptible to neurasthenia, the men to hysteria.

The American writer, Elaine Showalter, has suggested that there may have been some reluctance for military doctors to stigmatise men of their own social class with what was seen as the 'feminine' label of hysteria but for Myers the distinction was explained, to a large extent, by the officer being fully occupied issuing orders and organising his men until finally collapsing of nervous exhaustion.[26] The ordinary soldier, on the other hand, could do nothing but watch and wait until eventually 'snapping'. However, Myers also suggested that 'the forces of education, tradition and example make for greater self-control in the case of the Officer'.[27] But given sufficient degrees of stress for sufficiently long periods of time mere will power (or 'self-control') could not prevent the possibility of mental collapse.

The ambiguities and contradictions in opinions and attitudes expressed by witnesses to the enquiry are revealed in the committee's report, published in 1922. This can be seen as a reflection, not only of the differing attitudes to war-induced neurasthenia and hysteria and their appropriate treatment, but of the need to balance the recognition of the bravery of 'the glorious dead', prominently emphasised on memorials concurrently being erected throughout the land, with an acknowledgement of the strains placed on conventional constructions of 'manly' behaviour by unprecedented forms of stalemated trench warfare.

Not surprisingly perhaps, few war memorials depicted the obviously shell shocked soldier, though the strains of war are certainly apparent on the faces of some of the featured servicemen. Gilbert Ledward's impressive soldier at Abergavenny leans wearily forward, his right arm resting on the barrel of his gun, blocking its end as if to negate its purpose. Apparently lost in thought, his face is grim and unsmiling.

A similar figure, leaning against a rocky outcrop, 'a soldier ... not so much of the fighting unit, but rather a soldier deep in thought', is shown at Huntingdon, gazing contemplatively into the far distance.[28] Whilst Ledward had personal experience of the strain of battle having served in the Artists' Rifles, Huntingdon's memorial was designed by a woman, Kathleen Scott, who could only sympathise with the soldier's plight.[29] Born in 1878, Kathleen Scott, the widow of Robert Falcon Scott ('Scott of the Antarctic'), had studied at the Slade School of Art and later in Paris where she had met Auguste Rodin whose famous *Thinker* appears to have had some influence on the Huntingdon figure.[30]

Other examples of pensive soldiers include two in Scotland by William Birnie Rhind, at Kelty and Prestonpans, and Gilbert Bayes' figure at Broughton in Humberside. In each of these examples, as at Huntingdon, the soldier's chin rests on his raised hand as he stares into space, lost in thought. At Broughton, the soldier symbolically holds a martyr's palm leaf, as though his thoughts are on those comrades who lost their lives or, if we see it as the 'palm of victory', on the high cost of its achievement.

Another example of an obviously weary soldier, described by the sculptor Eric Gill as 'very tired, heavily burdened, walking towards the setting sun', can be found in the village of Trumpington near Cambridge.[31] Gill carved the figure, which is based on a design by his friend and fellow artist David Jones, at the base of a tall cross. In the course of his discussions with the representative of the local War Memorial Committee who had commissioned the memorial, he commented, 'I trust the committee ... will not ask for naturalism in a thing which obviously calls for symbolism'.[32]

Pl. 108
Huntingdon.
Kathleen Scott,
1923

Pl. 109
3rd Batl'n
Monmouthshire
Regt memorial,
Abergavenny.
Gilbert Ledward,
1921

Pl. 110
Broughton.
Gilbert Bayes,
1923

Although typical of his distinctively stylised approach, and clearly intended, as his words suggest, to symbolically represent the strains of war on all, the figure, now unfortunately badly weathered, can still be seen as a portrayal of a specific, war-weary individual, mechanically marching forward, with his rifle over his shoulder and his head bowed. No doubt it was based on Jones' own experiences. Unlike the older Gill who did not receive his call up papers until September 1918 and therefore saw no active service, Jones had enlisted in the Royal Welch Fusiliers in 1915 at the age of nineteen. He was wounded on the Somme in 1916 and later, following his recovery and return to the front, contracted trench fever. In the light of this it is hardly surprising that his depiction shows a man under stress.

The only other contemporary soldier carved by Gill had been produced a year earlier. Unveiled on 1 September 1920, the memorial for the village of Chirk in North Wales had been commissioned by Lord Howard de Walden who had specified a bas-relief of a soldier. (Lord Howard de Walden was the resident of Chirk Castle and a long-standing patron of Gill's). Although somewhat less weary-looking than the Trumpington figure, the soldier's expression here as he peers out between his helmet and the upturned collar of his greatcoat, is similarly grim. His left hand, raised as if to challenge an approaching figure, might even be seen as a gesture of resignation and despair, not so much a halt to who goes there as a hoped for halt to hostilities.

Pl. 111
left
Trumpington.
Eric Gill, 1921

Pl. 112
right
Chirk.
Eric Gill, 1920

At St Anne's-on-Sea, as we have already seen, the memorial depicts war-weary and injured troops on the reliefs at the base of the monument. In addition, the sculptor produced other figures in the round. Two seated figures, one a mother with small child on her lap, the other a soldier, are placed at the base of a tall, square column while a third, an allegorical female figure with outstretched arms, stands at its apex. The grim-faced figure of the soldier, with close-cropped, helmetless head, bulging neck muscles and staring eyes, sits on the left-hand side of the monument on an outcrop of barren rock. His right hand holds his rifle by the barrel like a club, as if to emphasise its uselessness, whilst his left fist is tightly clenched.

Pl. 113
St Anne's-on-Sea.
Walter
Marsden, 1924

Though we may see this figure as simply signifying grim and heroic determination, it is clear that Walter Marsden, the memorial's sculptor, intended something more. Marsden had served with distinction during the war and was undoubtedly drawing on his own observations of men under stress. The commemorative booklet, produced for the unveiling ceremony in October 1924, explained that with this figure the sculptor's aim had been to express the reality of his own experience: 'The constant nervous strain of continuous trench warfare, brought about the ever-present feeling that danger was lurking near, a state of tension which, in the opinion of the Artist, was the cause of more mental agony than any other phase of the War'.[33]

An awareness of the likelihood of death and its horrific nature contributed greatly to the stress of soldiers who could only wait impotently for it to happen, or who had to witness friends and relations literally destroyed before their eyes. Edmund Blunden, in *Undertones of War*, recalled one such incident:

> One shell had dropped without warning behind me ... [it] had burst all wrong. Its butting impression was black and stinking in the parados where three minutes ago the lance-corporal's mess-tin was bubbling over a little flame. For him, how could the gobbets of blackening flesh, the earth-wall sotted with blood, with flesh, the eye under the duckboard, the pulpy bone be the only answer? At this moment, while we looked with dreadful fixity at so isolated a horror, the lance-corporal's brother came round the traverse. He was sent to company headquarters in a kind of catalepsy.[34]

Whilst the healthy bodies shown on many war memorials provided a metamorphic substitute for the fragmented bodies of the dead, elsewhere a sense of loss or absence was emphasised. For Blackburn's memorial, the Australian sculptor Bertram MacKennal produced a symbolic figure said to represent 'the son, returning war-worn after the conflict, received by the Motherland, supported by her, and led to peace'.[35] Although this interpretation implies survival there is, in the depiction of the unnaturally semi-

nude male collapsed in the arms of a cloaked and hooded female, an overpowering sense of finality, of life's final journey to 'the other side'. It is an impression which must have been heightened for the four women who assisted at the unveiling ceremony, each of whom had lost at least three sons in the war.

A similar memorial, by Harold Brownsword, is at Allerton in West Yorkshire. Again we see the soldier, stripped to the waist, supported by an allegorical, hooded female but this time with the additional help of a youthful male nude, presumably representing future generations. As the naked youth proffers a wreath, at the base of the group can be seen the soldier's helmet and rifle from which emerges a serpent, symbolically crushed by the soldier's boot. As the hooded figure was at the time identified as 'Death', we may assume that, as at Blackburn, the intention was to suggest the soldier's sacrifice as being received, metaphorically, with the gratitude of the nation and, in this case, of the 'nation's sons'.

If the iconography of Blackburn's and Allerton's memorials hint at death, that of other memorials made more overt reference to it and Macclesfield's inclusion of a soldier who has succumbed to a gas attack or the Glasgow 'Cameronians' memorial with its slain soldier in the midst of battle have already been identified. At Portadown in Northern Ireland the suggestion is again made that the soldier here shown collapsing in the arms of an angelic figure, is the victim of a gas attack, his mask lying unused at his feet. The statue is by Henry Fehr. The angelic figure was one much used by Fehr, though elsewhere identified as Victory. Fehr adapted the figure at Portadown, not only by the obvious addition of the soldier, seen at no other location, but by a downward tilt of the head and the substitution of laurel for the Sword of Justice.

Similar images of soldiers in the arms of angels can be seen elsewhere, at Bearsden in Scotland and Queen's University at Belfast for example, where, at both locations the soldier is shown as a semi-nude 'warrior'. At Stalybridge there are two separate statues of slain servicemen in the arms of angels. The memorial here is rather unusually sited at one end of a bridge over the River Tame which runs through the town. Curving walls create a semicircular space bisected by the road leading up to the bridge. At the end of each wall is a carved lion and on either side of the road, at the head of the bridge, the walls culminate in pedestals, on top of which are pairs of bronze figures. On one side a soldier lies in the arms of

Pl. 114
Blackburn.
Bertram
MacKennal,
1924

a semi-nude angel who leans over him supporting his right arm; on the other, a barefoot sailor is similarly slumped against an angel who holds out a small lamp with flickering 'eternal' flame.

Although it would be possible, not only here, but at Portadown, Bearsden and Belfast, to read the servicemen as merely wounded, the presence in each case of angels clearly implies death. The relative rarity of the obviously dead is surely significant, reflecting, like the reluctance to depict the seriously injured, a reticence on behalf of the bereaved.

The designer of the Stalybridge memorial was Ferdinand Blundstone, a London-based sculptor but former resident of the town.[36] At the unveiling ceremony on 6 November 1921, attended by an estimated 24,000 people, calculated to be equal to the population of the town at that time, each sculptural group was separately unveiled, the naval pedestal by the wartime mayor, James Bottomley; the army pedestal by the current mayor, Ada Summers. The latter commented on what she felt it represented: 'The courage and devotion to duty, and the fine spirit of self-sacrifice of all those men of Stalybridge whose names, carved in granite, tell to all who pass this way that they died that we might live ourselves'.[37] The first wreaths laid were by two men, both of whom had been blinded in the war. Of the many wreaths and floral tributes subsequently laid against the curved walls, one stated briefly, 'These men played the game'.[38]

Blundstone was to adapt the Stalybridge scheme for another memorial which he produced the following year for the Prudential Assurance Company in London. This time a single figure of a dead soldier is accompanied by two angels who, as at Stalybridge, hover above and behind him, their spectacularly extended wings suggesting imminent flight.

The acknowledgement of death was of course central to the meaning of war memorials and, although the depiction of the dead and dying in memorial sculpture remained the exception, the reality of death in battle could hardly be denied. Death was frequently illustrated during the war, in magazines and even on film. As with the mutilation of the

Pl. 115
Portadown.
H.C Fehr,1925

131

132

serviceman it served as a powerful symbol of self-sacrifice which could be turned to patriotic advantage. Indeed the depiction of death was at times consciously contrived. The 1916 documentary film *The Battle of the Somme*, screened in more than two thousand cinemas across the country between August and October, and even at the front during the very battle it depicted, featured, in perhaps its most famous scene, a regiment going 'over the top' with soldiers clambering out of their trench and advancing through barbed wire towards the enemy lines. One man immediately falls dead at the edge of the trench and slides back down. As the troops slowly advance, others are seen to fall. Often shown in documentaries about the Great War, this scene was in fact one of the very few inauthentic moments in the film having, out of practical necessity, been specially staged for the cameras, though audiences at the time were unlikely to have been aware of this.

There was considerable criticism of this depiction of the moment of death: a letter in the *Manchester Guardian* suggested that suffering had been turned into 'a spectacle for the pleasure of those who like to gloat ... over the agonies of others' while the Dean of Durham wrote to *The Times* to attack the film as 'an entertainment which wounds the heart and violates the very sanctities of bereavement'.[39] The general consensus, of both public and press, was however extremely positive, the *Evening News* describing it as 'the greatest picture in the world' and *Kine Weekly* as 'the most wonderful battle picture that has ever been taken'.[40] For Lloyd George it was 'an epic of self-sacrifice and gallantry'.[41]

The producer of the film, Geoffrey Malins, certainly felt that to be genuine (or appear to be genuine) it had to be 'full of suffering and agony'.[42] In fact almost one third of the film concentrates on pain and suffering with extensive footage of the wounded returning from the battlefield and being treated in the field hospitals. Following the 'over the top' sequence, a further scene shows troops advancing across a distant no-man's land with some men inevitably falling (this time genuinely) to enemy fire whilst another extended scene concentrates on the dead bodies lying on the field of battle. Though identified as German, some are clearly British. To the editor of the *Manchester Guardian* the film's effects were intentionally pedagogic and purgative with the portrayal of death and dying essential: 'the people who help to make war should know what war really means and ... those who remain at home should realise how great are the sacrifices which others are called upon to make for them'.[43]

The Battle of the Somme and other similar documentary films made and shown during the war, placed the death and injury of the serviceman in an explanatory context. So did the regular, though sometimes misleading illustrations of battle scenes in the popular

Pl. 116
Prudential
Assurance Co.
London. Ferdinand
Blundstone, 1922

133

Pl. 117
Film frame -
'The Battle of
the Somme',
1916

illustrated magazines of the time, accompanied as they were by patriotic texts. Where such a context was apparently absent, as in the exhibition of paintings, their presentation was more open to criticism and overt censorship. Christopher Nevinson was one artist who fell foul of the 'Defence of the Realm Act' which had been passed on 8 August 1914 to provide wide-ranging powers of censorship of any materials felt to be detrimental to the war effort.

Nevinson was one of a number of 'official' war artists who had been appointed from 1916 onwards to record their personal impressions of the war. In addition to their officially published work, war artists also exhibited their work privately, though this was still open to censure, as Nevinson was to discover when he attempted to show a painting entitled, with apparently intended irony, *Paths of Glory*, at an exhibition held in March 1918 at the Leicester Galleries in London.[44] The painting showed two dead British soldiers sprawled, face down, between and in part entangled by rows of barbed wire.

Whilst there is no emphasis on suffering, both men's faces being hidden and their bodies showing no signs of serious injury let alone mutilation or dismemberment, it was clearly felt that pictures of dead bodies would undermine public morale. Consequently, Nevinson was told to

134

withdraw the picture from the exhibition. In fact he chose instead to exhibit it with a strip of brown paper on which the word 'censored' was written in large letters, effectively obscuring the offending figures.

Photographs were also censored, both by restricting access to what could be seen and by suppressing what might be construed as providing information beneficial to the enemy. [45] With photographs in newspapers and magazines a tacit agreement existed between the military, the propagandists and the press in deciding what was fit for publication, to comply with what was perceived as acceptable standards of decency and an understandable reluctance to cause distress. Nevertheless, quite explicit photographic images *were* sometimes shown. Photographs of battlefield action, including photos of the wounded and dead, were regularly featured in the press, though these tended to concentrate on the less badly injured or the German dead.

Pl. 118
'Paths of Glory'.
Christopher
Nevinson,
Oil on canvas,
1918
(Imperial War
Museum)

Photographic exhibitions were also held. The position of painters, however, was seen as different from that of photographers, even when photographs were exhibited in galleries. Painting was located as art rather than reportage and, whilst photography was seen as unmediated and objective, painting was not. Concurrent with the exhibition of Nevinson's work was an exhibition in the near by Grafton Galleries of greatly enlarged photographs of the battlefields, many of which included dead allied and enemy soldiers. These photos remained uncensored. The audiences for exhibitions of paintings and photographs, it was implied, engage with the images differently in each case, and even more so in the more usual presentation of photographic imagery in newspapers and magazines. When looking at paintings we are conscious of the artifice involved and naturally question the artist's intentions in the decisions he or she has made. This is not the case with documentary photography which, despite an awareness of selectivity, composition, lighting etc., we are more inclined to see as presenting an unmediated 'reality'.

When death was depicted on war memorials, like wartime press photography, it became acceptable by its contextualisation and by the fact that it was invariably sanitised and frequently sanctified. After the war censorship was of course no longer in place. The sculptors of war memorials nonetheless continued to be constrained by the understandable sensitivity, not to mention conventionality, of war memorial committees.

Effigies of obviously dead soldiers were rare and when allowed were often the centre of some controversy. At Macclesfield, the depiction of the dead soldier caused some disquiet when first submitted. Although John Millard's design was well received when a model of the proposed monument was presented to the war memorial committee, a number of voices were raised to object to the depiction of death. One committee member, agreeing with the suggestion that the figure of the soldier was 'harrowing' explained his feelings. "In all conscience we have had more than enough to harrow our feelings in and through the great war, and must in future avoid even the semblance of the perpetuation thereof". Another simply said that the soldier "should be taken off", adding, with some emotion, "Our soldiers are not dead".[46] It was agreed to ask the sculptor to present an alternative design which removed the fallen soldier. This he duly did, but on comparing both the original and the revised versions of his design, and listening to Millard's explanation of his intentions, it was unanimously agreed to accept the former, with the sculptor's assurance that 'the figure of the prostrate soldier would not be so staring or "gruesome"'.[47]

Lindsey Clark's Cameronians memorial in Glasgow has previously been referred to as one which also graphically depicts the soldier's death in a scenario similar to the 'over-the-top' sequence from the *Battle of the Somme* film. Such depictions on British war memorials are rare though one memorial which also shows men 'going over the top' is at Brierley Hill. The main focus of this memorial is a crudely carved conventional figure of a soldier, by local masons, George Brown and Sons, but around the monument's plinth are relief carvings illustrating scenes of the Artillery and Navy in action, the Royal Army Medical Corps tending the wounded, and soldiers going over the top. The carvings here are badly weathered and it is difficult to make out the detail, but the panel appears to show soldiers surging forward, in this case without any sign of injury or death.

Given that much of their time was spent there, it is perhaps surprising that soldiers are rarely shown in trenches. One memorial which does show this is at Bellshill and Mossend in Strathclyde where, on a small bronze plaque, three men are shown manning a machine gun. Another, on a similar scale at the base of a name panel can be found on John Cassidy's Heaton Moor memorial. But a more impressive example is in the interior of Birmingham's 'Hall of Memory' where one of the three carved reliefs by William Bloye depicts a line of soldiers firing at the enemy, their rifles resting on the top of the trench. On the right, one soldier, apparently just shot, has slumped to his knees.

At Brierley Hill, Bellshill and Heaton Moor the relief plaques simply represent servicemen in action; at Birmingham there is a more forceful message, with the bas-reliefs, both individually and collectively, presenting a more complex narrative. Each panel includes elements of optimism and grief. In the first the enthusiasm of the men marching off to war is countered by the sadness of departure from the featured wife. The final plaque reverses this: the weary return of injured men and a consequent emphasis on the tragedy of war is tempered by the woman and child who greet them and who can be seen to represent a return to

Pl. 119
Birmingham.
William Bloye,
1925

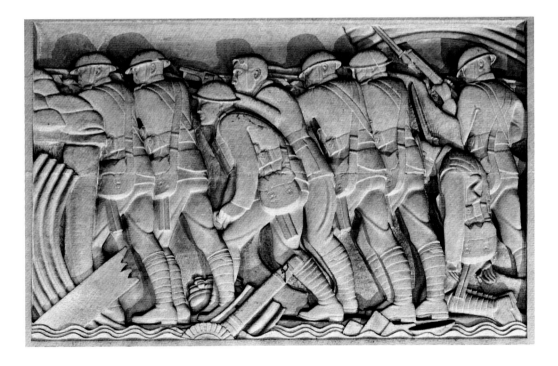

normality and potential happiness. And in the central panel of soldiers in the trenches the organised efficiency of the troops is qualified by the depiction of death.

Another illustration of trench warfare can be found at Alloa where the Scottish-based sculptor, Charles Pilkington Jackson, produced a striking memorial which combined the allegorical and realistic. The figure of St Margaret, her hand raised in benediction, stands over a group of four soldiers who emerge from a muddy trench, with only their heads and shoulders visible. A central figure with determined expression is shown with thick gloves and wire cutters, leaning forward in the act of cutting the barbed wire which blocks their path. To his side, with bayonets fixed, his comrades wait to surge forward when the path is clear.

Although reflecting an everyday reality for the front-line soldier, the barbed wire has additional symbolic significance, suggesting the difficult struggles towards victory and peace and personal survival. As a barrier to the soldiers' progress, it also hints at those who failed to survive, their names listed on eight narrow panels on the wall behind. The figure of St Margaret, in bestowing her blessing, seems also to be acknowledging the imminent deaths of the men below.

VI

The Great Sacrifice

The concept of the soldier's self-sacrifice had obvious religious implications and dying heroes had long been portrayed in such a way as to suggest this. Benjamin West's influential version of *The Death of General Wolfe* (1770), a picture shown at the Canadian War memorials exhibition at the Royal Academy in 1919, showed the event as a 'lamentation', with Christ replaced by Wolfe, the mourners at the foot of the cross by his fellow officers, and the Cross itself by the Union flag, providing an exemplar for subsequent depictions of heroic death.[1] This resonance of the soldier's self-sacrifice with Christ's own sacrifice on the Cross was frequently exploited both during and after the First World War. The presentation of the Red Cross nurse as a Marian figure, on posters or in newspaper appeals during the war, or on memorials after the war, also implied parallels between Christ and the injured or dying soldier.

Pl.121
The Great
Sacrifice.
James Clark.
The Graphic,
25th December
1914

    In these cases, like General Wolfe, the soldier is presented as a surrogate for Christ himself; elsewhere the analogy takes the form of a juxtaposition of the two. The Christmas 1914 edition of *The Graphic* included an illustration by James Clark entitled *The Great Sacrifice* which showed a soldier, shot through the temple, lying at the feet of the crucified Christ. Below Clark's picture were the familiar words 'Greater love hath no man than this'. Like the title, this deliberately ambiguous text, often inscribed on war memorials, could be seen to apply to both Christ and the soldier. All three elements, of illustration, title and text, implied an equivalence of sacrificial deaths.[2]

    The original painting, exhibited in a 'War Relief Exhibition' in aid of the Red Cross at the

Royal Academy in 1915, was bought by Queen Mary but reproductions were widely distributed to schools and churches throughout the country and some can still be seen in churches today. Many more were incorporated into street shrines. The painting itself now hangs in the church of St Mildred's in Whippingham on the Isle of Wight having been donated to the church as a memorial to Prince Maurice of Battenberg, the son of Princess Beatrice, after he was killed in action at Ypres in 1914.

More than one war memorial was based directly on Clark's popular picture. The two dimensional image translated easily into stained glass with versions to be found in a number of English churches. There are also examples in other countries. In St George's Church in Malvern, a suburb of Melbourne, Australia, there is a version which shows the dead soldier in Australian uniform, the original cap which lies at his feet replaced by the familiar Australian slouch hat. Relief panels were also produced. A carving of *The Great Sacrifice* can be seen on a cross in the churchyard of St Stephen's in Redditch and in the church of St John and St James on Merseyside is another carved panel of the painting.

Other memorials were based less directly on *The Great Sacrifice*. The war memorial outside the church of St Wilfred at Longridge in Lancashire shows the dead or dying soldier at the foot of the Cross. (A slight variation of this sculpture, by the same firm of masons, can be found outside another church in nearby Darwen). Unlike the oblivious

140

soldier in Clark's painting, where Christ is shown as a ghostly apparition hovering above him, at Longridge the soldier stares up, with half closed eyes, towards the here unavoidably solid figure of Christ who returns his gaze. Perhaps suggesting a redemptive vision in his dying moments, the equivalence of Christ's and the soldier's deaths is nevertheless clearly implied.

Such analogical implications in the imagery of the soldier's self-sacrifice were theologically problematic for the churches for whom Christ's sacrifice was uniquely significant but who wished nonetheless to reinforce the religiosity of memorialisation. The Church by tradition had a dominant role to play in the supervision of funeral services and, with the war memorial's function in the mediation of the grief of the bereaved, the clergy's involvement in the process of memorialisation was inevitable. The position of the Church of England during the conflict had, however, been fraught with theological difficulties, not least in the problem of how (or indeed whether) to provide support and encouragement for the fighting of the war. On 9 August 1914, just days after the declaration of war, the Archbishop of York, preaching in York Minster, declared "I hate War. I detest it. It is the bankruptcy of Christian principle". But he then went on to say that he believed this war to be righteous and that "We were bound in honour to enter it".[3]

Much was made of the concept of a 'just war'. For a religion whose philosophy was to love one's enemies and to 'turn the other cheek', and one of whose principal commandments was 'Thou shalt not kill', the concept of a just war had a long history of providing the justification for killing in battle. Without such an argument it would have been difficult for the Church to have provided the support for the Great War which, in the event, was widely forthcoming. Indeed for some in the Church it was not simply a just war but a holy war. The Bishop of London, Arthur Foley Winnington-Ingram, a belligerently outspoken advocate of the war who was fond of referring to it as 'the Nailed Hand against the Mailed Fist', argued, in the *Manchester Guardian* on 10 June 1915, that 'the Church can best help the nation first of all by making it realise that it is engaged in a Holy War, and not be afraid of saying so'.[4]

Those in the Church who most vociferously endorsed the war frequently drew parallels between Christ's sacrifice on the Cross and the soldier's sacrifice on the field of battle, suggesting that if they were to die in battle they were following in the footsteps of Christ. The Bishop of London went further, preaching a quasi-Islamic doctrine that soldiers dying in what he claimed was a holy war would immediately enter the 'Kingdom of Heaven', a doctrine admittedly condemned as absurd by others in the Church. A fascinating memorial at Sledmere in East Yorkshire appears to endorse the idea of Holy War, drawing parallels between the soldiers of the Great War and medieval crusaders. Sledmere's memorial is an Eleanor Cross, a copy of a thirteenth century monument in Northampton. Erected in the 1890s, it was adapted in 1919 as a war memorial by the addition of brass plates portraying each of the villagers who died in the war. Shown with hands clasped in prayer, in emulation of medieval church brasses, most are in contemporary uniform but two of the officers, including Sir Mark Sykes, the local landowner and commanding officer of the 5th Yorkshire Regiment, are depicted as crusaders. Beneath Sir Mark's feet is a dead infidel and behind him is the city of Jerusalem.[5]

It was inevitably assumed, and repeatedly suggested after the war, at unveiling ceremonies and elsewhere, that the dead had died willingly. At Stockport's war memorial unveiling ceremony it was said that they died 'without flinching, faced the horrors and deprivations of war, and willingly gave their lives for others and for the country they loved so well'.[6] Where inscriptions underlined the belief that the Great War had been fought 'for God' as well as for 'King and Country', the clear implication was that the self-sacrificing soldier believed in a religious as well as a patriotic imperative for his actions.

A literal illustration of religious backing, of 'God on our side', can be seen in a memorial in Exeter Cathedral to the men of the Devonshire regiment where an alert soldier is poised behind sandbags with rifle and fixed bayonet. In the landscape behind him is a crucifix, intact amidst the ruins of a village. A rather different and considerably grander exposition of this idea of theological endorsement can be found at Paisley where the memorial takes the form of a substantial plinth topped with larger than life size figures of a crusader on horseback flanked by contemporary soldiers. The local paper, commenting on the unveiling of the monument in July 1924, drew the obvious parallel: 'The idea which the group is intended to convey is that our men in the great war in their splendid determination were animated by the same spirit as the Crusaders, and were striving towards an ideal similar to that which stimulated them'.[7]

At the outbreak of war Lord Kitchener had made it clear that he did not expect the clergy to appeal for recruits from the pulpit and many,

Pl. 125
Tredegar.
Newbury
Trent, 1924

including the Archbishop of Canterbury, were certainly reluctant to go that far. (The Archbishop was nonetheless willing to give his endorsement in writing). Other clergymen did use their pulpits to urge men to enlist and to urge women to pressurise their men to do so, with the Bishop of London claiming that he was personally responsible for adding **10,000** men to the fighting force. However, whilst clergymen were often highly vocal in encouraging others to fight, they themselves were exempt from doing so and what was consequently seen by some as hypocrisy undoubtedly caused some resentment amongst the troops. A number of clergymen did in fact take up arms, though most who wished to take positive action became chaplains.[8]

Christian ideals could in fact be seen as positively unhelpful. The war correspondent Philip Gibbs commented on an Anglican chaplain who found it hard to reconcile the war with his Christian beliefs and continued to preach a 'Gospel of Love, and forgiveness of enemies'. When this fact was reported to the general, the chaplain was sent for and told in no uncertain terms "I can't let you go preaching 'soft stuff' to my men. I can't allow all that nonsense about love. My job is to teach them to hate".[9]

The blatant juxtaposition of the crucified Christ and slain soldier of *The Great Sacrifice* clearly implied a sanctification of the soldier's death. However, where soldiers are placed against plain crosses, the ideological connection between soldier and cross is rarely stressed. Typically the soldiers, whilst representing those who died, are themselves depicted as living. Involved in an act of remembrance, they are shown as contemporary survivors of the war rather than as dying soldiers or active combatants who may yet be killed. And even where the soldier is shown at the base of a crucifix, this is still the case. Nonetheless, where names are listed on the monument, it is to these men that our attention is directed and for whom the analogical point is made.

At Carnoustie in Scotland, Thomas Beattie's figure of a pensive, bareheaded and kilted soldier is shown placing a wreath on a cross. Again we read this imagery without theological implications. The cross is a battlefield cross and the soldier's gesture simply an act of mourning for a lost

144

comrade.[10] The aim with all of these works which combined soldier and cross would appear to have been simply to suggest the broad Christian principles for which it was implied the soldier was willing to fight and die. With the juxtaposition of Christ and the dying soldier however, the parallel between the soldier's sacrifice and that of Christ *is* made explicit. At Palmer's Green in London, outside the church of St John the Evangelist, the soldier is shown not only with the cross but in the arms of Christ himself. The cloaked and barefoot figure of Christ stands in front of a cross at the top of which is carved a crown and beneath this, behind Christ's head, the circular disc of his halo. Christ holds the soldier in his arms. Like Christ, the soldier is barefoot: his boots, puttees and helmet are missing though otherwise he is in uniform. He clings to Christ, his bandaged head resting against his saviour's chest. Around the base of the statue sit four small angels who bury their heads in their hands in sorrow.

Other memorials are similarly conceived. Ellen Rope's tiny bronze plaque in St Peter's church in Blaxhall to the fourteen men of this small Suffolk vilage who died in the war shows Christ on the field of battle, leaning forward to take the hand of the dying soldier who lies prostrate at his feet. At Eastham the dying soldier is supported by his companion, with the figure of Christ separated from them both spatially and materially. The soldiers here are carved in relief on the front of the stone pedestal on which stands the bronze figure of Christ. The carving shows one soldier, with some difficulty, assisting another. Kneeling behind his wounded companion on a rocky mound, his left arm stretches upwards towards a wreath carved on the pedestal, as if to acknowledge the impending death of the man he supports. The dying man, his arms raised in praise or prayer, looks to the heavens and we might imagine he sees a vision of the Christ who is shown directly above him. The figure of Christ holds in front of him a crown, as though to hand it down to those below. This gesture, and his greater physicality and prominent position, suggests a crowning in glory not only of the dying soldier, but of all 'from this Parish who gave their lives in the Great European War', as the inscription proclaims.

Pl. 126
Strensall,
George Milburn &
Son, 1922

145

Pl. 127
Eastham
C.J Allen, 1924

Pl. 128'
'The White Comrade'.
G.H Swinstead,
Illustrated London
News, 2 October 1915

The Eastham memorial, though not directly based upon it, reflects the influence of *The White Comrade*, a well known painting by George Hillyard Swinstead, popularly reproduced on postcards during the war and in October 1915, as a double-page spread in the *Illustrated London News*. (Copies of the painting were available for purchase at five shillings each, with ten per cent of the profits going to the British Red Cross).

Swinstead's painting shows a badly wounded soldier with bandaged head. He is supported by a colleague with Red Cross armband who looks up from offering water to the wounded man to a glowing vision of Christ - the eponymous *White Comrade*. Like Christ on the Eastham monument, he appears to bestow his blessing on the dying man, or him into his arms.[11] I know of no carving of The White Comrade, but at least one memorial window - for a church in Enniskillen in Northern Ireland- was produced.

Another memorial, similar in style to Eastham's and with similar implications, can be found at Limehouse in the East End of London, situated in the churchyard of St Anne in the East. Designed by Arthur Walker it again features a statue of Christ, his arm raised in benediction, with a bronze relief on the front of

146

the pedestal. This shows a remarkably realistic scene of the aftermath of battle, with burnt and blasted tree stumps and three dead soldiers in a shallow trench or shell hole.

Strongly reminiscent of Christopher Nevinson's *Paths of Glory* this is arguably the most explicit depiction of the horrors of modern warfare on any memorial to the Great War.[12] In the foreground a wounded but still living soldier, his uniform in tatters, struggles to sit up. The figure of Christ above bestows his blessing on both the dead (the figures on the left of the plaque and those named on the memorial) and on the survivors (the soldier on the right and the surviving servicemen who, at remembrance services, would stand in mourning in front of the monument).

With other memorials, the juxtaposition is again with the crucified Christ. In the little village of Lower Peover in Cheshire the memorial, by the Manchester sculptor John Cassidy, is placed on the outside wall of the Parish church of St Oswald's. This small but impressive work features a stone carved crucified Christ, traditional except perhaps for the fact that he is clean-shaven. More unusual, however, are the additional figures. Kneeling at his feet, though contained within separate square panels, are two servicemen, a soldier and a sailor with heads bowed in

Pls.129 and 130
Limehouse,
London.
A.G Walker,
1921

147

Pl. 131
Lower Peover.
John Cassidy,
1922

sorrow. In addition, at a lower level, are three bronze plaques. A central panel records the names of the sixteen men from the village who died in the war and this is flanked by panels depicting battle scenes - again one of soldiers and one of sailors.

The sculptor explained, in notes on the back of a photograph of the monument sent to the Imperial War Museum in the 1920s, that the memorial was 'deeply religious in character as befitting its position on [the] west side of [the] Parish Church, showing sorrow in the loss of the fallen (typified in panels of stone and bronze) overshadowed by the Divine Sacrifice'.[13] This suggestion of a parallel but humbler or 'overshadowed' sacrifice was echoed in the prayer read by the Rector at the opening ceremony of the Limehouse memorial: 'Help us to remember that the noblest sacrifice that men may make is but a shadow of the one perfect sacrifice offered for us upon the Cross by Jesus our Saviour'.[14]

A similar approach was used by Gilbert Ledward in his memorial at Stonyhurst College in Lancashire. On a marble panel with Gothic arched top Ledward has carved, in low relief, a Crucifixion, with the usual mourners at the foot of the cross replaced by four contemporary servicemen. All four gaze up at the figure of Christ. It is possible to read this simply as servicemen, perhaps visiting a church in France, admiring an effigy of Christ. But it is impossible not to read it as intentionally linking their exploits and their potential deaths with a Christian vindication.

Indeed we may well read the servicemen as already dead, like anachronistic, heavenly saints in a Renaissance altarpiece. Such details as the binoculars held by one and rifle by another, or the tin helmet of a third, are the attributes of servicemen in battle, denying the possibility of

Pl.132
Stonyhurst.
Gilbert
Ledward,1922

149

Pl. 133
Stonyhurst.
Gilbert Ledward
1922

reading this simply as men on leave. C.F Kernot commented on the panel in his book on public school memorials, published in 1927, 'The meaning of the figures is the teaching of St Paul that all Christians are at one with Christ, sharing His life through the gift of Grace'.[15]

The correspondence of the sacrifices of Christ and the serviceman had earlier been elaborated by Gilbert Ledward in his plans for a mausoleum for which he had produced a series of detailed drawings and notes in 1918. Ledward had served during the war as a Lieutenant in the Artillery, mainly on the Italian front, but had been recalled in May 1918 to be seconded to the Ministry of Information. Over the next year or so he worked on a series of reliefs for a proposed 'Hall of Remembrance'. (Although a number of large panel paintings were also commissioned, the plans for the hall eventually fell through).

Ledward's planned mausoleum, which was independent of the official hall (though presumably inspired by it) was to take the form of a massive classical temple, raised on a rusticated base with flights of steps zig-zagging up to the entrance. The interior was intended to contain a number of free-standing sculptural groups with carved reliefs around the walls which Ledward carefully planned in a series of separate drawings. These illustrated Ledward's equation of the soldier's wartime experiences with the Stations of the Cross. Noted in some detail in his sketchbook, the first Station sets the the tone: 'Jesus is condemned to death. He becomes a soldier'.[16]

Ledward's plans were never carried out and may always have been seen by him as a purely theoretical scheme and, with the exception of Stonyhurst, in none of the memorials he was to go on to produce - at Abergavenny, Witham, Blackpool, Harrogate and Stockport, or for the Guards' Division in London - were there any overtly religious elements.

One sculptor who did have the opportunity, in practical work, to make specific connections between the imagery of the Stations of the Cross and the recent experiences of front-line soldiers was Eric Gill. After spending most of the war years carving panels on this subject for Westminster Cathedral (finally installed and consecrated in March 1918) he was commissioned in 1919 to produce another series of panels on this theme for St Cuthbert's Roman Catholic church in Bradford. Completed in 1924, Gill's work on these fourteen panels coincided with the most productive period of memorialisation of the Great War, a process with which he himself was very much involved.

Clearly there was no scope here for overt references to the war dead, but it is interesting to compare the different treatments at Westminster and Bradford of the final panels which relate to the death and mourning of Christ. It is certainly possible to see at Bradford, in the choice of a pietà for the thirteenth station (with the words 'His Mother's Woe'), rather than the removal of the body from the cross shown at Westminster, an echo of imagery which was commonly used on war memorials. Similarly, the fourteenth station at Bradford, with Christ carried on a pallet at shoulder height, has unmistakable and surely intentional echoes of the stretcher-born soldier carried by his comrades, imagery which also coincides exactly with that suggested by Gilbert Ledward.[17]

Religious imagery was in fact highly visible on the Western Front. Most conspicuous of course were the simple wooden crosses which marked the battlefield graves. With the establishment of war cemeteries,[18] when the original wooden crosses were ultimately replaced by marble headstones, these simple grave markers were frequently collected and kept by grieving relatives. The Church Army, British Legion, Empire Services League and others, including individual churches, organised pilgrimages to battlefield sites during the 1920s with thousands of crosses being brought back to Britain. Those which remained uncollected were ceremonially burned and the ashes scattered in the cemeteries.

In many cases these original grave markers were used in churches as poignant memorials to individual soldiers. The United Kingdom National Inventory of War Memorials lists over four hundred examples including ones for Raymond Asquith, the son of the then Prime Minister, Herbert Asquith. Asquith's cross is in St Andrew's church in Mells, in Somerset. The same church contains a memorial to Edward Horner, designed by Sir Edwin Lutyens and Sir Alfred Munnings. Lutyens' plinth, on which stands Munnings' equestrian statue, incorporates Horner's original battlefield cross, built into one end of the base of the monument.

In some cases a collection of crosses for both named and unknown soldiers constitutes the local war memorial, as at St Mary's Church at Byfleet where twenty-two crosses are mounted on the wall of the South aisle of the church, or at St Mary's and St Michael's Church in Great Malvern which has eighteen.[19] Wayside crucifixes were also common in Belgium and France and such unfamiliar artefacts undoubtedly made a big impression on many English soldiers. In more than one English village, a crucifix, brought back from the battlefields, was used as a memorial.[20]

The cross, in a wide variety of styles, became by far the most popular form of public war memorial in the parks, churchyards, village greens and market squares of towns and villages across Britain.[21] Catherine Moriarty, the initial co-ordinator of the National Inventory of War Memorials, has suggested that this may reflect a reaction to the Government's controversial decision to replace the original crosses in the battlefield cemeteries with simple headstones which, unless specifically requested, lacked any religious symbolism.[22] Far more likely it simply reflects the traditional role of the church in funereal and remembrance rituals and its influence on post-war memorialisation. Furthermore, as Moriarty herself has pointed out, such was the demand for memorials that mass production was inevitable. Graveyard crosses produced by local stone masons could easily be scaled up to provide the village memorial and such monuments were commercially available and locally advertised.

For church memorials the crucifix was understandably a popular choice. Sometimes located inside the church but often outside, the vast majority were the work of anonymous local monumental masons or woodcarvers. Village war memorials were often placed close to the Parish church, or even in the churchyard itself, and in this context a crucifix was often seen as most appropriate. Even when the memorial was located on the village green, or some equally secular site, a crucifix was still frequently favoured. In fact, if we include church memorials, the crucifix had a popularity which exceeded that of any other figurative scheme for First World War memorials. Found as they frequently are in overgrown churchyards or in the church itself, and with their similarity to other, non-memorial crucifixes, they may, however, easily be overlooked.

The majority of these memorials followed the same traditional pattern with the figure of Christ carved in wood or stone, or occasionally cast in bronze, and frequently protected by a little roof over the cross. The memorial at Bisham in Berkshire, commissioned by a Mrs Kelly in 1919 in memory of her son Frederic and fourteen others from the village who died in the Great War, is of this type, though more distinguished than most being the work of Eric Gill.

Gill was born in Brighton in 1882 and learned decorative lettering at Chichester. Later, when apprenticed to the architect William Caroe, he studied letter cutting and stone masonry at Westminster Technical Institute and the Central School of Arts and Crafts. It was not until 1909 that he began to carve figures, and 1911 before he held his first solo exhibition of carvings in London.

Carved in Portland stone, in part *in situ*, Gill produced at Bisham a typically stylised Romanesque figure with slim, featureless torso and gaunt face. The cloth, swathed around his legs from waist to feet, is carved with elegant folds which sweep up and over his left knee. This, as the art historian Judith Collins has pointed out, is 'Christ the King', the figure shown as triumphant rather than suffering.[23] Collins suggests that Gill began to depict Christ in this way in the immediate post-war period in reaction to the widespread bereavement and suffering of those years and undoubtedly such depictions emphasised the belief in resurrection and redemption, that 'death was not the end', a message frequently repeated by the clergy throughout the war and sometimes carved onto the memorial itself.

Pl. 134
Bisham.
Eric Gill,1919

Between 1918 and 1921 Gill worked on war memorials for a number of villages around Britain: at Briantspuddle in Dorset, Chirk in North Wales, Trumpington in Cambridgeshire, South Harting in Sussex and the memorial at Bisham. In addition he carved memorial panels for Leeds University and Rossall School in Lancashire, produced numerous unadorned plaques and worked as stone mason or letter cutter on memorials by other designers.

The Rossall School War Memorial is unusually carved in wood. Gill described himself as 'a very inexpert wood carver' but this is an impressive piece.[24] The memorial is in the form of a triptych. A large, horizontal, central panel shows *The Crucifixion* with the crucified thieves, attendant mourners and a kneeling soldier. Narrower side panels depic *The Baptism of Christ* and *The Beheading of John the Baptist.* An interesting detail is the figure of the kneeling soldier in the central panel who wears what appears to be a First World War tin helmet, an anachronistic detail similarly used in his earlier carving of St George on the Trumpington memorial.

With the sole exception of Chirk, all of Gill's figurative memorials featured religious imagery. At both Trumpington and South Harting it was in the form of carved bas-reliefs at the foot of a cross. At Briantspuddle, more prominent figures of Christ and the Madonna and Child feature on either side of another tall cross. Contained within a small tabernacle at the base of the cross, the Madonna is shown suckling her child, one hand cupping her exposed breast, an image which Gill had repeatedly explored from the outset of his career in both religious and secular forms.

The figure of Christ is particularly impressive. The Briantspuddle memorial had been commissioned, by Ernest Debenham, a local landowner, as early as April 1915 and was unveiled on 12 November 1918, just one day after the declaration of the Armistice. The figure of Christ, the last part of the memorial to be produced and carved, again in situ, between January and August 1918, is once more gaunt and thin, no wider than the cross in front of which he stands. His left hand presses, rather than holds, a large broad sword against his body; his right hand is raised, ostensibly in blessing. Both hands are contrived to reveal the gashes made by the nails of the crucifixion, no doubt an intentional reference to the wounds of soldiers of the Great War.

Gill's Christ clearly derives from Medieval images of the *Man of Sorrows.* With its slender verticality there are also strong echoes of the *Risen Christ* of his former friend and collaborator

Jacob Epstein. Epstein's sculpture was a
personal project rather than a commissioned
work, but one clearly informed by the war. It
was completed the year after Gill's but started
around the same time. Epstein's work was
differently conceived however, evolving from a
portrait mask of the composer Bernard van
Dieren, and had different intentions, the
sculptor claiming that 'It stands and accuses
the world for its grossness, inhumanity,
cruelty, and beastliness'.[25]

A significant difference between the
two works is Gill's Sword of Justice in place of
the accusatory finger of Epstein's Christ.
Epstein's outright opposition to the war and
desperate attempts to avoid involvement were
not matched by Gill whose attitude to memorialisation was therefore somewhat different.
Although Gill did not fight in the war, unlike
Epstein he made no effort to avoid conscription
and whilst understandably showing no
enthusiasm for fighting was prepared to serve,
if and when asked. In fact he was called up,
too late to fight, in September 1918,
immediately after the completion of the
Briantspuddle memorial, his call up having
been deferred because of his work on the *Stations of the Cross* panels for
Westminster Cathedral.

Despite the fact that they were by this time no longer on speaking
terms, the art critic Richard Cork, who described the *Risen Christ* as 'the
most moving of all the British memorials', has suggested that Gill may
have been influenced by Epstein's work.[26] In fact the Briantspuddle Christ
appears to be based on an earlier design which Gill produced in 1916, in
collaboration with the architect Charles Holden, as a proposed 'Memorial
to Overseas Heroes'.

This was a memorial intended to commemorate those throughout
the Empire who had given their lives in the still current war. The scheme
coincided with a Civic Arts Association exhibition of designs for war
memorials currently being held at the Royal Institute of British
Architects in London. It was funded by the Overseas Club who commissioned designs for a memorial which they hoped would 'have in it some of
the virile energy and courage of the younger and somewhat rebellious

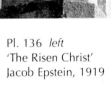

Pl. 136 *left*
'The Risen Christ'
Jacob Epstein, 1919

Pl.137 *right*
Briantspuddle.
Eric Gill,1918

Pl.135
(opposite)
Briantspuddle.
Eric Gill, 1918

155

THE MEN OF ENGLAND
TO THEIR DEAD KINSMEN
OF THE DOMINIONS &
CROWN COLONIES
HAIL
YOUR BODIES ARE BURIED
IN PEACE BUT YOUR NAME
LIVETH FOR EVERMORE
ABOVE ARE INSCRIBED
THE NAMES OF THE MEN FROM
THE BRITISH DOMINIONS OVERSEA
WHO GAVE THEIR LIVES IN THE WAR
AGAINST THE GERMANS
1914–1917
THIS COLUMN WAS BUILT BY PUBLIC
SUBSCRIPTION IN THE YEAR 1918
OF OUR LORD JESUS CHRIST
PRAY FOR THEM YOU WHO PASS BY

Monument to the Overseas Troops, detail showing Top of Column and suggested Inscription, also Plan showing Proposed Site in Kingsway

Pl. 138
Proposed
memorial for
the dead of
overseas
contingents.
Eric Gill,
The Graphic,
29 July,1916

school of artists'.[27] They appealed for £10,000 to be raised by public subscription to enable the project to proceed. Gill and Holden's proposal, published in *The Graphic* in July 1916, was for a 150 feet high monument to be located in central London, consisting of a stone pillar onto which the names of the fallen were to be cut. The giant figure of Christ was to be at the apex.

In Gill's designs, the end of the war is optimistically guessed at as 1917. In the event, the monument was never built, but Gill revived his figure in a much scaled-down version for his memorial at Briantspuddle. Indeed it is possible that the figure of Christ was actually devised for the Briantspuddle memorial and then offered for the Overseas Heroes memorial. However, his original sketch for Briantspuddle, made in 1915, shows a very different conception with a Holy Family group on one side and Christ with the Lamb of God on the other. Precisely when Gill decided to use the *Man of Sorrows* figure is not known.

The relationship to Epstein's *Risen Christ*, if any, is also difficult to establish. Certainly the intended scale of Gill's 'Memorial to Overseas Heroes' was matched by Epstein's ambitions for his own work. He had fantasised this as being made 'hundreds of feet high' and set 'on some high place where all could see it, and where it would give out its warning'.[28] Both artists had also previously planned to collaborate on 'doing some colossal figures together ... a sort of twentieth-century Stonehenge'.[29] However, their relationship had broken down by 1911. Whether their respective works had their origins in their earlier ideas, or Epstein simply based his work either on Gill's published plans, or coincidentally on similar Medieval prototypes, remains unclear. In discussing the *Risen Christ* and its origins in his autobiography, written many years later, Epstein makes no mention of Gill, but then the only references to Eric Gill in the whole book are brief and entirely disparaging.

Eric Gill's most impressive war memorial was for Leeds University. Commissioned in 1916, it featured the unusual, and for a war memorial, almost certainly unique subject of *Our Lord Driving the Moneychangers out of the Temple*. This was a subject first proposed by Gill in his submission that same year for a Civic Arts Association competition for a war memorial to the employees of London County Council. Gill was given second place in that competition on the grounds that his proposed choice of subject failed to meet the stated conditions - and possibly because the subject, as Gill himself admitted, failed to appeal.[30]

Gill explained his choice of subject matter by pointing out that 'The act of Jesus in turning out the buyers and sellers from the Temple when he did was really a most courageous act and very warlike'.[31] He concluded therefore that Christ's actions showed how 'The use of violence in a just cause is made lawful', adding that 'Violence may not always be expedient, it may always be the last resource, but it cannot be called forbidden'.[32]

The subject itself might merely have caused bewilderment, rather than outright opposition and outrage, had Gill not also chosen to depict the moneylenders as contemporary citizens. On a fifteen feet long panel of Portland stone Gill shows Christ wielding a seven corded whip, one chord for each of the deadly sins. He is accompanied by a leaping dog in front of an overturned table. Gill explained that this 'hound of the Lord' - Domini canes - was a reference to Dominicans because, as he put it, 'The Dominicans stand especially for Truth and it is untruth rather than ill-will which is damning the modern world'.[33] (Gill was himself, by this time, a member of the Dominican order). The moneylenders, in frock

Pl. 139
Leeds University war memorial.
Eric Gill, 1923

157

coats, spats and top hat, the woman with 'two beautiful feathers in her hat and nice bobbed hair', stumble with heads bowed away from Christ.[34] One man holds a pawnbroker's symbol, another clutches a ledger marked 'LSD' (Pounds, Shillings & Pence). At the feet of Christ sits a mother and child, said by Gill to be 'taking no notice of the ejection of the money men', knowing 'it is nothing to do with her'.[35]

Though Gill's work was much admired by many, others were less impressed. Critical letters and articles appeared in the press, with local merchants, some no doubt with sons killed in the war, understandably upset, feeling that they were the target of Gill's visual attack. The *Pawnbrokers' Gazette* was particularly outraged on behalf of its members, describing the memorial as a 'tasteless and tactless parody of a war memorial' and 'a sculptural monstrosity'.[36]

Eric Gill was in the fortunate position of being, for almost all of his war memorials, privately commissioned, thereby having no need to consider the requirements and imposed limitations of a local community's war memorial committee. At Leeds, he benefited from the patronage of an enlightened collector and defender of modern art, the Vice-Chancellor of the university, Sir Michael Sadler. Even Sadler was dismayed, however, when the artist published *A War Memorial* pamphlet to explain the rationale behind his work, which further fanned the flames of controversy.[37] 'Modern war', Gill wrote, 'in spite of the patriotism of millions of conscripts and their officers, is mainly about money'.[38] There were undoubtedly many who shared this view and who felt aggrieved that some, during the war, and because of the war, had prospered while so many suffered. The journalist Philip Gibbs, writing in 1919, was particularly bitter, and no doubt his views reflected those of many who had served at the front: 'Government contractors were growing fat on the life of war, amassing vast fortunes, juggling with excess profits, battening upon the flesh and blood of boyhood in the fighting lines'.[39] To have this as the focus of a prominent and public monument, supposedly intended to acknowledge the sufferers, was however considered inappropriate by many, and not only those who felt themselves thus criticised.

For Eric Gill, Christ and the moneylenders might have seemed a suitable subject for a war memorial. Other artists however were more inclined, when depicting Christ, to choose more predictable but more obviously relevant episodes relating to his death - the Crucifixion, Entombment, Pietà and, in one case at least, the Ascension (the subject of Doyle Jones' carved relief used both at Weymouth and Gillingham).

One impressive example of the Entombment of Christ can be found in a memorial by William Reynolds-Stephens at Saltburn by the Sea in North Yorkshire. Here the recumbent body of the dead Christ, attended by praying angels at head and foot, is shown on a bronze panel on the front of the memorial. The single and significant word, 'Sacrifice', is carved above the largely horizontal panel which, with extensions at top and bottom, echoes the cruciform shape of the monument itself.

The same design was also used for a marble altar the artist produced for a war memorial in the church of St Mary the Virgin at Great Warley in Essex where the words 'The gateway to life' are used instead of 'sacrifice'. The church, a masterpiece of Arts and Crafts architecture by Charles Harrison Townsend, is decorated throughout by Reynolds-Stephens, a man who, like George Frampton, considered himself an 'art worker' rather than simply a sculptor. The war memorial at Great Warley is dedicated to the memory of 'The gallant British fighting men who made the supreme sacrifice during the Great War', the names of whom are listed on either side of the central figural panel. The fine, delicate carving at Great Warley reveals details, of cloth and feathers and facial features, which the weathering and staining of Saltburn's bronze relief unfortunately obscures.

Although explicit depictions of religious subjects for municipal memorials were relatively rare (with the already noted exception of the

Pl. 140
Saltburn by the Sea.
Wlliam Reynolds-Stephens, 1920

Pl. 141
Great Warley.
William Reynolds-Stephens, 1920

Crucifixion) a variety of Christian iconography was reinterpreted in secular form by many memorial sculptors. The monument at Kidderminster takes as its model the traditional iconography of the entombment (very similar to Reynolds-Stephens' work at Great Warley), but with Christ replaced by a dead soldier. The artist, Alfred Drury, also used this design, derived from his Boer War memorial at Warrington, for other memorials at Pershore Abbey and at St Matthew's church in Dinnington, near Newcastle.[40]

A relief plaque shows the prostrate soldier, accompanied by an angel holding a small cross. She is about to place a laurel wreath on his lifeless body. At his feet, a young mother draws the attention of a small child to the soldier's sacrifice, a didacticism reinforced by the memorial's major focus of a free-standing figure of an angel, who cradles a baby in her arms. Both baby and child represent future generations.

Next to the crucifixion, the pietà was the most commonly used religious imagery for church memorials and was also occasionally used elsewhere. As with the entombment, it was also adapted in a secular form, as at Bolton where it is one of a pair of sculptural groups which flank an arched cenotaph, the central feature of which is large bronze cross.

Another interesting, more subtle suggestion of a pietà is the panel at Workington which shows one grim-faced soldier carrying another. The implication here is that the soldier being carried, with his right arm around the other's shoulder, is merely injured rather than dead. Nonetheless, there is, in his posture, with his head slumped and left arm limp, an unmistakable and no doubt deliberate echo of Michelangelo's famous *Pietà* at St. Peter's in Rome.

Pls. 142 and 143
Kidderminster.
Alfred Drury, 1922

The sanctification of the soldier's death clearly helped in the mediation of grief for some of the bereaved but it is doubtful whether any servicemen saw death on the field of battle as sacred. Even army chaplains found it hard to reconcile the romanticised image with the reality. One chaplain, writing in 1917, compared the soldier's death in Clark's *The Great Sacrifice* with his own experiences:

> Like the young lad in the picture, the man whom I saw die had a bullet wound in the temple, but there the likeness ceased. Here was no calm death, but a ghastly mess of blood and brains and mud, on his face and in the surrounding trench; and in the stark horror of the moment I could not see the Crucified at all.[41]

As previously noted, during the war the graves of servicemen overseas had been marked by simple wooden crosses, but in 1918 the Imperial War Graves Commission decided to replace these with uniform headstones in the permanent cemeteries at that time being established. In a statement issued by the Commission in January 1918, concern was expressed that if individual memorials were allowed in the cemeteries,

> costly monuments put up by the well-to-do over their dead would contrast unkindly with those humbler ones which would be all that poorer folks could afford. Thus the inspiring memory of the common sacrifice made by all ranks would lose the regularity and orderliness most becoming to the resting places of soldiers, who fought and fell side by side.[42]

In addition, it was argued that when choosing a standardised form, given the variety of religious beliefs of those who had served in the armed forces (or indeed the absence of belief of many), a simple headstone would be more appropriate than a cross.

Each headstone, two feet eight inches high, had engraved, at the top, a national emblem or regimental badge and below, the serviceman's rank, name, unit, date of death and age. Below this was carved, if requested, an appropriate religious symbol, a cross or Star of David for

Pl. 144
Workington.
Alexander
Carrick, 1928

161

example, and in many cases, at the bottom, an inscription chosen and paid for by the relatives.

There was considerable opposition to these plans. A report in *The Times* in December 1919 about a parliamentary debate on the matter noted the comments of Lord Cecil:

> There were some who attached the greatest importance to a symbol: many passionately desired to erect a cross ... it was no use telling people that something else would do just as well. These things touched the very depths of emotion and could not be treated officially. It was bureaucratic tyranny and nothing else.[43]

The Times went on to note, 'It is equally repugnant to British feeling that even in death the family should surrender all rights over the individual to the State, and that private memorials should therefore be prohibitive'.[44]

War cemeteries did not, however, entirely lack religious symbolism. In addition to the emblem carved on most headstones, all sites featured a 'Cross of Sacrifice' designed by the architect Sir Reginald Blomfield. The 'Cross of Sacrifice' came in a range of four sizes -

Pl. 145
'The Cross of Sacrifice'.
Sir Reginald Blomfield

fourteen, eighteen, twenty and twenty-four feet high - appropriate for a variety of sizes of cemetery sites. On a stepped, octagonal base, the tapering cross had, on the front of the octagonal shaft, a large bronze reversed sword 'to identify it with war'.[45]

Blomfield's design, though by no means universally admired - *The Connoisseur* describing it as 'more like a two-armed clothes-prop than a Christian symbol'[46] - was undeniably successful. The cross was erected not only at the battlefield cemeteries and in cemeteries at home but was also often used for the memorials of local communities, frequently being copied, with varying degrees of accuracy, by local masons in 'unofficial' versions, much to Blomfield's dismay.[47] Usually it was presented in isolation but sometimes with additional embellishments, as at Bury where a curving wall with bronze relief panels by Hermon Cawthra extends on either side of the central cross.

In addition to the cross, most cemeteries also featured Sir Edwin Lutyens' 'Great War Stone'. Initially proposed by Lutyens for use in battlefield cemeteries as early as May 1917 it was to be revived in August 1918 in the architect's designs for a War Shrine in Hyde Park. Each anniversary of the outbreak of war had been commemorated with patriotic rallies, in London and elsewhere, with the day becoming known as 'Remembrance Day', a title later to be transferred to the commemoration of the war's ending. On the fourth anniversary, to accompany a large rally held in Hyde Park, a temporary shrine had been built as a focal point and site for floral tributes. With calls to make the tempoarary shrine permanent, Lutyens was approached, but following objections from various quarters it remained unbuilt.

The Great War Stone (or 'Stone of Remembrance') provided the central feature of Lutyens' Hyde Park design. In his drawing, the architect had inscribed the word 'Amen' on the front of the altar. The precise wording to be used on the actual stone was the subject of some dispute. Rudyard Kipling had suggested a quote from Ecclesiasticus: 'Their bodies lie buried in peace but their name liveth for evermore'. Lutyens objected that, as he put it, 'someone will add an S and it will read pieces'.[48] In the event, only the second half of the quotation was used. As with the

Pl. 146
'The Great War Stone'.
Sir Edwin Lutyens

163

Cross of Sacrifice, in addition to its use in battlefield cemeteries the Great War Stone appeared in a number of provincial war memorials designed by Lutyens, but it also served as a prototype for numerous memorials by other people.[49]

The Great War Stone had the appearance of an altar and was discussed in these terms by Lutyens and others. With the architect's full approval it was occasionally used as such. In Christian ritual the altar provides conspicuous support for the display of the bread transformed into the body of Christ. In those cases where the figure of a dead soldier is added to a memorial plinth the allusion to the sacrificial altar and to the analogy between the soldier and the body of Christ become more obvious.

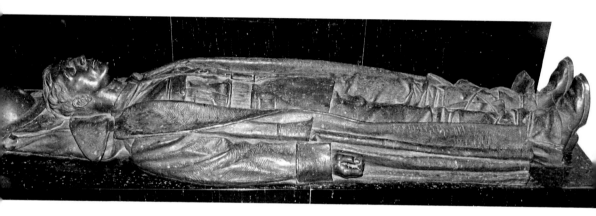

Macclesfield's memorial provides one example. More explicit still is a memorial by Francis Derwent Wood in the church of St Mary in Ditchingham, a small village in Norfolk.

Commissioned by William Carr of Ditchingham Hall at a cost of £1,100, the memorial was paid for by Carr with contributions from the writer, H. Rider Haggard and the families of the dead. (Rider Haggard, a local resident and former church warden, was subsequently buried in the chancel of the church). Wood's memorial, exhibited at the Royal Academy in 1920, features a lifesize bronze figure of a soldier in battledress and greatcoat, laid to rest on a black marble slab. His eyes are closed and he appears at peace, with no indication of injury or cause of death. His youthful appearance is emphasised by the smooth modelling of the face which contrasts with the distinct striations and roughened surface of the uniform. Tied around his calf and ankles are thick cloth pads, intended to protect against the cold and mud of the trenches. His head rests on his army backpack, as though placed there to support the dying man on the field of battle. His helmet is behind his head.[50] A square panel behind, which lists the names of the dead (including a nurse) and the reminder that 'They died for England in defence of Liberty and Justice', echoes the appearance of the traditional church altarpiece, an impression reinforced by the monument's ecclesiastical setting.

In a general sense, the war memorial can be seen as a form of altarpiece. Like the painted or sculpted panel traditionally placed behind the altar it acts as a focus for the thoughts and prayers of the bereaved. This is particularly the cases where the imagery of the memorial draws attention to, or parallels, acts of remembrance. One such location is Liverpool. Here the altar and altarpiece are effectively combined in one. The memorial takes the form of a long altar-shaped slab, on the face of which the bronze relief depicting the act of remembrance provides the illustrative focus traditionally provided by the altarpiece.

Although Lutyens was adamant that he wanted to avoid Christian symbolism in his memorial designs it was still possible to read specifically Christian signification into his work. For the national memorial, the Cenotaph, he produced a starkly abstract, essentially classical structure. Having been asked to produce a design for a 'catafalque', a structure for the support of a coffin or the display of the remains of the dead, Lutyens pointed out that what was actually required was not a catafalque but a 'cenotaph', literally an empty tomb to honour a person buried elsewhere. As the historian, Adrian Gregory, has pointed out, the idea of the empty tomb inevitably brings to mind the resurrection of Christ.[51]

Pl. 148
Liverpool.
Lionel Budden
(architect) and
G.H Tyson
Smith, sculptor,
1930

Pl. 149
The cenotaph.
London
Sir Edwin
Lutyens, 1920

The Whitehall cenotaph is topped by a simple, carved stone wreath (like the wreath on the side, the work of Francis Derwent Wood). Lutyens adapted his design for his monument at Manchester, and in more elaborate and therefore less striking versions at Southampton, Derby and Rochdale, by placing, on top of the cenotaph, an effigy of a dead soldier. In its elevated position, Lutyen's soldier literally distances us from the reality of death and indeed it is only with careful examination that the figure is likely to be noticed at all.

A similar figure adopted by Charles Sargeant Jagger for his Royal Artillery monument at Hyde Park Corner, though this time at ground level, was however criticised. Jagger's figure lies at rest, his head covered

166

by his greatcoat. There is no sign of injury. Despite
this, it was seen by some as inappropriate in 'forcing
home on the minds of the public the horror and terror
of war'.[52]

It has been suggested that Jagger may have
been influenced by effigies on nineteenth century
French tombs but such figures were also popular
with his British contemporaries in the years leading
up to the First World War and Jagger would
certainly have been aware of many of these works.[53]
Jagger's use of the recumbent figure could also be
seen to derive from English Medieval tomb
sculptures. Where the recumbent soldier is located
within a church the analogy with Medieval tombs
seems particularly pertinent. At Thrumpton in
Nottinghamshire the neatly carved stone effigy of a
dead soldier is placed within a niche on the outside
wall of the church, but again, we naturally equate
the scheme with the tombs usually to be found inside.
Here, as with Derwent Wood's memorial at
Ditchingham, the soldier, representing the three men
from the village who died, is shown in full uniform.
His right hand, which holds a small cross, is laid
across his chest. The fight of good against evil, for
which the men died, is symbolically referred to in
the spandrels of the framing tomb with tiny, facing
images of St George and the Dragon.

Pl. 152
Thrumpton

The specificity of nineteenth century and Medieval prototypes is replaced at Thrumpton with generality and, by Jagger, with anonymity by the covering of the head with the coat. This is not to dissipate emotional reactions but to more easily enable the soldier, like the 'Unknown Warrior' in Westminster Abbey, to symbolise all who had died. Lutyens made this point too about his Manchester figure, describing it as 'the figure of a fighting man with equipment at his side and feet and a greatcoat thrown over the whole, conveying to those who stand below no individual identity and so in truth 'every mother's son'.[54]

Such stark representations of the dead on war memorial sculpture are rare and are limited to these and very few other examples. In his book, *Sites of Memory, Sites of Mourning*, Jay Winter, suggests that the stark horizontality of such figures is too bleak for most sculptors who aim to present a message of hope.[55] Winter rightly sees in this imagery an evocation of Holbein's sixteenth century *Dead Christ in the Tomb* which, for Winter, shows 'no sign whatsoever of the Resurrection'. This was not an interpretation which Holbein himself would have hoped to have encouraged but was certainly a view shared by others.[56] Dostoevsky, on viewing the painting in 1867, was to comment that 'one could lose one's faith from that picture'.[57]

Holbein's panel had been a particular inspiration in the late nineteenth and early twentieth centuries: German artists were most obviously responsive and the suggestion has been made that the translation into German in 1889 of Dostoevsky's *The Idiot*, in which the painting is dramatically described and in which the author's own words about loss of faith are repeated by the central character, was of particular significance in influencing visual artists.[58]

Derwent Wood's depiction of the dead soldier at Ditchingham has been seen as similarly agnostic.[59] However, like Holbein's *Dead Christ*, whose tortured and mutilated body provides an image of suffering, not to deny Christian doctrine but to emphasise the magnitude of the sacrifice, so too the presentation of the dead soldier in apparent emulation of the body of Christ is surely intended, regardless of the sculptor's personal views, to underline the parallel between Christ and the servicemen and the significance of the latter's sacrifices.

Unlike Derwent Wood's Ditchingham figure, the dead soldier of the Royal Artillery memorial lacks an ecclesiastical context. Seen in isolation, Jagger's figure is a stark reminder of the inevitable repercussions of war, but in offering no apparent explanation or justification for his death, and no obvious analogy with Christian sacrifice, may appear gratuitous. However, to view the corpse in isolation is to deny the context of the memorial scheme: the bringing together of a range of sculptural, architectonic and textual elements to create a narrative of the war which, as the next chapter will show, played a significant role in the communication of the memorial's message.

Pl. 153
Royal Artillery
Memorial,
London.
Charles Sargeant
Jagger, 1925

VII

A Narrative of War

The Royal Artillery Memorial had its origins in the formation, in May 1918, of a War Commemoration Fund Committee which contained representatives from all ranks. As with the memorials of local communities, considerable discussion took place regarding the appropriate form the memorial should take, with various schemes, including the establishment of a hostel for wounded ex-soldiers or a memorial in Westminster Abbey, being considered but rejected. Initially the Committee favoured the proposal that the Royal Artillery's memorial should become a part of a National Memorial which would incorporate all branches of the armed forces. It was not until the end of 1919, by which time this idea had collapsed, that the Committee began

Pls. 154 and 155
Royal Artillery
Memorial, London.
Charles Sargeant
Jagger, 1925

to seriously consider an appropriate site for a monument of its own. Of
various locations offered, in July 1920 Hyde Park Corner was announced
as the one chosen and a number of sculptors and architects were then
asked to submit plans for a monument on this site.[1]

Sir Edwin Lutyens presented three proposals, all of which were
rejected. So too were schemes by his fellow architect, Sir Herbert Baker,
and the sculptor Adrian Jones. A concern with Lutyens' schemes, which
included the possible involvement of Francis Derwent Wood, was that they
were too similar to the Cenotaph. One of Lutyens' designs incorporated an
effigy of a dead soldier which was also a feature of a concurrent design for
Southampton's memorial and one to be revived in subsequent memorials
for other cities.[2] But as Lutyens and Wood were reluctant to incorporate a
sculpture of a realistic gun on top of their memorial in a form which
would satisfy the committee's request for such a feature, and as the
Commissioner of Works had also rejected Lutyens' schemes as being too
high for the intended site, the Committee was forced to consider alternative proposals. Charles Sargeant Jagger was consequently asked to submit
his designs for the Artillery Memorial.

Jagger was a Yorkshireman, born in Kilnhurst near Sheffield in
1885. His father was a colliery manager and amateur artist and all his
children, Charles, David, and Edith, proved to be gifted artists. Coming
from a relatively poor background, Charles - the name Sargeant was
adopted from his mother's maiden name - was discouraged by his father
from studying art and was instead apprenticed, at the age of fourteen, as a
metal engraver with Mappin and Webb.

After completing his apprenticeship he was offered a teaching post
at Sheffield Technical School of Art where, for the next two years, he
taught metal engraving. While he was there he took the belated opportunity
to study sculpture and in 1907 was awarded a scholarship to continue his
studies at the Royal College of Art where his fellow students included
Harold Brownsword and Gilbert Ledward. One of the men who taught
Jagger at the Royal College, William Goscombe John, was later to note
that he had been one of the most gifted students he had ever encountered.[3]

Jagger's success at the Royal College is indicated both by the
winning of a number of prizes, including a travel bursary which enabled
him to visit Italy and North Africa in 1911, and his appointment, on the
completion of his course, as studio assistant to Edouard Lantéri who was
the head of sculpture at the college. Lantéri was the former pupil of Aimé-
Jules Dalou who had also preceded him as modelling master at the Royal
College (or the National Art Training School as it was then called). Both
Dalou and Lantéri were inspirational teachers whose influence on many
of the men who later designed war memorials was considerable.

In 1913, Jagger applied for the first 'Prix de Rome' in sculpture from the British School in Rome, no doubt encouraged by Lantéri who was on the sculpture faculty there.[4] Although he failed to win, the prize going to Gilbert Ledward, he tried again the following year and this time was successful.[5] Unfortunately, just days after the announcement of the prize, war was declared. Jagger decided to forego the scholarship and instead joined the Artist's Rifles.

There can be no doubt that he was an enthusiastic recruit. When he finally set sail from Plymouth for Gallipoli in September 1915, as a Second Lieutenant in the 13th Battalion of the Royal Worcesters, he was to describe it in a letter written the following day to his future wife as 'one of the greatest days I shall live to see'.[6] After enduring six weeks of fierce fighting, Jagger was shot through the left shoulder and evacuated to a hospital in Malta before being sent to England to recuperate. On recovering from his wounds he was promoted to Lieutenant but for some time remained in England training new recruits on the Isle of Wight. Eventually he was sent back to fight, this time on the Western Front and, in April 1918, was again wounded and awarded the Military Cross at the Battle of Neuve Église. Later that year Jagger applied for employment as an official war artist and was accepted, being released from military service for four months, by which time the war had ended.

In the immediate aftermath of war Jagger was fully aware of the potential for the employment of sculptors, with the wide scale processes of memorialisation already underway. It was not long before he had been awarded his first commission for a war memorial on the recommendation of Sir George Frampton, a member of the panel who had awarded Jagger the 'Prix de Rome'. This was for a memorial at Hoylake and West Kirby on the Wirral, but his subsequent appointment as designer of the prestigious Royal Artillery memorial was the real breakthrough in his career. He had been recommended for this by John Singer Sargent whom he had first met in 1918 when the sculptor had approached him to ask for his support in his request for employment as a war artist.

Jagger's contract for the Artillery memorial stipulated that his design should consist of a group in bronze on an appropriate pedestal, to be unambiguously recognisable as an Artillery memorial and with the various branches of the Artillery 'remembered by the sculptor in thinking out the design'.[7] The cost of the work was not to exceed £25,000. By June 1921 Jagger and Lionel Pearson, the architect with whom he had chosen to collaborate, had produced a model which was quickly approved. An illustration of this now destroyed model shows a number of differences in the memorial finally built, most significantly a shift in the axis and positioning of the stone gun and the use of carved stone rather than bronze

for panels on the side. The sculptor later proposed a considerably larger monument with more free-standing figures which was readily agreed to. Another change, made at the instigation of the Fine Arts Commission, was to turn the gun 180 degrees to face South.[8]

      After some delay the monument was eventually unveiled in October 1925. The central feature is the lifesize stone 9.2 inch howitzer atop a massive, cross-shaped, stepped podium. Around the sides are a series of bas-reliefs, each depicting a different branch of the regiment and a different type of gun, all of which face South like the howitzer itself. On the East and West sides of the memorial are placed bronze figures of a shell carrier and a driver, the former with heavy shells in pouches around his legs, the latter with cape and arms outstretched and solid, leather protective pads strapped to his calves. At the southern end forming the head of the cross and the front of the memorial is an Artillery captain in a position of command, literally backed by the giant gun, the barrel of which towers above him.

Pls 156 and 157
Royal Artillery
Memorial,
London.
Charles Sargeant
Jagger, 1925

The dead soldier, described in the previous chapter, an even later addition to the scheme, is placed at the opposite end. Although creating an emotional focus, this figure is by no means dominant, the axial emphasis of the monument being away from him, as if to signify the determined continuation of battle despite the inevitability of death. The narrative scenes of battle on the stone reliefs provide a context for the iconic figures and most importantly for the dead soldier.

Pl. 158
(detail)
Blackpool.
Gilbert
Ledward, 1923

These bronze figures are differentiated from the reliefs by medium and scale and are presented as representative images of the heroic strength, stoic endurance and self-sacrifice of the artilleryman.

By placing depictions of dead and dying soldiers in a narrative context, acceptable justifications for their deaths are provided. However, as befits the national memorial of a major branch of the armed services, the Royal Artillery monument is of a scale and complexity rarely matched in provincial memorials. Lindsey Clark's Glasgow memorial to the 'Cameronians' is much smaller and simpler. It places the dead soldier clearly in the context of battle, but unlike the Artillery memorial it lacks the range of references to the broader conflict. Similarly, at Macclesfield, the dead soldier is depicted as though on the field of battle, the apparent

victim of a gas attack. His mask, which it is implied he had no time to put on, is still in his hand. His death is plainly symbolic, a sign of patriotic self-sacrifice in general, as Britannia's presence suggests. With the Royal Artillery memorial the dead soldier forms a part of a narrative more complex than that of Glasgow's memorial and more subtle than Macclesfield's.

Narrative depictions on memorials to the battlefield dead have a long history. Widely used in classical monumental art, their origins can be traced even further back and certainly to Mesopotamian art of the third millennium BC. Narrative has been defined by the American historian and academic, Hayden White, as 'a solution to ... the problem of how to translate knowing into telling'.[9] For those who used memorials, who visited, placed wreaths, searched for and touched the names, *their* knowledge was that their loved ones would not return and that for those who did return, life could not continue as before. Narrativity was a means for the designers and commissioners of war memorials to tell a story of the war which would provide for the bereaved both explanation and justification.

For White, the point about narrativization is that it 'produces meaning ... [by transforming] into a story a list of historical events that would otherwise be only a chronicle'.[10] According to White, this meaning is essentially moral. 'The demand for closure in the historical story is a demand, I suggest, for moral meaning, a demand that sequences of real events be assessed as to their significance as elements of a moral drama'.[11] Whether this is universally true or not, it is precisely in this ability to produce a much needed moral meaning that narrative has a place in the commemorative process.

Pl. 159
Stourbridge.
John Cassidy,
1923

Pl. 160
Hastings.
Margaret
Winser, 1922

The transformation of historical events from chronicle to narrative is most obviously found on war memorials in the relief panels which illustrate episodic events of men in battle. On the Victorian public monuments on which many war memorials are clearly based, the reliefs normally pay tribute to notable achievements in the lives of the 'great and good' depicted above. Around the base of the column supporting Edward Hodge Baily's statue of Lord Nelson in Trafalgar Square can be found relief panels of the battles of Trafalgar, Copenhagen, St Vincent and the Nile and similar scenes of battle are common on the numerous monuments to admirals and generals around Britain.

Such scenes, as supplements to the central effigy, were suitably popular for Boer War memorials and were again used on many memorials of the First World War. Where the scenes of triumph or achievement on Victorian monuments intentionally add glory to the memory of the soldier or statesman - and on Boer War memorials to the body of men commemorated - on First World War memorials there is more usually an indication of the endurance of physical hardships. The most common illustration here would appear to be that of soldiers marching (or trudging) across a barren landscape.

The narrative relief seldom depicts a specific moment of triumph or victory but serves instead to highlight an aspect of the day-to-day existence of the soldier. The fighting of battles was of course a part of this, but the nature of trench warfare was such that overt acts of heroism were relatively rare. We are far less likely to find on memorial reliefs the illustration of cavalier exploits and hand-to-hand fighting so familiar from the pages of the popular press during the war years, though at Banbridge in Northern Ireland such a scene is indeed shown. More often, however, the emphasis is on servicemen efficiently coping with difficult jobs.

Significantly, the depiction of the enemy is extremely rare. When shown it is almost always in symbolic form, as a serpent beneath the soldier's feet or 'German' eagle trampled by the 'British' lion, and of course the dragon slain by St George or St Michael. The caricatured exaggeration of snarling Germans seen on the Waggoners memorial at Sledmere is extremely unusual but seems, like the memorial itself, an almost amusing oddity. A realistically depicted dead German beneath the feet of British soldiers on the Blackpool memorial however, is really quite shocking, the more so for being so unexpected. The bayoneting of a fallen German at the feet of a British soldier at Banbridge is even more shocking.

Pl. 161
Southwark.
Philip Lindsey Clark, 1922

The depiction of soldiers marching is frequently paired with scenes of sailors loading and firing guns. At Smethwick marching men are paired with battleships and biplanes departing to engage with the enemy, a scenario also seen at Southwark where naval and aerial forays are shown on separate panels. At Hastings the memorial has three panels, the close-up of soldiers waving as they march away is matched with similar close-ups of an airman in the cockpit of his plane and sailors on board ship. All are preparing for battle rather than engaged in it. Arthur Walker's memorial at Dartford is similarly undemonstrative. Supplementing the main free-standing figure of a soldier are relief panels on either side of the plinth, one showing sailors carefully loading a gun, the other, four airmen watching a biplane being readied for takeoff.

Pl. 162
Dartford
A.G Walker, 1922

Where more obvious scenes of battle are shown, the emphasis is invariably on the arduous efforts and grim determination of men working under adverse conditions. This is well illustrated by Alexander Carrick's impressive relief plaques for the Scottish National War Memorial. His panel for the Royal Engineers shows men stripped to the waist, involved in strenuous construction work, with planning, surveying and communications emphasised as being of equal importance. For the Royal Artillery we again we see men stripped to the waist, their muscles straining as they manhandle, with considerable effort, a pallet of shells towards those who load the gun.

Carrick, who was born in Musselburgh in 1882, had served an apprenticeship as a stone carver with Birnie Rhind before studying at art schools in Edinburgh and London. He was later to become Head of the Sculpture Department at Edinburgh College of Art. Primarily a carver rather than a modeller, around half of his war memorials, including some of his most impressive works, were nonetheless in bronze and his work for the National Memorial is amongst his best.

Carrick had served for three years in the Royal Artillery and clearly knew his subject but both panels at Edinburgh achieve their impact not only from their attention to closely observed detail, but through their carefully contrived compositions, in particular on the Royal Artillery panel. Here

the inward leaning soldiers at bottom left are counterbalanced by the men at top right who drive home the shell into the barrel of the gun. The circularity of movement, from left to right and back again, suggests the relentless and repetitive nature of the struggle.

Pl. 164
Clay model.
Royal Artillery.
Scottish National
War Memorial,
Edinburgh.
Alexander
Carrick, 1927

The activities of the artillery did not involve face-to-face confrontations and the loading and firing of guns is invariably shown without overt emotion. The remoteness of the enemy is frequently emphasised by the inclusion of a soldier or sailor with binoculars or telescope locating targets, or checking on the distant effects of their actions. At Port Sunlight, in one of four high relief panels by Goscombe John showing scenes of battle, it is a machine gun which is being fired from the trenches, but the implication of close-up action is dissipated by the detail of the binoculars and the composure of the men.

Pl. 165
Port Sunlight.
William
Goscombe John,
1921

181

Pls.166 and
167
Submarine
Corps
Memorial,
London.
Frederick
Brook Hitch,
1922

As with the reluctance to depict images of aggression, there was a
preference to show the servicemen as threatened rather than threatening.
In a memorial to the Submarine Corps on London's Embankment, the
threat to lives is imaginatively and allegorically expressed. The
submariners are shown literally encircled by wraiths of the sea whose
aggression and attempts to ensnare them in nets is clearly intended to
symbolise not only the natural dangers of underwater warfare but of the
enemy above. The sailors themselves remain impassive. They go about their
work efficiently, unperturbed by the obvious dangers. At the unveiling
ceremony of this memorial on 15 December 1922, Rear-Admiral Sinclair,
Chief of Submarine Services, noted that one third of all submarine
personnel, some 138 officers and 1,225 men, lost their lives in the war, a
far greater proportion than any other branch of the armed forces.[12]

In many ways similar to Carrick's sculpture for the Royal
Artillery in Scotland is the relief panel by Gilbert Ledward on the reverse
of the Guards' Division Memorial in London. Once it had become obvious
that individual regiments would want to build their own memorials, and
following a meeting in February 1920, a Memorial Committee was
established under the chairmanship of the Duke of Connaught to organise
and co-ordinate the commissioning and planning of a memorial for the
Guards to be located on the edge of St James' Park, facing Horse Guards'
Parade.

It was decided to hold a competition, to be assessed by Sir Thomas
Brock, founding president of the Society of British Sculptors, and the
architect Sir Reginald Blomfield. The conditions set for contestants were
that the memorial should represent all five Guards' regiments and that
representative figures should be shown, not in action but in repose. Gilbert

Ledward, working with the architect Harold Bradshaw whose acquaintance he had first made when both were students at the British School in Rome, submitted a sketch model which was accepted by the committee in January 1922.

Ledward was the son of a sculptor who, like Albert Toft's father, had originally worked as a modeller in the ceramics industry in Staffordshire. Gilbert was born in Chelsea in 1888 and in 1905 he enrolled as a student under Professor Lantéri at the Royal College of Art, where he was later to become Professor of Sculpture himself. (One of his assistants at that time was a young Henry Moore). After further studies at the Royal Academy Schools, in 1913 Ledward applied for and won the Travelling Scholarship as the first Rome Scholar for Sculpture. Bradshaw, a former student of the Liverpool School of Architecture, had at the same time become the first Rome Scholar in Architecture.

Ledward's time spent touring Italy was cut short by the outbreak of war. As we know from his annotated sketchbooks, the work of Renaissance masters, particularly Donatello, made a considerable impression on the young sculptor but more recent work also impressed.

Pl.168
Guards Division
Memorial,
London.
Gilbert Ledward,
1926
(with architect
Harold
Bradshaw)

Ledward's early drawings of ideas for the Guards' memorial had an unquestionably Italian flavour and included sketches of Emilio Gallori's 1895 equestrian *Monument to Giuseppe Garibaldi.*

Pl.169
Guards
Division
Memorial.
Gilbert
Ledward, 1926

    Ledward's and Bradshaw's 1922 model, in contrast to the classically-influenced flamboyance of the sculptor's early sketches, was remarkably austere. The monument actually built was to differ very little from the model. One major change was the removal of sculptural groups flanking the central monument, but the row of five soldiers representing the Grenadiers, Coldstreams, Scots, Welsh and Irish Guards, remained. However, by the time that Ledward and Bradshaw had produced their model they had already had almost two years since the announcement of the competition to refine their ideas and as the early sketches showed, considerable changes to the initial concept had in fact taken place.[13]

    The evolution of the bronze relief on the back of the monument can be traced in an early drawing and a later photograph of Ledward working on a full-size plaster model. A receding row of field guns in the background, absent from the drawing and barely discernible in the plaster relief, is made more explicit, emphasising this specific action as a part of a greater effort. The most significant of a number of changes, however, is the removal of dead or dying figures. In both the drawing and the plaster relief, a dead soldier at bottom right is shown sprawled on his back. A second dead man in the drawing, lying trapped under a rafter or joist, his skull-like face frozen in an agonised scream, is reduced in the plaster cast to a rather less horrific arm emerging from the rubble. Both are omitted from the final bronze to be replaced by a kneeling soldier operating a field telephone. An explicit depiction of agonising deaths was no doubt ultimately considered unacceptable and some of the power of the earlier work is consequently dissipated in this final, less melodramatic version.

Like Ledward's panel for the Guards' Memorial and Carrick's for the Scottish National War Memorial, Charles Sargeant Jagger's reliefs for the Royal Artillery Memorial at Hyde Park Corner show the struggles of soldiers under hostile conditions. On either side of the bronze figures on both the East and West sides of the memorial are carved stone reliefs, one almost square; the other in a longer, horizontal format, with further, still narrower panels on the sides of the projecting 'arms' of the cruciform base. The smaller reliefs, of three men operating a trench howitzer on one side and a signaller and telephonist on the other, and the narrow panels of individual soldiers, show less action in the confined space but the larger reliefs provide adequate room for more complex scenes.

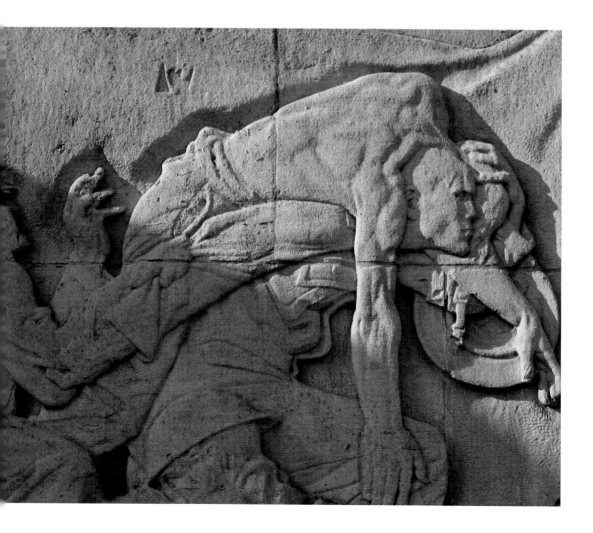

Amongst the soldiers frantically loading and aiming the heavy artillery is a man on the extreme right whose arm is in a crudely made sling with makeshift splint. Another man carries on his back a wounded colleague. Carried towards the back of the monument, away from the action, we might almost imagine him transformed into the bronze effigy of the dead soldier who lies there, particularly if we read the ghostly white carvings as memories of the recent war and the three-dimensional, free-standing bronze figures as representatives of the present.

Pls.170 and 171
Royal Artillery
Memorial,
London.
Charles Sargeant
Jagger, 1925

Where the Heavy Artillery relief concentrates on the difficulties and dangers of fighting the enemy, the Horse Artillery relief emphasises above all the sheer struggle for survival signified by the soldiers' difficulties in forcing the horse-drawn gun carriage through a shattered landscape of signposts and telegraph poles, mud and splintered trees. Whilst primarily acknowledging the men who fought, it is also a testament to the role of horses in the war.

Although the cavalry was little used, the British Army relied heavily on horses and mules for pulling gun carriages and wagons and carrying supplies and munitions. In the first twelve days of the war over 165,000 horses had been acquired for military service. By the end of the war close to half a million had been employed with more than 250,000 killed.[14] Significantly horses, and occasionally other animals, are featured on a number of British First World War memorials.

The Waggoners memorial at Sledmere specifically highlights, with appropriate imagery, the work of one particular army transport unit. In addition memorials acknowledging the deaths of animals in the war can be found throughout the country. 'The humble beasts that served and died' are acknowledged in the Scottish National War Memorial at Edinburgh, with

Pl. 172
RSPCA Memorial
Dispensary,
Kilburn, London.
Frederick Brook
Hitch, 1929

carved roundels by Phyllis Bone of animal heads, whilst at the RSPCA War Memorial Dispensary in Kilburn, opened in 1929, a particularly fine memorial plaque by Frederick Brook Hitch (who was also responsible for the Submarine Memorial) depicts, on the building's facade, army animals either side of a figure of Victory. An inscription notes the deaths of almost half a million animals and adds, 'In France alone 725,216 sick and wounded animals were treated in vetinary hospitals provided by the RSPCA'.

The inclusion of camels and elephants here reminds us that this was a world war. So too, Cecil Brown's well-known memorial to the Imperial Camel Corps in London's Embankment Gardens and indeed, a memorial to the Royal Gloucestershire Hussars Yeomanry outside Gloucester Cathedral. This depicts, in a series of finely detailed bronze panels by Adrian Jones at the base of a cross, their involvement, as part of the Imperial Mounted Division, in campaigns in Egypt and Palestine, with images of horses being watered and fed and trekked across a desert landscape.

On the Horse Artillery relief, a central figure, astride one of the two struggling horses, at first sight appears to be trying to restrain them, with his head tilted violently backwards and his face and outstretched arms in perfect line with the horses' reins. But, as we can see from the efforts of the other soldiers who strain every muscle and sinew to drag and force the carriage on, the horses need no restraint and we now see the mounted soldier in the instance of his death, shot by an enemy sniper. As with the inclusion of the bronze recumbent figure, by prominently featuring, in both these panels, dead or dying men, Jagger underlines the ultimate sacrifice of so many members of the Artillery which the monument more generally acknowledges.

By 1921, when Jagger was commissioned to design the Royal Artillery monument, he had already produced, or was concurrently working on memorials at Hoylake and West Kirby, Brimington, Portsmouth, Bedford and Manchester (for the textile firm S & J Watts) plus a memorial for the Great Western Railway Company at Paddington Station in London. None of these works featured relief sculpture but Jagger had nonetheless had earlier opportunities to explore the depiction of the war in the form of narrative reliefs.

In 1918 he was asked by the British War Memorials Committee of the Ministry of Information to produce a seven feet six by twelve feet bas-relief. This was intended for a Hall of Remembrance for which other sculptural reliefs by Gilbert Ledward and paintings by a range of artists, including John Singer Sargent, Percy Wyndham Lewis, Paul Nash, Stanley Spencer and many more, had also been commissioned.[15] Asked to base his work on either of the theatres of war of which he had personal experience, he chose the Western Front and entitled his work *The First Battle of Ypres, 1914.*

In contrast to the Royal Artillery reliefs, *The First Battle of Ypres* shows close engagement with the enemy, with British troops storming a desperately defended German gun pit. The scene depicted related to a bayonet charge at Gheluvelt by 'The Worcesters', Jagger's old regiment. Despite the explicit brutality of this scene, and perhaps because of its status as 'official' art, Jagger's approach, with its melodramatic extravagance of gesture and facial expression, is in many respects in line with more populist illustrations of hand-to-hand combat.

Pl. 173
Imperial Camel Corps Memorial. London. Cecil Brown, 1920

The British 'Tommies', with their soft caps contrasted with the aggressive appearance of the German spiked helmets, seem to be fighting a rearguard action, though the position of the gun on the German side refutes this. This is a British attack. Nonetheless, the emphasis is certainly on the suffering of the British troops. Although the German soldier in the centre of the relief tries desperately to fend off a British soldier's bayonet thrust, his face is hidden, and it is on the faces of the Allied troops that we see the agony of death, most obviously in the soldier

at bottom right who falls back screaming in pain, his left hand a rigid claw. Despite the populist melodrama of the scene, Jagger has made no distinction in his depiction of German and British faces, even apparently using the same model, with shaven head and broken nose, for combatants on opposing sides. He quite deliberately mirrors their postures and expressions as if to emphasise the similarity of experience for both German and Allied soldiers.[16]

When he received his commission for *The First Battle of Ypres,* Jagger was already working on another bas-relief for the British School at Rome. This work, *No Man's Land,* funded by the British School in lieu of the scholarship he had been unable to take up in 1914 and now in the collection of the Tate Gallery, was inspired by his experiences at Gallipoli. This time Jagger depicted the aftermath of battle with a macabre trail of corpses in various postures of ungainly death strewn across the barren landscape, from the disembodied naked legs hanging over a hummock on the left to a figure 'crucified' on a tangle of barbed wire on the right. On the far left of the relief, a roll of wire is coiled over broken fencing so as to resemble a wreath around a cross, this irony emphasised by the accompanying spade, equipment intended for the digging of trenches but now required to bury the dead.

Where *The First Battle of Ypres* was all action, *No Man's Land* is entirely static. Even the one living soldier, emerging from a listening post, remains motionless, stunned perhaps by what he sees or, more disturbingly, inured by the familiar sight of death. Amongst the debris of battle, a German helmet is identifiable, though the dead are clearly British. The original plaster included patriotic verse by Beatrix Brice-Miller: 'O little mighty band that stood for England that with your bodies for a living shield guarded her slow awaking' though this was removed from the subsequent cast, which was donated to The Tate in 1922.[17]

Neither the conventionally heroic nor the depressingly horrific approaches of Jagger's bas-reliefs would have been right for the Royal Artillery memorial. Here he adopted instead a less horrifying but ultimately more convincing heroic illustration of muscular artillerymen straining to cope with difficult conditions or carry on despite casualties. The figure types may be no less powerful but it is calm authority and stoic determination which is expressed here, rather than brutal aggression and appalling agonies. With the Royal Artillery Memorial, and with monuments abroad where he again used narrative relief, the sculptor was addressing an audience who would have approached the work with quite different expectations from those who visited a Hall of Remembrance. where the work of artists would be expected to be more personal and expressive.

Unlike many of the artists commissioned for the Hall of Remembrance, Jagger was no modernist. Indeed he was highly critical of much contemporary art, writing in 1933 of his disgust at the 'contortions and convulsions which have made the art of sculpture an object of derision and dismay'.[18] But neither was he an unquestioning traditionalist. Like those whose work he dismissed, he was more inclined to look to non-European sculptural traditions for inspiration, rather than the European

Pl. 175
'No Man's Land'.
Charles Sargeant
Jagger, 1919-20
Imperial War
Museum

191

sculpture of the previous century, about which he was similarly, if less vehemently critical. The twelve 'great works of sculpture' which he analysed in his 1933 book, *Modelling and Sculpture in the Making*, included African, Egyptian, Assyrian and Indian examples as well as Greek and Renaissance. The remaining examples were all by sculptors who were his contemporaries, with only Rodin who could truly be called a nineteenth century sculptor.[19]

It is perhaps in his later work for monuments in France and Belgium, on which he worked after completing the Royal Artillery memorial, that we see most clearly the influence of non-European art. Two reliefs for the Cambrai Memorial at Louverval in France have an almost Mayan quality. In one, soldiers are shown going 'over the top', only their feet and legs visible above the man crouching below. The detail of the revolver falling from the hand of a man we instantly understand to have been shot as he clambers out of the trench, eloquently and economically conveys the impression of the battle which rages unseen above. On the other relief - a deliberate counterpoint to the first panel, with a return to the trenches - the contorted hand and single bare foot of a man lowered into the trench on a stretcher, serves the same explicatory purpose.

The verticality of these panels is unusual but entirely appropriate for suggesting both a summary of the realities of trench warfare and a powerful metaphor for the struggle towards success. In both cases, the expression 'to emerge on top' might be used, but any suggestion of success is underplayed by the concentration on injury and death. For the stretcher-born soldier in particular, the lowering into a hole in the ground suggests the ultimate fate of so many more.

As with all of Jagger's reliefs the figures at Louverval occupy a shallow and claustrophobic space. In traditional history painting we are often encouraged to imagine ourselves as involved participants. In Benjamin West's *Death of General Wolfe* for example, the semicircle of spectators grouped around the dying soldier is effectively completed by the spectators of the painting. In Jagger's work, where soldiers are shown facing forwards or back, they are invariably engaged in heaving or dragging, lowering or loading from left to right, or right to left. There is no movement in depth nor figures looking out to make connections with the spectator. We might compare this with Arthur Walker's more conventional depictions of sailors and airmen at Dartford where, by the organisation of figures and objects in a receding space, he draws us into the picture, or with Margaret Winser's memorial at Hastings where the marching soldiers look back at us and raise their helmets in greetings as though we are there amongst the crowds who bid them farewell. With Jagger we remain remote. Those who were not there, he seems to be saying,

Pl. 176
Cambrai Tank
Memorial.
Louverval, France.
Charles Sargeant
Jagger, 1928

192

can only understand the facts, they cannot understand the experience or accurately imagine themselves as part of the action.

The Royal Artillery memorial has rightly come to be seen as a major achievement: not simply Jagger's most impressive work, nor even the most impressive of First World War memorials, but a major work of twentieth century sculpture and a monument which bears comparison with the very best. James Stevens Curl is an architectural historian who has written extensively on funereal and memorial monuments, including an essay on the Royal Artillery memorial. Curl says simply that this memorial is a work 'of the noblest conception and finest execution'.[20] For Curl, the works of Jagger, and especially the Royal Artillery memorial, 'remain in the mind's eye, their powerful compositions and stunning imagery as fresh and unforgettable as more familiar great works of art from antiquity'.[21] Alan Borg has simply described it as 'one of the outstanding examples of 20th century British art.[22]

But not all who viewed the monument when it was unveiled in 1925 saw it in such glowing terms. Much of the criticism was centred on the depiction of the howitzer. For Lord Curzon 'nothing more hideous could be conceived',[23] whilst the art critic of *The Times* suggested that it 'has neither the appeal of actuality, nor the more subtle and lasting appeal of monumental sculpture', adding that 'mere reproduction of machinery expresses nothing'.[24] Another critic, Selwyn Image, felt that the howitzer, and what it represented, was 'an offence'.

> Is it really a fine culminating symbol to have set high aloft over all, as finally expressive of our thankfulness to God for deliverance, and to keep green the blessed memory of those who sacrificed their lives for us, just this bare facsimile in stone of the latest mechanical invention of man's wit for blowing, on lamentable occasion, his fellow-creatures and their habitations to pieces? [25]

Significantly, many of those who wrote to *The Times* to refute these criticisms were military men who viewed the monument from a rather different perspective.

> Your critic cannot have been a 'gunner' during the Great War, otherwise he would not have given utterance to such a sentiment. The 'Gunner' Memorial is nothing if not real, and conveys nothing if not actuality . . . To all 'gunners' who knew those days in France and Belgium . . . the Memorial at Hyde Park Corner conveys the sense of actual power which 'gunners' felt when we could respond - and did respond - to every call from our infantry.[26]

> Many of us believe our fallen comrades would have been well
> content to know that a gun - a symbol to *them* of service, sacrifice,
> and affection - would crown their memorial, and this being so, not
> even the heaviest artillery of art and other critics will be likely to
> shake the dug-outs of our belief that the sculptor has been right in
> his conception.[27]

Although much of the argument, which continued in the press for many days, centred on the depiction of the gun, the significance of the broader scheme was also recognised, one letter writer asking, 'How many realize that the shape of the actual memorial is cruciform?'[28] Another, writing in the *Illustrated London News* of criticisms of the depiction of the dead soldier exclaimed, 'Let those who carp at what it is think rather what it means, and pass by on the other side'.[29] In its leader, the *Manchester Guardian* suggested that 'the soldiers who have never spoken frankly to their home folks of what they went through during those years were given a means of expression. Henceforth they can say 'Our story is written in stone. Look at it '.[30]

Each part of the memorial contributes to its broader meaning. In isolation, any one of the Royal Artillery panels may lack sufficient emplotment to qualify as true narrative. The panels however are not to be seen in isolation, but rather as parts of a visual scheme which involves not only the range of reliefs and the other more iconic sculptural elements, but also textual indications of the conflict. Inscriptions include the conventional slogans of self-sacrifice, a listing of campaigns from Macedonia to the Dardanelles and, perhaps most significantly, the ubiquitous dating of the war: 1914-1919. The organisation of the sculptural elements is itself significant, with all guns and efforts pointing away from the defeat of death, represented by the effigy of the corpse, towards a determined striving for victory.

It is equally possible, with other memorials which combine figuration and texts, to read into them narrative schemes of war and its after-effects. Like the Royal Artillery memorial, the memorial at Macclesfield combines a number of free-standing sculptures with inscriptions, dating and the listing of the locations of military campaigns. Here the linking of the free-standing figures which takes us from the soldier to Britannia to the figure of mourning, takes us also from death on the field of battle, through the nation's response, to the grief of the bereaved. These figurative elements are further supported by the textual scheme which also moves from the general to the specific and from the past to the present. Inscriptions list the arenas of battle, the time span of the war, an acknowledgement of self-sacrifice for King and Empire, a reference to the unveiling of the monument itself and finally, of course, the listing of the names of individuals who died.

The prominent display of the war's time span on almost all memorials of the Great War was, in itself, a means of encouraging a narrative interpretation, providing an obligatory beginning, middle and end. On some memorials the sense of the passage of time is reinforced, as at Lichfield where six separate plaques, either side of a figure of St George, record each year of the war, from 1914 to 1919.

Less obviously, the simple cross which forms the memorial for the village of Whitwick in Leicestershire is placed on a five-stepped base, each step intended to symbolically represent the five years of fighting. At Brockham Green in Surrey, where again the memorial is on a five-stepped base, the names of the dead are unusually listed in chronological order according to the year they died: one in 1914, four in 1915, nine the following year, then eleven and finally eight in the last year of the war.[31] The inexorable increase in numbers, which mirrors, until the final year, the increase in overall numbers of dead, provides a chilling picture of the progress of the war.

With similar effect a memorial in Rawtenstall cemetery, commemorating the dead of the two central wards of the town, was unveiled in June 1915 (making it the earliest of all memorials to the Great War). Donated by Carrie Whitehead, a local JP who was later to unveil the town's main memorial, it listed the names of nine men who had died. As the war progressed and more men were killed, their names were added to the memorial. The final total reached 332, their names filling all four sides of the substantial square plinth, spilling over onto the steps below.

Memorials elsewhere often explored a sense of before and after. Liverpool's cenotaph bracketed the marching off to war with the mourning of the dead while Bolton's was a more symbolic approach to the same idea. With Henry Fehr's memorials at Leeds, Colchester and Burton-upon-Trent we again see the contrast between beginning and end, though this time in allegorical form. On one side of the memorial St George, the symbol of patriotic endeavour, fights the enemy and on the other, Peace represents the results of his efforts.

Gilbert Ledward also adopted this approach for his memorials at Blackpool and Harrogate. In both locations, on opposite sides of massive obelisks built from giant blocks of Cornish granite, he placed reliefs depicting the contrasting emotions of war and peace. Both memorials were designed by the Lancashire architect Ernest Prestwich, a graduate of the

Liverpool School of Architecture. The obelisk at Blackpool is considerably taller and at close to 100 feet high is particularly imposing. Located on the seafront it can be seen from some distance along the coast, like a sombre echo of the famous tower, near to which it stands.[32]

At Harrogate the much simpler and smaller reliefs are carved into the granite face of the obelisk. On one side is a bugler and on the other a figure of Peace and at the feet of both we see only the helmets and bayonets of the troops, leaning forwards in the direction of battle in the one, vertical and at rest in the other.[33] At Blackpool the colossal reliefs, entitled *1914 the outbreak of War* and *1918 the end of War*, are cast in bronze. The former features a dominant central figure, similar to Harrogate's Peace, identified here as Britannia, but clearly intended as Justice with echoes of Frederick Pomeroy's famous Old Bailey figure holding in outstretched hands, both sword and scales. She is flanked by muscular figures, some of whom are already in uniform, brandishing weapons and clearly anxious for involvement. Others are civilians, including one with hammer and anvil, stripping for action. On the left is the familiar mother and child who must be left behind.

The complementary relief for 1918 shows a similar arrangement with, this time, a central figure of Peace with head bowed, holding in one hand a dove and in the other a wreath. Here, both combatants and civilians, to the left and right, are sombre and in mourning, though heads not bowed in respect for the dead are literally held high in pride of victory gained. The depicted eagerness of the men to take up arms in 1914 is echoed by the single figure of a semi-naked youth in the 1918 relief who, with his rifle on his shoulder and his clenched fist, seems to signify a willingness, despite the terrible consequences, to echo his elders if so required.

Pl. 178
Blackpool.
Gilbert Ledward,
1923

In other locations the story of the war is told in three acts. At both
Birmingham, on relief panels inside the Hall of Memory, and Colwyn
Bay, around the memorial's plinth, we see scenes of troops leaving and
returning which bracket depictions of fighting. Walter Marsden's
memorial at St Anne's-on-Sea, though lacking scenes of actual fighting,
presents a more complex narrative. On opposite sides of the massive stone
pillar are relief panels depicting the serviceman's progress from tearful
departure from wife and child to the weary return home.

The continual movement from left to right around the memorial
effectively suggests the circularity of the experience, the going out and
coming back. The matching pairs of servicemen either side of the listed
names on the front of the memorial might at first sight appear to be part
of a single movement. However, the careful contrasts in appearance
between those leaving, straight-backed and with heads held high, and
those returning, with weary looks and heads bowed, subtly summarises the
tragic effects of war. The stretcher-born soldier at the back of the
memorial is suggestive perhaps of those who failed to return.

Marsden's figures in the round, either side and on top of the
central pillar, reinforce the message of the reliefs below. Between the
departure of the soldiers on the front and the realities of war on the back

198

sits a mother with her child symbolising both defensive aims and future hopes, but also, according to the sculptor, 'intended to show the agony of mind caused by the tragedies of the War'.[34] Between the scenes of war and its successful conclusion sits, not a celebratory figure, but a weary, shell-shocked soldier.

Marsden was a former soldier who knew the realities of warfare and his message here is not one of celebration but of the necessity to acknowledge the grim truth and tragic consequences of war. The allegorical figure at the apex of the monument, with arms raised to the heavens, faces forward and is therefore seen to be placed above the names of the dead on the front of the monument. She both acknowledges society's gratitude and debt to these men and celebrates the peace they achieved. She, like us, 'will remember them'.

Pl. 180
St Anne's-on-Sea.
Walter Marsden,
1924

VIII

Peace

If the organisation of imagery, inscriptions and dating served to present a complete narrative of the conflict, the erection and unveiling of the memorial was itself the final act in the drama of the war. In those communities where the production of a permanent war memorial was considerably delayed, those involved often expressed frustration at the failure to achieve what is now referred to as 'closure'. When Liverpool eventually, in 1930, unveiled the city's memorial outside St George's Hall after considerable delays, a local paper commented on the sense of relief: 'At last Liverpool has a Cenotaph! ... there are still many thousands who gave their sons and daughters during that dread time, whose hearts feel the loss of blood so mercilessly shed'.[1]

Awareness of the needs of the bereaved for closure was combined with feelings of civic shame that a community should have taken so long to produce its official acknowledgement of the 'ultimate sacrifice' of so many of its citizens. In Londonderry plans for a monument had been put in place as early as February 1919 with the money to pay for it quickly raised. The subsequent political turmoil which eventually led to the partition of Ireland had inevitably delayed its production, but when the delays continued letters of complaint appeared in local newspapers. 'As a native of Derry I feel greatly grieved to see her so far behind as regards our long-talked of war memorial. Other cities have their memorials, and what is delaying Derry's memorial?' was one comment.[2] Another wrote of the Armistice Day ceremony that year: 'One felt that there was something missing, and that the scene would have been more impressive and complete could we have gathered around our War Memorial, in whatever form it may take ... to give those who have lost dear ones an opportunity of laying wreaths thereon in fond and loving memory of their fallen.[3]

For some recent commentators such as the American academic Samuel Hynes, writing in 1990, the production of war memorials was merely the ultimate official act, what he referred to as 'the C-major chords that bring a war and its emotions to a grand and affirming conclusion'. It

Pl. 181 *opposite* North Shields. John Reid, 1923

201

was an attempt, he suggested, to 'terminate the war finally and monumentally' and was intended simply to 'reassure non-combatants that the dead died willingly and do not resent or repent their sacrifice'.[4] This was to be contrasted with what Hynes called anti-monuments, the paintings, poems, novels, plays etc. which he claimed 'rendered the war without the value-bearing abstractions, without the glory, and without the large-scale grandeur'.[5]

For Hynes these two approaches, the production of monuments and anti-monuments, ran separately and in opposition during the 1920s, but not all who wrote critically about the war at this time reviled the production of monuments. Certainly there were many in the post-war years who condemned in particular the ceremonial rituals around memorials. This included many ex-servicemen who, in unemployment and lack of housing, saw scant reward for their wartime efforts, hardly compensated for by symbolic gestures. But others believed, or hoped, that memorials might serve as warnings to future generations of the folly and devastating costs of the act of war.

The tendency to see the war memorial merely as an official assertion of traditional values is to misunderstand (or simply to miss) the complexity of meanings they contained. Samuel Hynes' assessment of war memorials would seem to conform to Pierre Nora's idea of 'dominant' rather than 'dominated' sites of memory, as outlined in *Les lieux de mémoire* (Sites of Memory), Nora's exhaustive analysis of the national memory of France.[6] 'Dominant' sites were defined as grand and spectacular and imposed from above, usually by a national authority; 'dominated' sites were simply places of 'spontaneous devotion and silent pilgrimage'.

Undoubtedly some monuments, including those for various regiments, *were* imposed from above by a national authority. However, in many respects most British First World War memorials might seem to typify Nora's 'dominated' category. Organised independently of national government by local communities, paid for most frequently by public subscription and never by central government, and with decisions about siting and design often the result of public consultation, memorial building in communities throughout Britain certainly seemed the result of spontaneous reactions to a perceived need to remember the dead and to provide places of 'silent pilgrimage'.

However, regardless of the commissioning authority, whether local or national, it would be over-simplistic to see the war memorial either as exclusively imposed or entirely spontaneous. The bereaved still grieved for the men whose deaths the regimental memorials acknowledged and the memorials of local communities still acknowledged and reflected, in their inscriptions and in the organisation of commemorative ritual, the assertion of traditional, establishment values.

The iconography of many memorials serves to emphasise this complexity of public and private meanings. Macclesfield's monument, for example, visibly denotes the various bodies concerned with the process of remembrance. The military are personified in the figure of the dead soldier, the nation by Britannia, the clergy indicated by a cross carved on the pedestal (a late addition following complaints about the absence of religious symbolism) and the bereaved represented by the figure of mourning overseeing Britannia's act of tribute to the dead. Each element also illustrates a specific attitude or response to death: self-sacrifice, patriotic pride, religiosity and grief.

At Macclesfield, the names of the dead are listed on small pillars in the Garden of Remembrance in front of the monument. Elsewhere, names are more commonly listed on plaques around the base of the memorial. This is the case with Ashton-under-Lyne's war memorial. The main feature of this memorial is a tall pillar topped by a bronze group depicting a kneeling, wounded soldier passing the 'Sword of Justice' to a winged female intended to symbolise peace. On top of the base, either side of the pillar, are two bronze lions, symbols of the Empire, one shown fighting the 'serpent of evil'; the other, having killed it, is shown triumphant.

Pl. 182
Ashton-under-
Lyne.
John Ashton
Floyd, 1922

Ashton's memorial, unveiled on 16th September 1922 by General Sir Ian Hamilton, with wreaths laid by four girls whose fathers had died in the war, had its origins in a public meeting held at the Town Hall on 3 February 1919. This was attended by a typical cross-section of concerned parties: the mayor, several councillors, the town clerk, local representatives of the military and the churches and various others, including, as the local paper noted, 'a large number of ladies, many of whom were in mourning'.[7] After the usual discussion of possible utilitarian schemes, including an extension to the District Infirmary and the building of a YMCA, a monument was agreed upon.

The initial contract was given to J.H Cronshaw and J.L Robinson, two tutors at the local Art School, whose proposal for a cylindrical column surmounted by a bronze statue of St George and the Dragon, with additional statues of lions, was estimated at £10,000.

However, following difficulties in raising money, not least because of post-war problems in the local cotton trade, this scheme was abandoned and a new, somewhat cheaper design by local architect Percy Howard and Manchester-based sculptor John Ashton Floyd, was now selected. The final cost of the monument was £8,000 which was described as 'a mere bagatelle compared with the sacrifice of the 1,512 men whose names adorn the panels'.[8]

Catherine Moriarty, has written about Ashton's war memorial, pointing out the importance of the positioning of the names of the dead. She suggests that in the iconographic and textual organisation of the memorial, with the names at the base of a monument surmounted by Imperial lions, and at the apex by a soldier and figure of Peace, 'the dead thus literally uphold and support the values of Empire, service and honour, and it is through them that these values are to be understood'.[9] Yet it is also possible to view this rather less charitably, with the dead relegated to a subordinate position - literally a supporting role - with all emphasis on the glory and honour of the Empire.

At Macclesfield, in contrast, by listing the names of the dead in a non-hierarchical way within the Garden of Remembrance, they form a physically close connection with those members of the community who sit and stand and walk amongst them. Furthermore, unlike at Ashton, the clear focus of the monument is not a remotely elevated soldier who, by his glorious actions brings peace, but a dead soldier brought into close confrontation with the mourners for whom he is seen to have sacrificed his life. The bereaved are further represented by the figure at the top of the monument who oversees the events below. Instead of an emphasis on victory and peace, the emphasis is on the individual, personal tragedies which the country, in the guise of Britannia, must sorrowfully acknowledge. Our attention is directed towards the dead rather than away from them.

The allegorical figure of the winged female which we see at Ashton was only exceeded in popularity by images of soldiers or the crucified Christ as the figurative focus of First World War memorials in Britain. Allegorical figures were widely used in traditional memorial statuary to represent a range of interests and ideals. Britannia's popularity on war memorials reflected widespread feelings of patriotism before the war and symbolised the nation's post-war gratitude to its armed services. Figures of mourning or grief were also widely used to represent the bereaved, but in addition frequently ambiguous and usually female figures were used to reference the more abstract virtues of Peace, Honour, Justice, Freedom, and of course Victory. Their interconnectivity was to lead, in many cases, to nominal confusion.

John Floyd Ashton, the sculptor at Ashton-under-Lyne, had already, a year earlier, produced another different, and this time solitary winged figure, for a memorial at Royton near Oldham. Like his Ashton figure, this was also said to personify Peace. (Unfortunately the statue was stolen from its somewhat isolated country park location in the 1960s). The sculptor's only other war memorial was for the Post Office workers of Manchester and this too featured a figure of Peace, accompanied by two children. Here the memorial committee had made it clear that their memorial should emphasise peace not war, a fact particularly stressed by the Reverend Dr F.W Norwood in his speech at the unveiling ceremony and by the inscription - 'Strive for Peace' - on the monument's pedestal.

It was by no means unusual for the allegorical figure of the winged female to be identified as Peace. Equally common was her identification as angel, or indeed, quite frequently, 'Angel of Peace', as with Alexander Carrick's dignified figure at Berwick-upon-Tweed, or the impressive statue, by local mason Shirley Ward, in the small village of Ratby in Leicestershire. At North Shields an 'Angel of Healing and Peace' is shown holding a globe encircled by laurel, the world saved by the men who marched willingly to war, a representative group of whom (soldiers, sailors and airmen) are shown behind her, doing just that.

Pl. 183
Berwick-upon-Tweed.
Alexander Carrick,
1923

205

Pl. 184
Bridgwater. John
Angel, 1925

Pl. 185
detail at base of
Bridgwater
memorial.
John Angel, 1925

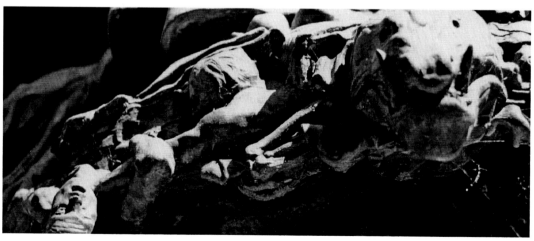

Of course the angel and Victory were closely connected. The winged Victory, the Nike of Greek mythology, goddess of victory and success, had survived in the post-Classical era in the form of the heavenly winged messenger, the angel. The conflation of victory and resultant peace, with the bringing of the welcome news of these achievements in the name of a just or holy war, blurred the distinctions between the female Classical Nike and traditionally asexual Christian angel. At North Shields the angel, her halo clearly identifying her as such, is unquestionably female, her form revealed by her dress blown back against her body like the traditional, wind-swept, flying Nike with whom she might easily have been confused.

Figures more readily identifiable as angels, both by their piety and by the accompanying Christian imagery (or by their location in church-yards) appear elsewhere on numerous First World War memorials. Usually the angel seems to have been transposed from the familiar funerary monument and was no doubt most often carved by a local mason, more usually employed in cemeteries or churchyards.

At Bridgwater in Somerset, a seated figure by the appropriately named, sculptor John Angel, said to represent Civilisation, holds a globe 'encircled with emblems of peace and commerce'.[10] She is accompanied, on either side, by angels, their subservience and childlike appearance confirming their identity. The angels help to hold, on Civilisation's lap, a book representing religious law while beneath their feet they trample the 'demons of war', identified as Strife, Bloodshed, Corruption and Despair and shown as intertwined male bodies, writhing in agony.

Pl. 186
Trumpington.
Eric Gill, 1921

Of the complex hierarchy of angels, from cherubim and seraphim to archangel, the Archangel Michael was understandably seen as particularly appropriate for war memorial sculpture. A militant saint traditionally shown in full armour vanquishing the devil, whether in semi-human form or the form of a dragon, and seen, like St George, as a symbol of the battle of good against evil, St Michael features on numerous memorials. Eric Gill shows him at the base of Trumpington's cross alongside images of a soldier, the Virgin and Child and St George, and here the saint is shown in the act of slaying the dragon.

As with St George, the potential to emphasise overt acts of aggression which, in more realistic form would have been discouraged, was frequently exploited but St Michael was also often shown in more iconic mode. A particulary striking example is A.G Wyon's figure at Shrewsbury where the saint is shown in medieval armour within a circular classical temple.

In memorial sculpture the angel, whether militant or passive, is presented merely as a signifier of spirituality or of religious approbation (of God having been on our side) but in the popular story of the Angel of Mons, a guardian angel was presented, and in many quarters surprisingly accepted, as having directly intervened in the course of battle. An angel clothed all in white, riding a white horse and brandishing a flaming sword, or in alternative versions, a curtain of angels protecting the retreating British, is said to have appeared during the Battle of Mons in August 1914. This episode was most likely derived from a short story of supernatural intervention on the battlefield, published in the *London Evening News* in September of that year.[11] It was also, no doubt, aided by mass hysteria. The story was widely believed as fact and was frequently illustrated in the early years of the war, with ex-soldiers many years later purporting to be witnesses to the events.

The Angel of Mons story and similar tales of spectral intervention on the field of battle chime with an increasing interest in Spiritualism which before the war had been in decline but which the current loss of life had helped to revive. The number of spiritualist societies in Britain in fact doubled between 1914 and 1920.[12] One of the movement's most famous and ardent apologists was Sir Arthur Conan Doyle, who lost not only his son but also his brother and brother-in-law in the war. Conan Doyle frequently lectured on spiritualism and saw the Angel of Mons story as significant. Whilst admitting that the extreme stress of retreat under fire could affect men's minds he argued it was 'at such times of hardship that the psychic powers of man are usually most alive'.[13]

In Liverpool's Anglican Cathedral a large, though easily missed memorial, designed by Walter Gilbert, is popularly thought to be based on the legend. Dedicated to the men of the 55th West Lancashire Division, the memorial, which is sited high above an arch supporting a gallery in the southern arm of the eastern transept, shows an angel holding a crown above a soldier who kneels before her. However, as the 55th Division played no part in the Battle of Mons, only arriving at the front in November, some months after the battle had ended, the suggestion that this memorial illustrates the famous myth would seem to be itself a myth.

Angels were not the only winged figures: Fame, History, Fortune, and of course Victory and Peace, were all regularly portrayed in this way from the Renaissance onwards. The precise categorisation of the winged figure was therefore usually dependent upon accompanying attributes or literary identification. The not uncommon and understandable confusion

Pl. 187
Shrewsbury.
A.G Wyon,
1922

of Victory and Peace, or the decision to name a memorial statue as Peace rather than Victory, emphasises a rhetorical reluctance in the ritual of remembrance (in the speeches, press reports and supportive booklets), to overtly celebrate military success, and a desire to avoid the triumphalism which the identification of the winged figure as Victory inevitably suggests. However, the visual equivocality of the Nike and angel permits a presumably deliberate interpretative ambiguity which could enable the sculptor to suggest victory while emphasising peace.

That said, the entirely appropriate figure of Peace on First World War memorials is more often shown as wingless, thus avoiding any questionable ambiguity. Harold Brownsword's bronze figure at Thornton near Bradford holds wreaths in both outstretched hands while at nearby Eccleshill the same artist's figure of Peace shows her with a wreath in one hand, the other holding the Sword of Justice, or 'sword of strife' as it was described at the time. The local paper suggested that the figure was 'taking away the sword of strife and bestowing the laurel wreath of honour'.[14]

At Leeds (and at Burton-upon-Trent and Colchester, the same figure being used at all three sites) Henry Charles Fehr has shown Peace releasing a dove, her most obvious attribute. At each corner of the base of the pillar in front of which she stands are carved owls. Owls are an emblem of Leeds, appearing on their coat of arms and elsewhere in the city and clearly their presence here is a reference to this. But the inclusion of this detail enables Fehr to suggest, or at least for us to read, additional layers of meaning. The owls, being nocturnal creatures, can be seen perhaps as symbols of the dark, from which, with the arrival of peace, the world emerged, and with wings outstretched they appear appropriately ready to fly.

As symbols of wisdom, owls are also traditionally associated with Athena, goddess of war, a fighter in defence of just causes and therefore the personification of wisdom.[15] She is usually depicted in armour, with spear, shield and helmet and Fehr's striking figure of Peace, with her military styled helmet, might almost be read as Athena were it not for the accompanying dove. Indeed, the two, Athena and Peace, are frequently confused or conflated, as Athena, in fighting wars, brings a just peace.

At other locations, allegorical figures are variously identified: at Luton she is seen as 'Courage bringing Victory', at Ramsgate as 'Destiny',

Pl. 188
Bexhill-on-Sea.
L.F Roslyn,
1923

Pl. 189
opposite
Leeds.
Henry Charles
Fehr, 1922

210

at Port Talbot as 'Victorious Peace' and at Armagh as 'Peace with Honour'. At Calverley the Britannia-like figure is named as 'Patriotism' while at Malvern and Hartlepool it is 'Youth' or 'Triumphant Youth'.

Charles Sargeant Jagger's memorial at Hoylake and West Kirby features two figures on either side of an obelisk: on one side is one of his familiar impassive soldiers; on the other is a figure identified as 'Humanity'. Jagger apparently rejected the suggested, more conventional idea of pairing a soldier and a sailor. The deliberate dichotomy of male and female, archaic and contemporary, allegorical and realistic, might suggest that if the draped figure represents humanity then the soldier signifies inhumanity - the inhumanity of war. And if the soldier represents war then humanity is equally representative of peace. With the style and iconography of this and other similar figures clearly referring back to the *fin de siècle* world of Alfred Gilbert and George Frampton (or, for that matter, Jagger's own pre-war student work) we are reminded of an earlier, happier era, one to which it is hoped we may now have returned.

Fehr's memorials at Leeds, Colchester and Burton also featured paired male and female figures either side of the pedestal, deliberately chosen to provide contrast and to carry specific, symbolic meanings. At Leeds, beneath the figure of St George, are the words 'Pro Patria' and beneath Peace, with which he is paired, the words 'Invictis Pax' (peace to the unvanquished). This is, in other words, the familiar pairing of war and peace, action and reward, aggressive male and passive female. St George looks down at the dragon

beneath his feet, but also in sorrow; Peace looks up to the dove she holds, but also in hope for the future. And, as the unveiling brochure at Colchester declared: 'As St. George represents the Manhood, so the figure of Peace represents the Womanhood of England, and reminds us all of the splendid work done by the women of England in general and Colchester in particular'.[16]

But although she also represents peace, Jagger's Humanity is no celebratory figure like Fehr's elated female. Admittedly the broken chains around her wrists suggest liberty, whilst a barely visible baby at her breast

is intended to represent the future of humanity freed from the chains of war. But in the crown of thorns, through which the baby looks down at us, and the dark hooded cloak, there are unmistakable intimations of death. Indeed, our inclination is to read the two figures of the soldier and Humanity in an entirely different way; to see the human barricade of the soldier as the defender of life and the darkly hooded allegorical female as a symbol of death, the broken chains around her wrist signifying liberty perhaps, but also hinting at shattered lives in the pursuit of peace.

Such details present a complex image, not easily categorised. She seems in particular to incorporate a Christian ideology, not only in the wreath or crown of thorns on her breast and the cross of lilies behind her head, but in the very idea of redemption which she is intended to represent. This deliberate complexity and ambiguity suggests that, however we look at it, peace has been gained but at a terrible cost to humanity.

Where Victory is denied, then Peace is most often preferred, both with and without wings. Nonetheless, in very many locations winged females were unambiguously identified as Victory. (The Welsh National Memorial at Cardiff, by the English sculptor, Henry Pegram, is unusual in featuring an obviously male winged Victory). The figure of Victory had both the weight of tradition and a contemporary popularity. With the rediscovery, in 1863, of a statue of Nike on a small Greek island, and with the subsequent installation of this *Victory of Samothrace* at the Louvre, the winged victory had enjoyed something of a popular revival at the end of the nineteenth century. This was appropriate for a goddess whose Roman name was Victoria in the era of a queen named after her. Sir Thomas Brock's 1911 memorial to Queen Victoria outside Buckingham Palace especially contributed to the growing popularity of the winged Victory in England in the pre-war years whilst her frequent portrayal on memorials commemorating the Boer War provided prototypes for later monument builders.[17]

Pl. 190
Hoylake and
West Kirby.
C.S Jagger,
1922

212

The natural flamboyance of flared wings provided, for most sculptors, an irresistible drama, which is occasionally countered by a more reserved demeanour, with bowed head and static pose. Charles Hartwell's Victory at Denbigh in North Wales (and also at Clacton) shows her with palm leaf in one hand and laurel wreath in the other. She looks down in sorrow towards the mourners who, at remembrance ceremonies, would be gathered in front of the memorial. The fictive wreath, held at arm's length, is shown as though ready to be handed down to be added to the real tributes placed at the base of the monument.

L.F Roslyn's Victory at Greengates also express a sombre mood, with the wreath held demurely in front of the static figure. Roslyn designed some two dozen First World War memorials of which more than half were winged Victories, although the same casts were often used in multiple locations. The Victory at Greengates, also used at Tottenham, is unusually demure; in a more typically vigorous version seen in Buxton, Bexhill-on-Sea, Port Talbot and Wetherby she holds a wreath above her head in one hand and the Sword of Justice in the other.

The figure of Victory was also much used by Henry Charles Fehr. At Keighley in Yorkshire she is somewhat confusingly wingless but elsewhere has a more conventional appearance. At Leeds, Burton and Colchester the figure strides forward with both a reversed Sword of Justice and a wreath held aloft. At all three locations she is presented in combination with the figures of Peace and St George but at Eastbourne, Hammersmith, Langholm, Lisburn and Lockerbie, the same figure is shown in isolation. At Portadown, most dramatically, the figure uniquely supports a dying soldier and here, in place of the sword, she holds a sprig of laurel.

Like Roslyn and Fehr, Sydney and Vernon March made extensive use of the figure of Victory on their First World War memorials. Sydney and Vernon were brothers, part of an extensive family of artists who jointly worked under the banner of 'Messrs. March Bros. of Farnborough'. Sydney was born in Kingston-upon-Hull in 1875 and Vernon, the youngest child, in 1891, the family moving south in 1901. During the war, Vernon, having already learned to fly, joined the Royal Flying Corps. Ironically, however, his poor eyesight was to prevent him from serving as a pilot.

Vernon's most elaborate, and by far his most impressive memorial was the Canadian National War Memorial in Ottawa. Winning a world-wide competition in 1925, which attracted 127 entries, including twenty-five from Britain, the sculptor was to work on this project with the help of

Pl. 191
Denbigh.
Charles Hartwell,
1922

213

his six brothers and his sister Elsie for the rest of his unfortunately short life. When Vernon died of pneumonia in 1930 aged thirty-eight, some nine years before the memorial was eventually unveiled, Elsie and his brothers completed the work, which featured twenty-two larger than life-sized figures of servicemen with two horses and an eighteen pounder field gun.

These figures, influenced perhaps by Goscombe John's 'Commercials' memorial in Newcastle and similarly intended to represent a 'great response' to the outbreak of war, pass through a massive arch on top of which are two colossal figures of Victory and Liberty. All of the figures, cast in bronze in the March's own foundry at Farnborough, were completed by 1932 and, as the arch had not yet been built, were exhibited in London's Hyde Park for six months before being placed in storage, ready for shipment to Canada.

Although based in the South of England, a number of the March brothers' memorials can be found in the North, in and around Manchester, with memorials by Vernon at Glossop and Hadfield and by Sydney at Radcliffe and Whitefield. Examples in the South include Sydney's memorial at Bromley - a slight variation of his work at Radcliffe - and Vernon's equally elaborate memorial at Lewes in Sussex. Vernon also produced a remarkable memorial for Londonderry in Northern Ireland, with figures of a soldier, a sailor and another winged Victory. All of the figures at each of the locations are spectacularly flamboyant.

Pl. 192 *left*
Lockerbie.
H.C Fehr, 1922

Pl. 193 *right*
Thornton.
Harold
Brownsword,
1922.

214

At both Glossop and nearby Hadfield, Derbyshire villages close to Manchester, an identical cast of Vernon's sculpture is used with Victory shown precariously balancing on a serpent-encircled globe and stretching up as if to pluck from the heavens the wreath she clasps in her hand. Variations of this figure were also used on memorials at Lewes and Londonderry. The prominently carved reference to patriotic incentive - *Pro Patria* - at the top of the plinth on which she stands at Glossop, Hadfield and Lewes, a by no means unusual inscription but here particularly pronounced, serves to add to a feeling that the overwrought imagery and its apparent glorification of military victory is somewhat inappropriate.

If Vernon's memorials now seem excessively ostentatious, Sydney's appear even more so. Of course, given the family business with the two brothers sharing a studio, and the close similarities of their work, to what extent they were individually conceived is open to question. Each artist did however sign their works individually.

At Whitefield near Manchester, Sydney's semi-naked figure of Victory, like Vernon's, balances with considerable agility on a globe encircled by laurel wreaths. Her wings are stretched thinly to either side as she strains, on tiptoe, upwards and back, to grasp in both hands the ubiquitous wreath. The same artist's monument at Radcliffe, also in Greater Manchester, is much larger, more elaborate and even more dramatic. This work features three life-sized allegorical figures arranged

Pl. 194 *left* Whitefield. Sydney March, 1922

Pl. 195 *right* Lewes. Vernon March, 1922

around a twenty-six feet high obelisk. The central figure, who grasps a laurel wreath in her raised left hand, is identified as Victory. Stretching round the obelisk, Victory's right hand clasps the left hand of a second standing figure who holds in *her* right hand the flaming torch which identifies her as Liberty. The third figure, on the opposite side to Liberty, is Peace. She is melodramatically slumped against the obelisk, with her attribute, the dove, held close to her face as if she is listening to its message of peace. (The same motif was used by Vernon at Lewes). On her lap is a garland of roses, said to be symbolic of remembrance. The fourth side of the obelisk contains an oval plaque inscribed with the words, 'To Our Glorious Dead, 1914-1918', the names of whom are listed on panels around the monument's base.

The intended meaning here is clear: victory has brought liberty and peace, the one leading inexorably on to the others, symbolically expressed by the linked hands. But as at Ashton-under-Lyne the emphasis seems to be on national interests and on the grand ideals for which the war was said to have been fought. Although the dead are acknowledged in the listing of names and described as 'glorious' on the plaque, our attention, rather than drawn to them, is entirely distracted by the rococo extravagance of the semi-naked cavorting women. The raising of the wreath in Victory's hand away from the dead, represented by their names, seems somehow significant, as though acknowledging God's role, rather than Man's, in achieving victory. This is in marked contrast to those more dignified memorials, such as that at Denbigh, where Victory appears to present the laurel tribute to those who mourn and, by implication, to the dead whose names are inscribed beneath her feet.

However, when the proposed design for Radcliffe's monument was presented to a public meeting in April 1920, it met with widespread approval, confirmed when photographs of the scheme, subsequently published in the local press, were similarly well received. Sydney March had been approached directly by the memorial committee to design the monument. No First World War memorials by the brothers had so far been erected but Boer War memorials and other prestigious public projects, in particular Sydney's 1914 statue of Lord Kitchener for Calcutta, would presumably have been familiar.

NAMES OF THE FALLEN

RIDER, W.V.	SMITH, H.	THOMAS, S.H.	WARD, G.H.
RIGBY, T.	SMITH, N.C.	THOMAS, W.	WARING, T.
RILEY, F.	SMITH, J.	THOMAS, S.	WARWICK, F.
RILEY, J.C.	SMITH, P.	THOMSON, R.	WATMOUGH, W.
		THORNLEY, A.	WATSON, A.E.

At Lewes, a competition was held which attracted thirty-five entries including ones from Henry Fehr and L.F Roslyn. The submissions, both drawings and models, were judged by Edward Prior, architect and co-founder (with W.R Lethaby) of the Art Workers' Guild and at that time Slade Professor of Fine Art at Cambridge University. Despite some reservations and suggested alterations, Prior decided in favour of March, noting that his submission 'gave proof of sculptural talent of a high order'.[18]

When the Lewes memorial was unveiled in September 1922, two months before the Radcliffe memorial, it too was well received. The Chairman of the Memorial Committee commented on the memorial's emphasis of the men's sacrifice for their country. March, he suggested, had 'made the bronze and the stone instinctive with meaning, speaking of those who gave their all for their country in the hour of need'.[19] The mayor, in turn, hoped that the monument 'might prove an example to those who followed and inspire them to emulate the noble sacrifice which their bretheren made in time of war'.[20] However, neither at Lewes nor Radcliffe are we encouraged by the imagery to consider the soldiers' sacrifices in terms of the impact on the bereaved.

In other towns however, our likely understanding of the winged figure as celebrating military victory is qualified, whether by her obviously sorrowful demeanour or by the additional figure of the soldier shown fighting and dying. The memorial at Oswaldtwistle shows a soldier with a wounded companion whilst in John Cassidy's more unusual memorial at Skipton in Yorkshire, a semi-naked allegorical 'warrior' symbolically breaks his sword across his knee. In both of these locations, a winged Victory stands remotely on top of a tall column acting merely as an adjunct to the major focus of the monument.

Many memorialists, and memorial committees, were in fact determined to avoid *any* suggestion of the celebration of military victory. At Newcastle it was argued that 'The addition of anything suggestive of the trappings of military might would be destructive of the deep emotions that should be stirred at the sight of the memorial'.[21] And at Euston Station, Reginald Wynn Owen declared that his monument in memory of the 3,719 men of the London and North West Railway Company killed in the war was essentially for the fallen and deliberately devoid of any element which might mark it as an emblem of victory'.[22] In this there was undoubtedly a reflection of mixed emotions at the declaration of the end of the war.

Certainly the announcement of an armistice in November 1918 was met with considerable, though not unqualified celebration. In Macclesfield, the local paper, published a few days after the declaration of peace, described how people who had left their place of work, and children released early

Pl. 198
Skipton.
John
Cassidy,
1922

218

from school, thronged the roads leading to the Town Hall to hear a formal announcement from the mayor. There were no scenes of rowdyism or exhibitions of horseplay, but the inhabitants, high and low, young and old, rich and poor, gave vent to their feelings of heartfelt gratitude in no unmistakable manner. When the news was announced the people went almost frantic with joy'.[23]

But at the front the response was more muted. As numerous ex-soldiers have recalled there was a feeling of anticlimax, exhaustion and sadness at the loss of life. As one man declared, 'On our side there were only a few shouts. I had heard more for a rum ration. The match was over, it had been a damned bad game'.[24]

The inscriptions on war memorials frequently make reference to the servicemen's deaths and to those for whom they died - for King, for Country, for Empire, for Civilisation, and certainly for 'us'. We also read of the causes for which they died - for Justice, Liberty, Freedom or Peace. Less common, however, is the use of the word 'Victory'. Where victory *is* referenced it is quite often in the form of praise to God for victory achieved. At Leominster the inscription reads, 'To the glory of the giver of victory and peace and in proud and grateful remembrance of the men of Leominster who laid down their lives in the cause of humanity in the Great War'. The monument here, by W.G Storr-Baker, a Hereford monumental mason who received numerous war memorial commissions, shows a winged Victory in an attitude of quiet contemplation with head slightly bowed and with raised arm holding the torch of Liberty.

More sombre still, at Liverpool, on the side of the memorial depicting a scene of mourning and remembrance, the inscription includes the words, 'and the victory that day was turned into mourning unto all the people'. As we have seen, the planning of Liverpool's memorial had been delayed until the second half of the 1920s and was only finally unveiled in 1930. By this time attitudes to the Great War - the war to end wars - had begun to change, not least because a second war seemed to many people increasingly likely.

But it is clear that in referencing victory in both the textual and figural elements of the memorial it is not only military achievement on the field of battle that is suggested. The death of the serviceman in action was seen as helping to achieve a victory over tyranny and injustice. The inscription on the memorial at Burton-upon-Trent refers to the men 'who gave their lives for the victory of honour and freedom over terror and oppression'. At Grangemouth in Scotland the 'fight for God and the right', as the inscription records, is expressed metaphorically by the depiction of a 'British' lion killing the 'German' eagle, imagery similarly deployed by Sir William Reid Dick on his 1920 memorial at Rickmansworth. A memorial for workers of the Metropolitan Railway Company at Baker Street Underground station shows the lion trampling a serpent and symbolic serpents trampled by soldiers are commonly featured on war memorials.

Often an inscription refers to victory over death itself. 'Death is swallowed up in victory' (Paul's assertion of life after death in Corinthians 15:54) is used on many memorials. Winnington-Ingram, the Bishop of London, had, during the war, produced a booklet, *Good Friday and Easter Day Thoughts*, 10,000 copies of which were distributed at the front in 1915. In this he urged the soldier to think, on Good Friday, that 'Christ died for others today; then if I am called to die for others I shall be only following Him'.[25] For Easter Day, the message was that 'Christ rose from the grave today, then death is not the end. My comrade who lies on the stretcher will live again . . . Death is the "gate of life" '.[26]

To the non-believer such sentiments would provide scant comfort, but in an age when, despite falling church attendance, most people in Britain would have considered themselves as Christian and would have received a basic religious education, if only at Sunday school, they did have real meaning.[27] As one historian writing in 1942 of his own growing disillusionment at 'the hollow words used too often at the unveiling of war memorials' was forced to admit, 'I know that in many cases these words were used with deep feeling by men who had lost their own sons'.[28]

For those attending the unveiling of the local war memorial who had lost sons or husbands, brothers or fathers, the allegorical figure of Victory or Peace, with its implication that those they mourned had died in a noble cause and had not died in vain, may have been a more anodyne choice than the figure of the soldier whose physical presence would only serve to emphasise the absence of their own loved ones. This would particularly be the case where the soldier was shown healthily and happily returning from battle.

As with enlistment, the representation of returning troops was a common theme on figurative memorials and reference has already been made to relief plaques which show this. Whilst with most memorials there was a resistance to any overt triumphalism, many did also show the soldier on top of the plinth striding confidently forward, often with helmet raised high in a gesture of apparent celebration at the end of the war. Sir George Frampton had produced a prototype for this in his Boer War memorials for Bury and Salford, where the same cast is used in both locations. It shows the soldier with rifle in one hand and busby in the other, held high in celebratory greeting.

The First World War equivalent is to be found in many places, including a repeatedly commissioned sculpture by Joseph Whitehead and Sons. This was described in the unveiling booklet at one of these sites as 'a

soldier in the ecstasy of victory'[29] and elsewhere as if he were crying 'Hurrah! Thank God the task is accomplished'.[30] Whitehead's soldier can be seen at Worthing, Chertsey, Ebbw Vale, Stafford and Truro and was also commissioned by the General Post Office for their memorial in London.

At Stafford there was apparently some reluctance on the part of some members of the war memorial committee to accept this celebratory figure, possibly because it was seen as too jubilant. However, variations of the Whitehead soldier by a number of other sculptors were also produced,

Pl. 199
Maxwelltown &
Troqueer.
Henry Price, 1921

notably by Frederick Pomeroy at Banbridge in Northern Ireland and George Thomas at three locations, Abertillery and Merthyr Vale in South Wales and Waterhead in Oldham. The *Oldham Evening Chronicle* described Thomas's figure as 'hailing the final victory and the end of the war'.[31]

Mortimer Brown's soldier at Twickenham wears both a trench coat and a broad smile and, like the others, holds his rifle in one hand and, in his case, with his helmet at his feet, a soft cap raised high in celebration. Adrian Jones' Bridgnorth figure is more ambiguous. He leans forward, with arm outstretched, as though greeting a distant friend, though he may merely have been meant to be waving his comrades forward. Similarly ambiguous is Henry Price's soldier for Maxwelltown in Scotland. He is shown with both arms raised to the heavens, an image open to more than one interpretation. His expression might suggest either relief or despair but there is certainly little sign of joy. Whether meant to be thankful for the end of the war, as seems most likely, or, as Derek Boorman perhaps imaginatively suggests, 'begging for an end to the slaughter', is unclear.[32] Either way, the absence of a rifle can be seen as significant.

Pl. 200
Stafford.
Joseph Whitehead & Sons, manufacturers.1922

Pl.201
Twickenham.
Mortimer Brown, 1921

In other towns the soldier simply strides confidently forward. John Tweed's figure at Bodfari in North Wales was later reused for the memorial to the Rifle Brigade in London's Grosvenor Square and, in a half life-size version, at the small Scottish village of East Wemyss. Most notable perhaps is Robert Tait McKenzie's figure for the memorial at Cambridge. Entitled 'The Homecoming', McKenzie shows the bareheaded soldier, his helmet in his hand and rifle, with laurel wreath around it, over his shoulder, jauntily striding homewards. The sculptor lengthened the normal stride by two inches to suggest both athleticism and the joy to be home. In this particular case the memorial was specifically intended to celebrate victory, with the self-sacrifice of the troops and the listing of the names of the dead being separately acknowledged on a memorial in Ely Cathedral.

Pl.202
Bridgnorth.
Adrian Jones,
1922

224

Whilst such gestures in all locations would no doubt be seen as celebrations of victory they could also, perhaps more accurately, be seen as acknowledging the sense of pleasure and relief, not only of the soldier himself but also of those to whom he returned. Of course, for those whose menfolk did not return, and for whom the memorial was primarily intended, such imagery might have been painful to view. As the author of an unveiling programme at Gateshead commented, 'It happened all too frequently that the "Welcome Home" greeting was not heeded. Men left and came home no more'.[33]

The depiction of the soldier striding home would be particularly poignant in those few cases where the memorial is dedicated to a specific individual. Many memorial plaques to individual soldiers can be seen in churches throughout the country, erected by family members and occasionally incorporating a portrait bust. Life-size free-standing statues are less common. In Knutsford in Cheshire, a statue by Sir William Thornycroft now stands in front of the local Red Cross Headquarters (built as a memorial hospital and paid for by public subscription). The statue, of Lieutenant Haron Baronian, was commissioned by his parents, in the grounds of whose family home it originally stood.

Pl. 203
Cambridge.
Robert Tait
McKenzie,
1922

Pl.204
Lt Haron Baronian
Knutsford.
Sir William
Thornycroft, 1918

The young Lieutenant, a slightly anxious smile on his face, has raised his hand to shield his eyes as though searching for a familiar face in the crowd of those whom we might imagine are waiting to welcome him and his colleagues home. But Lieutenant Baronian did not return. He was in fact killed in Mesopotamia in 1917. Like the depiction of the dead as still living in seventeenth and eighteenth century tomb sculptures, the effigy of the soldier in this case becomes the social body which continues to live in memory, as opposed to the natural body which rots and eventually turns to dust.

In the case of the First World War, not only did many men not survive, but nor were the bodies of those who died returned for burial at home. Many bodies were, of course, literally lost, having been blown apart or drowned at sea - or in a sea of mud - but in 1915 the decision had been taken, against considerable opposition, not to repatriate the bodies of any man killed on foreign soil.

It was a decision explained 'not only on the grounds of hygiene, but also on account of the difficulties of treating impartially the claims advanced by persons of different social standing'.[34] Unless the repatriation of all bodies was funded by the government it was argued, in practice only the rich would be able to afford to bring back their dead. Furthermore, so many men had no known grave that further discrimination would be created between those able to bring back identified bodies and those who lacked that choice. Instead, it was decided, all would be buried, or their deaths acknowledged, in battlefield cemeteries.

This was a decision which caused considerable distress for those who were left without a body to bury and, if unable to visit the cemeteries, without a focus for grief. And it was a decision which was to have a profound and defining impact on the production and nature of memorials after the war. War memorials provided a focus for grief, becoming surrogate graves, whilst the ceremonies of remembrance effectively replaced the funeral.

The figurative sculpture of the war memorial became a symbolic replacement of the missing body. The realistically detailed depiction of the individual soldier, though a permanently painful reminder of the absent dead, could be seen by grieving relatives and friends as a personal tribute. The anonymous figure, like that of the 'unknown warrior' in Westminster Abbey', came to represent, for each individual mourner, their own lost loved one and in so doing provided comfort for the bereaved.

IX

We Will Remember Them

An awareness of absence is reflected in the nation's memorial in Whitehall. Sir Edwin Lutyens had been asked, at very short notice, to produce a temporary structure for the Peace Celebrations on Saturday, 19 July 1919. Although the fighting had ended on 11 November 1918, the formal end of the war came only with the signing of a peace treaty, the Treaty of Versailles, on 28 June 1919 following months of negotiations. In anticipation of the signing of the treaty, plans for some form of celebration had been in place since the beginning of May.[1] They would include both a day of thanksgiving, including religious services, and a victory parade through the streets of London by Allied and Commonwealth troops. Similar celebrations were to take place in towns and cities throughout the nation.

When Lloyd George, the British Prime Minister, discussed with his French counterpart, Georges Clemenceau, their respective plans for Peace Day celebrations - the French celebrations to be held on 14 July - he was told that when *their* troops marched through Paris, 'They would pass a great catafalque, which they would salute in honour of the dead'.[2] This was to be erected adjacent to the Arc de Triomphe. The French memorial was actually equipped with wheels to enable it to be moved from its initial position under the Arc itself to the side of the Champs Elysée when the parade began.[3]

Lloyd George, impressed by these plans, recommended to the Peace Celebrations Committee that Britain should have a similar focal point for *their* victory parade and that some eminent artist or architect be appointed to produce an appropriate design. Alfred Mond, the Minister of Works, who had previously asked Lutyens to design a temporary war shrine to be constructed in Hyde Park on the fourth anniversary of the outbreak of war, again recommended the architect for this project. Early in July, Lutyens was summoned to 10 Downing Street and invited to design a catafalque for the victory parade in London. Realising that a catafalque was inappropriate, being a structure on which to place a coffin, Lutyens instead offered his designs for a cenotaph, a monument not actually containing the body commemorated, quite literally an empty tomb.

Lutyens apparently sketched out his initial ideas, which contained all the major elements of the completed work, that same day. In fact it is likely that he had already been thinking about this project for some time, possibly as a result of informal discussions with Alfred Mond. In addition, the architect was by this time working on a design for Southampton's war memorial, having been approached in January by the mayor of the city. (The Southampton memorial, unveiled in 1920, combined Lutyen's earlier Hyde Park design of Great War Stone and acorn topped pillars, with a prototype cenotaph). By 7 July he had drawn up his final design which was approved by Lord Curzon, Chairman of the Peace Celebration Committee.

The original structure, erected in Whitehall, was built of wood and plaster and was unveiled on 19 July, the morning of the parade. Originally intended purely as a temporary 'saluting point', such was the overwhelmingly enthusiastic response to the Cenotaph that almost immediately there were calls for it to become permanent. A letter to *The Times* on 21 July, from someone signing themselves R.I.P, suggested that 'The cenotaph in Whitehall is so simple and dignified that it would be a pity to consider it merely an ephemeral erection . . . it should be retained in granite or stone'.[4] The newspaper's leader concurred, commenting that 'Sir Edwin Lutyen's design is so grave, severe, and beautiful that one might well wish it were indeed of stone and permanent'.[5] Five days later the paper added:

> No feature of the Victory March in London made a deeper impression than the Cenotaph . . . it has been universally recognised as a just and fitting memorial to those who have made the greatest sacrifice; and the flowers which have been daily laid upon it since the march show the strength of its appeal to the imagination.[6]

By the end of July, following representations in Parliament, the decision had been taken to replace the wood and plaster structure with a permanent version in Portland stone, and despite suggestions by *The Times* and others to move it to a new location, it was decided also to retain its Whitehall siting. Lutyens himself argued strongly in favour of retaining the original site which, in his words, had been 'qualified by the salutes of Foch and the allied armies and by our men and their great leaders. No other site would give this pertinence'.[7] The temporary Cenotaph was retained as a focus for the Armistice Day commemoration in November and one year later the new permanent memorial was unveiled, at 11 a.m on 11 November 1920.[8]

Lutyens' cenotaph was to influence both the terminology and monumental form of memorialisation of many provincial towns. In numerous locations, regardless of the nature of the memorial, it was referred to as 'the cenotaph'. The same inscription - 'The Glorious Dead' - was also frequently used. In choosing the words 'The Glorious Dead' it seems clear that Lutyens intended to suggest that the dead were deserving of honour rather than to imply an idealisation of death in battle, or even, as is sometimes assumed, a glorification of war itself.[9] Furthermore, to avoid the suggestion of official appropriation in the one memorial sponsored by government, the definitive article rather than the possessive pronoun ('the' rather than 'our') was deliberately used, though elsewhere, where local communities honoured their own dead, the latter was more often preferred.

In the absence of bodies, and therefore of funerals, the erection of local war memorials and the potential for involvement in the organisation and decision-making processes of memorialisation helped considerably in the mediation of grief for the bereaved. A continuity with tradition was seen as an essential element of this process of mediation: if the war had been fought to preserve a way of life, as was claimed, it was natural that memorials, as 'sites of memory', should, in Jay Winter's words, have 'faced the past, not the future'.[10] Certainly there were well established commemorative traditions on which memorialists could draw and, both during and immediately after the war, considerable discussion around appropriate forms of memorialisation took place.

Intrinsic to the process of memorialisation was an idealisation, and as we have already seen in many cases, a sanctification of the dead. The monumental bodies of memorial sculpture became the social bodies which perpetuated memories of the dead, with the figurative statue representing for each individual mourner their own lost husband or son. The needs of post-war reconstruction and the desire to return to the pre-war status quo similarly encouraged a process of idealisation, with gender difference embodied in exemplary representations of the athletic male and maternal female.

In many communities the planning of memorials was well under way by November 1918 with designers inevitably looking for precedents to guide them. Boer War memorials provided obvious models, though the building of monuments to soldiers or sailors killed in the defence of their country did not of course originate with the war in South Africa. However, the commemoration of the dead from earlier conflicts had more usually been reserved exclusively for senior officers. One notable exception

to this is John Bell's Crimean War memorial to the Guards' Regiments at Waterloo Place in central London, the first publicly sited regimental memorial which refers to soldiers of all ranks.[11]

Memorials to officers were normally erected as funereal monuments by family members, usually in their local church. Generals and admirals were further honoured, not only by their burial in one of the national shrines, but also by the erection of public monuments. Financed by public subscription, they were an expression of civic as well as of national pride.[12] As such they provided a precedent for later communities planning monuments to the battlefield dead.

Both the public monuments and tomb sculptures for these national heroes provide the stylistic models for many First World War memorials. The iconography and composition of many memorials - at Macclesfield, Bootle, Ashton or Exeter for example - quite clearly derive from late eighteenth and early nineteenth century monuments. John Flaxman's

Pl. 205
Guards
Crimean
Memorial.
London.
John Bell,
1860

monument to Lord Nelson in St Paul's Cathedral, where the distinguished admiral is elevated above Britannia and a 'British' lion, is typical. The didacticism of Flaxman's work, with Britannia instructing two young sailor boys and, by implication, the youth of the nation, as she points towards the exalted hero, was also to have echoes in the rhetoric of subsequent memorialisation.

At the unveiling ceremony of Macclesfield's memorial, the mayor spoke of the monument as providing 'an inspiration to each and all of us, more especially the young, for them to emulate the great example set them by those men who have gone and passed away'.[13] The mayor, whose message was endorsed by the Vicar of Macclesfield writing in the local paper two weeks later,[14] was no doubt consciously echoing the words of the sculptor, John Millard, who had previously explained to the war memorial committee, including the mayor, his view of what a local community required of their war memorial:

> Something that was not merely beautiful but that would command reverence. Something that would remind the future generations - who had not felt the horrors of the terrible war as we had felt them - of all that their forbears had gone through . . . There were many beautiful monuments all over the country to-day which people only looked at and passed by, but they needed something that would arrest attention and would speak to future generations.[15]

After the Boer War, in addition to regiments and family members, local communities also erected memorials to the dead.[16] In a number of respects these provided exemplars for the memorialisation of the dead of the First World War. Firstly, it was clear that in many cases these memorials reflected a recognition of the involvement, not only of regular soldiers for whom death might be considered an occupational hazard, but of volunteers who should also, it was felt, be acknowledged as citizens. At Winsford in Cheshire, in addition to naming the six local men who had died in the South African war, those who had served and survived are also recognised and care is taken to acknowledge, and list separately, the names of volunteers and regulars.

Boer War memorials also provided a precedent in their adoption of the forms and siting of public monumental sculpture in places of civic importance which had been developed during the nineteenth century to commemorate the lives of 'great men'. Thirdly, and perhaps most significantly, they elevated (quite literally) the importance of the serviceman, depicting him as an 'ordinary' working class man.

The solitary soldier seen at Winsford was used for numerous Boer War memorials and was to reappear on even more memorials of the Great

Pl. 206
Winsford Boer
War Memorial.
Herbert Chatham,
1906

Pl. 207
Suffolk Men Boer
War Memorial,
Ipswich.
Albert Toft, 1906

Pl.208
Streatham, South
London. Albert
Toft, 1922

War. Indeed, it was by no means unusual for sculptors of later memorials to base their work on earlier solutions to Boer War memorial commissions, as for example in Albert Toft's soldier seen in five different locations (Streatham, Stone, Thornton Cleveleys, Leamington Spa and Smethwick) which was closely modelled on his previous Suffolk Men Boer War memorial at Ipswich.

With well established processes of remembrance and commemoration which could be drawn upon by communities faced with bereavement, almost from the beginning of the war local communities found ways of honouring the dead. Rolls of Honour, initially listing men who had joined the colours but later adapted to indicate those who had died, were widely produced. Plaques were placed in public buildings and places of employment and books published detailing individual companies whose workers had enlisted. At Milnrow in Rochdale, and no doubt elsewhere, a cinematic roll of honour was produced by, and shown at, the local cinema. Made a year before the end of the war, it featured a succession of still photographs of the 125 men who had lost their lives. When the town's permanent memorial was unveiled in 1924 the number listed had risen to 143.

During 1916, street shrines, listing the names of men from a single street or local area, also began to appear. Apparently originating in the

streets of a working class district of Hackney in April 1916, further examples could soon be seen throughout the country and by August cheap shrines had even been made commercially available.[17] Like the Roll of Honour, the street shrine developed from an initial concern with acknowledging enlistment rather than death. Indeed the street shrine movement can be seen as a grass roots response to the official commemorative process provided by employers, institutions and civic authorities in the more formal Roll of Honour.

That said, the shrines were very much encouraged by the clergy who helped to organise and administer services of intercession and remembrance. Services held to dedicate new shrines often attracted hundreds of people, mirroring the later unveiling of war memorials.[18] Such ceremonies were sometimes filmed and, like the Milnrow 'Roll of Honour', shown at the local cinema, as were the unveiling ceremonies of later, permanent memorials. But street shrines also provided a more intimate focus for the anxieties, and ultimately the grief, of local communities. Shrines, which frequently featured photographs of the men, were lavishly decorated with flowers and Queen Mary in 1916, on a visit to a 'mural roll of honour', added her own small bunch to the existing bouquets, an event reported in both the local and national press.

Pl. 209
'The Queen in the East End'.
Illustrated London News,
19 August 1916

233

Street shrines generally had little influence on the style and iconography of subsequent monuments, but they were in many ways to provide an important paradigm for the post-war processes and rituals of memorialisation. The visible expression of a community's patriotic support, the focus for shared grief and the privileging of women in the process of mourning were all to form crucial elements in the establishment of the local war memorial, as was their creation as sites of religious ceremony.

Few of these original shrines now remain, but in the immediate post-war period they continued to provide a focus for remembrance until replaced by more permanent memorials. Occasionally permanent memorials to very local communities were also erected after the war. On rare occasions such memorials featured figurative sculpture. One such example can be found at Dukinfield in Greater Manchester where the Victoria Street memorial, initially planned in 1917 and finally unveiled three years later, features a crudely carved soldier, produced by a local mason at a cost of £282. And in St Albans' Abbey parish, a number of stone memorials for individual streets, some plain unadorned plaques, but others with crucifix attached, were dedicated by the Bishop between 1920 and 1921 and have been carefully maintained ever since.

The significance for a small community within the larger urban body of commemorating 'its own' was generally lost in the permanent memorials erected by towns and cities, but on occasion this connection was maintained and at Portadown in Northern Ireland the listed names of the dead are grouped according to the street or neighbourhood from which they came.

The whole procedure of organisation, debate, commissioning and fund-raising formed essential elements in the production of meaning for a local community's act of memorialisation. How decisions were made, and by whom, were as important as the decisions themselves. In most communities the formation of a war memorial committee derived from the initiative of the local council. At Worthing, however, a war memorial committee was formed by the local paper, the *Worthing Gazette*, after the council's own scheme had been abandoned, this information being recorded on the memorial itself.[19] At Manchester it was the local branch of the British Legion who initiated the project.

Considerable importance was normally attached to the need to represent the views of a cross-section of the community, including the bereaved and ex-servicemen, though in some communities they were very much underrepresented or entirely absent. Committee members were usually drawn from a range of religious, civic, commercial and charitable organisations. How these members were chosen varied but the inclusion of many would normally depend on their influence or involvement in local politics. Working class men and women may have had little opportunity or confidence to be involved in the procedures. A failure, however, to adequately consult the wider population about what they saw as the most suitable form of memorialisation, or about details of imagery, siting or inscriptions, certainly led on numerous occasions to bitterness and protest.

In many locations important decisions were made at public meetings. At Macclesfield the mayor's preference for a utilitarian memorial was reversed by the wider demand for a monument. In contrast, at Lampeter in Cardiganshire, the memorial committee's decision to erect a monument was rejected by a public meeting. In this case a decision to consult the bereaved families, all of whom apparently preferred a monument, led to the committee's original suggestion being ultimately carried, the wishes of the bereaved being considered as paramount.[20] As a result, Sir William Goscombe John was appointed to provide a figurative monument.

Although memorials were sometimes financed entirely by prominent citizens they were more usually paid for by public subscription and again, as the notification of this fact on many memorials implies, this consequent conferring of communal ownership was seen as a significant aspect of their meaning for the local community. Those who contributed to the fund were usually invited to air their opinions at public meetings and thus to be a part of the decision-making process. But a willingness to contribute was sometimes dependent upon the intended form of memorialisation. At Macclesfield, the local firm of *Hovis* promised financial support, but only on condition that the money should not be spent on the erection of a monument. When a monument was in fact commissioned, the promised contribution was withdrawn.

There was of course a long tradition of raising money by public subscription for public monuments but during the war the public had become used to calls on their willingness to contribute to a wide range of war related 'good causes' and such appeals were to continue until well after the war had ended. With the economic recession of the 1920s, raising money was often difficult. Communal pride and civic rivalry were constantly brought to bear on prospective subscribers. In Macclesfield, when only £2,000 of a hoped for £10,000 had been collected, with the deadline rapidly approaching, concern was expressed that so little had been raised. Unfavourable comparisons were made with nearby Congleton, a significantly smaller town which had nonetheless been able to raise almost £5,000 towards its memorial.

Pressure for war memorials to be utilitarian rather than monumental was widespread and a variety of schemes, from memorial halls and hospital wards, cottages and recreation grounds, supplements for war widows to scholarships for the poor were suggested and considered. Not surprisingly, those with vested interests staked their claims and from as early as 1917 articles appeared in trade magazines promoting a variety of possibilities for utilitarian schemes.[21] Between December 1917 and July 1918 for example, the *Architectural Review*, stressing the need for the 'reconstruction of social life after the War', published a series of three articles entitled 'Homes of Rest: Almshouses as War Memorials'.[22]

Sculptors also promoted their own interests. William Reynolds-Stephens, in a letter to *The Times* in April 1919, stressed the enduring quality of sculpture and decried the 'utilitarian point of view':

> It should be our pride that money be devoted liberally and ungrudgingly for the needs of those mained [sic] or suffering by the war; that their children and dependents be educated and supported is essentially right, but all this should be as an act of gratitude, not as any war memorial.[23]

Such views found widespread support: in discussing the nature of Streatham's war memorial the local newspaper declaimed, 'Let utilitarianism for once stand aside and beauty take its place', adding, perhaps with some cynicism, 'homes, hospitals and the like will very soon be State supported, and the Ministry of Health in the new Socialist State to which we are gravitating will take charge of all'.[24] At Macclesfield the local newspaper's answer to the question 'What is a war memorial?' was clear. 'The only answer to this question is an object to perpetuate the memory of the fallen soldiers . . . It is not a question of the needs of the living but justice to the dead'.[25]

One concern frequently expressed about some of the suggested schemes was that the utility would have significance for only a minority of the population; an even greater concern was that lacking any direct relevance to the war the commemorative aspect would soon be forgotten. But the demand for help for ex-servicemen, both the many disabled and the increasing numbers of those unemployed and unable to afford decent housing, was less easily dismissed. One ex-soldier in Cambridge, describing himself as 'a grateful survivor', in response to the town's decision to erect a figurative sculptural memorial, wrote to the local press on behalf of the men who had fought and died to create 'a land fit for heroes' to demand decent housing rather than 'dumb effigies' as he put it.[26]

An unusual example of such provision occurred in 1918 in Lancaster where the local industrialist, Herbert Storey, donated land around his former home of Westfield House to build the Westfield

Memorial Village. Designed by the landscape architect Thomas Mawson, the village was intended to provide housing for ex-servicemen and their dependents. By 1924, when the village was formally opened by Earl Haig, thirty cottages had been built and paid for by public subscription, with more to be added over the years. At the centre of the village is a bronze statue by a local sculptor, Jennie Delahunt, of a soldier offering water to a wounded comrade, a deliberate echo perhaps of the help for ex-servicemen the larger scheme provided.

Whilst the building of a whole village may have been exceptional, many communities chose to erect memorial halls or build new hospital wards, as their surviving names continue to indicate, though it is not always clear to what commemoration the 'memorial' of their title refers. Sometimes the hall or hospital ward or almshouse was erected instead of a monumental memorial, but in very many cases money was split between monumental and utilitarian commemoration. Despite the comments of the 'grateful survivor', at Cambridge, the £13,000 raised was split between a donation for improvements to a local hospital, a memorial in Ely Cathedral listing almost 6,000 names of the fallen and a monument close to Cambridge railway station.

Pl. 210
Westfield
Memorial
Village.
Sculpture by
Jennie
Delahunt, 1924

At North Shields, £60,000 was spent on both the erection of a monument and an extension to the Tynemouth Royal Infirmary, though whilst the monument survives the hospital has now been demolished. This scenario was repeated on a smaller scale at Wallasey, where less than half of £6,000 raised was used for the town's monument, the rest going towards an extension to the Victoria Central Hospital. Again, the monument remains but the hospital does not.

Occasionally the utilitarian and the monumental were successfully combined. Stockport's war memorial takes the form of an art gallery which incorporates a memorial hall, the central feature of which is Gilbert Ledward's marble statue of Britannia with a naked warrior kneeling at her feet. An initial meeting held in February 1919 had considered the usual variety of possible schemes, including a museum, recreation grounds and the planting of an avenue of trees - one for each soldier killed. An art gallery had also been suggested and when the Borough Council received a donation of land with a proviso that it should be used to build an art gallery and exhibition space, this proposal was adopted.

The Manchester architect, Theo Halliday, was appointed and money raising began, a slow process during the post-war depression. In the meantime a temporary war memorial, a simple but carefully designed and quite substantial stone structure, was erected and unveiled in July 1921 on the boundary wall of the site of the permanent memorial.

At the suggestion of Halliday, a number of sculptors - William Reid Dick, Frederick Wilcoxson, John Cassidy, John Millard and Gilbert Ledward - were invited to submit designs for the sculpture which Halliday and the war memorial committee had, from the start, envisaged as a crucial aspect of the scheme. Each of their models was considered, anonymously, by the war memorial committee with the assistance of the former official war artist, Francis Dodd, with Gilbert Ledward's scheme being chosen as the winner. (The mayor declared Ledward's design to be 'head and shoulders above anything else shown to them').[27]

The Stockport War Memorial and Art Gallery was officially opened on 15 October 1925 by Prince Henry, the son of King George V. Below the pediment of the classical building are inscribed the words 'In Remembrance'. Few who now use the gallery are likely to notice this, or if so, to give it much thought, but on entering and immediately encountering Ledward's sculpture in the memorial hall opposite they can be left in no doubt as to the building's origins.

The art gallery is still used each year for remembrance services. The necessity of providing a focus for such ceremonies and a site of mourning for the bereaved were the main reasons for the production of monumental memorials and in those communities where memorial halls

238

or hospital wards were initially considered sufficient, monuments were often later erected to meet these needs. At an early stage in the planning of Macclesfield's memorial, one woman, a Mrs Walton Bushby, suggested that what women would require, on the anniversary of the death of their sons, was to go to the memorial to place flowers.[28]

As Mrs Bushby's words suggest, it was not only on the anniversary of the Armistice that people remembered the dead. Harry Patch, one of the last surviving combatants of the Great War, recently commented, 'My Remembrance Day is on 22nd September, when I lost three mates'.[29] In many towns this demand for a place for the bereaved to place flowers was echoed in letters to newspapers when the form of memorialisation had yet to be decided. At Merthyr Tydfil one letter writer declared,

> I am a war widow and feel very strongly on the matter. If we are to have a war memorial, let us have one that we can go and look at whenever we feel inclined and place our flowers on, as they do in every other town . . . whatever it may be, let us have it in the form of a cenotaph, so that we may look at it as we pass by, and say to ourselves that it commemorates our loved ones.[30]

Pl. 211
Stockport. Memorial Hall.
Theo Halliday, architect, 1925

The need for a suitable space for ceremony and mourning meant that the siting of monuments was frequently the subject of considerable

discussion and, on occasion, of serious disagreement. Most often, a prominent civic site was considered the best solution, usually in front of the Town Hall, on the market square or village green, or in a public park. Where a potential site had particular historical or social significance such locations were usually to be favoured. In Stanley Spencer's birthplace and home village of Cookham, the simple stone cross (the unveiling of which provided the subject of one of Spencer's best known works) was located on what was known as the 'marbles ground' where many of the dead would have played as children. At Cannock the site was chosen, in part at least, because the Market Place where the monument was erected was the place where enlistment of the town's men had first taken place. The monument built appropriately reflected the patriotic response of local men, with carved figures of proud servicemen holding a regimental flag.

In some cases the precise orientation of the memorial appears to have been used to add meaning to the imagery. At Oban, on the West coast of Scotland, Alexander Carrick's monument depicting two soldiers carrying an injured comrade is located on the shores of the loch on the outskirts of town. The figures face along the shoreline towards the centre of town and the impression is of the injured man being carried home.

On the other side of Scotland, the monument at Fraserburgh, also by Carrick, is again on the outskirts of town. At Oban the memorial depicts the aftermath of battle, with an emphasis on the suffering and compassionate comradeship of the troops, but at Fraserburgh it is the soldiers' heroism in preparation for battle which is stressed. Valour, a helmeted semi-nude figure, is guided by the cloaked figure of Justice, as he prepares for the fight ahead. The overriding validity of the soldier's fight is metaphorically suggested by Carrick in making the figure of Justice considerably larger than the figure of Valour. The soldier's bravery is encouraged by his knowledge that he has right on his side and it is the outsized Sword of Justice which he has just been handed to take into battle. Significantly, the figures here face the open sea, away from the town and towards the south and the battlefields of France and Belgium.[31]

Pl. 212
Oban.
Alexander
Carrick, 1923

In all but the largest locations the names of the dead are normally listed on the memorial. The collection of names to be included on war memorials was, like other forms of decision making, a significant aspect of the community's ownership of them. Often an advertisement would be placed in the local paper asking the relatives of those who had died to provide details to the memorial committee. At Evesham, when the production of the town's monument was close to completion, a list of the names to be inscribed on the bronze plaques to be attached to the memorial, was posted in the public library. An advertisement in the local paper asked for notification of any requests for additions, alterations or necessary modifications and spelt out the criteria for inclusion. Nonetheless, it is clear that some names were still omitted as two small plaques, each containing eleven names, have been added underneath the main panels.[32]

The inclusion of the names of the dead on war memorials was seen by most people as extremely important. This was highlighted at Worthing where more than one person who had donated money to the memorial appeal and who feared it would be merely ornamental made it clear in

Pl. 213
Fraserburgh.
Alexander
Carrick, 1923

241

letters to the local paper that they would demand their money back if names were excluded from the monument. As one local businessman wrote, 'Let every name be shown in endurable metal or stone so that the children's children of those who have fallen may have a memorial of the sacrifice of their fore fathers always before them'.[33]

The emotional impact of the listing of names was undeniable, and at those battlefield sites where tens of thousands are named - the nominal equivalent of the cemetery's vast sea of headstones - it is impossible not to be moved. At the Menin Gate almost 55,000 names are displayed on the walls of the monument, but to accommodate this number the memorial is 135 feet long by 140 feet wide and towers to a height of 80 feet. At Thiepval, the even larger Memorial to the Missing of the Somme contains over 72,000 names.[34]

The decision to include name panels necessarily affected the design of monuments. A curved wall to accomodate such panels, but also to create a precinct or sanctuary, was employed by many architects, often with a figurative monument or cenotaph at its heart. Portsmouth provides a particularly large and impressive example with both central cenotaph and carved figures by C.S Jagger flanking the entrance to the precinct. The names of literally thousands are listed on the wall behind.

In most large towns and cities the considerable space needed to display so many names would not have been available. In these cases, and in the case of regimental memorials where again thousands were being

Pl. 214
Portsmouth.
Messrs Gibson &
Gordon, architects.
Sculptures by C.S
Jagger, 1921.

commemorated, names were rarely included on the monument itself. Instead, alternative methods were used, most often Rolls of Honour or Books of Remembrance, usually, in the case of civic memorials, to be found in the Town Hall.

At Maesteg a 'Scroll of Honour' containing almost 400 names was placed in a sealed bottle in a cement chamber inside the memorial whilst the Royal Artillery memorial at Hyde Park has a Book of Remembrance buried within the structure. At some sites a readable book was incorporated into the town's memorial. At both Gateshead and Oldham, chambers were created within the base of the monuments to contain Books of Remembrance and provide spaces for people to pray.[35]

Pl. 215
Gateshead.
J.W Spink, architect.
Sculpture by Richard
Reginald Goulden,
1922

The significance of naming is emphasised in the design of a memorial at Hinckley in Leicestershire by the architect, J.A Gotch, and the sculptor, Allan Wyon. The focal point is a robed female figure with arms outstretched. Standing on top of a column in the centre of a garden, she faces a wall on which are six bronze plaques which list the names of the dead. Acting as a sundial, the statue casts a shadow in the direction of the names and at 11.00 a.m. on 11 November the shadow is said to fall exactly on the far-left-hand plaque, moving gradually across each plaque over the course of the next two hours, thereby directing attention to what is arguably the most significant aspect of the memorial's meaning.

The unveiling of memorials invariably attracted large crowds and the provision of space for ceremonies was another factor to be considered in the design of monuments. At Macclesfield, the unveiling was attended, according to the local newspaper, by as many as 20,000 people in a town with a population at the time of little more than 30,000. It was preceded by a service in the parish church at which the Lord Bishop of Chester commented on the involvement of the whole community who were 'all there in one way or another - either there in the church or in the rows of people that would wait in the streets or accompany them in the procession'.[36]

The organisation of this procession, and of the services in the church beforehand and at the memorial itself, tells us a great deal about the importance attached to the involvement of various civic, religious and

Pl. 216 and Pl.217 Hinckley. J.A Gotch , architect and Allan Wyon, sculptor, 1922

military bodies, as well as the roles of the ex-servicemen and the bereaved. The order of the procession from town hall to parish church and then to the memorial placed the greatest emphasis on civic and religious bodies with the mayor, the Lord-Lieutenent and the Lord Bishop of Chester leading the parade. Magistrates, representatives of the town council, ex-servicemen's associations and the members of various other civic and religious groups followed. Bringing up the rear were the relatives of 'the fallen' and other members of the public.

After the church service, the procession 'marched' to the memorial site where, already assembled, were further representatives of the community and the military including children from all of the elementary and secondary schools in the borough. Where the bereaved, in the church service, took quite literally 'a back seat', at the unveiling ceremony their involvement was far greater, in the laying of wreaths for example, though here too the wreaths of the mayor and civic authorities preceded theirs. The space to provide for these large numbers is incorporated into the design of Macclesfield's memorial in the Garden of Remembrance in which the monument stands. At other times the garden, of course, provides a place of quiet and contemplation.

Pl. 218
Macclesfield
Unveiling
Ceremony
1921

The appropriate forms and functions of memorialisation were widely discussed during the war. As early as 1915, Lawrence Weaver's book, *Memorials and Monuments*, served to 'focus attention on good examples, old and new', while articles in the professional journals and a series of pamphlets produced by the Civic Arts Association provided guidance for architects and builders.[37] In 1919 exhibitions of memorial designs were held at both the Royal Academy and the Victoria and Albert Museum.

The exhibition at the V & A in July was 'designed ... with the view of providing suggestions which may be of assistance to artists and the public who are interested in their promotion or execution'.[38] Amongst the artists whose work was featured were many who were to play an active role in the coming years in the production of memorial designs, including Stanley Babb, Gilbert Bayes, Percy Bentham, Harold Brownsword, Lindsey Clark, Doyle-Jones, Richard Goulden, Gilbert Ledward, Walter Marsden, Vernon March, Reynolds-Stephens, Louis Roslyn, Albert Toft and Newbury Trent.

The V & A exhibition was organised in co-operation with the Royal Academy War Memorials Committee which had been established in November 1918 to provide advice and assistance to those who wished to produce monumental memorials. Shortly afterwards the *Architectural Review* reported the committee's announcement of their aims. 'It is essential that memorials ... should express the emotion of the present and hope of the future without losing touch with the past; and that instead of being a rock of offence to future generations, they should be objects of veneration to those who follow us'.[39]

In October, the Royal Academy opened its own exhibition which again featured the work of many of the same artists to be seen at the V & A. Photographs and models of Boer War memorials by Hamo Thornycroft, Albert Toft, Doyle-Jones and others were included, as were models of First World War memorial projects already underway, including Roslyn's figure of Victory for Buxton and Ferdinand Blundstone's sketch model of the Prudential memorial. Also included, alongside tapestries, stained glass windows, plaques and Rolls of Honour, were models of Blomfield's Cross of Sacrifice and Lutyens' Cenotaph and Great War Stone, the latter described as 'the noblest work in the show'.[40]

Those who helped organise these exhibitions, and the sculptors and architects whose work they featured, were to exert a considerable influence on the decision-making process. Not only the Royal Academy but other associations such as the Arts and Craft Exhibition Society, the Civic Arts Association and the Art Workers' Guild provided advice and were willing to recommend suitable artists, whilst the Royal Institute of British Architects and the Royal Society of British Sculptors both attempted to regulate the organisation of competitions frequently held to select a memorial solution.

Members of the Royal Society of British Sculptors, which had been founded in 1904 with Sir Thomas Brock as its first President, were

Pl. 219 and
Pl.220
Beverley.
R.H Whiteing,
architect and
Vincent Hill,
sculptor, 1920

warned not to enter competitions without first checking whether it had
been organised according to the conditions the society laid down, which
included the stipulation that one of their members should act as an
assessor. The failure, or refusal, of war memorial committees to comply
with this regulation may have been one reason why ambitious local
stonemasons, without the competition of professional sculptors, were often
successful in gaining commissions. A notable case was that of W.G Storr-
Barber, a Hereford based monumental mason who received around a dozen

248

commissions for memorials as far apart as Kirkwall in the Orkneys and Plymouth on the South coast.

Many war memorials, particularly for smaller communities, were produced by local stonemasons or local architectural practices. In addition, companies such as R.L Boulton, H.H Martyn and The Bromsgrove Guild provided commemorative work throughout the country in a range of media from stained glass to bronze, and from the simplest of wall plaques (by far the most common form of war memorial) to highly ambitious monumental works.

In most places the production of war memorials was a collaborative effort involving both architects and sculptors, and often other craftspersons. The architect would most often have overall control, coordinating the contributions of others. At Beverley in Yorkshire, five different companies or individuals - masons, builders, architect, letter cutter and sculptor - were named as contributing to the scheme with the architect, R.H Whiteing in charge. The figurative sculpture here consists of four female figures representing the three branches of the armed services, plus the medical services, each one identified by the attributes they hold - ship, tank, aeroplane and Staff of Escalapius. These larger than life figures are seated on a decorative plinth beneath a tall, tapering column.

It might be assumed, given the relative simplicity and conventionality of these figures and their close integration into the overall scheme, that the sculptor, Vincent Hill, merely reproduced the design provided by the architect. However, Hill was a competent artist who had trained at the Royal College of Art under Professor Lantéri. Although the choice of subject was no doubt prescribed, he would almost certainly have expected, and was no doubt given, considerable freedom of interpretation. Similar assumptions might be made of the monument at Earl Shilton in Leicestershire though contemporary reports suggest otherwise. The memorial here was the work of Edward John Williams, a local architect, and Anthony Smith, a wood and stone carver. Both names appear on the monument which features a figure of Peace standing, somewhat awkwardly, on top of a tall, square pedestal around which are relief carvings. In newspaper reports at the time of the unveiling, whilst Williams' work was praised

Pl. 221
Mells.
Sir Edwin
Lutyens, 1920

Pl.222
Hove.
Sir Edwin Lutyens
and Sir George
Frampton, 1921

Pl.223
Fordham.
Sir Edwin Lutyens
and Sir George
Frampton, 1921

there was no mention of Smith. Presumably the assumption was that Smith was merely the interpreter of Williams' designs and therefore undeserving of special praise. This may indeed have been the case, though how detailed those designs would have been and how creative the interpretation, remain open questions.

Where sculptors of national repute were employed they would certainly have had a far greater degree of autonomy. The sculptor of the recumbent soldier who lies on top of Edwin Lutyens' cenotaph at Manchester is not recorded. (The monument was actually constructed by the Nine Elms Stone Masonry Works of London with whom Lutyens worked on more than one occasion). The concept however, we may confidently assume, was Lutyens' and the individual, or individuals, who actually carved the figure would certainly, in this case, have had limited creative input. This would certainly have been true of Lutyens' memorial at Mells in Somerset where a small, stocky, stone statue of St George, a close copy of a figure in the Henry VII chapel in Westminster Abbey, stands on top of a tall column. Lutyens used an identical scheme for his memorial at Wellington college and at both Wellington and Mells the figures were presumably carved by local masons from drawings or photographs of the original, provided by the architect.

Virtually identical columns were also used by Lutyens for memorials at Fordham and Hove, again featuring figures of St George. At these locations however, the architect collaborated with the eminent

250

sculptor, Sir George Frampton. One assumes that Lutyens requested a figure of St George, with Frampton providing a slight variation of an existing work, the architect's involvement extending no further than his approval of the sculptor's work.

Another of Lutyens' war memorials can also be found in Mells. In the church of St Andrew is a memorial in memory of Edward Horner, a Lieutenant in the 18th Hussars who died of his wounds in 1917 at the Battle of Cambrai. In this case the statue was specially commissioned. The memorial takes the form of an equestrian statue, approximately half life-size, for which Lutyens, a close friend of the Horner family, designed a white Portland stone plinth, reminiscent of his Whitehall cenotaph. Both horse and rider are appropriately at rest. The romantic image of the equestrian soldier, from a war in which such soldiering had proved largely ineffective, had some poignancy. If the efficacious employment of cavalry had ended with the Great War, so too, with the death of Edward Horner, had the Horner family line.

The statue was the work of Sir Alfred Munnings, the sculptor having been commissioned on the architect's recommendations precisely because of his expertise in equestrian portraiture. In 1918, Munnings had been attached as an official war artist to the Canadian Cavalry and had subsequently produced over forty paintings for the Canadian War Memorial Fund, including equestrian portraits. It was the exhibition of this work at the Royal Academy in 1919 which greatly increased Munnings' reputation and led not only to numerous commissions for equestrian portraits but to his election as an ARA that year. (Like Lutyens, Munnings would later become President of the Royal Academy).

The Horner memorial was however Munnings' first large scale sculptural work. Lutyens clearly believed him capable of carrying out the commission and no doubt,

Pl. 224
Horner Memorial, Mells.
Sir Edwin Lutyens and Sir Alfred Munnings, 1920

251

OSE WH
R ENGLAN
SET UP

RAYMON
FRANCIS
GEOFFRE
OLIVER
STANLEY
EDGAR

as a friend of the painter, knew (or at least knew of) his initial foray into sculpture, a small statuette of a friend's horse. Despite Lutyens' confidence in Munnings' sculptural talents, he was to remain a painter, producing only one other major three-dimensional work, a commission from the Jockey Club, for a statue of the racehorse 'Brown Jack'. This is surprising as the Horner memorial shows him as a sculptor of some talent.

Pl. 225 *opposite* Horner Memorial. Mells. Sir Alfred Munnings, 1920

The lieutenant is presented as a self-assured cavalryman. Munnings was an expressive painter of people as well as of horses, but here the rider's mask-like facial features, no doubt intended to suggest a calm and undemonstrative character, seem less confidently handled than the modelling of the horse which is particularly impressive. Overall, this is a finely crafted work and in his depiction of the young soldier in confident command of his horse, Munnings reveals his own assurance in the handling of his first sculptural commission.

The seemingly insatiable demand for war memorials in the immediate post-war period undoubtedly provided great opportunities for sculptors. A review in *Studio* of the Royal Scottish Academy's 1920 exhibition suggested that 'with the present day demand for war memorials, sculptors have not had the leisure necessary to do work that does not belong to this class'.[41] The article clearly implied the employment on war memorial commissions as a regrettable necessity which deprived the creative artist of opportunities for more self-expressive work. Most sculptors however did not have the luxury of working at leisure and most would have welcomed these opportunities to earn a living.

The Scottish sculptor, Pilkington Jackson, not one whose work was reviewed in the *Studio* article though he was a regular exhibitor at the Academy, was typical of the largely unknown journeyman sculptor who benefited from these opportunities. Charles d'Orville Pilkington Jackson, was actually born in Cornwall (in 1887) but was brought up in Edinburgh. He was a student of the Edinburgh College of Art where he later taught. Between 1919 and 1926 Pilkington Jackson, who had served in the Artillery during the war, contributed to over fifty war memorial projects, most notably for the Scottish National War Memorial in Edinburgh where he was the supervising sculptor.

Sometimes merely submitting rejected schemes (at Kirkcudbright and Denny for example), sometimes providing decorative carving or lettering on memorials for which other sculptors provided the central image, and often producing relatively simple wall plaques for churches, colleges, banks and individuals, most of his work remains unrecognised, and in truth unremarkable. By far his most impressive work was his depiction of contemporary soldiers at Alloa; less impressive his allegorical figures at a number of other sites. His contributions to memorial schemes

is often signalled by distinctive lettering, seen at Alloa and repeatedly used elsewhere, most notably throughout the National Memorial in Edinburgh.

For projects in villages and small towns a local mason would most often be employed without contest; for larger towns with more prestigious schemes (and more money) sculptors of greater renown would be commissioned, whether directly, as the result of reputation or recommendation, or as the winner of a competition. Whilst they frequently drew on the expertise of others, particularly in the design of pedestal or plinth, such sculptors were employed precisely because of proven skills and usually on the basis of presented designs. Whilst initial submissions may have been in the form of drawings, a sketch model or maquette would certainly be required once the commission had been granted. Most of these maquettes were later destroyed but a few have been retained, for example one of C.S Jagger's models for Portsmouth's memorial or Goscombe John's at Port Sunlight. Occasionally they are exhibited. Gilbert Ledward's model for the Stockport memorial is on show in the Memorial Hall in close proximity to the finished statue. A comparison of the model and the finished work reveals subtle alterations in the latter - the turn of the head from left to right, the replacement of a palm leaf for a wreath in Britannia's left hand and an accentuation of the folds in her cloak which consequently all but obscures the patterning of the Union Jack, clearly shown on the original maquette.

Original models were also often cast in bronze and exhibited at the Royal Academy and other venues. Again such models are occasionally on permanent display. Vernon March's three figures for Londonderry's memorial, exhibited at the Royal Academy in 1927 (and the figure of the sailor at the Walker Art Gallery that same year) are now, for example, proudly displayed in St Columb's Cathedral in the city.[42.]

Frequently changes would be suggested by war memorial committees which most sculptors would attempt to accommodate. At Macclesfield John Millard produced a second model when the suitability of the first was questioned. Millard was typical of the little known professional sculptor employed by most memorial committees. Born in Wigan in 1874 he had attended art schools in Warrington and Manchester before moving to Paris where he studied, and later taught, at the École des Beaux Arts. On his return to England he took a teaching post at Dover School of Art before, in 1905, becoming Principal Master of the Modelling School at

Pl. 226
Model for Stockport Memorial.
Gilbert Ledward

Manchester School of Art. He was to remain there until he retired in 1939.

Although described by a colleague as a 'modeller... rather than a sculptor' and as was then standard practice, teaching a syllabus with a heavy emphasis on modelling, Millard also taught a course in marble carving and a supplementary course in the history of sculpture.[43] In addition he gave lessons in anatomy at Manchester University's Medical School, his lectures including a practical course in the dissection of the human body. Little else is known of him except that he had, before the war, exhibited occasionally at the Royal Academy and regularly in Paris where he had been elected as a member of the French Academy.

Millard's memorial for Macclesfield is impressive, and though conventional in style is, in one respect at least, unusual. Although the reality of death on the field of battle lies at the heart of memorialisation, the actual depiction of death is relatively uncommon. In showing the soldier grasping a gas mask, implying the manner of his death, Macclesfield's memorial is exceptional.[44] Although Millard was asked to submit his designs for the competition for Stockport's war memorial he was unsuccessful and despite the quality of the Macclesfield memorial this seems to have been his only First World War memorial commission

Many artists undoubtedly had a favoured approach - Goulden's protective warriors, the March Brothers' flamboyant allegories, Tyson Smith's figures of mourning are obvious examples - and such schemes would no doubt be offered by them at every opportunity. And no doubt too sculptors would often be commissioned precisely because of their known predilection for a particular approach which chimed with a memorial committee's preference.

When choosing an artist or craftsman (other than the obvious local provider), war memorial committees frequently relied upon local suggestions, as at Macclesfield where John Millard was recommended by the head of the Macclesfield School of Art who had known him from his student days when both had studied together in Paris. Where particular artists had close connections with a town (often their birthplace) they were frequently asked to provide the memorial. Examples include Ferdinand Blundstone at Stalybridge, Harold Brownsword at Hanley, Derwent Wood at Keswick, Richard Goulden at Dover and John Angel at Exeter.

Pl. 227
Model for
Londonderry
Memorial.
Vernon March

Occasionally the war memorial committee would approach the local art school not merely for their recommendations but as prospective designers of the memorial, even for quite prestigious commissions. At Sheffield, the York and Lancaster Regiment commissioned the Sheffield Technical School of Art (Jagger's old art school) to produce their memorial in Weston Park to the 8,814 men of the regiment who had died. Designed by one of the students, Roy Smith, with the assistance of other students and a lecturer, it featured two servicemen poised for action, an officer with pistol in hand (by Smith) and a private with sleeves rolled up (by another student, George Morewood). They stand at the base of a tall obelisk, topped by a figure of Victory (the work of the lecturer, Francis Jahn). Perhaps encouraged by their success here, Smith and Jahn also entered the competition for Sheffield's municipal memorial, coming third out of an entry of thirty-four.

Occasionally the commissioning process seemed remarkably informal. The memorial at West Allotment on the outskirts of Newcastle is a stone figure of a Victory holding a wreath and a flag and was apparently designed by a local schoolboy who was asked to draw the figure with the promise of the payment of ten shillings (which it seems he never received).[45]

Sir George Frampton, the designer and sculptor of numerous First World War memorials, was also a member of the Royal Academy's Executive Committee on War Memorials and as such played a major role in recommending others for commissions. Frampton, whose son Meredith had served in the Artists' Rifles, was particularly sympathetic to the employment of those who had actually fought in the war.

> If we would truly commemorate the men who gave their lives for us, let us call for the work on those who saw those lives surrendered ... To them, far more than to us older men whom they have enabled to see the war through comfortably in our studios, must come the artistic vision we need.[46]

In an article published in April 1919 he referred to 'our soldier-sculptors, the artists who have fought, the craftsmen who have shaken hands with death', mentioning by name such 'brilliant men' as Gilbert Ledward, C.S Jagger, W. Reid Dick, J. Wilkinson, A.F Hardiman, J. MacDougald and R. Goulden.[47] Like other members of the Royal Academy War Memorial Committee, Frampton was to provide advice and recommendations to numerous committees, including recommending the employment of Charles Sargeant Jagger at both Hoylake and Bedford, and Richard Goulden for the Bank of England.

During the war however, Frampton had also been involved in denying the employment of one prominent sculptor, Jacob Epstein. Epstein

had applied to become an official war artist. Despite desperate attempts to avoid conscription he had by this time (1918) received his call-up papers and was waiting, with some trepidation, to be sent to France. His appointment as war artist appeared to be going ahead until a letter from Frampton, apparently objecting to Epstein's employment, was received by the War Office who promptly cancelled the expected commission. As the letter was subsequently removed from the files and has never been found it is difficult to know exactly what Frampton might have said to have convinced the War Office of his unsuitability, though it is likely that he was not alone in having reservations. The Major-General to whose unit he was to have been attached, on being told of the cancellation, apparently commented, 'Much relieved about Epstein'.[48]

Jacob Epstein was an extremely controversial, not to say notorious artist whose provocatively modernist work was the antithesis of Frampton's own and there was clearly no love lost between the two men. Frampton had previously intervened in a controversy about Epstein's employment when, in 1917, it had been suggested that Epstein might be asked to produce a

Pl. 228
York & Lancaster
Regt Memorial.
Sheffield.
George Morewood,
Francis Jahn and Roy
Smith, 1923

257

memorial to Lord Kitchener who had recently been lost at sea. The council of the Royal Society of British Sculptors had privately expressed concerns and suggested that, in justice to sculptors then serving at the front, no commissions should be given until after the war's end. Furthermore, they suggested, such a commission should be 'executed by a sculptor of purely British descent'.[49] (Epstein, although a naturalised Briton, had been born in the United States). Frampton, who was a past president of the society, wrote to *The Times* to warn of foreign sculptors being allowed to 'suck the juice from the grape' as he put it, 'leaving but the dry husk to the men of our race, whose development we have watched with such pride and pleasure'.[50]

Frampton's intervention in Epstein's employment as a war artist has been seen by some as professional jealousy, though given his earlier intervention he may well have objected, with more than a hint of anti-Semitism, to Epstein, as a 'foreigner', being employed. It is also likely that a major concern was that those who were to be appointed as official war artists should have had front line experience, like Ledward and Jagger, the two sculptors who *were* appointed.

He would also have been very aware of Epstein's widely reported attempts to avoid 'doing his duty' - of being 'swept into the oblivion of military training for which I am altogether unfitted' as Epstein himself put it.[51] This no doubt rankled and may well have been the core of Frampton's objections to Epstein's employment. '[The] returning soldiers', he had noted in 1919, 'deserve better at our hands than those who stayed at home'.[52] In the event, Epstein, on the eve of his transfer to fight in the Middle East, suffered a nervous collapse and was subsequently invalided out of the army.

Had Epstein been engaged as an official war artist he might, after the war, have expected to receive commissions for memorials, though it also seems likely that Frampton's antagonism, not only to Epstein but to his work, would have been shared by others and certainly, one imagines, by a majority of conventionally minded war memorial committee members. There was little room for avant-garde artists in memorialisation and Epstein, predictably, remained unemployed on the design and production of First World War memorials.[53]

X

Memory and Mourning

$\mathbf{M}$ost discussion, both during and immediately after the war, had assumed, as for previous campaigns, an essentially commemorative function for war memorials - a recording of the victory won and an acknowledgement of the sacrifice made by those who had 'given their lives'. The Royal Academy's war memorial committee had suggested that 'our war memorials should express the ideals fought for by the free nations of the world'.[1] This belief was echoed frequently over the years and engraved on the sides of many monuments, with occasional bitterness. At Brierley Hill the memorial is dedicated to those men who 'loyally gave their lives in defence of country and civilisation against the aggressive ambitions of Germany, Austria and Turkey'. At Burton-upon-Trent reference is made to 'the victory of honour and freedom over terror and oppression'.

It was frequently argued that war memorials were primarily for the common soldier and that their needs should therefore be uppermost in the minds of monument builders. In an editorial in the *Daily Mirror* in July 1918 the concern was expressed that this might not prove to be the case.

> Let us try to make our memorials of some comfort, in use or
> beauty, to the suffering men who will be left by the war: the
> wounded, the maimed, the permanently incapacitated. These men -
> to whom we owe all - will feel very bitter if they hear that a huge
> sum is to be wasted in a piece of emphasis in stone, or in yet
> another successful attempt to ruin one of the public parks where
> they go for rest and forgetfulness.[2]

The editorial was not necessarily opposed to the erection of monuments but was certainly concerned with their possible appearance, as a cartoon in the paper two days later emphasised.

The idea that war memorials were primarily intended for the returning soldier was also underlined in the planning and construction of Lutyens' Cenotaph. Intended as a saluting point for the troops in the

Pl. 229
'The War
Memorial: Will it
be like this?'
W.K Haselden.
Daily Mirror,
11 July 1918

'Peace Day' procession on 19 July 1919, it provided an opportunity for those who had survived to pay their respects to their fallen comrades. Such was its popularity, with photographs of the Cenotaph forming the focus of the following day's newspaper reports, that it was retained for the commemoration in November of the first anniversary of 'Armistice Day' and then replaced, a year later, by the present permanent stone monument.

It was on 11 November 1919 that much of the familiar ritual of Remembrance Day was initiated and it was at this time that the two minutes silence was introduced. The silence was on the recommendation of Sir Percy Fitzpatrick who, as High Commissioner in South Africa during the war, had been impressed by the observance there of a 'three minute pause' each day at noon. He suggested that a universally observed silence at eleven o'clock on 11 November would be an appropriate expression of the feelings of the people.

It is possible that Fitzpatrick was also influenced by a letter published in the *London Evening News* some months earlier, on 8 May 1919, written by an Australian journalist, Edward George Honey. Honey had served during the war in a British regiment before being discharged due to ill health and was now living in England. In his letter he suggested a five minutes silence.

There was no official response to this but on 27 October 1919 Fitzpatrick's suggestion was sent to King George V's private secretary, Lord Stamfordham. The King was evidently moved by the idea of a silence, but with a reduction of time from three minutes to just two, and on 7 November he issued a proclamation.

> At the hour when the Armistice came into force, the 11th hour of the 11th day of the 11th month, there may be for the brief space of two minutes a complete suspension of all our normal activities ... so that in perfect stillness, the thoughts of everyone may be concentrated on reverent remembrance of the glorious dead.[4]

The appeal of the silence rested on its dual nature as both public and private commemoration. The silence produced a visibly united response, in part enforced perhaps by a fear of shame at not complying, but at the same time it was intensely private; each person was alone with his or her thoughts for those two minutes. Fitzpatrick was clear about the aims of the silence: while intended to have a pedagogic role, particularly for children, and to be a tribute to veterans and to the dead, first and foremost it was for the bereaved.[5]

Its impact was considerable. As *The Times* reported, 'In the great awful silence that fell upon London's streets yesterday there was a glimpse into the soul of the nation ... the best tribute to the genuineness of the moments was to be seen in the bowed heads and streaming eyes of all too many men'.[6] The Cenotaph provided the focus for mourning ritual.

> A large proportion of the people here were wearing mourning, very many brought wreaths in memory of a fallen loved one, and some of these, despairing of ever getting near enough to deposit their wreaths raised them above their heads and they were passed from hand to hand over the heads of the people until they found a resting place at the foot of the Cenotaph.[7]

The significance for the bereaved of the two minutes silence and the obvious importance of the laying of wreaths meant that the following year they were given a much more prominent role in the Remembrance Day ritual. The published plans of the organisation of people in the area around the Cenotaph, which was officially unveiled in 1920, show that representatives of the bereaved were given extensive space and prominent positions.[8]

The ceremony that year was reinforced by the reinterment of the 'Unknown Warrior' in Westminster Abbey, where the bereaved, and particularly women, were again specifically catered for. Because of limited space in the Abbey, places were allocated firstly to those women who had lost a husband *and* a son; secondly to mothers who had lost all their sons or an only son; and thirdly to any other widows. Others, including fathers, were selected by ballot from applications received.

The idea of returning to England the body of an unknown serviceman to be buried with full military honours - a symbolic burial to represent all those lost on the battlefields with no known grave - first occurred to the Reverend David Railton in 1916 while serving as a padre on the Western Front. During the war he had written to Haig suggesting the idea but had received no reply. In August 1920 he wrote again, this time to Bishop Ryle, the Dean of Westminster Abbey, who approvingly passed on his suggestion to the government.

The actual tomb, topped by a simple marble slab on the floor of the Abbey, was less important than the ritual of selection and transportation and the idea that this unknown soldier could be anyone's husband or son. (And, one might add, for the Church, disappointed at the secular nature of Lutyens' Cenotaph, the siting of this memorial in Westminster Abbey had additional significance).[9]

For many days crowds queued, literally for miles, to place wreaths at the foot of the Cenotaph and to file past the tomb of the Unknown Warrior. The *Daily Mirror* reported this phenomenon:

> By 4 o'clock Whitehall presented an amazing scene, unparalleled in the history of London. From end to end it was one solid mass of slowly moving queues, passing in maze-like fashion up and down until they reached the object of their pilgrimage ... The Cenotaph is now lost in a mass of flowers.[10]

Within four days it was estimated that more than one million people had visited the Cenotaph and as many as 100,000 wreaths had been laid there, 'piled one on the other to a height of nearly ten feet'.[11] This reaction, a natural extension of the wartime ritual of placing flowers on street shrines (and on the 1918 Hyde Park shrine), encouraged a much broader view of the role of the war memorial which was to be incorporated into the production of provincial monuments.

Pl. 230
Liverpool.
G.H Tyson
Smith, 1930

Similarly the ritual and rhetoric which accompanied the commemoration of Armistice Day in 1919 and the unveiling of the permanent Cenotaph the following year were inevitably to influence the unveiling ceremonies and remembrance services held at provincial sites. The needs of the bereaved and the wider implications of the war's effects on communities had to be recognised. War memorials were to provide not only a commemoration and validation of military victory and of the bravery and sacrifice of the troops, but, of equal, if not greater importance, a site for the memories and mourning of the bereaved. In the design of many memorials there is a clear acknowledgement of their intended function.

Liverpool's cenotaph, as we have already seen, illustrates the act of mourning and the ritual of remembrance. The sculptor, George Herbert Tyson Smith, utilised the horizontality of the long bronze frieze which fills the front of the monument to depict two rows of mourners converging from left and right to place their wreaths and floral tributes on the central 'altar stone'. Carved above the relief are the words, 'To the men of Liverpool who fell in the Great War' and below it, 'And the victory that day was turned into mourning unto all the people'. Tyson Smith's mourners include men, women and children, and behind them can be seen row upon row of war cemetery headstones.[12] At the unveiling ceremony on Armistice Day 1930, wreaths were laid not only by the Lord Mayor and by Lord Derby on behalf of the British Legion, but also by a procession of widows and orphans, just as depicted on the memorial itself.

Figures of mourning can be found on numerous First World War memorials, though more usually in allegorical form rather than in contemporary dress. An exception is the serviceman with head solemnly bowed and rifle reversed, an image of the soldier both remembering and being remembered, which seemed particularly apt and was much deployed.[13] Albert Toft was one sculptor who adopted this approach, the same statue, a reworking of an earlier Boer War memorial figure at Ipswich, being used at various sites including Streatham, Stone and Thornton Cleveleys. Its first use, at Stone

in Staffordshire, in a memorial unveiled in January 1921, was criticised for showing the soldier as bareheaded as this was contrary to Army rules. Toft replied: 'The figure is the actual representation of what actually happened daily at the front, where a soldier coming across the grave of a fallen comrade has reverently taken off his hat and stood silently and reverently reflecting on his loss and the utter tragedy of war'.[14]

The bareheaded soldier was sometimes used by others but the serviceman in mourning is more often shown in a more formal pose. Wynn Owen's memorial at Euston to the men of the London and North Western Railway Company places four servicemen at each corner of a tall obelisk, exactly mimicking the frequent placing of living soldiers at remembrance services.[15] Wynn Owen was the chief architect of the LNWR and the figures were provided for him by R.L Boulton and Sons of Cheltenham. One of these figures was reused at Whitchurch in South Glamorgan and very similar figures by other sculptors can be seen in other locations. In most of these cases however, where the figure is shown in isolation on a raised plinth, some of the impact of four soldiers placed at each corner of a monument is undoubtedly lost.

The figure of the returned serviceman mourning his lost comrades is in many ways a more complex image than the depiction of the active front-line soldier who represents the absent dead. As a member of the victorious armed forces he is the deserved recipient of the country's gratitude and honour. But he is also a representative of the bereaved; he too has lost friends and frequently relatives. The allegorical figure of mourning symbolically denotes the grief and loss of millions but the realistic image of the surviving serviceman in mourning makes a more specific connection and reminds us of the wider tragedy for both those who fought and for whom they fought. The depiction of those who survived drawing attention to those who did not must have been particularly affecting for those who mourned lost loved ones.

Pl. 231
LNWR memorial
Euston Station,
London.
R. Wynn Owen,
1921

The laying of wreaths is regularly featured in war memorial sculpture. Sometimes the wreath is placed onto the head or body of a soldier, as at Macclesfield, but also onto the memorial itself in emulation of the ritual processes of remembrance. At Stourbridge, John Cassidy's allegorical figure, placed high up on top of a tall pedestal, stoops down and leans forward as if to place at the base of the monument the wreath held in her outstretched hand. More specifically, we may imagine it placed onto any one of the men whose names are listed on the front of the pedestal.

In similar fashion at Burnley, a female figure is shown in the act of placing a wreath onto the monument. Two women stand to the left and right of a twenty feet high cenotaph, one identified as 'the mother', the other as 'sister or wife'. The top of the stone structure is transformed into the carved heads and torsos of three men - soldier, sailor and airman - at whom the 'sister or wife' gazes in sadness, but also in admiration of their valour. The mother places her wreath at the foot of the monument. In the unveiling ceremony booklet it was explained that the memorial was

> Intended to express the emotion felt in the human heart at the ideals of those who have fallen in the Great War. The mother, overwhelmed in this emotion, places a wreath in memory of her son at the foot of the Cenotaph, and, as she stoops, the Cenotaph shapes itself in her heart into the features of her son ... To the sister or the wife bringing garlands and the palm of victory, the memory of the courage and prowess of the man fills her heart. She rejoices with shining eyes that her man was a man amongst men.[16]

The need to provide space for those who visited memorials to remember and grieve informed the design of a majority of monuments. Like many others, Macclesfield's war memorial is located in a small 'Garden of Remembrance' which is an essential element of the commemorative scheme, providing an area not only to accomodate the annual assembly but also for quiet meditation. In addition to the figure of Britannia, who stoops to place a wreath upon the head of the fallen

Pl. 232
Stourbridge.
John Cassidy,
1923

soldier, a third figure, who also holds a wreath and who represents 'grief and remembrance', stands on a tall pedestal gazing down at those below.

When the memorial was unveiled in 1921, this figure was described as 'symbolic of the wife, mother, sister and sweetheart who suffered in silent agony, alone and without complaint'.[17] As such she is central to the meaning of the monument. Her dominant position, physically separate and placed high above the other two figures, defines her as both mourner and spectator. Her bowed head is a sign both of deep sorrow and of observation of the scene below. Like the actual mourners around the monument she is lost in her own memories but is also witness to the ritual of remembrance intended to give meaning to her loss. Her dignified act of reverence provides an example for the bereaved spectators. Seen from a distance it is this figure we initially notice, silhouetted against the sky, and this prominence underlines the significance of the memorial as a site of mourning.

Pl. 233
Burnley.
Walter Gilbert,
1926

Pl. 234
(opposite)
Macclesfield.
John Millard,
1921

Figures such as these, whether intended as grieving widows or as more generalised personifications of mourning or sorrow, became popular during the eighteenth and nineteenth centuries on funerary monuments. Macclesfield's classically garbed figure is particularly reminiscent of Antonio Canova's well known statue from his funerary monument to *Maria Christina of Austria*, subsequently much copied, and indeed reused by Canova himself. Examples of similar figures of mourning exist throughout the country on war memorials as well as tombs.

Lindsey Clark's memorial at Southwark features relief carvings around the sides of the plinth on which an advancing soldier stands, and one of these reliefs shows a figure of mourning not dissimilar to John Millard's figure in the round at Macclesfield. Like her, the head is deeply bowed, the hood obscuring her expression of sorrow which her posture nonetheless elegantly implies. The symbolism of the small child at her feet, who reaches out towards a now badly weathered dove of peace, underlines the martial nature of this particular commemoration. The woman was said to represent 'the grief of the present generation' and the child, 'the hope of assumed peace of future generations'.[18]

Similarly, William Reid Dick's figure of mourning on the memorial at Bushey in Hertfordshire shows, like those at Macclesfield and Southwark, the woman in loose robes and with her hand raised to her chin in the conventional gesture of sorrow. Like the Macclesfield figure, in her other hand she holds a wreath.[19] At nearby Rickmansworth, the same sculptor provided two figures, again carved in stone, at either end of a cenotaph, the dates 1914 and 1918 engraved above their heads. Here the figure representing the end of war holds aloft a wreath of honour. It is her counterpart who appears to be in mourning. Perhaps intended merely to express sadness at the departure of the troops, she can also be seen to be expressing sorrow for the anticipated losses.

Pl. 235
Southwark.
Philip
Lindsey
Clark, 1922

268

Pl. 236
Rickmansworth.
William Reid
Dick, 1921

Pl. 237 *left*
Bushey.
William Reid
Dick, 1922

Pl. 238 *right*
Church. Walter
Marsden, 1923

Two allegorical, draped females by Walter Marsden, both identified as representing Peace, could equally, and perhaps more readily, be seen as figures of mourning. At Heywood near Rochdale, in front of a simple stone cenotaph, the bronze figure, holding a sprig of laurel, bows her head in sorrow. At Church, Marsden's home town, she again has a sorrowful expression, but with her arms outstretched along the top of the small stone cenotaph, she more unusually raises her head to the heavens.

A variation of the figure in mourning was produced at Todmorden in West Yorkshire where small children took on this role in an unusual monument by Gilbert Bayes. Here the memorial takes the form of an ornamental fountain, with a marble statue of St George in the centre. The saint is supported by allegorical figures carved in low relief around the sides of a rectangular pillar, very similar to his earlier, considerably smaller monument at Hythe where the carvings around the plinth show a continuous procession of servicemen. As at Todmorden, this memorial was originally a fountain, though it is no longer used as such, the basin now being filled instead with flowers.[20]

In the garden at Todmorden, some distance in front of the fountain, were two statues of cherubic children with heads bowed and holding wreaths. Placing them amongst the assembed mourners at remembrance ceremonies should have produced a particularly poignant effect. However, the dual nature of the monument, as both fountain and memorial, as though to provide an alternative future purpose for when memory may have faded, underlines its essentially ornamental nature. The cherubs are consequently too easily seen merely as additional decorative feature - or more accurately, would have been seen, as these figures were recently stolen.[21]

The Liverpool sculptor, Herbert Tyson Smith, frequently chose the theme of mourning in his designs for war memorials. Born in 1883, he lived and worked in Liverpool all his life and the majority of his memorials are in the Merseyside area. On leaving school he had been apprenticed as a letter cutter and had attended evening classes in clay modelling, stone carving and plaster casting at Liverpool College of Art. During the war he had served as a gunsmith in the Royal Flying Corps.

Pl. 239 and Pl. 240 Todmorden. Gilbert Bayes, 1924

271

Tyson Smith was essentially an architectural stone carver and he was to form a close association with Liverpool University's School of Architecture, a number of whose graduates, such as H.C Bradshaw, the first Rome Scholar in Architecture and designer of the Guards' Division memorial in London, were to make significant contributions to the design of war memorials. The Roscoe Professor of Architecture at Liverpool since 1904 was Charles Herbert Reilly and when, after the war, Reilly was commissioned to produce a memorial for Accrington, Tyson Smith was appointed as sculptor. Reilly was later to be an assessor and adjudicator for the competition for Liverpool's city memorial, won by Lionel Budden, another graduate of the School of Architecture. Again Tyson Smith was to provide the sculptural elements.

If the relief panels on the Liverpool war memorial were Tyson Smith's most prestigious and best known work, both stylistically and materially (being bronze casts) they were also atypical. As a stone carver, Tyson Smith's work elsewhere is far more typical of his usual approach. He was at his best when his work became an integral part of an architectural scheme in the form of reliefs or figures backed against pillars or obelisks. When placed on top of columns, at Bangor-is-y-Coed or Fleetwood for example, his figures in the round can seem uncertain in conception and heavy-handed in execution.

At Southport, next to Liverpool arguably his most important commission, relief panels of some assurance provide meaning to the scheme but are intentionally subordinate to the architecture. Taking the form of two classical, colonnaded pavilions with a tall, central obelisk, the monument dominates the junction of Neville Street and Lord Street, the town's main thoroughfare. Southport's imposing memorial was designed by the architectural firm of Grayson, Barnish and McMillan. The impact is entirely architectural with the sculptor's contributions very much subsidiary elements in the overall scheme.

Tyson Smith's willingness to assume a subordinate role was alluded to by Budden when commenting on his plans for Birkenhead's memorial, which he also designed and for which the sculptor again provided the carved panels. 'As the occasion has appeared emphatically not to be one for the employment of flamboyant and restless sculpture ... these figures alone are introduced into the design and are intended to be given a restrained and dignified treatment'.[22] The sculptor's contribution here was

Pl. 241
Accrington.
Herbert Tyson
Smith, 1922

272

two relief panels, again of figures of mourning. One holds both a wreath and a palm leaf, the other a plaque to the 'Next of Kin', engraved with the words 'He Died for Freedom and Honour'.

Tyson Smith was typical of the many architectural sculptors who, were it not for the war, would have remained largely unknown, earning a fairly steady but possibly precarious living in an age when the fashion was increasingly for relatively unembellished buildings. The demand for memorials after the war meant however that his work, at a number of locations, took centre stage.

At Accrington, Professor Reilly produced a tall obelisk, flanked for half its height by Ionic pilasters topped by classical urns. At the front of the monument is Tyson Smith's figure of mourning, holding, at arm's length by her side, a large palm leaf encircled by a wreath. Clearly inspired by Archaic Greek sculpture, the rigid, decoratively stylised treatment of the hair and the distinctive zig-zag pattern of the pleats of the drapery are features we see again in carvings by Tyson Smith for war memorials at Bangor, Wavertree, Birkenhead and the Liverpool Post Office. The Post Office memorial, again produced in conjunction with Professor Reilly, was of a seated figure of Britannia. It too can be seen as a figure of mourning and has indeed been identified as a personification of Grief.

In echoing those who attend memorial ceremonies, the figure of mourning provides a visual and conceptual link between the real and the representational. This signalling of the presence of the spectator is evident on numerous memorials. An unusual and subtle example of this can be found at Glasgow where the city's First World War memorial, designed by the architect Sir John Burnet, with sculpture by Ernest Gillick, takes the

Pl. 242
Glasgow
Sir J.Burnett,
architect and
Ernest Gillick,
sculptor, 1924

Pl. 243
Glasgow
Ernest
Gillick, 1924

form of a Lutyens-like cenotaph in front of which is placed a stone altar. The space in front of the cenotaph is incorporated into the scheme by an enclosing wall with seating and two stone lions on either side. In the centre of this space is a large horizontal slab on which is carved a wreath and a symbolic palm leaf.

Burnet originally proposed for this slab to be seven feet below ground level to create a vault with steps leading down to it, though this was not in fact allowed for safety reasons. The memorial committee had suggested, as a compromise, placing a railing around the vault which Burnet rejected. His intention was to encourage the spectator who approaches the cenotaph to look down at the slab and in so doing to bow the head as if in respect to the dead, a symbolism which remains but which, without the lowered slab intended (and even arguably with it), is perhaps too subtle to be recognised by most visitors to the monument.

The narrativity which I have suggested is an element, to a greater or lesser extent, of almost all memorials, frequently encourages the spectator's engagement with the monument. In some cases the full meaning is only evident through the viewer's movement, as if to reinforce the temporality of the narrative and of the experience of war. At Liverpool, Blackpool, Harrogate and Bolton, contrasting views of beginning and end are presented on opposite sides of the memorial; at St Anne's-on-Sea we follow a continuous narrative around the memorial, while at Port Sunlight we are presented with a complex arrangement of figures whose own movement is visible only through our own.

Albert Toft's large memorial for Oldham depicts a group of soldiers who stealthily work their way around a rocky outcrop, slowly spiralling upwards until one stands defiantly on top. The effect is of a single soldier's movement shown in sequence or, more symbolically, of the army's (and the country's) eventual attainment of success, a literal illustration of a rise to dominance and ultimate victory.

Pl. 244
Oldham.
Albert Toft,
1922

Many other memorials are however essentially frontal, with some presenting a direct reflection of their ritual function. L.S Merrifield's monument at Merthyr Tydfil signals, more obviously than most, an awareness of and response to the spectator's involvement in the ritual enacted before it. Reminiscent of a 'sacra conversazione', the three figures, a miner with his lamp, a mother and small child wrapped together in her shawl, and a Madonna-like central figure look down at, and gesture towards, the front of the monument, on which is carved an acknowledgement of gratitude to the dead and against which wreaths will be placed.

Contemporary comments suggest that the outstretched arms of the miner and the mother may originally have held garlands, now missing, as though being placed on the monument, though it may simply have been intended for them to hold actual wreaths placed there by mourners. Either way they both draw our attention to the memorial's acknowledgement of sacrifice and encourage our involvement in the ritual of remembrance.

The distinction made, in the use of materials, between the figural and architectonic elements of the memorial reinforces the suggestion of the figures as witnesses to the ritual. They occupy the same space as us and therefore seem separate from the monument itself. This same distinction is made at Port Sunlight where the bronze figures are arranged around the central stone cross as though around a pre-existent war memorial or village cross. So too in those memorials where bronze effigies of soldiers in mourning stand at the four corners of a stone column or cross.

And again, at Burnley, the dark, free-standing bronze figures placed at ground level are separate from, and occupy a different space to that of the contrastingly white stone cenotaph, a space clearly shared with the spectator who shares also the acts of reverence and remembrance. The implication here is that, like the figures whose memory and visualisation of lost sons, husbands or brothers is literally illustrated, we too remember and see lost loved ones in *our* mind's eye.

War memorials, by their very nature, encourage the act of remembering, providing a focus both for individual, private recollections, and for public, communal and politically shaped processes of commemoration. The word 'memory' is inscribed on many memorials: 'In Honoured Memory ...'; 'To the Glorious Memory ...'; 'In Proud Memory of Those Who Gave Their Lives'. At Broadstone in Dorset, an attractive memorial by Gilbert Bayes, with an inscription, 'To the Memory of the Officers and

Pl.245
Broadstone.
Gilbert Bayes, 1920

Pl. 246
opposite
Merthyr Tydfil.
L.S Merrifield, 1931

276

Men of Broadstone District Who Fell in the War', has, as its main figurative focus, a female figure of mourning, identified as the personification of 'Memory'. Those whom she remembers and to whom the memorial is dedicated are represented at the base of the column on which she stands.

The promise to remember is intoned at annual services of remembrance and the regular gatherings of men, women and children is evidence of the will to continue to remember. The two minutes silence, continued to this day, serves, as the French historian Pierre Nora puts it, 'as a concentrated appeal to memory by literally breaking a temporal continuity'.[23]

Covenants of remembrance were not of course directed at the bereaved but at later generations who might be expected to forget about the experiences of their forefathers. For the bereaved, no encouragement to remember was needed. As the mother of a soldier more recently killed (in Northern Ireland) commented at the opening in October 2007 of a new memorial to those killed in conflicts since the Second World War, "I don't think it's a place to remember loved ones. You remember them every day. It's a place where you feel their sacrifice has been recognised".[24] Unlike her, of course, the bereaved in the aftermath of the First World War had no grave to visit and had had no funeral to attend, both vital elements in the process of grieving and the public affirmation of loss. The war memorial at this time, and the ceremonies enacted before it, provided these functions for the parents and partners of the war dead.

James Young, an American professor of English and Judaic Studies, who has written extensively on the memory and memorialisation of the Holocaust, has suggested that the building of memorials is a way for societies to exonerate themselves from their responsibilities to remember.[25] Young argues that having built monuments to the dead we assume, or prefer to assume, that their presence will act as a constant reminder of past events, but that in reality we allow them to remind us only at our convenience. The monument all too often assumes an 'invisibility' he suggests; we pass them by almost without noticing and certainly without thinking.

There is undoubtedly some truth in this and the argument is not entirely countered by the continuance of remembrance rituals which in some respects themselves become the focus of memory. As Young again suggests: 'Once ritualised, remembering together becomes an event in itself that is to be shared and remembered'.[26]

The expression 'Lest We Forget' was occasionally inscribed on war cemetery headstones, though less frequently on public monuments where the concept of remembrance was usually preferred to that of 'not forgetting'. The acknowledgement that 'we will remember' is a positive and confident assertion; the concern 'lest we forget' sounds a note of pessimism that remembrance (by society and future generations) may be in doubt. But part of the function of the First World War memorial was actually to encourage and facilitate the act of forgetting. In the immediate post-war period the need, not only to remember the dead, but also ultimately to forget the horrors and personal pain, was an important concern. It was however, in a very real sense, necessary first to remember in order to forget.

This was particularly apparent for the hysteric suffering amnesia, or the neurasthenic for whom the desperate desire to hide unwelcome memories could be seen to perpetuate recurrent nightmares. Opinions on shell shock during and even after the war differed greatly, with suggested methods for the cure and rehabilitation of sufferers being equally varied. W.H.R Rivers, who famously treated Siegfried Sassoon's alleged shell shock at Craiglockhart Military Hospital in 1917, argued strongly, against the beliefs of many of his colleagues, that it was essential to confront the disturbing memories which had triggered or contributed towards the serviceman's breakdown.[27]

Rivers, born in 1864 and a Lecturer in Psychology at Cambridge before the war, had joined the staff of Mughill Military Hospital in Lancashire in July 1915. The following year he obtained a commission as a Captain in the Royal Army Medical Corps and in October was transferred to Craiglockhart near Edinburgh. Whilst acknowledging that it was natural to thrust aside painful memories, Rivers claimed that such repression was extremely harmful. Such memories could not be expected to disappear, so instead he recommended to his patients, 'No longer to try to banish them, but ... see whether it was not possible to make them into tolerable, if not even pleasant, companions instead of evil influences'.[28]

Rivers gives as an example, a man buried from an explosion who is able to carry on for two more months until finding a fellow officer literally blown apart. This, not surprisingly, gave the man nightmares. Rivers suggests that he should think that the officer died instantly and consequently did not suffer. The patient is then able to say that he would 'no longer attempt to banish thoughts and memories of his friend from his mind, but would think of the pain and suffering he had been spared'.[29] The next time the dreams occurred, 'he knelt beside his friend to save for the relatives any objects of value which were upon the body'.[30]

The war memorial was not of course intended primarily for the shell-shocked soldier. Nonetheless, for the bereaved and returning ex-servicemen the need to translate distressing realities and painful experience into manageable memories was similar. The need to remember, to 'psychically prolong' the existence of a loved one, to use Freud's term, was an essential part of the process of grieving. For Freud, mourning involved 'a turning away from reality ... and a clinging to the object [of loss] through the medium of an hallucinatory psychosis'.[31] Gradually, reality is regained but in the meantime 'the existence of the lost object is psychically prolonged'.[32]

The collection of mementoes - photographs, letters, uniform and personal effects - by grieving parents or wives helped in this process of prolongation, as the officer referred to above instinctively understood. An equivalent can occasionally be seen on war memorials, as at Burnley where the grieving mother has, at her feet, the objects which remind her of her lost son.

We also see a version of this on regimental memorials such as the monument in Sheffield to the York and Lancaster Regiment with, at the front and back of the memorial, still life groups of military equipment, regimental flags and uniforms. Similarly, at Ipswich, the memorial takes the form of a cenotaph in front of which is placed what appears to be a bronze sarcophagus, in fact the accoutrements of war - machine gun, lances, Stokes gun with tripod and shells - bound together and draped with the Union Jack and the banner of St George.

The accumulation of emblematic objects of war on military monuments derives from antiquity, though for the Romans, it was the spoils of the enemy which were displayed. The medieval practice of displaying on his tomb the helmet and armour of the deceased knight may

Pl. 247
Ipswich
E.Adams, 1923

Pl. 248
(detail)
Guards Division
Memorial, London.
Gilbert Ledward,
1926

have more relevence here; even more so the presentation of artefacts appropriate to the deceased which is a feature of eighteenth century tomb sculpture.[33]

The emphasis on militarism at Sheffield and Ipswich would no doubt bring little comfort to the bereaved onlooker, but in the centre of the arrangement at Ipswich more personal items have been included - haversack, water bottle, gas mask, rifle and helmet - items more suggestive of the individuals commemorated rather than merely of the mechanics of war.

Two impressive relief panels on Gilbert Ledward's Guards' memorial are closer to the classical approach to the display of trophies of war where the trophy was sometimes hung upon a column, with cuirass below and helmet above, thereby suggesting a human presence.[34] In front of the cenotaph of the Guards' memorial stand a row of five Guardsmen and on the back, a previously described relief depicting soldiers in action, loading and firing a field gun, all strong reminders of the healthy, living soldier. But at either end of the cenotaph are smaller relief panels, each one featuring arrangements of military paraphernalia.

The conglomeration of artefacts of active service - the rifle, machine gun and bullets of one, and sword, saddle and rifle of the other - are draped over and around the Guardsmen's coats, the sleeves and collars strongly hinting at the now absent bodies which once wore them. On top of these piles are helmets, visibly and significantly dented and punctured by bullets. All that is missing are the soldiers themselves, an apt metaphor for the absent dead who remained on the field of battle, leaving behind only these poignant echoes of life.

If the collection of mementoes helped the bereaved to prolong their memories of loved ones, so too did the locating of the dead in specific places, such as a room left untouched, or a favourite chair - or indeed a grave - such locations becoming shrines which helped to mitigate grief during a particularly difficult period. In the absence of a grave for the dead serviceman, the war memorial came to perform this function for millions of grieving relatives and friends who, by managing their memories, were eventually able to overcome their grief.

XI

Regeneration

If Walter Gilbert's depiction of the female figures of the Burnley memorial was intended to reflect the feelings of the mourners who stand before it, it was equally indicative of their assumed attitudes. Gilbert's women are shown remembering, literally seeing their men as they once were.

> By [the mother's] side and touching her is the rosemary bush for
> remembrance and under the rosemary is the cricket bat and ball,
> for the son is the boy to the mother always - the boy who never
> grows up in her eyes, and who is loved and remembered best in the
> days when he was mothered by her.[1]

The post-war concern with reconstruction and regeneration, with building a 'land fit for heroes', included the perceived necessity for the re-establishment of gender roles which the war had to some extent undermined and at Burnley we see a clear representation of gender difference in the idealisation of the 'manly', imagined stone figures and the adoring women.

Pl. 249
Burnley.
Walter Gilbert,
1926

Pl. 250
Eccleston.
Walter Gilbert,
1922

The same sculptor, Walter Gilbert, had previously produced a memorial scheme at Eccleston near Liverpool with similar implications: again we see the woman looking up to the man who stands in an heroic, active pose, binoculars in one hand, pistol in the other. Whilst we might again assume a representation of her retrospective vision of a lost loved one, the similarities of materials and scale at Eccleston make this less obvious, encouraging a more straightforward interpretation of the elevation, both literally and metaphorically, of the positive, dynamic male over the subservient female.[2]

The pedagogic restoration of a pre-war ideology also provided an important narrative closure, a third act in the drama of war, signalling an end to the chaos and disruption of the war years and a return to stability where the woman's role was the passive support of men. This final chapter aims to show how the presentation of positive images of the male body in memorial statuary, and more dependent images of women, was a part of that discourse of regeneration in the immediate post-war period.

Even before the war had ended, the suggestion was frequently voiced that women's position in the workplace was purely temporary and that at the war's end it would once again be in the home. In a leader in *The Times* in May 1916, the paper had warmly welcomed women's contribution to the war effort, noting that in wartime, 'she has no separate sphere' and that 'the more she branches out in new directions, the better'.[3] In the same article however it had been felt necessary to reassure their readers that 'the new woman of 1915-16 is still womanly. She has kept her softer qualities for all that she has stepped into man's place'.[4] Later that year the paper emphasised that 'A large proportion of the women will go back to their former occupations and to their homes. They are engaged on emergency work and they regard it as such. It is their contribution to the war; it will come to an end with the war'.[5]

This confident prediction proved correct. *The Restoration of Pre-War Practices Act* of 1918 which restored jobs to men, combined with the drastic reduction in demand for munitions or specifically war-related services, ensured a reversal of the employment situation for women. A year after the Armistice some 775,000 women had left work or been forced out of their jobs and by 1921 fewer women were in work than had been ten years earlier.[6]

Working women, previously praised, were now more often negatively portrayed as depriving ex-soldiers of a livelihood. It was a situation hinted at even before the war had ended. A letter to *Woman Worker* in May 1917 exclaimed, ' Let every woman be prepared to give up any situation she may hold to our soldiers, wounded and otherwise', optimistically adding that 'by doing so I feel certain that after the war other spheres of industry will open up where women will be indispensable'.[7]

However, despite the partial enfranchisement of women in 1918, a range of discourses in the immediate post-war period, from advertising imagery to newspaper editorials, revived the idea that the appropriate sphere for women was domestic. Where the wartime advert may have featured a female munitions worker, after the war it was more likely illustrated by the image of wife or mother in the home. Deirdre Beddoe in her book, *Back to Home and Duty*, a study of the role of women between the wars, gives the example of an advertisement in *Everywoman's* magazine for 'Glitto', used for removing oil and dirt from hands. As late as April 1919 it was 'portrayed as a gift to the munition worker' but by May was said to make 'the kitchen glitter'.[8]

The launch of numerous women's magazines from the 1920s onwards (some sixty new titles between 1920 and 1945) further helped to reinforce the image of women's domesticity, as numerous titles - *My Little Home, Woman and Home, Good Housekeeping* - suggest.[9] Although, in the post-war years, there was also an increase in the work carried out by men in the home, this was invariably in the form of heavier, more 'manly' work such as gardening or household repairs rather than an extension of other domestic skills such as sewing and darning and simple cookery which, of necessity, had had to be learned in the trenches.

The discourse of memorialisation, in the main, allied itself to this view of women's position in post-war society. The range of meanings of maternal images ensured their popularity on figurative war memorials and reference has already been made to a number of examples: women and children in need of protection, the mother and child who must be left behind, or the woman who waits anxiously and passively, with babe in arms, for news from the front, having encouraged her man to go. All of these images reinforced notions of difference in wartime gender roles. In contrast, images of working women sharing the tasks of men blurred the boundaries.

Underlying these images of anxious and reliant women during the war, and of those gratefully welcoming the homecoming of their men at the war's end, is the implication of a desire to return to 'normality'. The need to replace a 'lost generation', the 'cream of British manhood', became a national priority and the raising of the coming generation a patriotic act which was promoted while the war still raged. Millicent Fawcett, President of the NUWSS, noted that 'the care of infant life, saving the children, and protecting their welfare was as true a service to the country as that which men were rendering by going into the armies to serve in the field'.[10] The Bishop of London, commenting in 1917 on the fact that more babies than soldiers died every hour, suggested that 'the loss of life in this war has made every baby's life doubly precious'.[11] Significantly, between 1919 and 1921 the marriage rate was thirty percent higher than pre-war levels.[12]

If the war memorial contributed to the discourse of regeneration, it was not simply in the representation of images of motherhood and the hegemony of gender difference but in the rehabilitation of the male body emasculated by war. The Great War has been seen by some as creating 'a crisis of masculinity'. The American writer and feminist, Elaine Showalter, has suggested that shell shock in particular involved 'intense anxieties about masculinity, fears of acting effeminate, even a refusal to continue the bluff of stoic male behaviour'.[13]

The often discussed 'comradeship of the trenches' and the physical and emotional closeness of an all-male society has also been seen as sexually destabilising, though Joanna Bourke is surely right in questioning the degree to which this was true. As Bourke says, 'while the war provided an intimate environment for love between men, it at the same time exposed the fragility of brotherhood'.[14] Bonds of friendship formed could, in an instance, be shattered by a bullet or bomb and men on the field of battle soon learned that to stop to help their badly wounded comrades was both dangerous and often futile. Lyn MacDonald, a military historian, best-known for her books detailing the wartime memories of ex-combatants, quotes one doctor telling stretcher bearers to leave the seriously injured to die, and to bring back only those there was a hope of saving.[15] For Bourke, 'wartime experiences proved too stressful to result in an expansion of masculine love' and after the war men were only too ready to return to a reassuring, reinstated domesticity.[16]

Both the physically and mentally disabled did however threaten conventional constructs of manly appearance and behaviour and, in their

physical and emotional dependency and their inability to act 'appropriately', were seen to have been feminised by their disablement. Jay Winter
has outlined the way some of the shell shocked were nursed back to health,
being taught 'first to sew, then to weave, then to farm, then to carry a gun
and then to shoot it again'. It was, he suggested, 'as if they were moving
from a kind of feminine recuperation to masculine combat status and then
they could go back to the men's war'.[17]

Physical mutilation too provided unwelcome 'sites of remembrance'
which needed to be concealed. But it was not only the devastating effects of
modern warfare which threatened conventional constructs of the
masculine body. Disturbing realities had been revealed by the extensive
surveillance, in the process of recruitment, of men's bodies during the war.
Almost all men between youth and middle age had had their bodies
surveyed at some time between 1914 and
1918 and categorised in one of four grades
of which only the first indicated fitness for
general service and the last two unsuitability for combat.[18] The results were
highly disturbing for both the military and
the men themselves, with forty-two per cent
of recruits revealed to be unsuitable for
combat.[19]

Despite this, the male physique had
continued to be presented positively
throughout the war, prescribed by a
carefully controlled and highly organised
system of propaganda and censorship. The
official war artist Christopher Nevinson
had problems with the censor, already
described, when attempting to exhibit his
ironically entitled *Paths of Glory*, a picture
which graphically depicted dead British
soldiers on the field of battle. At the same
exhibition from which he had been forced
to withdraw (or at least censor) this
picture, Nevinson also met with criticism of
another of his works, this one blandly
entitled *A Group of Soldiers*. The painting
depicted just that, four men, relaxed and
talking together in a moment of inactivity.

Nevinson had described his
paintings of this period as 'straightforward,

Pl. 251
Specimens of
men in each of
the four grades.
Parliamentary
Papers 1919,
XXVI, p.308

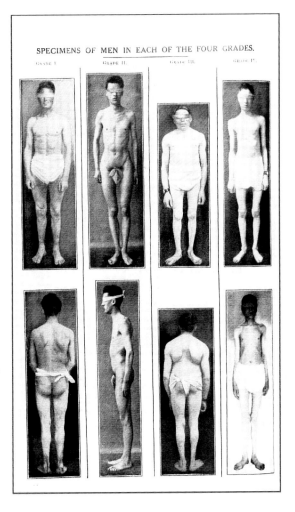

SPECIMENS OF MEN IN EACH OF THE FOUR GRADES.

GRADE I.   GRADE II.   GRADE III.   GRADE IV.

honest performances', a reflection not only of his intentions but of the obvious stylistic change from an earlier, overtly modernist approach.[20] For the official censors however, *A Group of Soldiers* was initially considered *too* honest, the suggestion being made that 'the type of man represented is not worthy of the British Army' and that the enemy might consequently choose to use the picture for their own propaganda purposes 'as evidence of the degeneration of the British soldier'.[21] In the event the picture *was* allowed and was in fact published ahead of the exhibition in the first volume of *British Artists at the Front*, a four-part series illustrating the work of official war artists.

Any image, during the war, considered less than flattering or suggesting inadequate conditions, was likely to meet with the disapproval of the censor. In truth, the military regime of training and drill actually had an improving effect on men's bodies, with many recruits adding inches to their chest measurement and pounds to their weight.[22] However, as Joanna Bourke wryly comments, 'the proposal that military service improved the shape of men's bodies obscured an important issue: the war improved only those bodies that were not completely or partially decimated'.[23]

The literal embodiment of the country's physical, and by implication moral strength in the encouraged imagery of wartime propaganda was to be echoed after the war by the presentation of positive images of powerful manhood in memorial statuary. There are many fine, if relatively indistinguishable examples of the 'manly' soldier on First World War memorials. Amongst the more memorable are the somewhat war-weary but 'gritty' soldiers of Frederick Wilcoxson at Hale or Gilbert Ledward at Abergavenny, previously described.

More typically however, the soldier is shown in calm and confident pose, standing 'at ease' and staring assuredly into the distance, for which we can read, looking optimistically into the future. This pose had numerous precedents in Boer War memorial sculpture and was to prove popular with First World War

Pl. 253
Guards' Division
Memorial.
London.
Gilbert Ledward,
1926

memorialists of varying levels of expertise and renown. Just such a figure by John Cassidy, seen in a number of locations including Colwyn Bay, Heaton Moor and Clayton-le-Moors was described by the sculptor as typical of the majority of soldiers. 'Called from the uneventful civil pursuits by the voice of duty, he carries with him the refinement of his ordinary life, whilst the knowledge of the horrors of war enhances his valour'.[24]

Gilbert Ledward's row of five Guardsmen across the face of the memorial in Horse Guards' Parade in London are shown in this familiar pose, though here rather more formal and less relaxed. Each slightly different soldier represents one of the five branches of the Guards. Like most sculptors, Ledward took great care to ensure accurate representations, sketching and modelling his figures from actual Guardsmen, borrowing the relevant uniforms and equipment and working in the traditional manner from nude studies to clothed end product (somewhat to the consternation of the soldiers who posed for him). Despite this, *The Times* commented, rather harshly, that the soldiers were 'lacking the colour of life'.[25]

Other notable statues in very similar vein to Ledward's and Cassidy's include Albert Toft's at Chadderton, Frederick Pomeroy's at Coleraine, Alfred Drury's outside the Royal Exchange in London, and Arthur Walker's soldier at Dartford. Walker's statue was commissioned after the war memorial committee there had seen the same work at nearby Sevenoaks. (Other versions of this work can be found at Chesham, Heath Town and Ironbridge, though it was initially produced in 1918 in a stone carved version at Heston in Middlesex).

Like Gilbert Ledward, sculptors depicting the common soldier invariably took great care to present with some accuracy the uniform, weapons and accoutrements of active service. It was a requirement frequently specified by commissioning committees. The attention to detail of Henry Poole's sculpture for Evesham's memorial was commented on at the time of its unveiling. Poole shows a soldier alert but relaxed, stepping forward, his rifle on his shoulder and his tin hat at a jaunty angle. A contemporary report noted:

Pl. 254
Evesham.
Henry Poole,
1921

> The Tommy is not heroic in the generally accepted sense of the term, but is truly typical of the average British infantryman during the war with a face which still carried the hard-bitten imprint of overseas service. The feature of the figure is its remarkable accuracy with regard to details of military arms and equipment. It is complete even to the cigarette end behind his ear and to the rat-bitten haversack.[26]

Pl. 255
Sutton Coldfield.
F.W Doyle-Jones,
1922

A similar concern with realism was expressed at Sutton Coldfield. Following a public debate about the form the memorial should take it was determined that the chosen design should be intended to represent a typical Tommy.

> A private soldier, the type of those who have gone from nearly every home in the place and the symbol of our common sacrifice. He should be graven as he went up into the trenches and as he came home on leave, with rifle, bayonet and full kit, each thing an emblem of what he had to do and to bear.[27]

The winner of the competition subsequently held to find a suitable sculptor for this memorial was Francis Doyle-Jones. Before the Great War, Doyle-Jones had produced memorials for the Boer War, not only in his home town of West Hartlepool and the nearby towns of Middlesbrough and Gateshead, but also in Llanelli and Penrith. After the war he was able to build on his reputation as a designer of memorials, with commissions from numerous First World War memorial committees across the country. Quite often, like other sculptors, Doyle-Jones was successful

in offering the same sculpture for more than one location. The Sutton Coldfield memorial committee was no doubt aware of this and consequently specified that this model should not be used elsewhere in Warwickshire and that no more than two others be offered anywhere else in the country.

Similar stipulations were made by other memorial committees though often it was they who specifically asked for a reproduction of an existing design, something with which most sculptors were only too happy to comply. In the event, Doyle-Jones' sculpture of a soldier was used at only one other location, at Elland near Leeds. A majority of his memorials featured a winged Victory (or Peace as they were most frequently identified).

The Sutton Coldfield memorial, unveiled in 1922, shows the soldier, like so many others, standing at ease but this time wearing his heavy greatcoat. Soldiers in greatcoats were often depicted.[28] The greatcoat can be seen as a realistic indication of the necessary protection against the very real problems of cold and rain. Pneumonia, bronchitis and hypothermia caused serious problems on the Western Front with tens of thousands of victims of the cold and wet having to be invalided out.

As an additional, armour-like protective layer the coat can also be seen as a metaphorical signifier of the need for protection against the far more serious assaults on the soldier's body, and as such as an indicator of his resilience and resistance. The greatcoat was standard army issue, worn in camp or in transit to and from the front line but not in actual fighting. The depiction of soldiers so attired was indicative therefore of moments of calm, adding to the preferred presentation of the defensive rather than aggressive combatant.[29]

Undoubtedly the most impressive images of powerful manhood in memorial sculpture are the various single soldiers by Charles Sargeant Jagger at Hoylake and West Kirby, Paddington Station, Manchester (for the Watts' warehouse) and, of course, on the Royal Artillery memorial. It is significant that Jagger too was fond of placing his men in heavy protective uniforms with the bulky clothing adding to the already considerable sense of great muscularity. The pattern established in his earliest

Pl. 256
S & J. Watts,
Manchester.
C.S Jagger, 1921

work is repeated in almost all subsequent statues and, regardless of whether the man is on guard, reading a letter or preparing for action, he stands with legs apart and feet firmly and defiantly planted.

Jagger's claimed intentions were to show the Tommy 'as I knew him in the trenches' and this appears to be how others saw them.[30] At the unveiling of the Royal Artillery memorial the *Manchester Guardian* reported the reactions of onlookers. "See that man carrying the shells. He is real". And of the driver: "Look at his expression. See what he's saying to himself. 'Fed up and far from home'. That's what he says".[31] But in reality, Jagger's figures are more symbolic than realistic, representing no one individual soldier but attitudes of grim determination and stoic resistance, their obviously muscular physiques signifying the fortitude of fighting men generally and, by implication, their moral strength and the moral strength of the nation.

At Manchester the figure is enveloped by a cape which hangs heavily in soft angular folds from his shoulders and arms, and by the sacking wrapped in swirls around his legs to give protection from the mud and water of the trenches. *The Sentry*, as this work is known, now stands in the entrance lobby of The Britannia Hotel in Manchester.[32] Built in 1857 and converted into a hotel in 1984 after standing empty for some years, the building had originally been a textile warehouse, the head offices of S & J Watts for whose employees the memorial was erected. When converted, the entrance lobby was thankfully retained in its original form. In 1923, two years after it was unveiled, the Liverpool architect Charles Reilly had this to say of the sculpture:

Pl. 257
Hoylake and
West Kirby.
C.S Jagger, 1922

Such a figure makes one understand the rock of national character against which the German flood broke in vain. It is truly monumental in its combined steadfastness and power. It is sculpture like this, and this only, free from any trivial suggestions, that can at all express the depth of feeling the war called forth.[33]

At Hoylake the soldier, described by Sir George Frampton who was instrumental in obtaining this commission for Jagger as 'certainly one of the best, if not the best statue I have seen of recent years', is similarly, though less obviously, cocooned in an extra layer of protective clothing.[34] The high neckline and voluminous folds of cloth around shoulders and legs, reminiscent of protective pieces of medieval armour, again create a sense of impenetrable invincibility. The German helmet at the soldier's feet, like Goliath's head at the feet of David, suggests the victory ultimately achieved but hints also at the necessary cost in human lives on both sides.

Jagger's memorial to the men of the Great Western Railway Company was erected halfway along Platform One at Paddington Station. When conscription was introduced in 1916, the railway worker was classified as a reserved occupation; by 1916, however, over 25,000 men from this railway company alone had already enlisted, with more than 2,500 having been killed.[35] In November 1919 the decision was made to erect a memorial to these men and the following November, after determining that this should take the form of a statue, a shortlist was drawn up of many of the best known sculptors of the time, including some of the knighted elite: Goscombe John, Hamo Thornycroft, Thomas Brock and George Frampton.

In January 1921, the memorial committee sought the advice of Sir Reginald Blomfield who suggested a number of younger, and at that time largely unknown men such as Gilbert Ledward and William Reid Dick. Jagger's name had not yet been mentioned but he was subsequently approached and was quick to accept the commission. Whether any other sculptors were also approached is not known, but by 21 February 1921 a sketch model had been submitted by Jagger and Thomas Tait, the architect with whom he had chosen to work.[36]

The statue of a soldier reading a letter was closely related to an early study for an unused figure on the Royal Artillery memorial on which the sculptor was concurrently working. In both cases the soldier stands with unbuttoned coat loosely draped around his shoulders. It was a scheme proposed by Jagger only after three earlier ideas, all of single soldiers, one with a 'trench catapult', one with a cross, and one waiting for a train, had all been rejected.[37]

Typically lacking any overt expression of emotion (though Jagger himself described his look as 'wistful') the Paddington soldier nonetheless hints at underlying feelings.[38] The home-knitted scarf he wears around his neck serves not only to indicate the need for protection against the cold, also suggested by the sheepskin jerkin, but additionally as a signifier of a physical and emotional connection with home. We can imagine the scarf as a gift from the mother or wife who waits at home and from whom the letter he reads has also been received.

We have seen elsewhere, at Bury and Croydon, images of women with letters from their menfolk, but the exchange of letters was equally of importance for the morale of the men at the front, as Jagger himself knew only too well. By 1916 the Army postal service was handling around eleven million letters and 875,000 parcels a week and to the ex-servicemen who

saw the memorial, the reminder of this familiar emotional lifeline would have been quite affecting. For those who wrote letters to men who never returned there would, of course, be even greater poignancy.[39] The soldier's letter would remind them not only of communications with the living but of news of the dead so recently received. An easily overlooked detail of one of Jagger's smaller reliefs for the Royal Artillery memorial featured a Madonna and Child, the Virgin holding in her hand what appears to be a letter, an echo of the position of thousands of women receiving news of their husbands' deaths on the field of battle. The gaze exchanged with the squirming child in her arms suggests a prefiguration of Christ's impending death which in turn suggests a parallel between Christ's and the soldier's self sacrifice.

The soldier at Paddington stands in front of a black marble slab. Jagger explained that he required this to more closely relate the figure to its architectural setting and that it was intended 'to create an impression of stability, to isolate the soldier from the surrounding area and to "stop out" the gap between the soldier's legs'.[40] We may read this in realistic terms as the entrance to a trench dugout, but Ann Compton, in her book on Jagger, suggests an additional, more metaphorical reading, as the entrance to a tomb. If so it is not a tomb that he appears about to enter, but one whose entrance he blocks, symbolically emphasising his defensive role rather than intimating his own fate.

The production of war memorials throughout the 1920s was naturally seen by sculptors as a great opportunity to establish or reinforce their professional reputations. On receiving the commission for the Royal Artillery memorial, Jagger himself had commented to the commissioning committee that he saw this 'as an opportunity to make his name'.[41] Sculptors often prepared designs in anticipation of possible commissions or competitions to be entered. Given that only a few weeks might separate the announcement of a competition and the date for the submission of proposals, those sculptors with pre-prepared designs would obviously be at an advantage. At Lewes in Sussex, where thirty-five entries were received for the competition held, the assessor was critical of the numbers who merely sent in drawings, preferring to see a model, or at least a photograph of a model; those with such models to hand were most likely to be successful.[42]

Gilbert Ledward was one sculptor who regularly sketched out ideas for memorials and even, as we have seen, prepared detailed, ambitious designs for an imagined Hall of Remembrance. Jagger too produced numerous sketches in both two and three dimensions for possible war memorial commissions. In many of these studies the soldier is shown as active; in completed schemes however, the free-standing figures are most often entirely still, with movement reserved for accompanying reliefs. The only exception to this was at Portsmouth, where a soldier and a sailor both man machine guns. The usual stasis of Jagger's soldiers conveys a sense of calm authority, absent from his more active figures, and his servicemen at Portsmouth were significantly his least successful.

The suggestion of the defiant human barricade, made explicit by the horizontally held gun at Hoylake, is implicit in many of these figures to a greater or lesser degree. Indeed, the Hoylake figure is remarkably similar to a French wartime poster, entitled *On ne passe pas*, and may well have been influenced by it.[43] With other memorials the horizontal obstruction is created by folded or outstretched arms or an actual physical barrier against which the soldier stands.

A particularly impressive example of the human barrier is the Anglo-Belgian memorial in Brussels (a gift from the British to the Belgian people) with its massive, granite soldiers, one British, one Belgian. They stand side-by-side, their mirrored, folded arms and the deep shadow cast creating a horizontal accent which reinforces the facial expressions of grim determination that 'they shall not pass'.

Similar in style to Jagger's Belgian memorial, though rather less impressive, is the Soissons Memorial in France, designed by Eric Kennington. Here the line of three stylised, robotic figures stand undemonstratively to attention, a neatly folded uniform with helmet and rifle in front of them as an indication of those colleagues who died.

Pl. 259
Anglo-Belgian
Memorial.
Brussels.
C.S Jagger,
1923

Kennington had begun his artistic career as a painter and was employed in this capacity as an official war artist. His first venture into three dimensional art had been a bas-relief carving exhibited at the Alpine Club Gallery in London in 1920. It showed soldiers relaxing in a dugout and was entitled *P.B.I* (soldiers' slang for 'Poor Bloody Infantry'). The following year he was approached by Lieutenant-Colonel Hill of the 9th Battalion Royal Sussex Regiment, to which Kennington had been attached as an official war artist, who asked if he could recommend a sculptor for a memorial to the 24th Infantry Division to be located in Battersea Park. Kennington not only volunteered to produce the memorial himself but to do so for free.

Described by Alan Borg as having 'a totemic simplicity, at the expense of realism and accuracy of detail', the sculpture, as in his Soissons memorial, features three servicemen, a sergeant, corporal and lance-corporal, 'crunched together and looking straight to their front', as one critic put it.[44] The same critic commented of the memorial that the 'limited

Pl. 260
Soissons
Memorial, France.
Eric Kennington,
1928

group of people who admire "futuristic" art will doubtless highly approve of this monument'.[45] In reality the work, though certainly stylised, is no more 'futuristic' than many other statues of soldiers produced at this time, though Kennington clearly has not aimed at realism, intending it to have broader signification.

> All three [figures] have boundless strength, courage and resolve and their progress is unimpeded by the common danger at their feet. They are British soldiers in uniform and also men journeying through life - the enemies which they overcome are not so much German soldiers as the internal, inner, enemies of all of us.[46]

Kennington's first design had featured a single soldier but this was changed to three as he felt that 'the various natures of British soldiers could not be presented by one man'.[47] Facial features differ slightly, each figure having been modelled on a different man. (The left-hand figure was based on Robert Graves, whom the artist had known for some years and whose portrait he had recently drawn). Otherwise there is little to distinguish the separate figures and Kennington's intention was presumably to suggest a united fighting force of individuals quite literally bonded together into a single entity. Certainly this was the impression for Field Marshall Lord Plumer who commented at the unveiling of the memorial that 'the three figures were joined together in a union that was indissoluble in life, and was sanctified in death - a union which could only be described as the brotherhood of service'.[48] At the men's feet the common danger which impedes them is symbolically represented by a serpent entwined around their ankles.

The memorial was unveiled in October 1924 and was generally well received, the main criticism being reserved for the relationship of figures to plinth with the latter seen as too small. *The Observer* commented that Kennington had achieved 'the investment of solid matter with rhythmic and emotional significance' suggesting that 'it is intensely human and, without being sentimental, intensely tender'.[49] Kennington himself described the figures as 'young, strong, fearless and one in purpose'.[50] The fact that they are shown holding hands may have been intended to convey the idea of being 'one in purpose', and it has been suggested that this detail was a reference to what was apparently the common practice of men shaking the hands of those either side of them in the trenches immediately prior to an attack.[51] Nonetheless, it is a strange detail which, with the figures' physical closeness, hardly suggests fearlessness.

Far from 'futuristic', Kennington's work now seems, if anything, insufficiently abstracted. The angled posts between the soldiers' feet may

Pl. 261
opposite
24th Division Memorial, London. Eric Kennington, 1924

be suggestive of Cubist sculpture, but the handling of space seems uncertain rather than deliberately ambiguous. The three figures appear to occupy too little space, whilst details such as the lefthand figure's rifle truncated by his tin hat seem odd and even inept and may well betray Kennington's inexperience of direct carving.

For most sculptors, normal practice at this time involved the production of a clay maquette, cast in plaster and scaled up to the required size with the aid of a pointing machine, to then be cast in bronze or carved from stone or marble, usually by assistants. Direct carving, which Kennington employed on this memorial, involved, in contrast, the working out of the final look of the work in the act of carving by the sculptor himself and without the help of detailed models.

This was more than merely a technical choice; for Eric Gill, the man most often credited with the reintroduction of a technique unused since the Middle Ages, it was a question not only of 'honesty to materials' but of reuniting 'the artist as man of imagination and the artist as workman'.[52] Kennington knew and admired Gill's work and was a personal friend of others, such as Frank Dobson and Ossip Zadkine, who held similar views. Undoubtedly he was guided by them and indeed, before embarking on this project, Kennington wrote to Gill to ask his advice about the best stone to use.

The 24th Infantry Division memorial was an ambitious project for an inexperienced sculptor. Working directly on a large block of stone (the figures being slightly larger than lifesize) and with only a small, one foot high plaster model to guide him, may have been unwise and the memorial, though refreshingly original, is ultimately somewhat unsatisfactory. Kennington's Soissons memorial was in many ways less ambitious but is the more successful work. With far greater stylisation, to the point of oversimplification perhaps, Kennington produced at Soissons a

powerful statement of military unity, the subtle variation of pose and facial features subsumed into an image of common resolve.

With their memorials at Soissons and Brussels, both Kennington and Jagger present their soldiers as undemonstrative fighting machines. They were not alone in seeing the First World War Tommy in this light. In *Realities of War*, first published in 1920, the journalist and war correspondent Philip Gibbs wrote of soldiers who became 'automata at the word of command, [and who] lost their souls, as it seemed, in that grinding machine of military training'. [53] Christopher Nevinson, writing in 1919, explained that ' I began, like everybody else, to see the war as a thing of mechanics, a tremendous machine. Men were just creatures of routine'.[54] Later, in his 1937 autobiography, he reiterated his views: 'My obvious belief was that war was now dominated by machines and that men were mere cogs in the mechanism'.[55]

Nevinson had declared himself an English Futurist and was consignatory in 1914 of 'A Futurist Manifesto [of] English Art'. His well-known picture, *Returning to The Trenches*, shows a closely-packed body of French troops welded into a single entity, determinedly forging forwards, with individual figures reduced to a series of repeated and interlocking arcs and angles in true Futurist style. Such extremes of abstraction are unsurprisingly absent from memorial sculpture. Nonetheless the depersonalised corps of

Pl. 262 'Returning to the Trenches'. Christopher Nevinson. Etching, 1916. Imperial War Museum

stylised marching men of Liverpool's memorial, or the slightly more individualised soldiers of William Bloye's panels for Birmingham's Hall of Memory - in particular, *The Front Line*, with its anonymous and repetitive line-up of marksmen along the side of a trench - provide examples of what has been referred to as the 'troop machine'.[56]

The association of masculinity with mechanisation which we see in Jagger's and Kennington's stolid figures and in the depiction of marching men as a dehumanised, unified body, clearly represents a return to a pre-war gender division which saw masculinity as 'hard' (and related to the worlds of science and engineering) and femininity as 'soft' (and associated with the natural and intuitive). A rather different exposition of masculinity is evident in Francis Derwent Wood's 1925 memorial to the men of the Machine Gun Corps.

Although born in Keswick in the Lake District in 1871, to an American father and English mother, Francis Derwent Wood's family moved to Switzerland, and later to Germany, when he was still a child. Having studied art in Karlsruhe in Germany, Wood returned to England in 1889 where he worked briefly as a modeller for the tile manufacturers, Maw & Co of Ironbridge, a company owned by his father-in-law. The following

Pl. 263
(detail)
Liverpool.
G.H Tyson Smith,
1930

year, having won a scholarship to the National Art Training School, he moved to London and in 1895 became a student at the Royal Academy Schools, winning a Gold Medal and a Travelling Scholarship, which enabled him to spend a year in Paris. Subsequently he worked as an assistant to both Alphonse Legros and Sir Thomas Brock and, following a brief spell as modelling master at Glasgow School of Art, in 1900 he established his own studio in Chelsea. By 1918 he had succeeded Edouard Lantéri as Professor of Sculpture at the Royal College of Art.

The Machine Gun Corps was a quintessentially modern fighting force formed in 1915, though disbanded only seven years later. During the war, almost 14,000 officers and men of the Machine Gun Corps had been killed, with more than 48,000 wounded, missing or prisoners of war, as an inscription on the reverse of the memorial confirmed. The main focus of the Machine Gunners' memorial is a nine feet tall bronze figure of David. In his nakedness and confident pose, with right hand resting on his hip and left hand holding the outsize sword of Goliath, he is most immediately reminiscent of Donatello's fifteenth century version, though the influence of Alfred Gilbert is also clearly evident. (One thinks in particular of that sculptor's studies of 'Icarus' from the 1880s).[57]

More muscularly athletic and dependent on classical prototypes than either of its more androgynous, adolescent predecessors, Derwent Wood's David nevertheless retains something of the sensuousness of both Donatello's and Gilbert's work. This strikes a somewhat incongruous note, as does the inscription: 'Saul has slain his thousands, but David his tens of thousands'. This quotation from the Book of Samuel was unquestioned at the design stage but subsequently resulted in outraged letters to the press and even questions in Parliament. 'Is it really the opinion that memorials to the dead in the War should contain references to the amount of slaughter?' was one disapproving critic's comment.[58]

Both the Royal Artillery and Machine Gun memorials are sited close to Hyde Park Corner. The close proximity of the two has encouraged comparisons, by some recent commentators, of the contrasting approaches of Jagger and Wood, invariably to the detriment of the latter. Susan Beattie, in her book on *The New Sculpture*, goes so far as to suggest that Jagger's work 'represents a violent gesture of revulsion against the aesthetic cliché embodied by its neighbour'.[59] The brutal honesty of the inscription and the realistic depiction of machine guns on either side of the central figure suggest however a rather more ambivalent attitude than might be immediately apparent. Like Jagger, Derwent Wood was not averse to the realistic depiction of death, clearly shown by his Ditchingham soldier which certainly bears comparison with the younger sculptor's recumbent figure on the Royal Artillery monument.[60]

The figure of David was of course a recognised symbol of the victory of justice over tyranny, but perhaps because of what might be construed as an imprecise, or not entirely flattering parallel, of the underdog triumphing against all odds, it was not one widely used in war memorial statuary. Indeed, I know of no other overt example, though the figure of David, as we have seen at Hale, is occasionally alluded to elsewhere.[61] Of course Germany had frequently been portrayed as brutish and uncivilised whilst the idealised classical nude signified the very essence of civilisation. The parallel with David and Goliath as presented here could therefore be seen as appropriate.[62] It is, however, the incongruity of the confident and victorious adolescent nude, with whom it is difficult to imagine many ex-servicemen empathising, which seems particularly inapt.

For memorialists depicting the semi-nude male body, less specific but more active allegorical 'warriors', such as Richard Goulden's various muscular males, or John Cassidy's Skipton figure, who symbolically breaks

his sword across his knee, usually proved a more popular approach. Such figures were clearly seen, by some at least, as appropriate representations of the contemporary male. Goulden's semi-naked warrior at Gateshead was described in the souvenir booklet, produced when the memorial was unveiled, as depicting 'our "Manhood" in an attitude of "Defence", strong, motionless and unconquerable'.[63] A similarly muscular, semi-naked figure on Bolton's war memorial representing 'Youth' was recognised as 'characteristic of the best manhood of our Town - clean and fit, with unbounded energy'.[64]

At Birmingham, the use of nudity lacks the justification of a particular or imagined narrative. Here the memorial took the form of a massive, octagonal 'Hall of Memory'. Placed on low granite pedestals on four sides of the building are bronze figures by Albert Toft representing the different branches of the armed services, including the Womens' Services. These overtly Michelangelesque, semi-nude figures are based on Toft's earlier allegorical figures for his Welsh National Boer War memorial at Cardiff.

Pl. 265 and Pl.266
Birmingham.
Albert Toft, 1925

The single male figure at Cardiff holds a sword and a shield, but at Birmingham the men clasp the markedly contemporary attributes of their particular branch of the services, including machine gun and aircraft propellor.

Each of the lean, muscular figures is crouched rather than seated on the blocks which half support them, indicating their potential for action. The representation of the three branches of the armed services plus a variously identified female figure - nurse, Womens' Services, Peace, and so on - is a conventional scheme common to many memorials. The allegorisation and semi-nudity of Birmingham's version is far less common and can therefore be seen, as with the Machine Gunners' memorial, as a deliberate concern with exposing the muscular male physique.

John Angel's Exeter memorial has four figures disposed around a central pedestal: a soldier, a sailor, a nurse and a prisoner of war. (The inclusion of the prisoner of war was in recognition of relief work for prisoners in Germany carried out by Exonians headed by Lady Owen, the wife of the then mayor of Exeter, Sir James Owen). The figure of the soldier wears a heavy trench coat whilst the nurse is dressed in a capacious, long-sleeved tunic which covers her from head to feet.

Two of the Exeter figures are presented as nude, or semi-nude figures - the sailor and the prisoner of war - but here we might explain their appearance as having more specific significance. The former, with

Pl. 267
and
Pl.268
Exeter.
John Angel, 1923

rolled-up trouser legs and bare feet, sitting astride an emblematic boat, can be seen as dressed (or undressed) in a manner appropriate to his trade; the latter, identified by chains around his wrists, is shown as nakedly vulnerable in his state of captivity.

Exposure of the manly, muscular physique was in other cases justified by the demands of realism. Alexander Carrick's panels at the Scottish National War Memorial in Edinburgh, and Gilbert Ledward's figures on the Blackpool memorial show, for example, men stripped to the waist, engaged in strenuous physical activities. At Watford, there is no such justification. The memorial consists of three males nudes, the work Mary Pownall Bromet, a Lancastrian by birth but a long-time local resident.[65] Each figure, clearly influenced by Rodin under whom the sculptor studied, is used to represent aspects of the war: the fallen, the wounded and victory.

Although unveiled in 1928, the figures were produced during the early years of the war: of the two dated works, one is inscribed '1914', the other '1916'. They must therefore have been produced independently of the memorial scheme, though were no doubt informed by thoughts of war. The nudity of the figures may indicate mere conventionality in works originally intended to be exhibited in a gallery, but in the context of memorialisation it suggests something more, both vulnerability and moral integrity. In late Victorian and Edwardian moral discourse it was widely held that 'will power' was decisive in the formation of 'character' and that the mind was the 'seat of the will'. As mind and body were believed to be directly related it was assumed that strengthening the body consequently strengthened the will and so helped the development of character. Furthermore, the finely honed body served as a metaphor for the effectual society and it is in this sense that memorialists who revealed the exposed male body as muscular and athletic, literally laid bare their images of manhood, suggesting not only physical, but moral strength.

Robert Tait McKenzie's idealised figure for the Cambridge war memorial, though fully clothed, was similarly intended, not only to provide an exemplar at a time of reconstruction, but also to draw parallels between physical and moral strength. McKenzie was both a sculptor and a qualified surgeon. He was born in Ontario in 1867, the son of a Scottish minister who had emigrated to Canada a few years earlier. After studying medicine at McGill University he had accepted, in 1894, the post of Medical Director of Physical Training and Lecturer in Anatomy at the university. The appointment reflected not only his belief in exercise as an aspect of preventative medicine but also his own enthusiasm for, and accomplishments in, a range of sports. (As an undergraduate McKenzie had won the All-round Gymnastic Championship and become Canadian

Intercollegiate Champion in the high jump). In 1904 he moved to
Philadelphia to become Professor of Physical Education and Physical
Therapy at the University of Pennsylvania.

McKenzie initially began to sculpt as a way to illustrate aspects of
the athleticism of his students, producing, whilst still in Montreal, four
studies to show the accumulative effects of exertion on the face of an
athlete. His sculpture of a sprinter, exhibited at the Royal Academy in
1904, was based on measurements of seventy-four leading American
athletes, a technique intended to reveal the embodiment of the ideal and
one to be reused the following year in his sculpture of a *College Athlete*,
this time based on the measurements of some 400 men.

Pl. 269
Watford.
Mary Pownall
Bromet, 1928

311

Tait McKenzie's commission for the Cambridge memorial followed from a visit by the war memorial committee to an exhibition of his sculptural work held at the Fine Art Society in London in 1920 which included his studies of athletic male bodies. The Cambridge statue, entitled *The Homecoming*, and as such forming a counterpoint to his later Edinburgh memorial *The Call*, depicts a youthful, bareheaded soldier, exuberant on his return from the front. His own helmet is in his hand and a German helmet as a trophy of war is on his back. Over the barrel of his rifle, which he carries on his shoulder, is a laurel wreath which encircles the German helmet. As well as his helmet, he carries in his hand a rose, caught from those thrown by welcoming citizens. Another rose lies at his feet. In McKenzie's own words, 'His head is turned to the side, his expression is alert, happy and slightly quizzical, and his lips are slightly parted as if he has recognised an old friend in the welcoming crowd and is about to call to him'.[66]

The figure was based, in contrast to his earlier working methods, on one man alone, Kenneth Hamilton, a Cambridge University undergraduate. In the circumstances this was a somewhat ironic choice. The Cambridge memorial was one of three commemorative responses proposed by the Lord Lieutenant of Cambridgeshire on behalf of the county and the Isle of Ely: firstly a donation on behalf of the living to Addenbrooke's, a local hospital; secondly a memorial in Ely Cathedral listing the names of the dead; and finally the monument in Cambridge, as an acknowledgement and celebration of victory.

Efforts were made throughout the county to raise £30,000 to cover the costs of these ambitious plans, though less than half the amount was eventually collected. Whilst there was a satisfactory response from the townspeople, elsewhere contributions to the fund were slower in coming, with alternative, local schemes often having taken precedence. More sluggardly still was the response from the university. When the Vice-Chancellor had made an appeal to the university colleges, the resulting contribution had been a mere £600. This did not reflect an objection to the scheme or any reluctance to contribute financially to acts of commemoration but rather a belief that the Cambridgeshire memorial was for those who had served in Cambridgeshire regiments, which included very few of the university's men. Furthermore, the almost 2,500 men from Cambridge University who had died in the war would be honoured by their own colleges and by the memorials of those towns and cities throughout Britain (and elsewhere) from where they originally came.

Nonetheless the university had been included in the plans for the memorial and a number of heads of college became members of the war memorial committee.[67] Therefore, despite the limited financial

involvement of the university, the institution had a significant influence on decision making. It was on the recommendation of one of the university's representatives, Sir Arthur Shipley, Master of Christ's College, that Robert Tait McKenzie, whom he almost certainly knew personally and whose work he unquestionably admired, was commissioned to provide the sculpture for the proposed monument. This followed a visit to McKenzie's London exhibition, again on Shipley's recommendation. It was also from Shipley's college that Hamilton, the undergraduate who was the model for the soldier, had come. The sculptor clearly felt the young man typified a particular, and most appropriate sort of English manhood. 'I have tried to express the type on whom the future of England must depend. Blond, with hair wavy rather than curly, head well rounded, forehead slightly flat, the boss over the eyes large, but not so developed as it will be in later life'.[68]

During the war, McKenzie had served in the Royal Army Medical Corps. He had travelled to England in 1915, hoping to obtain a commission in the Canadian Medical Service, but following frustrating delays he decided instead to join the RAMC. On their discovery of his particular expertise, and that he was the author of a familiar book on

Pl. 270
Cambridge.
Robert Tait
MacKenzie,
1922

313

physical training, he was asked to undertake a tour of inspection of training camps and hospitals. Subsequently placed on the staff of the Director of Medical Services at the War Office, he was charged with supervising the physical training of convalescent men. When the United States entered the war, McKenzie returned to America and in 1918 he was appointed as inspector of Canada's convalescent military hospitals.

In addition to devising programmes of physical training, working in particular with shell shock victims whose paralysed limbs had to be coaxed back into use, McKenzie also worked closely with orthopaedic and plastic surgeons, where his work included the designing of masks for the facially disfigured. McKenzie's handbook, *Reclaiming the Maimed*, which detailed appliances and treatments for the seriously wounded, was to become the official manual of the United States Army and Navy.

Significantly perhaps, more than one of those sculptors whose memorial work illustrated an idealised male body was involved in the reclamation of the maimed. Derwent Wood, the sculptor of the Machine Gunners' Memorial, was instrumental in setting up the 'Masks for Facial Disfigurements Department' (more commonly referred to as the 'Tin Noses Shop') at the Third London General Hospital in Wandsworth. Here he produced carefully sculpted metal masks to conceal disfigurement and enable the maimed to face, with at least some confidence, their fellow men. As he explained:

> My work begins where that of the surgeon ends. When the surgeon has done all he can to restore function, to heal wounds, to support fleshy tissue by bone grafting, I endeavour by means of the skill I happen to possess as a sculptor to make a man's face as near as possible to what it would look like before he was wounded.[69]

When Derwent Wood joined the RAMC in 1915, as an orderly in the Territorial Division, he was attached to the Wandsworth hospital, initially working in the Plaster and Splints department, designing and making splints moulded directly from the patients' bodies. With the establishment of the 'Tin Noses Shop' he was given a commission and was joined by three other sculptors including his studio assistant Frederick Wilcoxson. The team also included a plaster mould maker and a casting specialist.

The devastating nature of the injuries that men like Derwent Wood and Tait McKenzie were helping to hide is revealed in a remarkable series of pastel drawings by another artist-surgeon, Henry Tonks. Like Tait McKenzie, Tonks, who was a few years older than the Canadian, had studied medicine, becoming a Fellow of the Royal College of Surgeons in

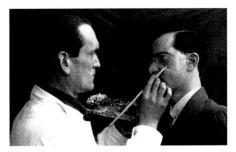

Pl. 271
Derwent Wood
fitting a mask.

Pl. 272
Derwent Wood
painting a mask.

1892. Unlike McKenzie, his interest in art took precedence over a potential career in medicine and in that same year he accepted a position as Assistant Professor at the Slade School of Art.

After initial work with the Red Cross in France and Italy, in 1916 Tonks joined the RAMC and was based at a hospital in Aldershot. It was here that he began to record the facial injuries of the patients. The head surgeon, Sir Harold Gillies, had developed new techniques, involving skin grafts from other parts of the body to cover severely scarred areas and Tonks was employed to produce diagrammatic records of operations. He also began to produce pastel drawings of the heads of the patients. In a letter to a friend he explained, with serious understatement, 'I am doing a number of heads of wounded soldiers who had their faces knocked about'.[70]

When Gillies and his team moved to a new specialist facial unit at Sidcup, Tonks was asked to recommended a sculptor to work there. He suggested Kathleen Scott, whom he had taught at the Slade. Scott's role was to create models of men's faces, with missing features reinstated, to help the surgeons plan and practise the procedures of plastic surgery. As Gillies explained: 'A plaster cast of the face is made and thereon the sculptor, aided by photographs if available, models the missing contours ...the surgeon now has data for adequate diagnosis'.[71] Like Tonks, Scott seemed able to view the appalling injuries of the servicemen with some dispassion, noting in her diary 'These men with no noses are very beautiful, like antique marbles'.[72]

Despite the claim of Tait McKenzie that the masks they provided enabled the 'horribly disfigured men [to be] able to accept and hold any position involving appearance among their fellows, who are quite unconscious of the grisly gap beneath [their] fair exterior', the injured ex-servicemen were still understandably self-conscious when wearing them.[73] Derwent Wood admitted: 'To wear an artificial substitute for any feature must necessarily be always a burden added to the consciousness of the man or woman so sorely stricken'.[74]

Considerable skill was used to carefully blend the painted surfaces of the masks to match the skin tones of the disfigured recipient, and they were normally attached to the face as inconspicuously as possible by spectacle frames. But they remained unmistakably oil paint on metal, and although the masks could also incorporate, where necessary, absorbent pads inside the shell to assuage discomfort, clearly they were as much for the benefit of the people with whom the wearer interacted, to appease their sensitivities to horrific injury, as they were for the wearers themselves. Nonetheless, as Derwent Wood described, 'Ithe patientl acquires his old self-respect, self-assurance, self-reliance, ...His presence is no longer a source of melancholy to himself nor of sadness to his relatives and friends'.[75]

Both Derwent Wood and Tait McKenzie were obviously more aware than most of the horrific impact of modern weapons on flesh and bone. It is understandable therefore that in their memorial work after the war they were inclined to turn (or return) to the depiction of a masculine ideal. As the historian, Ken Inglis, has commented of Tait McKenzie, 'after the terrible years of reclaiming the maimed, the sculptor-professor could once again represent young male strength and beauty'.[76]

Where the nude or semi-nude body is depicted, the nudity, an indicator of sexual identity, acts as a signifier of sexual difference. As such it is suggestive of the restoration of pre-war constructs of gender which had been partially undermined during the war. But the nude figure can also be seen as representing innocence and virtue, a literal 'laying bare' of moral integrity and honest intent. The strength and beauty which Tait McKenzie and other sculptors represent is clearly meant to be more than skin deep, serving to suggest not only physical strength but also moral certitude.

The Cambridge memorial was unveiled on the 3rd July 1922 by the Duke of York. (The bronze casting had not in fact been completed in time and instead, unknown to all but a few of the participants at the unveiling ceremony, a full-size gilded plaster model was actually displayed). The happy, striding soldier might easily have been mistaken for an enthusiastic recruit unaware in the early months of the war of what lay in store were it not for the German helmet he carries as a trophy of war. At the unveiling ceremony, the mayor, George Hawkins, no doubt accurately identified the sculptor's intentions. The thoughts of the soldier, he imagined, were 'firstly, he was happy to be home; secondly, he is proud of victory won; and, thirdly, best and most satisfying, with duty done'.[77]

The commemorative process at Cambridge was unusual in providing separate sites of mourning and memory to help the living, honour the dead and celebrate victory. The soldier is therefore unusual in being intended as an entirely celebratory figure. But he soon became seen as something more. Public monuments in all locations became *the* memorial for all of the people and at Cambridge, as elsewhere, the monument was to become the focus for annual Armistice Day ceremonies. To the commemoration of victory was therefore added, as in other towns, the memory and mourning of the dead.

The Cambridge figure may have been intended to represent all who served, including those who safely returned, but for those whose husbands or sons had failed to return the representation became singular, personal and posthumous. An avoidance of the 'bitter truth' of death and dismemberment, and the idealisation explicit in depictions of 'young male strength and beauty', was validated by the nation's desire for regeneration and a return to 'normality'. But the smile of the Cambridge soldier which indicates, not only a happiness to be home, but the pride and satisfaction with duty done, would, in addition, have provided for those who mourned, some pride and satisfaction of their own that their sons, husbands, brothers or betrothed had not died in vain.

Pl. 273
Cambridge.
Robert Tait
McKenzie, 1922

XII

Summary

The French refer to war memorials as 'monuments aux morts', a significant term which indicates both form and intent. Whilst memorialisation in Britain most often took the form of erecting a monument and was certainly concerned with the commemoration and mourning of the dead, this was by no means an exclusive approach. Many monuments commemorate not only those who died but also those who fought and survived, and sometimes those who contributed to the war effort on the home front. Furthermore, in many communities, memorialisation, as we have seen, took the form of utilitarian schemes. Both of these aspects - the utilitarian and the acknowledgement of all who served - can be seen in the village of Nethy Bridge in Scotland. Here the war memorial is a simple slab of stone which provides seating at the bus stop in the centre of the village. It is created from a stone step of the former village hall and, as the inscription records, is 'In proud memory of every man of Nethy Bridge and District who trod on this threshold step of the village hall when he enlisted in the forces, 1914-1918'.

As this suggests, memorials took many forms. Most large towns and cities would normally have a number of monumental war memorials representing different boroughs or parishes, but the public monument, even in quite small towns, was often only one of a range of commemorations. War memorials were provided by, and represented, all sections of the community. Social and political organisations, clubs and societies, schools and colleges, places of work and recreation, local regiments and churches and chapels, all produced their own tributes to the dead.

At Cambridge, in addition to Tait McKenzie's public monument, there were memorials in each of the University's colleges with others erected for postal, gas, bank and local government workers, for members of University boating clubs, for schools and for the parishioners of churches of various denominations. Even much smaller towns would have had numerous memorials. In Macclesfield, more than three dozen separate memorials were produced, between them representing a range of responses which included stained glass windows, a Memorial Hall, cricket pavilion, churchyard cross, statues and wall plaques in churches, Town Hall, schools and clubs.

The iconography of the public monument and its significance in representing a range of interests - civic, military, religious, political or personal - and its function in encouraging and reflecting appropriate responses in both individual and communal acts of remembrance have already been detailed. Only the public monument could provide this range of meanings. Other memorials, in churches, schools and clubs, were limited to their particular members and parishioners. The public monument represented all of these constituents.

What public monuments also provided was a site for the civic rituals of remembrance. Such rituals originated with the unveiling ceremony which would establish the pattern for subsequent services of remembrance and set a precedent for the involvement of particular parties, most obviously of local government, the clergy, ex-servicemen and, of course, the bereaved. Opportunities were also provided at these ceremonies, in speech making and unveiling ceremony booklets, to reinforce the intended didacticism of the act of remembrance and, not infrequently, an explanation of the iconography of the monument itself.

Frequently filmed and shown at local cinemas, unveiling ceremonies were invariably conducted with considerable pomp and pageantry. Those officially invited were carefully orchestrated and no doubt well rehearsed, as published plans for numerous ceremonies reveal. For the memorials of the largest towns and cities the highest ranking officers of the Armed Forces, and even Royalty, were imposed upon to officiate. At Newcastle, where the monument in Eldon Square was unveiled by Earl Haig in September 1923, over one thousand people were officially involved in the ceremony.

But even at such extravagant events the involvement of 'ordinary' people was often seen. At Manchester, where Lutyens' impressive cenotaph was unveiled by the Earl of Derby, he was accompanied by a Mrs Bingle, described as 'a citizen of the working-class district of Ancoats'.[1] She had been chosen to assist because all three of her sons had died in the war. This direct involvement of the bereaved was common and in many other places those with multiple losses were invited to participate in the unveiling of the memorial.

The involvement of the seriously maimed was also common and reference has previously been made to the laying of wreaths at Macclesfield, Port Sunlight and other locations by blind or disabled ex-servicemen. Given such ceremonies, often attended by thousands, and in larger locations by tens of thousands, a site sufficiently spacious to accommodate considerable numbers was clearly an important factor in the siting and design of memorials. At Macclesfield, the choice of a relatively quiet location for the public monument on the town's periphery was indicative of a secondary requirement, the provision of a contemplative space for the bereaved to sit quietly with their thoughts.

Public monuments became the memorial for all of the people. In Cambridge, where the monument was initially intended to reflect only one aspect of memorialisation, it too, inevitably, was seen to incorporate much broader signification. The meaning of monuments cannot be fixed. As the art historian, Ernst Gombrich, has said: " 'Meaning' is a slippery term, especially when applied to images rather than to statements. Images apparently occupy a curious position somewhere between the statements of language, which are intended to convey a meaning, and the things of nature, to which we can only give a meaning".[2]

Gombrich goes on to quote the writer, D.E Hirsch, in introducing the terms 'significance' and 'implication' into the examination of meaning. Hirsch stresses that whilst the significance and implications of a work may change, original intention does not.[3] He therefore rejects, as Gomrich says, 'the facile view that a work simply means what it means to us'.[4] Interpreting the significance of the work of art is, however, an open-ended process.

What is implied by war memorials and the figurative sculpture used to convey the intended meaning of those who erected them will continue to be questioned, whether by those who place wreaths or those who daub anti-war slogans. At Cambridge, no sooner had the memorial been unveiled than intended meaning, significance and implications began to separate.[5] But, as Gombrich went on to say of the interpretation of meaning, 'In looking at a work of art we will always project some additional significance that is not actually given', adding, 'Indeed we must do so if the work is to come to life for us'.[6]

The monumental bodies of First World War memorials symbolically replaced the absent bodies of literally hundreds of thousands of British men buried, fragmented or obliterated on numerous foreign fields. The decision to refuse to repatriate the battlefield dead had meant that the war memorial could not be limited to the commemoration of victory or become a quickly disregarded emblem of establishment gratitude and respect for the dead. For the millions who mourned, the memorial signified much more and provided a much needed site for grief and personal remembrance.

I have argued that the palliative function of the war memorial was paramount and that it is precisely this function rather than mere conservatism which encouraged the traditional and anodyne nature of much of the figurative imagery. The idealisation of the serviceman was validated both by the needs of the bereaved and by the nation's desire for regeneration. Nonetheless, as we have seen, many memorials did acknowledge to some extent the dreadful repercussions of 'total' warfare as well as stressing a more compassionate and concerned image of masculinity and more positive images of femininity.

It is all too easy, decades later, to be dismissive of memorialisation and to see, as some have, merely sentimentality or pomposity. It is easier still to give memorials no thought at all. But, as I hope has been shown in the preceding pages, any serious appraisal of what amounted to the most extensive project of public sculpture the country has seen reveals many outstanding examples of work by a wide range of talented sculptors. In its entirety, what this project presents is a remarkable picture of a nation's response to war, of its devastating impact on ordinary men and women, and of the struggle to come to terms, in the aftermath of the conflict, with a changed society.

In the post-war years, an anxiety to promote a new art for a new era, which favoured personal expression above all, left little room to admire, what seemed for many, outdated expressions of an earlier age. However, the passage of time allows a more considered appraisal of memorial forms than has hitherto taken place. It also provides an opportunity to reassess the development of sculptural practice in the early years of the twentieth century. This can now be seen as something more complex than a simple choice between conservatism and modernism, with previously ignored or disregarded sculptors being seen to take a more vital place in the history of British sculpture.

For many millions who mourned in the aftermath of the First World War, monuments to those who fought and died provided a place for public acclamation and for personal memories and quiet meditation. The sculpture which adorned so many, a metaphorical remembering of lost loved ones, presented the bereaved with fitting tributes to husbands, sons, brothers and friends - and sometimes wives and mothers - the men and women they were encouraged to call, with pride and sorrow, 'The Glorious Dead'.

The facts of that first 'Great War' continue to shock and fascinate, and significantly we retain the date and timing of the armistice of 1918 in remembering the dead of more recent conflicts. That memorials continue to be used and, for many, continue to impress, is an indication of the success of those who designed and built them and whose achievements this book acknowledges.

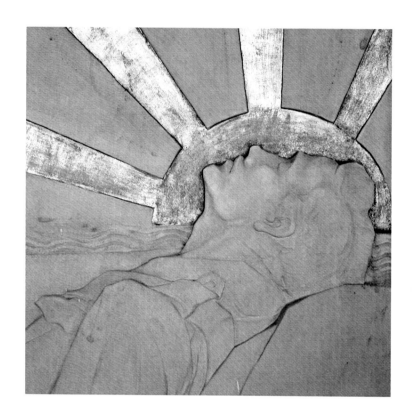

Pl. 274
Aldeburgh.
Gilbert
Bayes 1919

NOTES

Introduction

1   The inscription on the front of the memorial.
2   Farr, D., 'The Patronage and Support of Sculptors' in Nairne & Serota (1981) p 19.
3   Crellin (1995), p 40.
4   On modernism and the Great War see Silver (1989) & Cork (1994).
5   Borg (1991) p xi.
6   Ibid.
7   For an invaluable listing of all types of war memorials see the UK National Inventory of War Memorials (www.ukniwm.org.uk). For an analysis of obelisks as war memorials see Barnes, R., (2004).
8   It might be argued that memorial building was not a single project but rather a series of individual schemes. However, given the national mood, organisational encouragement and assistance, and awareness of nationwide responses, it is not unreasonable to discuss this as a 'single project'.

Chapter One: Pro Patria

1   *Manchester Guardian*, 31 August 1914.
2   See Stedman (1994).
3   Reader (1988), p 15.
4   By a group of Manchester industrialists meeting at Manchester Town Hall on 28 August 1914. For discussion of the formation of Pals' battalions see p 56-58.
5   Hall (1994), p 7.
6   Rosen, D., 'The Volcano and the Cathedral: Muscular Christianity and the Origins of Primal Manliness' in Hall (1994) p 26.
7   Ibid. p 36.
8   See Parker (1987), p 63.
9   Ian Beckett, 'The Nation in Arms, 1914 - 18', p 5 in Beckett & Simpson (1985).
10   In 1911 the Church Lads' Brigade, like the O.T.C., was accepted by the War Office as part of a Territorial Cadet Force. Rifle drill was a common part of their activities.
11   Ian Beckett, 'The Nation in Arms, 1914 - 18', p 5 in Beckett & Simpson (1985).
12   See Springhall (1977), p 57.
13   Ibid. p 122.
14   See Roberts (1996), pp 20-21.
15   See Mangan & Walvin (1987) and Mangan, J.A. 'Athleticism: A Case Study of the Evolution of an Edwardian Ideology' in Simon & Bradley (1975)
16   Haley, B., *The Healthy Body and Victorian Culture*, (Cambridge 1978), p 119.
17   Private Frederick James Hodges in van Emden (2005), pp 254 - 255).
18   *The Times*, 24 November 1914.

19 Roberts (1996), p 125.

20 See Peter Hart, *The Somme*, (London 2005), p 187. This incident also inspired a poem, *The Game*, by Claude Burton (See Roberts (1996), p 166). Philip Gibbs noted the incident at the Battle of Loos in his book Realities of War, and quotes the comment of a watching French officer, 'He is not mad … It is a beau geste. He is a sportsman, scornful of death. That is the British sport'. (Gibbs (1920), p 140).

21 From the 'Morning Post', 22 January 1915 quoted in Reader (1988), pp 96 - 97.

22 H.G. Wells, 'The Daily Chronicle', 9 September 1914 in Hynes (1990), p 20.

23 Kernot (1927), p 136.

24 See Gudmundsson (2005), pp 48 - 49.

25 *The Times*, 3 March 1924, p 9.

26 St. George's Church in Stockport provides one example with which I am personally familiar.

27 See Gosse, E., 'The New Sculpture: 1879 - 1894' in the *Art Journal*, (1894) pp 138 - 142 and Beattie (1983).

28 In addition he produced a private memorial for the parents of Haron Baronian which is now at the Red Cross Headquarters in Knutsford.

29 From Joseph Hatton, 'The Life & Wok of Alfred Gilbert RA, MVO, LLD', *Easter Art Annual*, 1903, quoted in Dorment, R. (1986), p 162.

30 See Gaffney (1998) on Welsh nationalism and the memorialisation of the 'Great War in Wales.

31 Colchester War Memorial Souvenir, unveiling ceremony booklet, 1923. *Scouting For Boys* actually featured an illustration of St George slaying the dragon, the figure of the saint dressed in the uniform of the scouts.

32   *Yorkshire Observer*, 15 August 1914.

33 Quoted in the *Macclesfield Courier And Herald*, 14 October 1916, p 8.

34 See Colley (1992), p 5.

35 For discussion of Britannia see Warner (1985) & Samuel (1989).

36 See Whittaker (1985), pp 2 -3.

37 H.H Martyn and Co. had showrooms in London, Glasgow, Manchester and other large cities in the United Kingdom. (The company were also to expand their business after the war into the production of prosthetic limbs for amputees).

38 In some cases whole figures were added. L.F Roslyn's standing soldier at Portstewart and Dromore has a wounded comrade at his feet in other locations. And Henry Fehr's often used Victory has, uniquely at Portadown, a dying soldier in her arms.

39 The poster was designed by Bernard Partridge.

40 Compton (2004), p 114.

41 One example is the 'Memorial Plaque' presented to the families of every soldier killed on active service in the war which featured Britannia. It was designed by E. Carter Preston.

42 From 'For the Fallen' by Laurence Binyon, published in *The Times*, 21 September 1914.

43 See Moriarty (University of Sussex 1995), p 186.

44 *The History of Stockport War Memorial and Art Gallery*, Stockport Metropolitan Borough Council leaflet.

45 See Cavanagh (1997), pp 246 - 248.

Chapter Two: Men Who March Away

1   The chapter title is taken from Thomas Hardy's poem 'Men Who March Away (Song of
        the Soldiers)', published in *The Times Literary Supplement*, 10 September 1914.
2   H.O. Arnold Foster in Reader (1988), p 6.
3   See Colley (1992), p 287.
4   Other examples of memorials of this sort include the 'Commercials' memorial in
        Newcastle and his Boer War memorial for the King's Regiment in Liverpool.
5   The hooded crow (the corvus comix) was apparently so common in the district that it
        became known as the Royston Crow and local inhabitants became known as 'crows'. The
        local newspaper is still popularly known as the Royston Crow and local sports teams
        (known as 'the Crows') wear black and white as their colours and feature the bird on
        their badges. See the North Hertfordshire District Council website, www.north-herts.gov.uk.
6   If church memorials are included, the Crucifixion is probably the most popular subject
        of all.
7   See Chapter Seven.
8   South London Press, 28 April 1922, p 6, quoted in Cavanagh (2007), p 214.
9   The same figure was also used for a memorial to the 41st Division at Flers in France.
10   Hale War Memorial Committee booklet.
11   Quoted in Wyke & Cocks (2004), p 392.
12   Also used at Builth Wells.
13   Figures from Winter (1986), p 72.
14   Ibid. p 73.
15   Cunningham (1975), p 70.
16   Samuel (1989), p 238.
17   Ibid. p 237.
18   Wolseley in Cunningham (1975), p 97.
19   Figures from Winter (1986), p 28. Conscription was eventually introduced early in 1916,
        though not in Ireland.
20   See pp 161 -162 for discussion of the controversy surrounding the design of headstones.
21   The figures for the Llandaff memorial were exhibited at the Royal Academy in 1924:
        the two flanking figures were entitled 'Workman' and 'Student'.
22   Moriarty (University of Sussex 1995), p 214.
23   Pevsner, N. & Neave, D., *The Buildings of England. Yorkshire: York & the East
        Riding*, (Yale, New Haven & London, 1972), p 693.
24   *Daily Post and Mercury*, 16 October 1926.
25   From the Liverpool Cenotaph official programme quoted in Cavanagh (1997), p 99.
26   Bolton War Memorial, unveiling ceremony booklet.
27   Public Monument & Sculpture Association, National Recording Project notes, ref.
        MR/BOL25. (see PMSA. website: pmsa.cch.kcl.ac.uk/MR/MR-BOL25.htm).
28   Quoted in Wyke & Cocks (2004), p 221.
29   *Bolton Evening News*, 27 December 1927.
30   These words are inscribed on the memorial.
31   See Simkins (1988).
32   See Usherwood, Beach & Morris (2000), pp 91 - 92.

Chapter Three: Women of Britain Say "Go!"

1   *The Graphic*, 22 August 1914, p 314.
2   See Conway, J., 'Stereotypes of Femininity in a Theory of Sexual Evolution' in Vicinus (1972), p 144.
3   See Vicinus (1972), p 141.
4   See Arthur (2002), p 19.
5   See Van Emden, (2005).
6   Demuth in Arthur (2002), p 22.
7   From the song 'Your King and Country Wants You'.
8   MacDonald (1980), p 22.
9   Lieutenant R.A. Chell in Brown (1978), p 72).
10   Ibid.
11   In Bourke (1999), p 140.
12   Ibid.
13   Grenfell's attitude was clearly shared by others. See for example Henry de Man's comments quoted in Bourke (1999), p 31: "One day ... I secured a direct hit on an enemy encampment, saw bodies or parts of bodies go up in the air, and heard the desperate yelling of the wounded or the runaways. I had to confess to myself that it was one of the happiest moments of my life".
14   Bourke (1999), p 1.
15   *Yorkshire Observer*, 6 July 1922.
16   *Bradford Daily Telegraph*, 3 July 1922 in King (1998), p 208.
17   *Yorkshire Observer*, 3 July 1922.
18   *Bradford Daily Telegraph*, 3 July 1922 in King (1998), pp 207 - 208.
19   *Keighley News*, 6 December 1924 in King (1998), p 176.
20   *Derry Standard*, 25 May 1927. A very similar memorial was produced by March for Cape Town in South Africa.
21   Bourke (1999), p 2. However, as one military historian recently explained ' What you want to do is to knock a soldier out of the battle and you want him to be a real drain on the resources. Killing him is actually relatively cheap. You just bury him in a blanket ... as the war progresses it's more about disabling soldiers than it is about killing them'. (Taff Gillingham in 'Wilfred Owen: A Remembrance Tale', B.B.C. TV, 11 Nov 2007.)
22   Gilbert in a letter to Burnley's Town Clerk, 8 November 1926.
23   Blunden (1935), p 215.
24   McKenzie (2002), p 244.
25   Figures from Winter (1978), p 40.
26   Quoted in Brown (1978), p 73.
27   Hynes (1990), p 116.
28   See Hayward (2002), pp 101 - 137.
29   From 'The Old Lady of Threadneedle Street', December 1921, Memorial Supplement, quoted in Ward-Jackson (2003), p 29.
30   From the unveiling booklet, 5 August 1923.
31   This information is inscribed on the monument.
32   *The Builder*, 12 November 1920, p 539, quoted in Ward-Jackson (2003), p 90.
33   Frampton, G., 'Our Shrine of Memory', *The Quiver*, April 1919, p 427.

34   Public Monument & Sculpture Association, National Recording Project notes, ref. MROLD06. (see PMSA. website: pmsa.cch.kcl.ac.uk/MR/MR-OLD06.htm).

35   Jagger interviewed in the 'Daily News', 14 July 1921, quoted in Compton (1985), p 69.

36   Compton (2004), p 114.

37   These included his memorial to the King's Liverpool Regiment from 1905 and the Engine Room Heroes memorial of 1916. The latter was originally intended to commemorate the thirty-two engineers who perished in the sinking of the Titanic in 1912, the year the memorial was planned, though it was also intended to leave space 'to receive at some future time the records of other heroic deeds done by seagoing engineers'. Following the outbreak of the First World War, with the memorial still in the planning stage, it was felt by some to be inappropriate to continue with the scheme, given the numbers currently being lost at sea in the war. Rather than abandon it however the inscription was amended to 'a tribute to the Engine Room Heroes of all time', with the added motto 'the brave do not die'. (Quotation from *The Engineer*, 5 July 1912, quoted in Cavanagh (1997), p 138.)

38   *Macclesfield Courier and Herald*, 29 November 1919, p 6.

39   Quoted in Moriarty (University of Sussex 1995), p 199.

40   Quoted in Boorman (1988), p 134

41   Ibid.

Chapter Four: Strong, Sensible and Fit

1   Title from Jessie Pope's poem *War Girls* - see p 101.

2   Bishop & Smart (1981), p 89.

3   Gorham (1996), p 89.

4   Bishop & Smart (1981), p 102.

5   Ibid.

6   Gorham (1996), p 89.

7   Vera Brittain was born in Newcastle-under-Lyme in 1893. In 1895 the family moved to Macclesfield where she lived until she was eleven. At that time, in 1905, the family moved again - to Buxton in Derbyshire.

8   Fountain (2002), p 22.

9   Ibid.

10   Elsie Maud Inglis was born in India in 1864. She established a maternity hospital, staffed entirely by women, in Edinburgh in 1894. She died of cancer in 1917.

11   Other women who worked as doctors at the front included Elsie Knocker and Mairi Chisolm who set up an advanced dressing station close to the trenches, working for the Belgian Red Cross (the British, French and American having rejected them).

12   The UK National Inventory of War Memorials lists ten separate memorials to Edith Cavell, including the naming of a locomotive (housed at the National Railway Museum in York).

13   For example Frederick Pomeroy's memorials at Kensington and Coleraine. This was an iconography with its origins in eighteenth century tomb sculpture.

14   *The British Journal of Nursing*, 27 March 1920, p 190.

15   'New Statesman', 10 April 1920, quoted in Sue Malvern's 'For King & Country:

Frampton's Edith Cavell (1915 - 20) and the Writing of Gender in Memorials to the Great War' in Getsy (2004), p 224.

16   The British Chaplain, the Reverend H. Stirling Gahan met Cavell the night before her execution and related her final words, quoted in Penny (1981), p 37.

17   Other villages awarded 'prizes' for the numbers who enlisted included Daldeby in Lincolnshire and Barrow-on-Trent in Derbyshire - see King (1998), p 46.

18   Knowlton is one of what came to be known in the 1930s as 'thankful villages', where all who went away to war safely returned. There were probably forty or more 'thankful villages'; memorials in such villages sometimes attest to the safe return of all who served. One example was at Harley in Shropshire where a memorial inside St. Mary's Church names 20 men and has the inscription 'By the Grace of God every one of these men returned to the Parish after the War'.

19   Anti-German feeling which resulted in businesses with German sounding names being attacked during the war led to various name changes, most famously perhaps the Royal family's change of name from Saxe-Coburg-Gotha to Windsor.

20   'The Greatest Mother' poster was actually American with some ten million copies being distributed in the United States but it was also printed in Britain. Designed by the mural artist Alonzo Foringer it was issued as part of a Red Cross appeal in 1918, one year after the U.S.A. entered the war. The model for the nurse was Agnes Tait, a sculptor. Seeing the same turn of the head and slightly ethereal look, and indeed a similar positioning of the arm, in both the Red Cross nurse of *The Greatest Mother in the World* and in Roslyn's Darwen relief suggests a possible prototype for the latter.

21   Between July 1914 and November 1918 the number of women at work rose from 3,277,000 to 4,936,000, an increase of 1,659,000. Figures from Beddoe (1989), p 48.

22   For example *Women's Land Army* of December 1917, *A Day in the Life of a Munitions Worker* (1917), *Mrs. John Bull Prepared* (1918) & *Woolwich Arsenal* (March 1918).

23   *The Times*, 18 May 1916, p 9.

24   *The Times*, 5 October 1916, p 7.

25   Yates (1918), p 12.

26   Ibid.

27   Roberts (1996), p 189.

28   See Adie (2003), p 43 & Lee (2005).

29   Adie (2003), p 66.

30   Ibid. p 48.

31   Ibid.

32   Ruby Ord in Fountain (2002), p 81.

33   See Adie (2003).

34   Ibid. p 48.

35   Yates (1918), pp 7 - 8. See also Braybon (1981) & Woollacott (1994).

36   For example at Attenborough and Chilwell in Nottinghamshire, Oare and Faversham in Kent and Low Moor in West Yorkshire.

37   The Daily Chronicle, 16 August 1918 quoted in Braybon (1981), p 159.

38   The Morning Post, 16 July 1915, quoted in Higonnet (1987), pp 119 - 120.

39   Mary Brough-Robertson in Arthur (2002), p 170.

40   Gibbs (1920), p 32.

41   Ibid. pp 436 - 437.

42   Locations where munitions workers are acknowledged include St. Luke's Church in
     Weaste, Greater Manchester, Kirkurd in the Scottish Borders and Beverley in
     Humberside. Here a street shrine erected in 1916 lists the names of all from the area
     who had served, with an indication of those killed, wounded, discharged or 'in
     munitions', an approach no doubt mirrored on numerous shrines elsewhere.

43   The inscription on the memorial.

44   Re: the 'Cross of Sacrifice', see p 162.

45   Merthyr Express, 14 November 1931, quoted in Gaffney (1998), p 42.

46   See Gaffney (1998), pp 110 - 111.

Chapter Five: Under Fire

1   Brittain (1933), p 339.

2   Tylee (1990), p 60.

3   Bagnold (1918), pp 12 - 13.

4   Kent (1993), p 67.

5   Bagnold (1918), p 56.

6   Gorham (1996).

7   Bourke (1996), p 31.

8   Figures quoted in Bourke (1996), p 33.

9   Joanna Bourke's book, *Dismembering the Male*, deals with this at some length.

10   'Maimed Soldiers Entertained at Windsor Castle', *The Graphic*, 4 November 1916 and
     'Our Wounded in their Hour of Ease', a drawing by Helen McKie, *The Graphic*, 23
     December 1916.

11   Brittain (1933), p 442.

12   Private R. Richards quoted in Arthur (2002), p 106.

13   Brittain (1933), p 371.

14   Ibid. p 356.

15   From Wilfred Owen's poem 'Dulce et Decorum Est'.

16   Sassoon (1937), p 538.

17   Smith & Pear (1917), p 30.

18   *The Times*, 8 April 1915. See also *The Times*, 24 August 1915.

19   Smith & Pears (1917).

20   Ibid.

21   Lord Southborough in Bogacz, T., 'War Neurosis and Cultural Change in England,
     1914 -1922:   The Work of the War Office Committee of Enquiry into Shell Shock' in
     the *Journal of Contemporary History*, Vol. 24 (1989), p 227.

22   Bogacz (1989), p 231.

23   Ibid. p 239.

24   Smith & Pears (1917), p 8.

25   Myers (1940), p 28.

26   Showalter (1985), p 174.

27   Myers (1940), p 40.

28   Mayor's address at the unveiling of the memorial.

29   Her maiden name was Edith Agnes Kathleen Bruce. During the war she had worked on the production of masks for the seriously maimed (see Chapter 11).

30   Rodin's Thinker, though not intended as such, was used as a memorial statue for his own tomb.

31   Collins (1998), p 122.

32   Ibid.

33   St Anne's-on-Sea unveiling ceremony booklet, 12 October 1924.

34   Blunden (1935), p 67.

35   Quoted in Boorman (1988), p 137.

36   Blundstone was actually born in Switzerland but returned to England as a child and studied art at Ashton-under-Lyne (near Stalybridge) before moving to London to study at the South London Technical Art School and the Royal Academy. Later he worked closely with Gilbert Bayes: both worked as assistants in the Modelling Department of the Sir John Cass School. The two also collaborated on a memorial in St.Johns, Newfoundland, unveiled in 1924.

37   From The Stalybridge Reporter, 12 November 1921 in Wyke & Cocks (2004), p 377.

38   Wyke & Cocks (2004), p 377.

39   *Manchester Guardian*, 15 August 1916, p 10. *The Times*, 1 September 1916, p 7.

40   Quoted in Reeves, N., 'Film Propaganda and Its Audience: The Example of Britain's Official Films During the First World War' in the *Journal of Contemporary History*, Vol.18, No. 3, (July 1983), p 480.

41   Sillars (1987), p 21.

42   Reeves (1983), p 468.

43   *Manchester Guardian*, 15 August 1916, p 10.

44   The title, 'Paths of Glory', is taken from Thomas Gray's 'Elegy Written in a Country Churchyard' (1751).

45   At the start of the war there had in fact been a prohibition on all press photogrpahy, only relaxed in 1916 by the initial appointment of just two official photographers.

46   *Macclesfield Courier and Herald*, 29 November 1919, p 5.

47   *Macclesfield Courier and Herald*, 20 December, 1919, p 6.

Chapter Six: The Great Sacrifice

1   There are in fact a number of versions produced by West of this famous image including one in the Royal Collection. Paintings inspired by *The Death of Wolfe* included John Singleton Copley's *The Death of Major Peirson* and Arthur William Devis' *Death of Nelson at Trafalgar*. West's own painting of the *Death of Nelson* is also derived from his earlier work.

2   James Clark produced a sequel to *The Great Sacrifice*, entitled *The Greater Reward*, which showed the dead soldier ascending to heaven, holding an angel's hand. Other paintings during the war presented similar imagery. Henry Lintott's *Avatar* (1916) for example depicted four angels carrying on their shoulders a dead soldier on a stretcher.

3   Wilkinson (1978), p 16.

4   *The Guardian*, 10 June 1915, quoted in Wilkinson (1978), p 253.

5   This imagery was appropriate for a man who was a Middle Eastern expert. As a

politician, Sykes was very much involved in wartime policy making for the Middle East. His inclusion on the memorial might be considered an anomaly; he died, not in the war, but of Spanish flu in 1919, whilst involved in peace negotiations in Paris.

6   *The History of Stockport War Memorial and Art Gallery*, Stockport Metropolitan Borough Council leaflet.

7   *Paisley Daily Express*, 28 July 1924.

8   At the outbreak of the First World War there were 117 chaplains in the British Army, 89 of them Anglicans; by the end of the war the number had risen to 3,475 with 172 chaplains being killed on the field of battle. See Wilkinson (1978) p.124.

9   Gibbs (1920), p 82.

10 Identical imagery was used by Morris and Alice Meredith-Williams on their memorial to the men of the London, Liverpool, Tyneside and South African Scottish Regiments in the Scottish National War Memorial at Edinburgh.

11 In fact Swinstead supposedly based his painting on a soldier - Rifleman Frederick Charles Taylor - who survived his wounds. Swinstead apparently visited him in hospital. (See Laffin (1988), p 112).

12 This same relief was also used in 1923 on a memorial to 'Old Salopians' at Shrewsbury.

13 Moriarty (1992), p 73

14 Ibid. p 72. 26

15 Kernot (1927), p 68.

16 1 - Jesus is condemned to death / He becomes a soldier, 2 - Jesus carries his cross / He marches with his rifle, 3 - Jesus falls the first time beneath his cross / To the front, 4 - Jesus meets his afflicted mother / Behind the lines he meets the afflicted inhabitants of destroyed villages, 5 - Simon helps Jesus to carry his cross / He is helped by the guns, 6 - Veronica wipes the face of Jesus / He is wounded and helped by a comrade, 7 - Jesus falls the second time / He is shelled in the front line, 8 - Jesus meets the women of Jerusalem / Behind the lines, 9 - Jesus falls the third time / He is shelled in a communication trench, 10 - Jesus is stripped of his garments / He is a prisoner and tormented by his captors, 11 - Jesus is nailed on the cross / He goes over the top, 12 - Jesus dies on the cross / No man's land. Death, 13 - Jesus is laid in the arms of his blessed mother / Three mourning figures over the soldier's body, 14 - Jesus is placed in the sepulchre / He is carried to the grave by stretcher bearer. Quoted in Skipworth, P., *Gilbert Ledward*, The Fine Art Society exhibition catalogue, (London 1988).

17 Gill's carvings at Bradford were in fact based on designs provided by his friend and fellow artist (and recently ordained Catholic priest) Desmond Chute - though the 14th station would itself appear to be based on, or at least strongly influenced by, William Blake's painting of *The Body of Christ Borne to the Tomb* in the collection of the Tate.

18 The Imperial War Graves Commission, founded in May 1917, was charged with the maintenance of these graves. The commission had its origins in the work of Fabian Ware, Commissioner of the British Red Cross, who had begun to mark and record military burials as early as October 1914. In February 1915 his unit was renamed the Graves Registration Commission and later that year given military status.

19 Other examples include St Mary's Church in Cavendish, Suffolk with thirteen crosses and St Peter's and St Paul's Church in Deddington, Oxfordshire which has nine. The twelve crosses which formed the memorial in St Chrysostom's Church in Bradford were unfortunately lost when the church was subsequently demolished.

20   Examples of crucifixes used as village memorials include Nympsfield in Gloucestershire and Edwinstone in Nottinghamshire.

21   The U.K. National Inventory of War memorials lists over 5,000 examples. Plaques and 'Rolls of Honour' far exceeded this number but were of course mainly found inside buildings.

22   Moriarty (1992), p 69

23   Collins (1998), p 21.

24   In a letter to William Rotherstein quoted in Collins (1998), p 44.

25   These comments were made in retrospect when Epstein also claimed the figure as 'prophetic', accusing the world 'for the First World War and for the later wars in Abyssinia, China, and Spain which culminated in the Second World War'. Epstein (1955), p 102.

26   Cork, R., 'War of Remembrance' in *The Times* Magazine, (12 November 1994), p 47.

27   Joseph Thorp, *The Graphic*, 29 July 1916, p 136.

28   Epstein (London 1955), p 102. His comments about the scale of the work were made retrospectively; this was not necessarily the original intention.

29   In a letter from Gill to William Rothenstein, quoted in Collins (1998), p 35.

30   Gill commented 'P'raps they took fright, or were insulted at the awful suggestion that London were a commercial city or that England were a temple from which a money-changer or two might not be missed'. Shewring (1947), p 98.

31   From Gill's pamphlet 'A War Memorial', 23 May 1923.

32   Ibid.

33   Ibid.

34   Ibid.

35   Ibid.

36   From *The Leeds Mercury*, 28 May 1923.

37   Sadler was to write, 'He departed egregiously (without telling me until it was too late) from the earlier design he had chosen. And he broke his word by publishing at the worst moment of acute controversy, and sending down to Leeds, a contentious political interpretation of the Memorial's significance. He behaved like a vain, wilful child". Quoted in Speaight, R., *The Life of Eric Gill*, (London 1966), p 133.

38   From Gill's pamphlet 'A War Memorial'.

39   Gibbs (1920), p 437.

40   At Warrington the main figure is a soldier, at Pershore Abbey it is a winged Victory; and at Dinnington the relief is used in isolation.

41   Geoffrey Gordon quoted in Bourke (1996), p 212.

42   In Longworth (1985), p 33.

43   *The Times*, 18 December 1919, p 15.

44   Ibid. p 18.

45   Blomfield (1932), p 178.

46   From an anonymous review of the War Memorials exhibition at the Royal Academy in *The Connoisseur*, Vol. 55, No. 220, December 1919.

47   See Blomfield (1932), pp 179 - 180. 'My only complaint of its popularity is that it has also been freely pirated all over the country. The design is, of course, my copyright, but I have come across horrible travesties of it in many local memorials apparently executed by the local mason from illustrations of the Cross given in the papers'. Blomfield's

concerns were less that the design had been 'pirated' but rather that the detailing and proportions were inaccurate.

48   Percy & Ridley (1985). The line is from Ecclesiasticus 44 : 14.

49   For more on Lutyens and the Great War Stone see Skelton & Gliddon , (2008).

50   I am grateful to Richard Barnes for information on Ditchingham's memorial.

51   Gregor (1994), p.47/

52   Colonel Lewin in Compton (1985), p 94.

53   Goscombe John was one sculptor (and former tutor of Jagger's) who exhibited a number of examples of such work.

54   From a description of the memorial prepared for the Manchester War Memorial Committee, *Proceedings of the City of Manchester Council*, 6 August 1924, p 403.

55   Winter (1995), p 163.

56   Ibid.

57   From Anna Dostoevsky's memoirs, quoted in Gatrall, J., Between Iconoclasm and Silence: representing the Divine in Holbein and Dostoevskii, *Comparative Literature*, (Summer 2001).

58   Hofstatter, H.H., 'Faith and Damnation: religious Depictions in Symbolism' in Ehrhardt. I. & Reynolds, S., (eds.), *Kingdom of the Soul: Symbolist Art in Germany 1870 - 1920*, Munich, London, New York (2000), p 137.

59   See Crellin (2001) p 88.

Chapter Seven: A Narrative of War

1   Other sites suggested included the Mall and Buckingham Palace Gardens - see James Stevens Curl, 'The Royal Artillery Memorial at Hyde Park Corner' in Compton (1985), p 83. See also Compton (2004).

2   At Manchester, Rochdale and Derby.

3   From The Yorkshire Post, 17 November 1934, quoted in Black, *The Bite of War's Reality* (2003), p 30.

4   Other members of the Sculpture Faculty included George Frampton, Thomas Brock, Goscombe John, Bertram Mackennal, Frederick Pomeroy, Derwent Wood and Havard Thomas.

5   Jagger's winning piece was entitled 'A Bacchanalian Scene', now in a private collection.

6   In Compton (1985), p 15.

7   Quoted in James Stevens Curl, 'The Royal Artillery Memorial at Hyde Park Corner' in Compton (1985), p 83.

8   See Compton (1985) & Compton (2004).

9   White (1987), p 1.

10   Ibid. p 42.

11   Ibid. pp 42 - 43.

12   *The Times*, 16 December 1922, p 14.

13   Sir Reginald Blomfield apparently had a major influence on changes made to the designs for the Guards' memorial asking for at least sixteen revisions - see Moriarty (2003).

14   Figures from the article by Simon Rees, *The Forgotten Army*, 19 June 2004,

www.firstworldwar.com.

15   For a detailed discussion of the Hall of Remembrance see Harries & Harries (1983). When the scheme collapsed the work passed to the newly created Imperial War Museum.

16   See Moriarty (2003). When both Jagger and Gilbert Ledward were employed producing sculptures for the intended Hall of Remembrance they, for a time, shared a studio at the Royal College of Art. Both men used the same models; the man with broken nose and shaven head was also used by Ledward for his panel, *Germans Violate the Neutrality of Belgium*.

17   From 'To the Vanguard' - see Roberts (1996), p 207.

18   Jagger, C.S., 'The Sculptor's Point of View', *The Studio*, Vol. CVI, No. 488, November 1933, p251.

19   The others were Bourdelle, Mestrovic, Metzner and Henry Poole.

20   In addition to the memorial at Louverval and the Anglo-Belgian memorial in Brussels, Jagger worked on monuments at Port Tewfik in Egypt and Nieuport in Belgium, carving tigers at the former and lions at the latter.

21   In Compton (1985), p 81.

22   Ibid. p 82.

23   Quoted in *The Times*, 29 October 1925.

24   *The Times*, 19 October 1925, p 15.

25   *The Times*, 22 October 1925, p 8.

26   Major MacGregor Knox, *The Times*, 20 October 1925, p 15.

27   Ex-Gunner, A.B. Thornton, *The Times*, 29 October 1925, p 15.

28   Elizabeth Gillman, *The Times*, 27 October 1925, p 15.

29   Lieutenant-General Sir Herbert Uniacke in the *Illustrated London News*, 14 November 1925, pp 956 - 957.

30   *Manchester Guardian*, 19 October 1925, p 10.

31   Although unusual, this is a pattern sometimes used elsewhere, for example at Armitage in Staffordshire and Lower Peover in Cheshire.

32   For information on the use of obelisks as war memorials see Barnes (2004).

33   The image of the bugler was surprisingly little used but two can be found in Northern Ireland - at Moy in County Tyrone and Glendermott in Londonderry - whilst Margaret Winser depicted a bugler for her memorial at Wakefield Grammar School.

34   From St Anne's-on-Sea inveiling ceremony booklet, 12 October 1924.

Chapter Eight: Peace

1   *Liverpool Review*, undated.

2   *The Sentinel*, 11 November 1924.

3   *The Sentinel*, 13 November 1924.

4   Hynes (1990), p.270

5   Ibid. p.283

6   Nora (1989), p 23.

7   In Wyke & Cocks (2004), p 358.

8   From The Ashton Reporter, 23 September 1922, quoted in Wyke & Cocks (2004), p 359.

9   Moriarty (1997), p 135.
10   As described in the U.K. National Inventory of War Memorials.
11   The story, *The Bowmen*, was written by Arthur Machen.
12   See Jalland, P., 'Victorian Death and Its Decline: 1850-1918', p 251 in Jupp & Gittings (1999).
13   See Sir Arthur Conan Doyle's *The History of Spiritualism*, Vol. II, (London 1926).
14   Yorkshire Observer, 12 June 1922, quoted in King (1998), p 179.
15   See Warner (1985).
16   Colchester War Memorial Souvenir, unveiling ceremony booklet, 1923.
17   See Gildea (1911) plus the U.K. National Inventory of War Memorials.
18   Moriarty (University of Sussex 1995), p 95.
19   *East Sussex News*, 8 September 1922.
20   Ibid.
21   Public Monument & Sculpture Association, National Recording Project notes, ref. TWNE37. (see P.M.S.A. website: pmsa.cch.kcl.ac.uk/NE/TWNE37.htm.)
22   King (1998), p 176.
23   *Macclesfield Courier and Herald*, 16 November 1918, p 8.
24   Colonel W.M. Nicholson quoted in MacDonald (1988), p 316.
25   Wilkinson (1978), p 180.
26   Ibid.
27   Wilkinson notes that in 1888 it was calculated that three out of four children attended Sunday School in England and Wales and adds the comment that this is a remarkable figure considering the relatively low attendance of members of the higher social classes. Wilkinson (1978), p 7.
28   Sir Llewellyn Woodward in Wilkinson (1978), pp 305 - 306.
29   Moriarty (University of Sussex 1995), p 208
30   Noszlopy & Waterhouse (2005), p 125.
31   *Oldham Evening Chronicle*, 19 April 1920.
32   Boorman (1988), p 89.
33   In Moriarty (University of Sussex 1995), p 218.
34   Fabian Ware in Longworth (1985), p 14.

Chapter Nine: We Will Remember Them

1   See Greenberg (1989).
2   Ibid. p 7.
3   Unlike the British Cenotaph, the French version, designed by André Mare, Gustave Laulmes and Louis Sue, was highly elaborate, with four Victories on each of the sides, a giant brazier on top and copious decoration throughout. After the war it was demolished.
4   *The Times*, 21 July 1919.
5   Ibid.
6   *The Times*, 26 July 1919.
7   In a letter from Lutyens to Sir Alfred Mond quoted in Greenberg (1989), p 10.
8   See Greenberg (1989) for a detailed analysis of the Cenotaph.
9   In May 2000 the Cenotaph was daubed in red paint with the slogan 'Why glorify war?'

which suggests that for some, more recently at least, Lutyens' intentions were misunderstood.

10   Winter (1995), p 223.

11   See Barnes, R., *John Bell: The Sculptor's Life and Works*, (Norwich 1999).

12   See Yarrington, A., 'Nelson the Citizen Hero: State and Public Patronage of Monumental Sculpture, 1805 - 18' in *Art History*, Vol. 6, No. 3, (September 1983) pp 315 -329 and Yarrington, A, 'Public Sculpture and Civic Pride: 1800-1830' in Curtis (1989).

13   *Macclesfield Courier and Herald*, 24 September 1921, p 3.

14   *Macclesfield Courier and Herald*, 8 October 1921, p 3.

15   *Macclesfield Courier and Herald*, 20 December 1919, p 6.

16   See Gildea (1911).

17   Wilkinson (1978), p 171.

18   See King (1998), pp 47 - 60.

19   See www.worthing.gov.uk.

20   See Gaffney (1998), pp 34 & 35.

21   See for example articles in *Architectural Review*, December 1917, June 1918, July 1918, July to October 1919, and January and February 1920.

22   Macartney, M.E., 'Homes of Rest: Almshouses as War Memorials - II', *Architectural Review*, Vol. XLIII, No. 259, (June 1918) p 119.

23   *The Times*, 4 April 1919, p 7.

24   Quoted in Cavanagh (2007), p 116.

25   *Macclesfield Courier and Herald*, 31 May 1919, p 3.

26   Inglis, *Journal of Contemporary History* (1992), p 598.

27   Public Monument & Sculpture Association, National Recording Project notes, ref. MR.STO02. (see PMSA website: pmsa.cch.kcl.ac.uk/MR/MR-STO02.htm). Ledward's original model is displayed in the memorial hall at Stockport.

28   *Macclesfield Courier and Herald*, 29 November 1919, p 6.

29   Quoted in *The Observer*, 1 July 2007, p 23.

30   Merthyr Express, 24 November 1923, quoted in Gaffney, (1998), p 34.

31   As Jim McGinlay has pointed out Alexander Carrick was particularly sensitive to the siting of his work and took the trouble to visit towns which commissioned memorials to view the intended site or discuss with memorial committees the best location for the monument. See McGinlay's excellent website www.alexandercarrick.webeden.co.uk.

32   In a number of cases, names discovered to be missing from the memorial have been added much later. At Dromore in County Down, Northern Ireland, a bronze plaque listing over sixty additional names, omitted when the monument was erected in 1926, was added as recently as 2007. Although the situation in Ireland may have been exceptional, with names deliberately withheld for political or sectarian reasons, it seems likely that the omission of names, for whatever reason, was quite common.

33   See www.worthing.gov.uk.

34   The Thiepval memorial was designed by Sir Edwin Lutyens; Menin Gate by Sir Reginald Blomfield

35   The Book of Remembrance at Gateshead has now been moved to what is considered a safer location while at Oldham, after the Second World War, the chamber was changed to create a window which revealed a Book of Remembrance for those killed in that war, the pages of which are automatically turned each day.

36   *Macclesfield Courier and Herald*, 24 September 1921, p 3.

37   Weaver (1915), p 2. Civic Arts Association booklets included A.C. Benson's *Lest We Forget* (1917), A. Clutton-Brock's *On War Memorials* (1916), C. Jack's *War Shrines* (1918), E. Warren's *War Shrines* (1917) and the same author's *War Memorials* (1919).

38   Victoria and Albert Museum, *War Memorial Exhibitions catalogue*, (London 1919).

39   *Architectural Review*, January 1919, p 20.

40   Royal Academy of Arts, *War Memorial Exhibition*, catalogue, (London 1919).

41   *Studio*, Vol. LXXX, 1920.

42   Other examples where the models of work discussed in this book were exhibited at the Royal Academy include Blackpool, Bootle, Bridgwater, Bridlington, Bury, the Cameronians, Captain Albert Ball, the Cavalry memorial, the Cavell memorial for Norwich, Exeter, the Guards memorial, Hoylake & West Kirby, Llandaff, the Machine Gunners, Newcastle, Paddington, Port Sunlight, S & J Watts, St Anne's-on-Sea, Southwark, Stockport, Todmorden and Wrexham.

43   All works exhibited at the Royal Academy were portrait busts.

44   Henry Fehr's memorial at Portadown is one other which implies death by gas. At the foot of a dying soldier supported in the arms of a winged Victory, can be seen his gas mask.

45   Usherwood, Beach & Morris (2000), p.155.

46   Frampton (1919), p 426.

47   Ibid.

48   Major-General Donald in Gardiner (1993), p.179.

49   Minutes of the Royal Society of British Sculptors, quoted in King (1998), p.156.

50   *The Times*, 28 July 1917, p.9.

51   Gardiner (1993), 172.

52   Frampton (1919), p 426. These views were clearly widespread. Paul Montford felt his employment opportunities were so limited by his age and non-combatant status that he decided, in 1923, to emigrate to Australia.

53   Epstein's one official war memorial was produced after the Second World War, for the TUC in London.

Chapter Ten: Memory and Mourning

1   *Architectural Review*, January 1919, p 20.

2   *Daily Mirror*, 9 July 1918, p 6.

3   *London Evening News*, 8 May 1919 - under the pseudonym Warren Foster.

4   Statement published in the press, 7 November 1919.

5   Gregory (1994), p 10.

6   *The Times*, 12 November 1919, pp 15 - 16.

7   Ibid. p 16.

8   See *The Times*, 11 November 1920.

9   The procedure for selecting the body was explained by Brigadier-General Wyatt, the officer in charge, in a letter to the *Daily Telegraph* in November 1939. See MacDonald (1988), p 325. & Hanson (2005), pp 355 - 364. Great care was taken in the selection of the body to ensure anonymity: on the night of 7 November, one unidentified body was exhumed from each of four main areas of battle - the Aisne, the Somme, Ypres and

Arras. Each body was covered with a Union Jack and placed on a stretcher. Wyatt then chose at random one of the bodies which was placed in a coffin and transported the following day to Boulogne and from there, with military escort, across the Channel to Dover. Here it received a nineteen gun salute before being transferred to a train for the journey to London. On the morning of 11 November the body was carried to the Cenotaph on a gun carriage drawn by six black horses followed by twelve pallbearers who included Lord Haig, Sir John French and Admiral Sir David Beatty. At the eleventh hour the King released the flags which veiled the Cenotaph and then followed the two minutes silence. The body then continued down Whitehall to the Abbey.

10   *Daily Mirror*, 15 November 1920, p 3.

11   *The Times*, 16 November 1920, p 14 & 17 November 1920, p 14.

12   Tyson Smith included a self-portrait amongst the mourners.

13   A far less common variation of his idea is the occasional depiction of a bugler sounding The Last Post (as for example at Moy and Glendermott, both in Northern Ireland).

14   Moriarty (University of Sussex 1995), p 185.

15   This was a sculptural scheme which Lutyens was encouraged to adopt for the Cenotaph. See Greenberg (1989), p 12.

16   Unveiling ceremony booklet, 12 November 1926.

17   *Macclesfield Courier and Herald*, 24 September 1921, p 3.

18   From the unveiling ceremony booklet, 16 November 1922.

19   The same figure was used for a private memorial to Lieutenant H.G.E. Hill-Trevor at Givenchy-de-la-Bassée on the Western Front.

20   In his 1946 book, *War Memorials*, intended as inspiration for prospective memorialists after the Second World War, Arnold Whittick had suggested that the 'war memorial, at its best, must have a sense of life, of re-creation and renewal' and in this context he saw the fountain as a most appropriate form. Whittick (1946), p 11.

21   Bayes was very interested in the decorative arts and in garden sculpture in particular and in this capacity worked closely with the Doulton ceramics company for many years.

22   Public Monument & Sculpture Association, National Recording Project notes, ref. MSWR0049. (see P.M.S.A. website: pmsa.cch.kcl.ac.uk/LL2MSWR0049.htm.)

23   Nora (1989), p 19.

24   Rita Roestorick, speaking on B.B.C. television news on 12 October 2007. The Armed Forces Memorial - to those who have died since the Second World War - was unveiled on 12 October 2007 at the National Memorial Arboretum at Alrewas in Staffordshire.

25   Young (1993), p 5.

26   Ibid. p 7.

27   See Rivers (1924), p 189. Sassoon was sent to Craiglockhart after writing a 'Soldier's Declaration' in which he condemned the execution of the war claiming that it was being 'deliberately prolonged by those who have the power to end it' and stating that 'I can no longer be be a party to prolong these sufferings for ends which I believe to be evil and unjust'. The statement, written whilst convalescing after being wounded in battle, was sent to his commanding officer and to the press and was read out in Parliament. On the intervention of his friend Robert Graves it was agreed to declare him shell shocked and he was sent to Craiglockhart rather than to a court martial. Whether he was actually suffering from neurasthenia may be questioned. He was clearly under considerable stress and certainly had nightmares. Rivers' sympathetic 'treatment' was greatly

appreciated by Sassoon who subsequently returned to the trenches.

28   Rivers (1924), p 193.

29   Ibid.

30   Ibid.

31   Freud, S., 'Mourning and Melancholia' in Strachey, J. & Freud, A. (eds.) *The Complete Psychological Works of Sigmund Freud, Vol. XIV,* (London 1957), p 244.

32   Ibid.

33   See Bindman & Baker (1995), pp 159 - 161.

34   See Bernard de Montfaucon's description - from his *Antiquity Explained,* Book VI, (1719 -1721) quoted in Bindman & Baker (1995), note 41, p 380.

Chapter Eleven: Regeneration

1   Unveiling ceremony booklet, 12 December 1926.

2   The inscription on the memorial reads ' The laurels of the sons are watered from the hearts of the mothers' which seems to imply the depiction of mother and son, though the visual evidence would tend to deny this. Indeed, Catherine Moriarty notes that 'the memorial was financed by Mr. Dixon-Nutall, the owner of a local glass works, who had lost a son in the war. Local people believed the soldier was modelled on another son and that the female figure represented the son's wife'. She does however go on to add 'as the Inventory record states "there is no written evidence of this"' - Moriarty (University of Sussex 1995), pp 201 - 202.

3   *The Times,* 18 May 1916, p 9.

4   Ibid.

5   *The Times,* 5 October 1916, p 7.

6   See Beddoe (1989), p 48.

7   A. McGregor in 'Woman Worker', May 1917 in Braybon (1981), p 170.

8   Beddoe, (1989), p 13.

9   See Beddoe (1989).

10   Quoted in Kent (1993), p 16.

11   The Bishop of London in Winter (1985), p 193.

12   Before the war roughly 13% of all males and 19% of females remained unmarried; in the inter war years these figures declined significantly. (Figures from Winter 1985, p 261).

13   Showalter (1985), p 172.

14   Bourke (1996), p 145.

15   MacDonald (1988), p 247.

16   Bourke (1996), p 145.

17   Quoted in programme five of the television series, 1914 -18: *The Great War and the Shaping of the Twentieth Century,* K.C.E.T. Los Angeles & B.B.C. co-production.

18   The four grade system was introduced in March 1915 but was later revised in June 1916 to provide five categories with subsections, A1 at this time becoming the highest classification, indicating fully trained and physically fit for overseas service.

19   Bourke (1996), p 172.

20   A letter in the *Connoisseur,* June 1920, p 110.

21   Harries & Harries (1983), p 45.

22   Bourke (1996), p 175.

23   Ibid.

24   Unveiling ceremony booklet, 11 November 1922.

25   *The Times,* 19 October 1926.

26   Quoted in Quinlan (2005), p 336.

27   Letter from K. Rathbone in the Sutton Coldfield News, 22 July 1919, in Noszlopy &
        Beach (1998), p 77.

28   Other examples illustrated here include Paisley, Workington, Broughton, Twickenham,
        Chirk, Trumpington, Euston and Liverpool.

29   See Moriarty (2004), pp 291 -309.

30   Compton (1985), p 21.

31   *Manchester Guardian,* 19 October 1925, p 10.

32   Seven casts of a reduced version of this figure were made.

33   Wyke & Cocks (2004), p 122.

34   Compton (2004), p 112. A small, independent version of the Hoylake figure, entitled
        'Wipers' is in the collection of the Imperial War Museum. In all, six casts were made.
        Another cast is in the Royal Collection.

35   Numbers quoted in Black, *The Bite of War's Reality* (2003), p 38. Between 1914 and
        1916 over a quarter of a million transport workers nation-wide enlisted. (See Beckett &
        Simpson (1985), p 9.

36   See Black, *The Bite of War's Reality* (2003).

37   The difficulties of arriving at an acceptable solution were to lead to Jagger at one point
        offering his resignation.

38   In a letter to Viscount Churchill, November 1922, quoted in Black, *The Bite of War's
        Reality* (2003), p 44. Jagger apparently felt some dissatisfaction with the figure,
        believing it overly sentimental. (Sheffield Daily Independent, 17 January 1936, quoted
        in Black. p 47).

39   Figures quoted in Bourke (1996), p 22.

40   Compton (2004), p 116.

41   King (1998), p 107.

42   See Moriarty (University of Sussex 1995), pp 95 - 97.

43   The poster was designed by Maurice Neumont in 1918.

44   Borg (1991), p 76. Gleichen (1928), p 171.

45   Gleichen (1928), p 171.

46   From notes by Kennington in 1924, quoted in Black, *The Real Thing* (2003), p 857.

47   From the Kennington archives at the Imperial War Museum, quoted in Cavanagh
        (2007), p 284.

48   *Daily Telegraph,* 6 October 1924, p 9.

49   *Observer,* 5 October 1924, p 15.

50   *Daily News,* 4 October 1924, p 5..

51   See Black, *The Real Thing* (2003), p 857. Frederick Pomeroy's memorial for Larne in
        Northern ireland features a similar detail. Here a soldier and a sailor clasp hands.

52   From Eric Gill's *Autobiography,* (London 1940), p 162.

53   Gibbs (1920), p 59.

54   *The New York Times,* (25 May 1919) section 7, p 13.

55   Nevinson (1937), p 87.

56 See Theweleit, K., *Male Fantasies, Vol. 2: Male Bodies - Psychoanalysing the White Terror*, (Minneapolis 1989), p 162.

57 Gilbert was almost certainly influenced himself by Antonin Mercié's version of David , now in the Musée d'Orsay.

58 Quoted in Penny (1981), p 39.

59 Beattie (1983), p 236. See also Cork, '*The Bitter Truth*' (1994).

60 Derwent Wood was also the author of a particularly gruesome and controversial bronze sculpture, *Canada's Golgotha* which showed a Canadian soldier crucified with bayonets which pinned him to the side of a barn - an illustration of a widely-believed story of just such an event having taken place during the war.

61 Interestingly enough the Hale memorial was designed by Derwent Wood's studio assistant Frederick Wilcoxson. Another memorial which seems to have been influenced by Michelangelo's *David* was Alexander Carrick's statue of a kilted soldier at Killin in Scotland. (Another memorial by Carrick, at Workington, seemed to referece Michelangelo's St Peter's *Pietà*).

62 Robert Graves wrote a poem in 1916 entitled *Goliath and David*, which saw Goliath as victorious and David vanquished - a counter to the trite assumptions of the inevitability of victory for the 'righteous'.

63 From the unveiling ceremony programme, quoted in Usherwood, Beach & Morris (2000), p 65.

64 Bolton War Memorial, unveiling ceremony booklet.

65 Mary Pownall was born in Leigh in Lancashire sometime during the second half of the 19th century. She studied at Frankfurt, Paris and Rome and exhibited at the Paris Salon between 1893-1899 and at the Royal Academy from 1897 to 1925. In 1902 she married Alfed Bromet and moved to Oxhey near Watford. In 1910 she became President of the Society of Women Artists.

66 Hussey (1929), p 67.

67 The committee was composed of three representatives from each of the four interested parties - the borough, the two counties of Cambridgeshire and the Isle of Ely, and the university. In addition to the three heads of college representing the university, the deputy mayor, one of the representatives of the borough, was himself Master of Corpus Christi college.

68 *Studio*, Vol. 84, No. 353, (August 1922), pp 111 - 112. When McKenzie was later commissioned to produce another version of this figure for Woodbury in the USA he made significant changes - to the uniform and the substitution of a laurel branch for the English rose, but also to what he considered were more typically 'American' facial features.

69 Derwent Wood (1917), pp 949 - 951.

70 Freeman (1985) p 286.

71 Quoted in Young (1995), p187.

72 Ibid. p 188.

73 Tait McKenzie in Moriarty *The Absent Dead and Figurative First World War Memorials* (1995), p 158.

74 Derwent Wood (1917), pp 949-951.

74 Ibid.

76 Inglis, *Journal of Contemporary History* (1992), p 600.

77   Cambridge Chronicle, 5 July 1922 in Inglis *Journal of Contemporary History* (1992),
p 600.

Twelve: Summary

1   Public Monument & Sculpture Association, National Recording Project notes, ref.
MR/MCR07. (see P.M.S.A. website: pmsa.cch.kcl.ac.uk/MR/MR-MCR07.htm.)

2   Gombrich, E.H., *Symbolic Images: Studies in the Art of the Renaissance II*, (Oxford &
New York 1972), p 2.

3   Hirsch, D.E., *Validity in Interpretation*, (New Haven 1967).

4   Gombrich (1972), p 4.

5   See Inglis, *Journal of Contemporary History* (1992), p 603.

6   Gombrich (1972), p 18. One example where intended meaning and subsequent
interpretation separated in a particularly negative way was at Londonderry in Northern
Ireland. For many years the monument was seen as relevant only to the Unionist
community; for Nationalists it merely symbolised British occupation. Recent
researchers have revealed that many of the 700+ names on the monument were, in fact,
from the Catholic community and their efforts have resulted in gates in the fencing
around the memorial being unlocked and the monument being opened up to the whole
community, stressing the continuing relevance of the war memorial as part of the
history of the city and its people.

BIBLIOGRAPHY

Adie, K., *Corsets to Camouflage: Women and War*, (London 2003)

Alberti, J., *Beyond Suffrage: Feminists in War and Peace, 1914-28*, (London 1989)

Anderson, O. 'The Growth of Christian Militarism in Mid-Victorian Britain' in the *English Historical Review*, (January 1971) pp 42-49.

Anon, 'The Sculpture of Gilbert Ledward' in *Architects' Journal*,(16 Aug 1922)pp 208-213

Arthur, M., *Forgotten Voices of the Great War*, (London 2002).

Ayris, I. et al, *A Guide to the Public Monuments and Sculpture of Tyne & Wear*,(Newcastle 1996)

Barnes, R., *The Obelisk: A Monumental Feature in Britain*, (Norwich, 2004).

Batten, S., 'Forgetting the First World War', *Journal for the Centre for First World War Studies*, Vol. 2, No. 2, July 2005.

Bagnold, E., *A Diary Without Dates*, (London 1918).

Baldry, A.L, 'The Work of W.Reynolds-Stephens', *The Studio*,Vol. 17 (1899),pp 74-84.

Beattie, S., *The New Sculpture*, (New Haven & London 1983).

Beckett, I.F.W. & Simpson, K. (eds.) *A Nation in Arms: A Social Study of the British Army in the First World War*, (Manchester 1985).

Beddoe, D., *Back to Home and Duty: Women Between the Wars, 1918-1939*, (London, Boston, Sydney & Wellington 1989).

Bindman, D. & Baker, M., *Roubiliac and the 18th Century Monument: Sculpture as Theatre*, (New Haven & London 1995).

Bird, J., 'Representing the Great War' in *Block*, No. 3 (1980) pp 41-52.

Bishop,A & Smart,T(eds)*Chronicle of Youth:Vera Brittain's War Diary 1913-1917*,(London 1981)

Black, J., 'War Without the Gloss?: Masculinity, the Feminine Ideal and the Image of the Vulnerable British Soldier in First World War Memorial Sculpture c1919-25', *Object*, University College London , (Nov. 1999), pp 28-46.

Black, J,*The Sculpture of Eric Kennington*,(Much Hadham, Aldershot & Burlington VT 2002)

Black, J., 'The Bite of War's Reality: 'Letters From Home', Charles Sargeant Jagger's First World War Memorial for the Great Western Railway Company, Paddington Station (1921-22), *Firestep*, Vol. 4, No. 2, (Nov. 2003), pp 29-49.

Black, J., 'The Real Thing: Eric Kennington's 24th Infantry Division Memorial in Battersea Park, London (1921-24)', *Burlington Magazine*,Vol. CXLV,(December 2003),pp 854-859

Black, J. et al, *Blasting the Future!: Vorticism in Britain 1910-1920*, Estorick Collection exhibition catalogue, (London 2004).

Blomfield, R., *Memoirs of an Architect*, (London 1932)

Blunden, E., *Undertones of War*, (London 1935).

Bogacz, T., 'War Neurosis and Cultural Change in England, 1914-22: The Work of the War Office Committee of Enquiry into Shell Shock' in the *Journal of Contemporary History*, Vol. 24 (1989) pp 227-256.

Borg, A., *War Memorials : From Antiquity to the Present*, (London 1991).

Boorman, D,*At The Going Down of the Sun: British First World War Memorials*,(York 1988)

Boorman, D., *For Your Tomorrow: British Second World War Memorials*, (York 1995).

Bourke, J., *Dismembering the Male: Men's Bodies, Britain and the Great War*, (London 1996).

Bourke, J., *An Intimate History of Killing: Face to Face Killing in Twentieth Century Warfare*, (London 1999).

Bourne, J.M., *Britain and the Great War, 1914-1918*, (London 1989).

Braybon, G, *Women Workers in the First World War: The British Experience*, (London 1981)

Brittain, V., *Testament of Youth*, (London 1933).

Brod, H & Kaufman, M.(eds.), *Theorizing Masculinities*, (Thousand Oaks, London & Delhi 1994)

Brown, J., *Lutyens and the Edwardians: An English Architect and his Clients*, (London 1996)

Brown, M., *Tommy Goes to War*, (Stroud & Charleston 1978).

Brown, M., *The Imperial War Museum Book of the First World War*, (London 1991).

Brown, M., *The Imperial War Museum Book of the Western Front*, (London 1993).

Bruce, A., 'War Memorials' in *The Historian*, (November 1990) pp 17-20.

Burnett, C., *Britain and Her Army, 1509-1970: A Military, Political and Social Survey*, (London 1970).

Bushaway, B., 'Name Upon Name: The Great War and Remembrance' in Porter, R. (ed.), *Myths of the English*, (Cambridge 1992).

Cannadine, D., 'War and Death, Grief and Mourning in Modern Britain' in Whaley, J. (ed.), *Mirrors of Mortality: Studies in the Social History of Death*, (London 1981).

Carmichael, J., *First World War Photographers*, (London & New York 1989).

Cavanagh, T., *Public Sculpture of Liverpool*, (Liverpool 1997).

Cavanagh, T., *Public Sculpture of Leicestershire & Rutland*, (Liverpool 2000).

Cavanagh, T., *Public Sculpture of South London*, (Liverpool 2007).

Clutton-Brock, A., *On War Memorials*, Civic Arts Association, (London 1916).

Coetzee, F. & Shevin-Coetzee, M. (eds.), *Authority, Identity and the Social History of the Great War*, (Providence & Oxford 1995).

Colley, L., *Britons: Forging the Nation, 1707-1837*, (New Haven & London 1992).

Collins, J., *Eric Gill: Sculpture*, Barbican Gallery exhibition catalogue, (London 1992).

Collins, J., *Eric Gill: The Sculpture, A Catalogue Raisonne*, (London 1998).

Compton, A., *Charles Sargeant Jagger: War and Peace Sculpture*, Imperial War Museum exhibition catalogue, (London 1985).

Compton, A., 'Memorials to the Great War' in Curtis, P. (ed.), *Patronage and Practice: Sculpture on Merseyside*, (Liverpool 1989).

Compton, A., *The Sculpture of Charles Sargeant Jagger*, (Much Hadham, Aldershot & Burlington 2004).

Compton, S. (ed.), *British Art in the Twentieth Century: The Modern Movement*, Royal Academy exhibition catalogue, (London 1987).

Condell, D. & Liddiard, J., *Working For Victory? Images of Women in the First World War, 1914-18*, (London 1987).

Cooke, M. & Woolacott, A. (eds.), *Gendering War Talk*, (Princeton 1993).

Cork, R, *The Bitter Truth: Avant-Garde Art and the Great War*, (New Haven & London 1994)

Cork, R., 'War of Remembrance' in *The Times* Magazine, (12 November 1994) pp 44-47.

Cork, R., *Jacob Epstein*, (London 1999).

Corke, J., *War Memorials in Britain*, (Princes Risborough 2005).

Crellin, S., *Hermon Cawthra FRBS, ARCA 1886-1971 Sculptor*, Unpublished Sculpture Studies dissertation (Leeds 1995).

Crellin, S., 'Hollow Men: Francis Derwent Wood's Masks and Memorials, 1915-1925' in
     The Sculpture Journal VI (2001) pp 75-88.

Cross, T. (ed.), *The Lost Voices of World War One*, (London 1988).

Cunningham, H, *The Volunteer Force: A Social and Political History,1859-1908,*(London 1975)

Cunningham, H., 'The Language of Patriotism, 1750-1914' in the *History Workshop Journal*,
     Vol. 12 (1981) pp 8-33.

Cunningham, J.A., *Adrian Jones: His Life and Work (1845-1938)*, Sladmore Gallery
     exhibition catalogue, (London 1984).

Curl, J.S., *A Celebration of Death*, (London & New York 1980).

Curtis, B., 'Posters as Visual Propoganda in the Great War' in *Block*, No. 2, (1980) pp 45-57.

Curtis, P. (ed.), *Patronage and Practice: Sculpture on Merseyside*, (Liverpool 1989).

Curtis, P., *Sculpture 1900-1945*, (Oxford 1999).

Darracott, J. & Loftus, B., *First World War Posters*, (London 1972).

Dawson, G., *Soldier Heroes: British Adventure, Empire and the Imagining of Masculinities*,
     (London & New York 1994).

Degroot, GJ, *Blighty: British Society in the Era of the Great War,*(London & New York 1996)

Dickenson, D. & Johnson, M. (eds.), *Death, Dying and Bereavement*, (London 1989)

Doherty, C.E., 'Paths of Glory' in the *Art Journal*, (Spring 1992) pp 64-71.

Dorment, R. (ed.), *Alfred Gilbert: Sculptor and Goldsmith*, Royal Academy of Arts exhibition
     catalogue, (London 1986).

Dyer, G., *The Missing of the Somme*, (London 1994).

Eksteins, M., *Rites of Spring: The Great War and the Birth of the Modern Age*, (London 1989).

Epstein, J., *Epstein: An Autobiography*, (London 1955).

Fountain, N. (ed.), *Women at War*, (London 2002).

Frampton, G., 'Our Shrines of Memory: Some Suggestions For Suitable War Memorials',
     The Quiver, (April 1919), pp 425-428.

Fraser, T.G. & Jeffrey, K. (eds.), *Men, Women and War*, (Dublin 1993).

Freeman, J,'Professor Tonks: War Artist' in the *Burlington Magazine*, (May 1985) pp 284-291.

Freeman, J., 'No Easy Grace: The Great War Sculptures of Charles Sargeant Jagger' in
     Military Illustrated, (February / March 1987) pp 15-21.

Fussell, P., *The Great War and Modern Memory*, (London & New York 1975).

Gaffney, A., *Remembering the Great War in Wales*, (Cardiff 1998).

Gardiner, E.N., 'The Revival of Athletic Sculpture: Dr. R. Tait McKenzie's Work' in *Studio*,
     Vol. 80 (1920) pp 133-138.

Gardiner, S., *Epstein: Artist Against the Establishment*, (London 1993).

Garrett, R., *The Final Betrayal: The Armistice, 1918 … and Afterwards*, (Southampton 1989).

Getsy, D.J. (ed.), *Sculpture and the Pursuit of a Modern Ideal in Britain, c 1880-1930*,
     (Aldershot & Burlington VT 2004).

Gibbs, P., *Realities of War*, (London 1920).

Gibson, E. & Ward, G.K., *Courage Remembered*, (London 1989).

Giddings, R., *The War Poets*, (London 1988).

Gildea, J., *For Remembrance and in Honour of Those Who Lost Their Lives in the
     South African War, 1899-1902*, (London 1911).

Gillis, J.R. (ed.), *Commemorations: The Politics of National Identity*, (Princeton 1994).

Gleichen, Lord E., *London's Open-Air Statuary*, (London 1928).

Glanfield, J., *Bravest of the Brave*, (Stroud 2005).

Godfrey, W.H., 'War Memorials: Suggestions From the Past. I - Wall Tablets', *Architectural Review,* Vol. XLVI, No. 272, (July 1919) pp 10-13.

Godfrey, W.H., 'War Memorials: Suggestions From the Past. II - Table Tombs and Headstones', *Architectural Review,* Vol. XLVI, No. 273, (August 1919) pp 35-39.

Godfrey, W.H., 'War Memorials: Suggestions From the Past. III - Market Crosses and Halls', *Architectural Review,* Vol. XLVI, No. 274, (September 1919) pp 63-69.

Godfrey, W.H., 'War Memorials: Suggestions From the Past. IV - Almshouses', *Architectural Review,* Vol. XLVI, No. 275, (October 1919) pp 93-99.

Godfrey, W.H., 'The War Memorials Exhibition at the Royal Academy', *Architectural Review,* Vol. XLVI, No. 277, (November 1919) pp 163-164.

Godfrey, W.H., 'Some Examples of Modern Memorials - I', *Architectural Review,* Vol. XLVII, No. 278, (January 1920), pp 13-16.

Godfrey, W.H., 'Some Examples of Modern Memorials - II', *Architectural Review,* Vol. XLVII, No. 279, (February 1920), pp 38-41.

Gorer, G., 'The Pornography of Death' in *Encounter,* (October 1955).

Gorer, G., *Death, Grief and Mourning in Contemporary Britain,* (London 1965).

Gorham, D., *Vera Brittain: A Feminist's Life,* (Oxford & Cambridge 1996).

Gosse, E., 'The New Sculpture: 1879 - 1894' in the *Art Journal,* (1894) pp 138-142.

Graves, R., *Goodbye To All That,* (London 1929).

Graves, R. & Hodge, A., *The Long Weekend: A Social History of Great Britain, 1918-1939,* (London 1940).

Grayzel, S.R., *Women and the First World War,* (Harlow & London 2004).

Greenberg, A., 'Lutyen's Cenotaph' in the *Journal of the Society of Architectural Historians,* (March 1989) pp 5-23.

Gregory, A., *The Silence of Memory: Armistice Day, 1919 -1946,* (Oxford 1994).

Grundy, A.R., 'Rubbish for the War Museum: The Exhibition at Burlington House' in the *Connoisseur,* (March 1920) pp 119-120.

Grundy, A.R., 'Satan Rebuking Sin: Mr. Nevinson Repudiating Advanced Art' in the *Connoisseur,* (June 1920) pp 110-111.

Gudmundsson, B., *The British Expeditionary Force 1914-15,* (Oxford & New York 2005).

Hall, D.E. (ed.), *Muscular Christianity: Embodying the Victorian Age,* (Cambridge 1994).

Hall, J., *Hall's Dictionary of Subjects and Symbols in Art,* (London 1974).

Hamer, J., 'Our Rising Artists: Mr. Albert Toft' in the *Magazine of Art* (1901).

Hanson, N., *The Unknown Soldier: The Story of the Missing of the Great War,* (London, Sydney, Auckland 2005).

Hantover, J.P., 'The Boy Scouts and the Validation of Masculinity' in the *Journal of Social Issues,* Vol. 34, No. 1, (1978) pp 184-195.

Harries, M. & S., *The War Artists: British Official War Art of the 20th Century,* (London 1983).

Hart-Davis, R., *The War Poems of Siegfried Sassoon,* (London 1983).

Haste, C., *Keep the Home Fires Burning: Propaganda in the First World War,* (London 1977)

Hay, I., *Their Name Liveth: The Book of the Scottish National War Memorial,* (Edinburgh 1985)

Hayward, J., *Myths and Legends of the First World War,* (Oxford 2002).

Hearn, J., *Men in the Public Eye: The Construction and Deconstruction of Public Men and Public Patriarchies,* (London & New York 1992).

Hichberger, JWM, *Images of the Army: The Military in British Art, 1815-1914,* (Manchester 1988)

Higonnet, M.R. et al (ed.)*Behind the Lines: Gender and the Two World Wars*(London 1987)

Higonnet, M.R., 'Women in the Forbidden Zone: War, Women and Death' in Goodwin, S.W & Bronfen, E. (eds.), *Death and Representation*, (Baltimore & London 1993).

Hildred, A., C.R.W. *Nevinson, War Paintings 1914-1918*, Graves Art Gallery exhibition catalogue, (Sheffield 1972).

Hill, D., *For King's and Country*, (London 2003).

Homberger, E., 'The Story of the Cenotaph' in *Times Literary Supplement*, (12 Nov 1976)

Houlbrooke, R. (ed.), *Death, Ritual and Bereavement*, (London & New York 1989).

Hussey, C., *Tait McKenzie, a Sculptor of Youth*, (London 1929).

Hussey, C., *The Life of Sir Edwin Lutyens*, (Woodbridge, Suffolk 1950).

Hynes, S., *A War Imagined: The First World War and English Culture*, (London 1990).

Inglis, K.S., 'Men, Women and War Memorials: Anzac Australia', in *Daedalus*, Vol.116, No. 4 (1989) pp 35-59.

Inglis, K.S., 'War Memorials: Ten Questions for Historians' in *Guerres mondiales et conflits contemporains*, No. 167 (July 1992) pp 5-21.

Inglis, K.S., 'World War One Memorials in Australia' in *Guerres mondiales et conflits contemporains*, No. 167 (July 1992) pp 51-58.

Inglis, K.S., 'The Homecoming: The War Memorial Movement in Cambridge, England' in the *Journal of Contemporary History*, Vol. 27 (1992) pp 583-605.

Irwin, D., 'Sentiment and Antiquity: European Tombs, 1750-1830' in Whaley, J. (ed.) *Mirrors of Mortality: studies in the Social History of Death*, (London 1981).

Jagger, C.S., *Modelling and Sculpture in the Making*, (London & New York 1933).

Jagger, C.S., 'The Sculptor's Point of View' in *Studio*, Vol. CVI, No. 488 (Nov 1933) pp 251-254.

Jupp, P.C. & Gittings, C. (eds.) *Death in England: An Illustrated History*, (Manchester & New Jersey 1999).

Kahn, E.L., 'Art From the Front, Death Imagined and the Neglected Majority' in *Art History*, Vol. 8, No. 2 (June 1985) pp 192-208.

Kemp, B., *English Church Monuments*, (London 1980).

Kennedy, A., *Soldiers of Labour*, (London, New York & Toronto 1917).

Kent, S.K., 'The Politics of Sexual Difference: World War One and the Demise of British Feminism' in the *Journal of British Studies*, Vol. 27, No. 3 (July 1988) pp 232-253.

Kent, S.K., *Sex and Suffrage in Britain, 1860-1914*, (London 1990).

Kent, S.K., *Making Peace: The Reconstruction of Gender in Interwar Britain*, (Princeton & Chichester 1993).

Kernot, C.F., *British Public Schools War Memorials*, (London 1927).

Kidd, W. & Murdoch, B. (eds.), *Memory & Memorials: The Commemorative Century*, (Aldershot 2004).

King, A.M., *The Politics of Meaning in the Commemoration of the First World War in Britain, 1914-1939*, Unpublished PhD thesis, (University of London 1993).

King, A., *Memorials of the Great War in Britain: The Symbolism and Politics of Remembrance*, (Oxford & New York 1998).

King, A., 'Monuments With No Fixed Meaning', *The Independent*, 23 March 1999, p 7.

Knowles, E, *C.R.W. Nevinson 1889-1946*, Kettle's Yard Gallery exhibition catalogue, (Cambridge 1988).

Koureas, G., *Memory, Masculinity and National Identity in British Visual Culture, 1914-1930: A Study of Unconquerable Manhood*', (Aldershot & Burlington VT 2007).

Laffin, J., *World War I in Post Cards*, (Gloucester 1988).

Laffin, J., *The Western Front Illustrated 1914-1918*, (Stroud 1991).

Lee, J., *War Girls: The First Aid Nursing Yeomanry in the First World War*, (Manchester & New York 2005).

Leed, E.J., *No Man's Land: Combat and Identity in World War One*, (Cambridge, London, New York & Melbourne 1979).

Lewis, P.W., *Blasting & Bombardiering*, (London 1937).

Licht, F., *A History of Western Sculpture - 19th & 20th Centuries*, (Ed. Pope-Hennessy, J., (London 1967).

Llewellyn, N., *The Art of Death: Visual Culture in the English Death Ritual c. 1500 - c. 1800*, (London1991).

Longworth, P., *The Unending Vigil: A History of the Commonwealth War Graves Commission, 1917-1984*, (London 1985).

Lutyens, M., *Edwin Lutyens*, (London 1980).

McAllister, I-G., 'A Rising British Sculptor: Charles Sargeant Jagger' in *Studio*, Vol. 63, No.260, (14 Nov. 1914) pp 84-99.

Macartney, M.E., 'Homes of Rest: Almshouses as War Memorials - I', *Architectural Review*, Vol. XLIII, No. 253, (December 1917) pp 117-125.

Macartney, M.E., 'Homes of Rest: Almshouses as War Memorials - II', *Architectural Review*, Vol. XLIII, No. 259, (June 1918) pp 119-128.

Macartney, M.E., 'Homes of Rest: Almshouses as War Memorials - III', *Architectural Review*, Vol. XLIII, No. 260, (July 1918) pp 9-12.

MacCarthy, F., *Eric Gill*, (London, 1989).

MacDonald, L, *The Roses of No Man's Land*, (London 1980).

MacDonald, L., *1914-1918: Voices and Images of the Great War*, (London 1988).

MacDonald, S., *The History and Philosophy of Art Education*, (Cambridge 1970).

McIntyre, C., *Monuments of War: How to Read a War Memorial*, (London 1990).

McKenzie, R., *Public Sculpture of Glasgow*, (Liverpool 2002).

Malvern, S., 'War As It Is: The Art of Muirhead Bone, C.R.W. Nevinson and Paul Nash' in *Art History*, (December 1986) pp 487-515.

Malvern,S.,*Modern Art, Britain and the Great War: Witnessing, Testimony and Remembrance*, (New Haven & London 2004).

Mangan, J.A. & Walvin, J. (eds.), *Manliness and Morality: Middle Class Masculinity in Britain and America, 1800-1940*, (Manchester 1987).

Manning, E, *Marble and Bronze: The Art and Life of Hamo Thornycroft*, (London 1982).

Marlow, J. (ed.), *Votes for Women: The Virago Book of Suffragettes*, (London 2001).

Marwick, A., *The Deluge: British Society and the First World War*, (London 1965).

Marwick, A., *Women at War: 1914-1918*, (London 1977).

Mayo, J.M., *War Memorials as Political Landscape: The American Experience and Beyond*, (New York, Westport & London 1988).

Michalski, S., *Public Monuments: Art in Political Bondage 1870-1997*, (London 1998).

Mitchell, C, 'Benjamin West's "Death of General Wolfe" and the Popular History Piece' in the *Journal of Warburg and Courtauld Institute*, (1944).

Mitchell, D., *Women on the Warpath: The Story of the Women of the First World War*, (London 1966).

Mitchell, W.J.T. (ed.), *On Narrative*, (Chicago & London 1981).

Montague, C.E., *The Western Front: Drawings by Muirhead Bone*, 10 Vols., (London 1916-1917)

Montague, C.E., *The Front Line*, (London 1917).

Montague, C.E., *British Artists at the Front - Part 1: C.R.W. Nevinson*, (London 1918).

Montague, C.E., *British Artists at the Front - Part 2: Sir John Lavery*, (London 1918).

Montague, C.E., *British Artists at the Front - Part 3: Paul Nash*, (London 1918).

Montague, C.E., *British Artists at the Front - Part 4: Eric Kennington*, (London 1918).

Moriarty, C., 'Christian Iconography and First World War Memorials' in the *Imperial War Museum Review*, No. 6, (1992) pp 63-75.

Moriarty, C., 'The Absent Dead and Figurative First World War Memorials' in *Transactions of the Ancient Monuments Society*, Vol. 39 (1995).

Moriarty, C., *Narrative and the Absent Body: Mechanisms of Meaning in First World War Memorials*, Unpublished PhD thesis, (University of Sussex 1995).

Moriarty, C. 'Private Grief and Public Remembrance: British First World War Memorials' in Evans, M. & Lunn, K. (eds.), *War and Memory in the Twentieth Century*, (Oxford & New York 1997).

Moriarty, C., *The Sculpture of Gilbert Ledward*, (Aldershot & Burlington 2003).

Moriarty, C., 'Remnants of Patriotism: The Commemorative Representation of the Greatcoat After The First World War', *Oxford Art Journal*, Part 27, (2004), pp 291-309.

Moriarty, C., *The Commemorative Sculpture of Paul Montford*, (University of Brighton,2007).

Morley, J., *Death, Heaven and the Victorians*, (London 1971).

Mosse, G.L., *Fallen Soldiers: Re-Shaping the Memory of the World Wars*, (London 1990).

Myers, C.S., *Shell Shock in France: 1914-1918*, (Cambridge 1940).

Nairne, S. & Serota, N. (eds.), *British Sculpture in the Twentieth Century*, Whitechapel Art Gallery exhibition catalogue, (London 1981).

Nevinson, C.R.W., *The Great War: Fourth Year*, (London 1918).

Nevinson, C.R.W. 'Painting War as a Soldier Sees It' in *The New York Times*, (25 May 1919) section 7, p 13.

Nevinson, C.R.W., *Paint and Prejudice*, (London 1937).

Nora, P., 'Between Memory and History: les Lieux de Memoire' in *Representations*, (Spring 1989) pp 7-25.

Noszlopy, G.T. & Beach, J. (ed.), *Public Sculpture of Birmingham including Sutton Coldfield*, (Liverpool 1998).

Noszlopy, G.T., *Public Sculpture of Warwickshire, Coventry & Solihull*, (Liverpool 2003).

Noszlopy, G.T., & Waterhouse, F., *Public Sculpture of Staffordshire & the Black Country*, (Liverpool 2005).

O'Day, A. (ed.), *The Edwardian Age: Conflict and Stability, 1900-1914*, (London 1979).

Oliver, N., *Not Forgotten*, (London 2006).

Ouditt, S., *Fighting Forces, Writing Women: Identity and Ideology in the First World War*, (London & New York 1994).

Panofsky, E., *Tomb Sculpture: Its Changing Aspects from Ancient Egypt to Bernini*, (New York & London 1964).

Parker, P., *The Old Lie: The Great War and the Public School Ethos* (London 1987).

Parkes, K., 'Modern English Carvers, IV: H. Tyson Smith' in the *Architectural Review*, (October 1921) pp 151-152.

Pearson, F., *Goscombe John at the National Museum of Wales*, (Cardiff 1979).

Penny, N., *Church Monuments in Romantic England*, (New Haven & London 1977).

Penny, N., *Mourning the Arts and Living*, (London 1981).

Penny, N., 'English Sculpture and the First World War' in *The Oxford Journal*, (November 1981), pp 36-42.

Penny, N., 'Amor Publicus Posuit: Monuments for the People and of the People' in the *Burlington Magazine*, (December 1987) pp 793-800.

Percy, C. & Ridley, J. (eds.), *The Letters of Edwin Lutyens to his Wife Emily*, (London 1985).

Poovey, M., *Uneven Developments: The Ideological Work of Gender in Mid-Victorian England*, (London 1989).

Price, R., *An Imperial War and the British Working-Class: Working-Class Attitudes and Reactions to the Boer War, 1899-1902*, (London & Toronto 1972).

Prost, A., 'Memoires locales et memoires nationales: les monumentes de 1914-1918 en France' in *Guerres mondiales et conflits contemporains*, No. 167, (July 1992) pp 41-50.

Putkowski, J. & Sykes, J., *Shot at Dawn* (London 1989).

Quinlan, M., *British War Memorials*, (Hertford 2005).

Rawson, A., *British Army Handbook, 1914-1918*, (Stroud 2006).

Read, B., *Victorian Sculpture*, (New Haven & London 1982).

Reader, W.J., *At Duty's Call: A Study in Obsolete Patriotism*, (Manchester 1988).

Reddie, A., 'Albert Toft' in *Studio*, Vol. 66, (October 1915) pp 18-28.

Reese, P., *Home-coming Heroes: An Account of the Reassimilation of British Military Personnel into Civilian Life*, (London 1992).

Reeves, N., 'Film Propaganda and Its Audience: The Example of Britain's Official Films During the First World War' in the *Journal of Contemporary History*, Vol. 18, No. 3, (July 1983) pp 463-494.

Richardson, A. & Phillips, R.R., 'Memorials of War-I Ancient' in the *Architectural Review*, Vol. 37 (1915) pp 27-30.

Richardson, A. & Phillips, R.R., 'Memorials of War-II Renaissance' in the *Architectural Review*, Vol. 37 (1915) pp 46-50.

Richardson, A. & Phillips, R.R., 'Memorials of War-III Napoleonic' in the *Architectural Review*, Vol. 37 (1915) pp 64-71.

Richardson, A. & Phillips, R.R., 'Memorials of War -IV Modern' in the *Architectural Review*, Vol. 37 (1915) pp 95-104.

Richardson, A. & Phillips, R.R., 'Memorials of War- V Modern French', *Architectural Review*, Vol. 38 (1915) pp 7 -12 & 21-25.

Richardson, A. & Phillips, R.R., 'Memorials of War- VI Modern Italian' *Architectural Review*, Vol.38 (1915) pp 73-78.

Richardson, A. & Phillips, R.R., 'Memorials of War- VII American' in *Architectural Review*, Vol. 38 (1915) pp 107-113.

Rivers, W.H.R., 'The Repression of War Experience' in *The Lancet*, (2 February 1918).

Rivers, W.H.R., *Conflict and Dream*, (London 1923).

Rivers, W.H.R., *Instinct and the Unconscious: A Contribution to a Biological Theory of the Psycho-Neurosis*, (Cambridge 1924).

Roberts, D, *Minds at War: Essential Poetry of the First World War in Context*, (Burgess Hill 1996)

Roper, M. & Tosh, J. (eds.), *Manful Assertions: Masculinities in Britain Since 1800*, (London & New York 1991).

Roszak, B. & Roszak, T. (eds.), *Masculine / Feminine: readings in Sexual Mythology and the Liberation of Women*, (New York, Evanston & London 1969).

Royal Academy of Arts, *War Memorial Exhibition*, catalogue, (London 1919).

Samuel, R. (ed.), *Patriotism: The Making and Unmaking of British National Identity, Vol. 1*, (London & New York 1989).

Sassoon, S., *The Complete Memoirs of George Sherston*, (London 1937).

Scarry, E., *The Body in Pain: The Making and Unmaking of the World*, (Oxford & New York 1985).

Scott, J.W. *Gender and the Politics of History*, (New York 1988).

Shewring, W. (ed.), *Letters of Eric Gill* (London 1947)

Showalter, E., *The Female Malady: Women, Madness and English Culture, 1830-1980*, (London 1985).

Silber, E., *The Sculpture of Epstein*, (Oxford 1986).

Silber, E. et al (eds.), *Jacob Epstein: Sculpture and Drawings*, (Leeds 1989).

Sillars, S., *Art and Survival in First World War Britain*, (London 1987).

Simkins, P., *Kitchener's Army: The Raising of the New Armies, 1914-16*, (Manchester & New York 1988).

Simon, B., & Bradley, I. (eds.), *The Victorian Public School: Studies in the Development of an Educational Institution*, (Dublin 1975).

Silver, K.E., *Esprit de Corps: The Art of the Parisian Avant-Garde and the First World War, 1914- 1925*, (London 1989).

Sitwell, O., *Contemporary British Artists: C.R.W. Nevinson*, (London 1925).

Skelton, T. & Gliddon, G., *Lutyens & the Great War*, (London 2008).

Skipworth, P., 'A Synthesis of War - The Paintings of C.R.W. Nevinson 1914-1916' in the *Connoisseur*, (October 1972) pp 100-103.

Skipworth, P., 'Gilbert Ledward R.A. and the Guards' Division Memorial' in *Apollo*, Vol. CXXVII, No. 311, (January 1988).

Skipworth, P., *Gilbert Ledward*, The Fine Art Society exhibition catalogue, (London 1988).

Smith, G.E. & Pear, T.H., *Shell Shock and Its Lessons*, (Manchester 1917).

Spielmann, M.H., *British Sculpture and Sculptors of Today*, (London 1901).

Spiers, E.M., *The Army and Society: 1815 - 1914*, (London & New York 1980).

Springhall, J., *Youth, Empire and Society: British Youth Movements, 1883-1940*, (London 1977).

Stamp, G., *Silent Cities: An Exhibition of the Memorial and Cemetery Architecture of the Great War*, (London 1977).

Stamp, G., *The Memorial to the Missing of the Somme*, (London 2007).

Stedman, M., *Salford Pals: A History of the Salford Brigade*, (London 1993).

Stedman, M., *Manchester Pals*, (London 1994).

Stevens, T., 'George Frampton' in Curtis, P. (ed.), *Patronage and Practice: Sculpture on Merseyside*, (Liverpool 1989).

Summers, A., 'Militarism in Britain Before the Great War' in the *History Workshop Journal*, No. 2, (Autumn 1976) pp 103-123.

Terraine, J., *The Impact of War: 1914 and 1918*, (London 1970).

Tickner, L., *The Spectacle of Women: Imagery of the Suffrage Campaign, 1907-14*, (London 1987).

Toft, A., *Modelling and Sculpture*, (London 1924).

Tylee, C.M., *The Great War and Women's Consciousness: Images of Militarism and Womanhood in Women's Writings, 1914-64*, (London 1990).

Usherwood, P. & Spencer-Smith, J., *Lady Butler, Battle Artist: 1846-1933*, (London 1987).

Usherwood, P., Beach, J.& Morris, C., *Public Sculpture of North East England*, (Liverpool 2000)

Van Emden, R., *Britain's Last Tommies: Final Memories from Soldiers of the 1914-18 War - In Their Own Words*, (Barnsley 2005).

Van Emden, R., *Boy Soldiers of the Great War*, (London 2005).

Vellacott, J., 'Feminist Consciousness and the First World War' in Pearson, R.R. (ed), *Women & Peace: Theoretical, Historical and Practical Perspectives*, (London, New York & Sydney 1987)

Vicinus, M. (ed.), *Suffer and be Still: Women in the Victorian Age*, (London 1972).

Victoria and Albert Museum, *War Memorial Exhibitions catalogue*, (London 1919).

Viney, N., *Images of Wartime: British Art and Artists of World War One*, (London 1991).

Ward-Jackson, P., *Public Sculpture of the City of London*, (Liverpool 2003).

Warner, M., *Monuments and Maidens: The Allegory of the Female Form*, (London 1985).

Weaver, L., *Memorials and Monuments Old and New: 200 Subjects Chosen from Seven Centuries*, (London 1915).

Whinney, M., *Sculpture in Britain, 1530-1830*, (London 1964).

Whitaker, J., *The Best: A History of H.H. Martyn & Co.*, (Cheltenham 1998).

White, H., *The Content of the Form: Narrative Discourse and Historical Representation*, (Baltimore & London 1987).

Whitelegg, E. et al (ed.), *The Changing Experience of Women*, (London 1982).

Whittick, A., *War Memorials*, (London 1946).

Wilkinson, A., *The Church of England and the First World War*, (London 1978).

Wilson, T., *The Myriad Faces of War: Britain and the Great War, 1914-1918* (Cambridge 1986).

Wiltshire, A., *Most Dangerous Women: Feminist Peace Campaigners of the Great War*, (London, Boston & Henley 1985).

Winter, D., *Death's Men: Soldiers of the Great War*, (London 1978).

Winter, J.M., *The Great War and the British People*, (London 1986).

Winter, J.M., *Sites of Memory, Sites of Mourning: The Great War in European Cultural History*, (Cambridge 1995).

Winter, J.M. & Baggett, B., *The Great War and the Shaping of the 20th Century*, (New York, Ringwood, Toronto, Auckland & London 1996).

Winter, J.M. & Sivan, E. (eds.), *War And Remembrance In The Twentieth Century*, (Cambridge 1999).

Wood, F.D., 'Masks for Facial Wounds' in *The Lancet*, (23 June 1917) pp 949-951.

Woolf, S. (ed.), *Nationalism in Europe: 1815 to the Present*, (London 1996).

Woollacott, A., *On Her Their Lives Depend: Munitions Workers in the Great War*, (Los Angeles & London 1994).

Woollacott, A., 'Khaki Fever and Its Control: Gender, Class, Age and Sexual Morality on the British Home Front in the First World War' in the *Journal of Contemporary History*, Vol. 29, (1994) pp 325-347.

Wootton, G., *The Official History of the British Legion*, (London 1956).

Wyke, T. & Cocks, H., *Public Sculpture of Greater Manchester*, (Liverpool 2004).

Yates, L.K., *The Woman's Part: A Record of Munitions Work*, (London, New York & Toronto 1918).

Yorke, M., *Eric Gill: Man of Flesh and Spirit*, (London, 1981).

Young, J.E., *The Texture of Memory: Holocaust Memorials and Meaning* (New Haven & London 1993).

Young, L., *A Great Task of Happiness: The Life of Kathleen Scott*, (London & Basingstoke, 1995)

APPENDIX I

FIGURATIVE MEMORIALS OF THE FIRST WORLD WAR IN THE UNITED KINGDOM

The following is a list of civic and regimental memorials featuring figurative sculpture. Memorials for churches, clubs, workplace etc., and memorials to individuals are excluded. Whilst every attempt has been made to produce as accurate and definitive a list as possible, omissions are inevitable, with some memorials remaining unrecorded. Furthermore it is not always clear whether memorials in churchyards are for the congregation of the church or for the wider population and what are listed here as crucifixes (*ie.* featuring the figure of Christ) may, in one or two cases, have been misnamed and may in fact lack figurative imagery. All of those listed as sculptors have been identified as such except where otherwise indicated.

Includes masons (M), architects - where no other designer or sculptor is identified (A), designers (D), manufacturers (Man), builders (B), artists (Art) and wood carvers (W) + Relief (R), Eleanor Cross (EC), Lantern Cross (LC).

Date	Sculptor	Imagery +
1918		
Briantspuddle, Dorset	E Gill	Christ / Virgin & Child
East Clevedon, Avon	J Ninian Comper (A)	Crucifix
Heston, Greater London	A G Walker	Soldier / battle scenes (R)
Hickleton, S. Yorkshire	-	Crucifix
Royston, S. Yorkshire	J Mitchell Bottomley (A)	Crucifix
Stansfield, Suffolk	G Maile & Son Ltd. (Man)	Crucifix
Tring, Hertfordshire	P M Johnstone (A)	Crucifix
1919		
Aldeburgh, Suffolk	G Bayes	Soldier dying+ allegorical figs (R)
Almeley, Herefordshire	W G Storr-Barber (M)	Soldier (mourning)
Ashby de la Launde, Lincs	Hart, Son, Pears & Co. (M)	Crucifix
Bisham, Berkshire	E Gill	Crucifix
Boxford, Suffolk	-	Crucifix + Soldier (R)
Castleton, Derbyshire	J Beresford & Son (M)	Cross+ Angel of Victory (R)
Cottingley, West Yorkshire	-	Crucifix
Footdee, Grampian	A Watson (D)	Soldier & sailor (R)
Hightown, Merseyside	G H Tyson Smith	Kneeling winged female figure
Keyhaven, Hampshire	-	Crucifix
Knowlton, Kent	G Frampton	Soldier / nurse / Victory / casualty
Leiston, Suffolk	D Rope	Crucifix
Lochmaben, Dumfries	-	Soldier (mourning)
Muston, Leicestershire	W S Frith	Crucifix
Newton St. Loe, Avon	M A Green (A)	Crucifix /Virgin/ St John (LC)
Northaw, Hertfordshire	-	Cross + St George (R)
Rushall, West Midlands	-	Crucifix
Saddleworth, W. Yorks	B Corner (M)	Angel (kneeling)
Sledmere, E. Yorks	Gawthorp & Sons (Art)	Eleanor Cross + portraits (R)
Stepney, E. London	-	Crucifix

Sudbury, Derbyshire	Bodley & Hare (A)	St George
Tean, Staffordshire	M. Brown	Christ bestowing his blessing
Whippingham, Isle of Wight -		Crucifix

1920

Albrighton, Shropshire	W Aumonier	Crucifix
Alsager, Cheshire	-	Soldier
Arlesey, Bedfordshire	-	Soldier
Auchtermuchty, Fife	A Carrick	Soldier
Audenshaw, Lancs	P G Bentham	Soldier
Bampton, Oxfordshire	A Miller	Market Cross + St George
Belton, Lincolnshire	-	Soldier
Berriedale & Braemore, Highland	B Gotto	St Andrew
Beverley, Yorks	V Hill	Servicemen+medical service
Bexhill, East Sussex	L F Roslyn	Victory
Bilton & Bickerton, N. Yorks	-	Crucifix
Bodfari, Clwyd	J Tweed	Soldier
Bollington, Cheshire -		Saints/ Christ/ St George (R)
Bridport, Dorset	F Burlison	Column + St George
Broadstone, Dorset	G Bayes	Allegorical Female + soldiers (R)
Bucklesham, Suffolk	Messrs. Clary & Wright (M)	Crucifix
Burnham, Bucks	L S Merrifield	Soldier + Celtic cross
Bury, Lancs	H Cawthra	Cross + combatants / civilians (R)
Bury St Edmunds, Suffolk Regt	C E Whiffen	Cenotaph with angels
Buxton, Derbyshire	L F Roslyn	Victory
Carlton, S. Yorks		Crucifix
Carnforth, Lancs	P G Bentham	Soldier + marching soldiers(R)
Chalfont St Peter, Bucks	W Acworth(A)	Christ /Madonna /St Peter/Crucifix
Chapel Allerton, W. Yorks		Crucifix
Chatteris, Cambs	A Robinson &Son(M)	LC + St George /St Michael
Chirk, Clwyd	E Gill	Soldier (R)
Chopwell, Tyne & Wear	-	Soldier (arms reversed)
Clayton-le-Moors, Lancs	J Cassidy	Female + soldier
Clyro, Powys	-	Crucifix
Coggeshall, Essex	L J Watts (M)	Victory
Cornhill, London	R Goulden	St Michael, children + beasts
Cound, Shropshire	L A Turner (B)	Crucifix
Cowpen, Northumberland -		Soldier (mourning)
Cudworth, S. Yorks -		Crucifix
Dennington, Suffolk	H Binney (A)	Christ / Soldiers (R)
Ditchingham, Norfolk	F Derwent Wood	Soldier (dead)
Ditton, Kent	Sir Giles Gilbert Scott (A)	Crucifix
Dukinfield, Manchester -		Cross + angel
Dukinfield,(Victoria St.)	Wiloughby, Wilde & Co. (M)	Soldier
Dullingham, Cambs -		Infant Christ with Ox & Ass (R)
Earl Shilton, Leics	A Smith	Mourner, saints + woman, child (R)
East Hendred, Oxon -		Cross with St George (R)
East Malling, Kent	W D Gough	Crucifixion+Virgin &
		Child /Saints & Soldier (LC)
East Riddlesden, W. Yorks	-	Soldier (mourning)
Eastbourne, E. Sussex	H C Fehr	Victory
Eastergate, W. Sussex	M Harding	Lion
Edgmond, Shropshire	-	Crucifix /Soldier /Nurse (LC)
Ellesmere, Shropshire	Haswell & Son (M)	Crucifix + Saints (LC)

Location	Designer/Maker	Subject
Emberton, Bucks	Farmer & Brindley (M)	Soldier (mourning)
Forest Row, E. Sussex	E G Gillick	2 children (LC)
Fulham, W. London	A Turner	Female + winged child
Gawsworth, Cheshire	-	Crucifix
Glenelg, Highland	R Deuchars	Soldier, Victory & Stricken Humanity
Gosberton. Lincs	-	2 Figures (LC)
Grangetown,S.Glamorgan	H C Fehr	Victory
Grantham, Lincolnshire	Mr Phillips	Cross+Virgin & Saints
Great Warley, Essex	W Reynolds-Stephens	Entombment
Hadlow, Kent		Soldier
Hartford, Cheshire	Messrs. Powell & King (A)	Lantern Cross + Crucifix
Hawarden, Clwyd	Sir Giles Gilbert Scott (A)	Obelisk + Crucifix
Heath Town,W.Midlands	A G Walker	Soldier + reliefs
Heysham, Lancashire	-	Cross + St George (R)
Higham on the Hill, Leics	-	Crucifixion+ St George + St Michael(R)
Hurst Hill, W.Midlands	-	Crucifix
Ingatestone & Fryerning, Essex -		Crucifix
Iwerne Minster, Dorset	G Gilbert Scott (A)	Cross + relief (soldier)
Johnstone, Dumfries	F J Currie	Female (Peace)
Kettlethorpe, Lincs -		Crucifix
Killin, Central Scotland	A Carrick	Soldier (kilted)
Kirton, Suffolk	-	Crucifix
Leadenham, Lincolnshire	-	St George / knight/ pilgrim/ tree of knowledge (LC)
Lichfield, Staffordshire	R Bridgeman & Sons (M)	St George
Little Bealings, Suffolk	W D Caroe (A)	Column + St Michael
Littlewick Green, Berks	S Slingsby-Stallwood (A)	Crucifix
Lochawe, Strathclyde	A Carrick	Soldier
London (Imperial Camel Corps)	C Brown	Soldier on camel+reliefs
London (Women War Workers)	W H Gilbert	Nurse(R)
Lound, Suffolk	J Ninian Comper (A)	Crucifix
Martley,Worcs		Crucifix
Mells, Somerset	E Lutyens (A)	St George
Metheringham, Lincs	-	Soldier (mourning)
Morriston, W.Glamorgan	-	Female (Peace?)
Mortlake, Grampian	A Marshall Mackenzie & Sons (D)	Cross + Angels
Mossley, Lancs	-	Robed female
Moulton, Cheshire	Sir William Thornycroft	Soldier
New Seaham, Durham	-	Winged female + Soldiers
Newlyn, Cornwall	L S Merrifield	Cross + Soldiers/Sailors(R)
N. & S. Wheatley, Notts	-	Crucifix
Oakenshaw , W.Yorks	Wright & Son	Soldier (mourning)
Odiham, Hampshire	P Morley Horder (A)	Cross +St George(R)
Old Leake, Lincolnshire	-	Crucifix
Penpont, Dumfries	Kellock Brown	Soldier (mourning)
Pirbright, Surrey	F Brook Hitch	Crucifix
Pockley, N.Yorks	-	Crucifix
Pontyclun,Mid Glamorgan	-	Soldier/ sailor/ airman/ nurse (EC)
Prestatyn, Clwyd	R L Boulton & Sons (M)	Mourning soldier (EC)
Quorn, Leicestershire	-	Obelisk + St George(R)
Radclive cum Chackmore,Bucks -		Crucifix
Ramsgate, Kent	G Bayes	Draped, semi-nude female
Ratby, Leicestershire	S Ward (M)	Angel (Peace)
Rhynie & Kearn,Grampian	R Morrison (M)	Soldier (mourning)
Rockcliffe, Cumbria -		Stele + cross + soldier(R)

Rogate, West Sussex	W D Gough	Crucifix+ 2 Marys +St George
Saltburn by the Sea, N.Yorks	W Reynolds Stephens	Cross + relief
Sandwich, Kent	C L Hartwell	St George (R)
Sevenoaks, Kent	A G Walker	Soldier
Shacklewell, E. London	-	Crucifix + St John +Virgin
Shildon, Durham		Kneeling soldier
Sleaford, Lincs (cemetery)	F Clarke (M)	Angel of Peace
Sledmere,E.Yorks(Waggoners)	C Magnoni	Column+ Civilians/ Soldiers(R)
Southampton, Hants	E Lutyens (A)	Cenotaph + dead soldier
Soyland, W. Yorks -		Soldier
Staines, Surrey	-	Winged female + 4 servicemen
Stowlangtoft, Suffolk	F D Howard (A)	Crucifix
Thorpe Hesley,S.Yorks	Messrs. Tyas & Guest(M)	Soldier
Uppingham, Leics	WD Gough,	Saints, mother & child/ crucifix (LC)
Wainfleet St. Mary, Lincs	H C Wood (M)	Crucifix
Wanlockhead, Dumfries	-	Soldier (mourning)
Waterhead,Gt Manchester	G Thomas	Soldier (helmet aloft)
Weaste,Gt Manchester (Cemetery)	-	Angel of Peace
Westerham, Kent	-	Crucifix
Westhorpe, Suffolk	J H Bartlett (B)	Crucifix
Willersey, Glos	-	Crucifix
Wimblington, Cambs		Victory
Wing, Buckinghamshire	F D Howard (A)	Market Cross + Christ + Saints
Witham, Essex	G Ledward	Cross + soldier, St George(R)
Yateley, Hampshire -		Crucifix

1921

Abergavenny, Gwent	G Ledward	Soldier
Abertour, Grampian -		Market Cross + 'Heraldic Lion'
Abingdon, Oxfordshire	J G T West (A)	Mourning soldier (R)
Alderley Edge, Cheshire	Sir Hubert Worthington (D)	Cross with St Michael
Amersham, Bucks	P M Johnstone (A)	Crucifix
Annan, Dumfries	H Price	Soldier
Appleton Thorn,Cheshire	-	Soldier
Bamburgh, Northumberland	-	Crucifix
Barrow-in-Furness,Cumbria	Major Oakley	Figures (Army/Navy/Liberty/Peace)
Barrow-upon-Soar, Leics	W D Caroe (A)	Cross + St George
Batsford & Moreton in Marsh,Glos	Sir E G Dawber (A)	St George
Beaconsfield, Bucks	J O Cheadle (A)	Cross + Crucifixion(R)
Beckenham, Kent	Newbury Trent	Pillar + St George(R)
Bellshill & Mossend,Strathclyde.	Messrs. Scott & Rae (M)	Soldier
Bishopthorpe, N.Yorks	Brierley & Rutherford (A)	Cross + St George
Blackley, Gt Manchester	L F Roslyn	Victory, army/ navy/airforce/ nursing
Blairgowrie, Tayside	A Carrick	Soldier (mourning)
Brierley Hill,W. Midlands	G Brown & Sons (M)	Soldier + reliefs
Bridgend, Mid Glamorgan	H H Martyn (Man)	Brittania
Bridlington, Humberside	S N Babb	Cenotaph + Victory/ sailor(R)
Brightlingsea, Essex	R R Goulden	Cenotaph+ soldier/ sailor(R)
Brimington, Derbyshire	C S Jagger	Brittania
Briton Ferry,W Glamorgan	-	Soldier (mourning)
Burbage, Leics	-	Soldier
Burslem, Staffordshire	C Wallet	Cenotaph + Mourning soldier (R)
Bushmills, Co Antrim	C L Hartwell	Soldier
Canonbie, Dumfries T	J Clapperton	Soldier

Castle Donnington, Leics	C G Hare (A)	Crucifix
Chadderton, Lancs	A Toft	Soldier
Chalvey, Berkshire	H C King (A)	Crucifix
Cheadle Hulme, Cheshire	B Clemens	Cross + 2 figs/ soldier & sailor
Chelford & Wichington, Cheshire	-	Crucifix
Chertsey, Surrey	J Whitehead (Man)	Soldier
Chesham, Bucks	A G Walker	Soldier (rifle reversed)
Chipping Campden, Glos	F L Griggs (D)	Crucifix
Compton, Leek, Staffs		Crucifix
Cottenham, Cambs	F Baccus (M)	Soldier (mourning)
Cowbridge, S.Glamorgan	-	Soldier (mourning)
Croydon, Surrey	P R Montford	Cenotaph + Soldier + Woman & Child
Cullercoates, Northumberland	R Beall	Crucifix
Darwen, Lancs	L F Roslyn	Victory+ soldier/sailor/nurse(R)
Denny & Dunnipace,Stirling	G.H Paulin	Seated draped female
E. Barnet Valley,Gt London	Newbury Trent	Victory, lion & eagle on obelisk
East Bergholt, Suffolk	C E Eden (A)	Crucifix
East Brent, Somerset	A R Emery (M)	Soldier/sailor/airman/merchant seaman
East Wemyss, Fife	A Drury	Soldier
Echt, Grampian	W MacMillan (A)	Soldier
Egerton & Dunscar, Lancs	Gaffin & Co (Man)	Soldier (mourning)
Elgin, Grampian	P Portsmouth	Draped figure
Evesham,Worcs	H Poole	Soldier
Eversholt, Beds	E A Green	St Michael
Farsley, W.Yorks	-	Soldier (mourning)
Fernigair, Strathclyde	-	Soldier
Finsbury, N.London	T Rudge	Victory+ battle scenes (R)
Fishponds Park, Avon	-	Soldier (helmet aloft)
Fordham, Cambs	G Frampton	St George
Forsbrook , Staffs	R Bridgeman & Sons (M)	Soldier (mourning)
Freston, Suffolk	F Rogers (W)	Victory
Glynde, E.Sussex	R Bridgeman & Son (M)	2 figures (LC)
Greengates, W.Yorks	LF Roslyn	Victory
Llangefni,Gwynedd(School)	Brindle (D) / Williams (D)	Soldier (mourning)
Hackney, E.London	J H Cawthra	Female robed figure
Hartlepool, Co Durham	P Bennison (D)	Winged female (triumphant youth)
Hawick, Borders	-	Winged male nude
Haydon Br,Northumberland	P G Bentham	Soldier
Heaton Moor, Gt Manchester	J Cassidy	Soldier
Hertford, Herts	A Drury	White Hart
Higham Ferrers, Northants	Talbot, Brown & Fisher (A)	Column + Angel(R)
Highworth, Wiltshire	-	Cross + Soldier + sailor
Hints, Staffs	-	Crucifix
Holytown, Strathclyde	Scott & Rae (M)	Soldier (kilted)
Houghton-on-the-Hill, Leics	-	Crucifix/St George /St Catherine/ Peace
Hove, East Sussex	G Frampton	St George
Hungarton, Leics	-	Crucifix
Hunsworth,W.Yorks	Farmer & Brinsley (M)	Victory
Hythe, Kent	G Bayes	Victory+ servicemen/lions(R)
Jarrow, Co Durham	F W Doyle Jones	Peace
Kelso, Borders	Pilkington Jackson	Cross + St George
Kelty, Fife	Birnie Rhind	Soldier
Kendal, Cumbria	C W Coombes	Soldier
Ketton, Leics	Sir J Ninian Comper (A)	Crucifix+ Virgin & St John
Kingsthorpe, Northants	A Turner	St George

Kirkcudbright, Galloway	G H Paulin	Bare chested warrior + child
Knotting, Bedfordshire	Talbot, Brown & Fisher(A)	Crucifix+St George/ Virgin & Child/ St Margaret of Antioch
Knottingley, W.Yorks	-	Victory
Lampeter, Dyfed	W Goscombe John	Soldier
Langholm, Dumfries	H C Fehr	Victory
Largo, Fife	Sir Robert Lorimer (A)	Cross+ reliefs (inc. St George)
Largs, Strathclyde	Kellock Brown	Soldiers / sailor
Leigh on Sea, Essex	Art & Book Co. (D)	Crucifix
Limehouse, E. London	A.G Walker	Christ +trench scene (R)
Llanwenog, Dyfed	-	Soldier
Lockinge, Oxon	A Miller	Crucifixion (LC)
Lothersdale, N.Yorks	A M Smith	Angel + Lion
Macclesfield, Cheshire	J Millard	Dead soldier + Brittania + mourner
Madeley, Staffs	-	Soldier
Malvern Wells, Worcs	C F A Voysey (D)	Pelican
March, Cambs	W G Storr-Barber (M)	Soldier (mourning)
Market Harborough, Leics	-	Cross+ figs of Justice, Temperance, Fortitude, Prudence, Hope, Charity, Faith & Obedience
Matlock Bath, Derbyshire	J Beresford (M)	Soldier / Sailor + flag
Maxwelltown & Troqueer, Dumfries	H Price	Soldier
Monmouth, Gwent	W Clarke (M)	Soldier
Mortimer, Berks	H Maryon (A)	Cross+ Soldier/Sailor/ Honour / Justice/ Fortitude / Victory(R)
Morton, W.Yorks(Cemetery)		Soldier + angels + lions(R)
Much Hadham, Herts	H Wilson (D)	Crucifix
Nantwich, Cheshire	-	Crucifix
Naseby, Northants	J G Pullen & Sons (M)	Lion
Newmains Cross,Strathclyde	-	Soldier
North Berwick, Lothian	A Carrick	Column + unicorn
Pencarreg, Dyfed	J Coates-Carter (A)	Soldier
Penysarn, Gwynedd	-	Crucifix
Pershore Abbey, Worcs	A. Drury	Victory
Port Sunlight, Merseyside	W Goscombe John	Cross, servicemen/ women, children
Portsmouth, Hants	C S Jagger	Cenotaph, soldier & sailor
Pudlestone, Herefordshire	W G Storr-Barber (M)	Crucifix
Quorn, Leics	J H Morcom (M)	St George
Radyr, S.Glamorgan	A Turner	Cross + female + winged child
Ramsey, Cambs	F W Pomeroy	St George
Richmond, Surrey	W J Pickering	Column+ soldier/ sailor (R)
Rickmansworth, Herts	W Reid Dick	Lion, eagle+ female mourners
Royton, Gt.Manchester	J Ashton Floyd	Winged female (stolen)
St.Margaret's Hope,Orkney	A Carrick	Soldier
Sandon Estate, Staffs	A Toft	Soldier
Selkirk, Borders	-	Female
Sheffield, S.Yorks(Belgian Refugees)		Cross + Crucifixion(R)
Solihull, West Midlands	W H Bidlake (A)	Soldier/ Sailor/ Airman/ Nurse (LC)
South Harting, W.Sussex	E Gill	Cross + St George & St Richard/ draught of fishes (R)
Stalybridge, Gt Manchester	F V Blundstone	Winged angels holding Soldier +sailor
Stoke by Nayland, Suffolk	W D Caroe (A)	Crucifix
Stokesay, Shropshire	W G Storr-Barber (M)	Soldier
Stone, Staffs	A Toft	Soldier (mourning)
Sutton-in-Ashfield, Notts	-	Soldier (mourning)

Taddington, Derbyshire	S Hancock (A)	Cross+ child with sword(R)
Tarland, Grampian	R W Morrison (M)	Soldier
Tarporley, Cheshire	P S Worthington (A)	Lantern Cross with Christ
Taynuilt, Strathclyde	R W Morrison (M	Soldier (mourning)
Tow Law, Durham -		Soldier
Troedyrhiw, Powys	C Pryce	Soldier (mourning)
Trowbridge, Wiltshire	P G Bentham	Soldier
Trumpington, Cambs	E Gill	St George & St Michael/ Soldier/ Virgin & Child
Twickenham, Gt London	Mortimer Brown	Soldier+ Navy/ Air force/ women's services(R)
Wales, S. Yorks		Soldier
Walker,(5th Batt'n Northumberland Fusiliers) -		St George
Walkerburn, Borders	A Carrick	Soldier (mourning)
Wallasey, Merseyside	Birnie Rhind	Soldier+ sailor+ colonial soldier
Wallingford, Oxon	G Dawber (D)	Draped female
Warlingham, Surrey	J E Taylerson	Soldier + woman & child
Waterloo, Merseyside	F W Doyle Jones	Victory
West Hallam, Derbyshire	J Beresford (M)	2 Soldiers + machine gun
Weymouth, Dorset	F W Doyle Jones	Christ + angels
Whalley, Lancashire	P Scott Worthington (A)	Crucifix
Whetstone, Leics	A Smith	Crucifix
Wimbledon, Gt London	C L Hartwell	Obelisk+cross+Peace(R)
Worfield, Shropshire	-	Crucifix
Worthing, W. Sussex	J Whitehead (M)	Soldier
Wybunbury, Cheshire	-	Crucifix

1922

Acaster Selby, N. Yorks	G W Milburn (B)	Christ + Nurse & wounded soldier
Accrington, Lancs	G H Tyson Smith	Draped female
Allerton & Daisey Hill, W. Yorks	H Brownsword	Hooded female +soldier + naked youth
Alnwick, Northumberland	R Hedley (M)	3 Soldiers (mourning)
Ashover, Derbyshire -		Cross + 2 Angels
Ashton-under-Lyne, Lancs	J Ashton Floyd	Soldier+ female+ lions
Asplet Guise, Beds	Messrs. J Day & Son (M)	Crucifix
Auchterderran, Fife	A Murdoch	Army, Navy & Airforce
Bedford,	C S Jagger	Justice
Billy Row, Durham -		Soldier
Bishop Stortford, Herts	E.G Gillick	Shepherd, lamb, farmhand
Bottesford & Yaddlethorpe, Lincs -		Winged female (Peace)
Bradford, W. Yorks	H H Martyn Ltd (M)	Cenotaph +Soldier+Sailor
Bridgnorth, Shropshire	A Jones	Soldier
Brighouse, W. Yorks	F W Doyle Jones	Victory
Buckhaven & Innerleven, Fife	T Good	Soldier
Burton-on-Trent, Staffs	H C Fehr	Victory +St George +Peace
Burton Latimer, Northants -		St George
Bushey, Hertfordshire	W Reid Dick	Draped female
Calverley, W. Yorks	L F Roslyn	Draped female (Patriotism)
Cambridge	R Tait Mckenzie	Soldier
Chalford, Glos	-	Crucifix
Charlcombe, Avon	M A Green (A)	(LC)+ nurse + 2 Soldiers(R)
Chatham, Kent (R. Engineers)	A Proudfoot	Victory /Soldiers / Britannia + Youth /'Resignation' & 'Hope'(R)

Location	Sculptor	Description
Chester, Cheshire	A Miller	Cross + Saints
Cleckheaton, W.Yorks	G Frampton	2 females (mourning) + nude male
Cockermouth, Cumbria	F W Doyle Jones	Victory
Coleraine, Londonderry	W F Pomeroy	Soldier+daughter of Erin
Craghead, Durham	-	Winged figure
Cribyn, Dyfed	-	Soldier
Croydon,(Queen's R W.Surrey Regt)	C M Oldrid Scott (A)	Officer + soldier
Cupar, Fife	H S Gamley	Victory
Cwmcarn & Pontywaun,Gwent	Gaffin & Co (Man)	Soldier (mourning)
Dartford, Kent	A G Walker	Soldier /rifle reversed + reliefs
Denbigh, Clwyd	C L Hartwell	Victory
Denholme, W.Yorks	L F Roslyn	Soldier (mourning)
Dingwall, Highland	J.A Stevenson	Soldier
Dornoch, Highland	A Carrick	Soldier
Drefach, Dyfed	E Jones	Soldier (with cannon)
Dringhouses, N.Yorks	Brierley & Rutherford(A)	Market Cross+ Crucifix/Saints
Dronfield, Derbyshire	G Platts (M) / J Syddall (A)	Soldier
Dukinfield, Gt Manchester	P G Bentham	Soldier
Dumfries, Dumfriesshire	-	Soldier (mourning)
Dungannon, Tyrone	W F Pomeroy	Soldier
Eccleshill, W.Yorks	H Brownsword	Draped female
Eccleston, Merseyside	W H Gilbert	Soldier + female + reliefs
Elland, W. Yorks	F W Doyle Jones	Soldier
Elworth, Cheshire -		Soldier
Enniskillen, Fermanagh	Gaffin & Co (Man)	Soldier (mourning)
Folkestone, Kent	F V Blundstone	Mother+cross+soldiers(R)
Forres, Grampian	A Carrick	Soldier
Gainsborough, Leics	A Young Nutt (A)	Crucifix
Gateshead, Tyne & Wear	R R Goulden	Cenotaph + Semi-nude warrior(R)
Glossop, Derbyshire	V March	Victory
Gloucester, R.Glos Hussars Yeomanry	A Jones	Cross + soldiers & horses(R)
Gravesend, Kent	F W Doyle Jones	Victory
Grindleford, Derbyshire	S Hancock (A)	Cross + Angel
Hadfield, Derbyshire	V March	Victory
Hammersmith, W.London	H.C Fehr	Victory
Hanley, Staffordshire	H Brownsword	Brittania
Hastings, Sussex	M Winser	Victory+ troops/pilot/sailor (R)
Hereford, Herefordshire	Bromsgrove Guild (Man)	Eleanor Cross + Servicemen
Hinckley, Leics	A G Wyon	Draped female
Holywood, Co Down	L S Merrifield	Soldier
Hoylake & W.Kirby, Merseyside	C S Jagger	Soldier +Humanity
Ilford, Gt London	Newbury Trent	Soldier
Ilfracombe, Devon	C Pollock	Winged figure
Inveraray, Strathclyde	Kellock Brown	Soldier
Kensington, W.London	W F Pomeroy	Cross + female (Remembrance)
Keswick, Cumbria	F Derwent Wood	Britannia (R)
Kidderminster, Worcs	A Drury	Angel, dead soldier/ widow & child(R)
Kildalton, Islay, Argyll	-	Soldier (kilted)
Larne, Co Antrim	W F Pomeroy	Cenotaph+ Soldier+ Sailor
Leamington Spa, Warwicks	A Toft	Soldier (mourning)
Leeds, W. Yorks	H C Fehr	Victory+ St George+ Peace
Leominster, Herefordshire	W G Storr- Barber (M)	Winged female
Lewes, E.Sussex	V March	Victory + Peace + Liberty
Llanddewi Brefi, Dyfed	-	Soldier
Llandrindod Wells, Powys	B Lloyd	Soldier (mourning)

Llandovery, Dyfed	-	Soldier (mourning)
Lockerbie, Dumfries	H C Fehr	Victory
London (Submarine Corps)	F B Hitch	Submarine interior + sea nymphs(R)
Lossiemouth, Grampian	-	Seated semi-nude figure
Lower Peover, Cheshire	J Cassidy	Crucifix + reliefs
Luton, Bedfordshire	Sir W Thornycroft	Courage bringing Victory
Maidstone, Kent	G Frampton	St George
Milngavie, Strathclyde	G H Paulin	Female figure
Mountain Ash, Mid Glamorgan	J H Thomas (& G H Thomas)	Draped female + slain male nude + servicemen / nurse(R)
Mytholmroyd, W. Yorks	-	Soldier
New Elgin, Grampian	R W Morrison (M)	Soldier (mourning)
New Stevenston, Strathclyde	A Young	Soldier (mourning)+ lion
Newburgh, Fife	A Carrick	Soldier
Newburn, Tyne & Wear	-	Soldier
Newton Abbot, Devon	C Pollock	Freedom w. broken chain
Oakham, Leics	Sir J Ninian Comper (A)	Market Cross w. Crucifix / Mother & Child/St Martin/St George
Oldham, Lancs	A Toft	5 Soldiers on mound
Oswaldtwistle, Lancs	L F Roslyn	Victory + 2 Soldiers
Pencader, Dyfed	E Jones	Soldier
Portrush, Londonderry	F Ransom	Victory
Pudsey, W. Yorks	H Poole	Soldier
Radcliffe, Gt Manchester	S March	Liberty / Victory & Peace
Renfrew, Strathclyde	J Young	Lion + soldier / woman & child(R)
Rochdale, Lancs	E Lutyens (A)	Cenotaph with dead soldier
Royston, Hertfordshire	B Clemons	Soldier, crow+ soldiers from past (R)
St Johns Chapel, Durham	Beattie & Co.	Soldier (mourning)
Salisbury, Wiltshire	H H Martyn (Man)	Lion
Sandwich, Kent	C L Hartwell & O Ramsden(D)	St George (R)
Sheerness, Kent	R L Boulton & Sons (M)	Draped female
Shrewsbury, Shropshire	A G Wyon	St Michael in round 'temple'
Silksworth, Tyne & Wear	-	Soldier
Skipton, W. Yorks	J Cassidy	Victory+ nude warrior (breaking sword)
Sleaford, Lincs	Maxey & Son (M)	Winged fig / Knight / Fig with Ship (MC)
Southwark, S.London	P Lindsey Clark	Soldier + battle scenes/ St George/ woman mourning(R)
Stafford, Staffs	J Whitehead (Man)	Soldier
Stonyhurst, Lancashire	Gilbert Ledward	4 Servicemen + Crucifixion
Streatham, S.London	A Toft	Soldier (mourning)
Strensall, N. Yorks	G W Milburn (B)	Cross+ mourning soldier(R)
Sunderland, Tyne & Wear	R Ray	Victory
Sutton Coldfield, W. Midlands	F W Doyle Jones	Soldier
Thornton, W. Yorks	H Brownsword	Draped female
Treeton, S. Yorks	Bingley Bros (B)	Soldier (arms reversed)
Truro, Cornwall	J Whitehead (Man)	Soldier (helmet aloft)
Tunbridge Wells, Kent	S N Babb	Soldier
Walthamstow, E.London	-	Draped female mourning figure
Wanstead, E.London	Newbury Trent	Victory
Weston-super-Mare, Somerset	A Drury	Victory
Wetherby, W. Yorks	L F Roslyn	Victory + lions
Wimblington, Cambs	-	Victory
Winchester, Kings R Rifles	J Tweed	Soldier
Woking, Surrey	F W Doyle Jones	Victory
Wolverhampton, Staffs	W C H King	Obelisk + servicemen/St George

1923

Aberbanc, Dyfed	E J Jones	Soldier (rifle reversed)
Abercarn, Gwent	-	Draped female
Aberystwyth, Dyfed	M Rutteli	Victory + Nude female
Ardrossan, Strathclyde	J Young	Cross + St Columba/ Robert Bruce + Sir A Wood/ David Livingstone + Robert Burns+ James Watt(R)
Arsley, Bedfordshire	-	Soldier (mourning)
Bargoed & Gilfach, Mid Glamorgan	-	Soldier (mourning)
Basingstoke, Hants	L F Roslyn	Victory
Batley, W. Yorks	Wright & Son (M)	Soldier (mourning)
Benenden, Kent	A Toft	Seated female
Berwick on Tweed	A Carrick	Winged female
Blaydon, Co Durham	R W Morrison (M)	Soldier (mourning)
Bonnyrigg, Lothian	-	Soldier
Broadstairs, Kent	E M C Pollock	Soldiers, Crucifix/ battle(R)
Broughton, Humberside	G Bayes	Soldier (seated, deep in thought)
Blackpool, Lancs	G Ledward	Obelisk + War /Peace (R)
Burgess Hill, W.Sussex	W Gough	St George
Burley in Wharfedale, W. Yorks	-	Soldier/ Sailor(R)
Church, Lancs	W Marsden	Draped female (Peace)
Cinderford, Glos	J Swift	Soldier
Clitheroe, Lancs	L F Roslyn	Soldier (mourning)
Colchester, Essex	H C Fehr	Victory + St George + Peace (female)
Colwyn Bay, Clwyd	J Cassidy	Soldier
Comber, Co Down	L S Merrifield	Soldier
Crompton, Gt Manchester	R R Goulden	Nude male, beasts+children
Dale, Dyfed	W Jones	Soldier
Dodworth, S. Yorks	-	Soldier
Doncaster, S. Yorks	J & H Patterson (M)	Robed female (mourning)
Dudley, W.Midlands	-	Draped female
Ellon, Aberdeen	-	Soldier
Exeter, Devon	J Angel	Victory+ soldier, sailor+ prisoner + Nurse
Failsworth, Gt Manchester	Sellars of Manchester (M)	Column + Victory
Fraserburgh, Aberdeen	A Carrick	Justice + Valour
Gwersyllt, Clwyd	H Cawthra	Victory carrying wreath
Harrogate, N. Yorks	G Ledward	Obelisk + reliefs
Henllan, Clwyd	-	Soldier
Holyhead, Gwynedd	L F Roslyn	Cenotaph + soldier / sailor(R)
Huntingdon, Cambs	K Scott	Soldier
Ironbridge, Shropshire	A G Walker	Soldier
Kinghorn, Fife	A Carrick	Soldier + kneeling sailor
Kingston upon Thames, Surrey	R R Goulden	Nude male + 2 children
Laughton en le Morthern, S. Yorks	Tyas & Guest (M)	Soldier (mourning)
Lisburn, Antrim	H C Fehr	Victory
Llangeitho, Dyfed	E Jones	Soldier
Llanwrda, Dyfed	-	Soldier (mourning)
Llanelli, Dyfed	W Goscombe John	2 Soldiers (Artillery, Infantry)
London (RAF)	W Reid Dick	Eagle
London (London Troops)	A Drury	2 Soldiers
Malvern, Worcs	R R Goulden	Winged figure (Youth)
Marnhull, Dorset	-	Crucifix/ Archangel/ St George (MC)
New Tredegar, Mid Glamorgan	-	Soldier + wounded comrade
Newcastle upon Tyne	C L Hartwell	St George + Peace/ Justice (R)

Newcastle (Commercials)	W Goscombe John	Enlisting men, women + children
North Shields,Tyne & Wear	J Reed	Angel of Healing + servicemen(R)
Oban, Strathclyde	A Carrick	Soldiers carrying wounded comrade
Plymouth, Devon	Birnie Rhind	Female
Pontrhydfendigaid, Dyfed	H H Jones (B)	Peace
Portsoy, Grampian	Stewart & Co (M)	Soldier (mourning)
Reigate & Redhill, Surrey	R R Goulden	Nude male + child
Rothwell, W.Yorks	Stainer Bros (M)	Soldier (mourning)
Seven Sisters, W.Glamorgan	-	Soldier (mourning)
Sheffield, S.Yorks	G Alexander	Flag pole+ 4 Soldiers
Sheffield,(York & Lancs Regt)	R Smith/G Morewood/ F Jahn	Victory+ Soldier+ Officer
Slaidburn, Lancs	L F Roslyn	Soldier (mourning)
Stafford, (County memorial)	W.R Colton (& L S Merrifield)	Horse + Victory
Stourbridge, W.Midlands	J Cassidy	Female +Army /Navy(R)
Stretford, Manchester	J & H Patterson (M)	Cenotaph + lion
Thornton Clevelys, Lancs	A Toft	Soldier (mourning)
Thurso, Caithness	P Portsmouth	Draped male+ small child
Tottenham, N.London	LF Roslyn	Victory
Welshpool, Powys	Sir Aston Webb (A)	Lantern Cross + 4 figures of Saints
Welton, Lincs	A J Tuttle (M)	Soldier (mourning)
West Bromwich, W.Midlands -		Victory
Weybridge, Surrey	Boulton & Sons (M)	Soldier
Whitchurch, S.Glamorgan	R L Boulton (B)	Soldier (mourning)
Whittlesey, Cambs	T W Ford (M)	St George
Wick, Caithness	P.H Portsmouth	Victory

1924

Alloa, Central Scotland	Pilkington Jackson	St Margaret + Soldiers in trench, one cutting barbed wire)
Bearsden, Strathclyde	A Proudfoot	Victory holding semi-nude male
Belfast, Antrim(Young Citizens Volunteers)		Soldier
Blackburn, Lancs	B MacKennal	Female + semi-nude male
Bodmin,(D. of Cornwall Light Inf)	L S Merrifield	Soldier
Carmarthen, Dyfed	W Goscombe John	Soldier
Clacton on Sea, Essex	C L Hartwell	Victory
Coedpoeth, Clwyd	-	Soldier (mourning)
Crewe, Cheshire	W Gilbert	Brittania
Derby, Derbyshire	A G Walker	Cross + Woman & child
Douglas, Isle of Man	E Crellin (A)	Soldier
Dover, Kent	R R Goulden	Nude youth with flaming cross
Duffryn, Graig & Rogerstone, Gwent	G Bayes	Lych gate + St George
Earsdon, Tyne & Wear	-	Sailor (mourning)
Ebbw Vale, Gwent	J Whitehead (Man)	Soldier
Farnworth, Gt Manchester	J & H Patterson (M)	Peace
Gillingham, Kent	F.W Doyle-Jones	Christ + angels (Ascension)
Glasgow, (Cameronians)	P Lindsey Clark	Soldiers + dead comrade
Glenfinnan, Highland	-	Soldier (mourning)
Greenock, Strathclyde	A Proudfoot	Victory (on prow of ship)
Gwaun Cae Gurwen, W.Glamorgan	W J Williams	Soldier (mourning)
Haslingden, Lancs	L F Roslyn	Soldier + wounded comrade
Keighley, W. Yorks	H C Fehr	Victory + Soldier + Sailor
Kidwelly, Dyfed	G Moxham (A)	Soldier
Lancaster,	Bromsgrove School of Art (D)	Victory
Llandaff, S.Glamorgan	W Goscombe John	Female+ Schoolboy + Worker

London (Cavalry Division)	A Jones	St George
London (Rifle Brigade)	J Tweed	Soldier+ 2 historical soldiers
London (Royal Fusiliers)	A Toft	Soldier
London (Middlesex County)	R R Goulden	Soldier + battle+ airman+ sailor(R)
London (24th Division)	E H Kennington	3 Soldiers
Manchester	E Lutyens (A)	Cenotaph+ dead soldier
Milford Haven, Dyfed	E Jones	Soldier + Sailor
Milnrow, Manchester	G H Thomas	Soldier
Newcastle,(Northumberland Fusiliers)	J Reed	St George
Paisley, Strathclyde	A Meredith Williams	Mounted crusader+ 4 soldiers
Penarth,S.Glamorgan	W Goscombe John	Victory
Pencoed, Mid Glamorgan	W G Storr-Barber (M)	Winged figure
Portstewart, Londonderry	L F Roslyn	Soldier
Rhayader, Powys	B Lloyd	Clock tower and soldier /Peace / Welsh dragon defeating German eagle
Pwllheli, Gwynedd	J Summers (D)	Soldier
St.Annes on Sea, Lancs	W Marsden	Female+ Soldier+ Mother & child+ soldiers (R)
Shiremoor,Northumberland	W Endean & Sons (M)	Soldiers (R) (mourning)
Todmorden, W.Yorks	G Bayes	Fountain, St George, children
Tredegar, Gwent	Newbury Trent	Soldier
Troon, Strathclyde	W Gilbert	Brittania
Uxbridge, Gt London	A Jones	Victory
Wrexham,(R Welsh Fusiliers)	W Goscombe John	Soldier + 18th century soldier

1925

Aberdeen, Grampian	W McMillan (A)	Lion
Annfield Plain, Durham	Messrs A F Menwelle (Art)	Crucifix
Bangor-Is-Y-Coed, Clwyd	G H Tyson Smith	Robed female (mourning)
Barnsley, S. Yorks	J Tweed	Soldier +Victory(R)
Birkenhead, Merseyside	G H Tyson Smith	Cenotaph + grieving women(R)
Birmingham,	A Toft / W Bloye	Hall + 4 figures of armed services, nursing + reliefs inside
Bridgwater, Somerset	J Angel	Civilisation + angels
Buckie, Grampian	Birnie Rhind	Soldier + kneeling Sailor
Builth Wells, Powys	A R Emery (M)	Cross + 4 servicemen
Canterbury,(Cathedral - Carabiniers)	E Burton (A)	Soldier (dead)
Carnoustie, Tayside	T Beattie	Soldier laying a wreath on cross
Downpatrick,Co Down	T Hastings (M)	Soldier
Eastham, Merseyside	C J Allen	Christ + 2 soldiers (R)
Eccles, Gt Manchester	J Cassidy	Victory + mourning soldier(R)
Galashiels, Borders	T J Clapperton	Clocktower + mourning female(R) + equestrian statue
Heywood, Gt Manchester	W Marsden	Female (Peace)
Houghton le Spring, Durham	F W Doyle Jones	Cross + soldier(R)
Kenfig Hill & Pyle, Mid Glamorgan	L F Roslyn	Victory
Kingsbridge & Dodbrooke, Devon	-	Draped female
Llanbradach, Mid Glamorgan	T J Durbin	Draped female
London (Royal Artillery)	C S Jagger	Carved gun + Soldiers + Dead soldier + battle scenes(R)
London (Machine Gun Corps)	F Derwent Wood	Male nude (David)
Millom, Cumbria	A Miller	St Michael + Servicemen (R)
Olrig, Caithness	P H Portsmouth	Allegorical male
Pontardulais, W.Glamorgan	D Morgan (D)	Angel + cross

Port Talbot, W.Glamorgan	L F Roslyn	Peace, woman & child, male nude & battle scene / female(R)
Portadown, Armagh -	H.C Fehr	Angel + wounded soldier
Rhosllanerchrugog, Clwyd -		Soldier (mourning)
Ruthin, Clwyd	H Hughes	Cross+ St Michael(R)
Sale & Ashton on Mersey, Cheshire	A Sherwood	St George
Stockport, Cheshire	G Ledward	Brittania + semi-nude male
Trelewis, Mid Glamorgan	D Williams (B)	Soldier (mourning)
Walford, Herefordshire	L Boulton	St George
Wallsend, Tyne & Wear	Newbury Trent	Victory
Westfield Village, Lancaster	J Delahunt	Soldier & wounded comrade
Wigan, Gt Manchester	Sir Giles Gilbert Scott (A)	Medieval cross + females

1926

Abertillery, Gwent	G H Thomas	Soldier
Armagh, Armagh	C L Hartwell	Female (Peace with Honour)
Bournemouth, Dorset	G Maile (Man)	Female + servicemen (lost)
Burnley, Lancs	W Gilbert	Cenotaph+ 3 servicemen+ 2 females
Haltwhistle, Northumberland	R Beall	Cross + Animals / Birds
London (Guards Division)	G Ledward	Obelisk +Soldiers +reliefs
London (St Bartholomew's -Rough Riders)	A Webb (A)	Female + angels
Lye, Worcs	G Brown & Sons (M)	Soldier
Maesteg, Mid Glamorgan	L F Roslyn	Soldier + wounded comrade
Preston, Lancs	H Pegram	Obelisk + Victory(R)
St. Peter Port, Guernsey	-	St George
Scourie, Highland -		Soldier (mourning)
Scunthorpe, Humberside	J Beresford (M)	Soldier + Sailor + Flag
Smethwick, Staffs	R Lindsey Clark	Female+ Army/Navy/ RFC (R)

1927

Alfreton, Derbyshire	W Aumonier	Soldier with child
Bangor, Co Down	T E Macklin	Obelisk + Lion + Figure (Erin)
Brynmawr, Gwent	R Price (M)	Soldier
Catshill, Worcs	-	Soldier (mourning)
Dalry, Strathclyde	K Brown	Angel
Derry, Londonderry	V March	Victory + Soldier+ Sailor
Edinburgh,(Scottish-American)	R Tait McKenzie	Soldier + civilians & marching troops(R)
Edinburgh,(National Memorial)	various	Hall + individual memorials / reliefs
Fleetwood, Lancs	G H Tyson Smith	Nude male
Kilmarnock, Strathclyde	D McGill	Seated male youth (Victory)
Morley, W.Yorks	W Gilbert	Brittania

1928

Bolton, Lancs	W Marsden	2 figure groups -Struggle/Sacrifice)
Cardiff,(National Memorial)	H A Pegram	Winged figure +4 servicemen
Hackney, E. London	R R Goulden	Female
Lurgan, Armagh	L S Merrifield	Winged figure(Victorious peace)
Watford, Herts	M Bromet	3 nude males (2 seated)
Workington, Cumbria	A Carrick	Soldiers, mother & child, workers(R)

1929

Rawtenstall, Lancs	L F Roslyn	Obelisk + Servicemen & home front (R)

1930

Eastleigh, Hants		Victory
Liverpool, Merseyside	G H Tyson Smith	Soldiers / mourners (R)

1931

Clydebank, Strathclyde	W Gilbert	Robed female (Peace)
Merthyr Tydfil, Glamorgan	L S Merrifield	Female + Miner, Mother & child
Quarry Bank, Staffs	G. Wade	Christ

1934

Llanharan, Mid Glamorgan	-	Soldier
Newtownards, Co Down	-	Obelisk + female

1936

Marylebone, C. London	CL Hartwell	St George

Date unknown

Aberdour, Fife	-	Victory
Aldershot, Hants(8th. Division)	-	Lion
Alderton, Glos	-	Crucifix
Allenton, Derbyshire	-	Soldier
Almondsbury, Glos		Crucifix
Alton, Staffordshire	-	Crucifix
Alyth, Tayside	-	Female (Brittania?)
Ardgay, Highland	-	Soldier
Ardrossan, Strathclyde	-	Cross + Christ / Soldier(R)
Armitage with Handsacre, Staffs	-	Crucifix
Ashford, Surrey	-	Victory
Axminster, Devon	-	Cross + St George
Bagillt, Clwyd	-	Soldier (mourning)
Balcombe, W. Sussex	-	St George
Ballachulish, Highland	RW Morrison (M)	Soldier (mourning)
Balsham, Cambs	F E Howard (A)	Crucifix
Banbridge, Down	F.W Pomeroy	Soldiers and reliefs
Barham, Kent	-	Crucifix
Barlow, Derbyshire	-	Crucifix
Barnt Green, Worcs	The Bromsgrove Guild (Man)	Cross + Soldier / Sailor
Barrington, Cambs	-	Crucifix
Barton Seagrove, Northants	-	Crucifix
Bawtry, S. Yorks	-	Crucifix
Bayford, Hertfordshire	-	Cross + St George
Beckenham, Kent	-	Crucifix
Beckenham, (Crematorium)	-	Soldier
Belvoir Castle, Leics	-	Female
Berrick Salome, Oxon	-	Crucifix
Bersham, Clwyd	-	Soldier (reversed rifle)
Biddulph, Staffs	-	Soldier (mourning)
Binton, Warwickshire	-	Crucifix
Birdholme, Derbyshire	-	Crucifix
Blaenporth, Dyfed	-	Soldier

366

Location	Designer/Maker	Subject
Boroughbridge, N.Yorks	-	Female (bowed head)
Bourock, Strathclyde	-	Soldier (kilted)
Bracknell, Berkshire	-	Angel
Brading, Isle of Wight	-	Crucifix
Branston, Leics	-	Crucifix
Brean, Somerset		Soldier/dead eagle(R)
Brent Knoll, Somerset	-	Crucifixion (LC)
Brewood, Staffs	-	Cross + St George
Bridgetown, Staffs	-	Obelisk + soldier's head(R)
Brockley, Gt London	-	Soldier + Sailor
Brodick, Strathclyde	-	Soldier
Broughshane, Antrim	-	Soldier (reversed rifle)
Brown Candover, Hants	-	Crucifix
Bury & West Burton, W.Sussex	-	Crucifix
Butetown, Cardiff,	-	Crucifix
Butleigh, Somerset	-	Crucifix
Callander, Central Scotland	-	Lion + soldier holding cross(R)
Cannock, Staffs	J Beresford (M)	Soldier + Sailor
Canongate, Lothian	L R Deuchars	Mourning soldier/sailor(R)
Cantley, S.Yorks	Sir J Ninian Comper (A)	Crucifix
Cambuslang, Strathclyde	-	Soldier
Canterbury, Kent	-	Cross+ servicemen(R)
Canterbury, (Cathedral -9th Queen's Royal Lancers)		Knight + angel
Carbrooke, Norfolk	-	Crucifix
Cardenden, Fife	-	Mourning soldiers(R)
Carlton, W.Yorks	-	Crucifix
Carleton in Craven, N.Yorks	-	Cross +Crucifixion(R)
Cassington, Oxon	A Miller	Cross + Crucifixion/ Virgin & Child
Castlefields, Shropshire	-	Crucifix
Cheddar, Somerset	-	Market Cross+ Crucifix/Virgin & Child/ St George/St Michael
Chelmsford, (Cathedral - Essex Yeomanry)		Soldier (mourning)
Chiddingstone, Kent	-	Lantern Cross with Virgin Mary
Childe Okeford & Hanford, Dorset		Market Cross with Figures
Chirbury, Shropshire	-	Crucifix
Church Leigh, Staffs	-	Crucifix
Christleton, Cheshire	-	Lantern Cross + Crucifix
Clifton, Manchester	-	Obelisk + Lion
Clowne, Derbyshire	-	Soldier
Coleshill, Warwickshire	-	Cross + soldier / sailor
Colwall, Herefordshire	-	Crucifix
Conisbrough, S.Yorks	Messrs. Tyas & Guest (M)	Soldier
Copford, Essex	-	Crucifix
Cornholme, W.Yorks	-	Angel
Cramlington, Northumberland	-	St George
Cranworth, Letton & Southburgh, Norfolk		Angel
Crawley Down, W.Sussex	-	Cross + Christ
Creswell, Derbyshire	-	Soldier
Crewkerne, Somerset	-	Soldier
Crianlarich, Central Scotland	-	Soldier
Cromford, Derbyshire	-	Crucifix
Dalmally, Strathclyde	-	Soldier (kilted)
Danesmoor, Derbyshire	G Platts (M)	Soldier
Darlaston, W.Midlands	-	Soldier
Dedham, Essex	W D Caroe (A)	Crucifix + Virgin & Child /Shepherd

Deanshanger, Northants	-	Crucifix
Deeping St. Nicholas, Lincs	-	Cross +St George(R)
Derry Hill, Wiltshire	-	Lantern Cross + St George
Dilwyn, Herefordshire	W G Storr-Barber (M)	Soldier
Donnington, N.Yorks	-	Crucifix
Dore, S.Yorks		Soldier
Dromore, Tyrone	LF Roslyn	Soldier
Dufftown, Highland	-	Victory
Dunbar, Lothian	-	Crucifix
Durisdeer, Dumfries	-	Soldier (R)
Earls Croome & Hill Croome,Worcs		Crucifix (lost)
East & West Somerton, Norfolk	-	Lion
East Brierley, W.Yorks	-	Female
Ebchester, Durham	-	Cross + St George(R)
Effingham, Surrey	-	Crucifix
Egremont, Cumbria C W Coombes		Soldier
Elsenham, Essex	-	Crucifix
Elton, Cambs	-	Crucifix
Elton, Humberside	-	Crucifix
Elsworth, Cambs	-	Angel
Epsom, Surrey	-	Crucifix
Eston, Normanby & Barnaby Moor,N.Yorks		Soldier (mourning)
Farndale, N.Yorks	-	Crucifix
Fartown & Birkby, W.Yorks	-	Soldier
Fernhurst, W.Sussex	-	Crucifix
Ferryhill, Durham	-	Soldier
Finningham, Suffolk	-	Crucifix
Flookburgh, Cumbria	-	Crucifix
Fordcombe, Kent	-	Crucifix
Forse, Latheron & Latheronwheel, Highland		Soldier
Fort William, Highland	-	Soldier (mourning)
Freeland, Oxfordshire	-	Crucifix
Freshwater West, Dyfed	J Coates-Carter (A)	Crucifix
Fulford, Staffordshire		Crucifix
Fylingdales, N.Yorks	-	Cross + St George & St Stephen(R)
Garboldisham, Norfolk	-	Cross + St George
Gedney Hill, Lincs	-	Crucifix
Glandford, Norfolk	-	Crucifix
Gleadless, Hollinsend & Intake, S.Yorks		Soldier
Glencoe, Highland	-	Soldier (mourning)
Gloucester		Cross + soldiers (R)
Grangemouth, Central Scotland	-	Lion + eagle
Great Billing, Northants	-	Crucifix
Great Chesterford, Essex	-	Crucifix
Great Offley,Hertfordshire	-	Crucifix
Great Shefford, Berks	-	Crucifix
Guiting Power, Glos	-	Soldier/sailor/crucifixion/figure(LC)
Halkirk, Highland	-	Woman & girl
Hardwick, Notts	-	Crucifix
Harlow Moor, N.Yorks	-	Crucifix + dying soldier (R)
Harrogate,N.Yorks (Ex-Servicemen)		Crucifix+ soldier/ nurse + soldier/ airman/ Naval gun crew (R)
Hartlepool,(Old Hartlepool)	-	Angel
Hasland, Derbyshire	-	Soldier
Hassocks, W.Sussex	-	Semi-nude youth with dove

Haverfordwest, Dyfed (Men of Pembroke)		Welsh dragon
Haxey, Humberside	-	Soldier (mourning)
Headcorn, Kent	-	Cenotaph with Soldier & Sailor
Headington Quarry, Oxon	-	Crucifix
Helmsley, N.Yorks	-	Crucifix
High Ham, Somerset	-	Crucifix + Angels
Hinton Martell, Dorset	FC Eden (A)	Cross + Pieta
Hoghton, Lincolnshire	-	Crucifix
Hollington, Staffordshire	-	Crucifix
Hopton on Sea, Norfolk	-	Crucifix
Hooton Pagnall, S.Yorks	-	Cross + Angel
Horfield, Bristol	-	Crucifix
Horndean, Hampshire		Victory
Horsley, Glos	-	Crucifix
Hunmanby, N.Yorks	-	Obelisk with soldier(R)
Huntley, Glos	-	Crucifix
Huyton with Roby,Lancs	-	Winged female
Ickburgh, Norfolk	-	Grieving woman
Invercharron, Highland	-	Soldier
Inveresk, Lothian	-	Cross + angel
Inverurie, Grampian	-	Soldier
Jacksdale, Notts	J Beresford (M)	Soldier
Johnstone, Strathclyde	-	Soldier (kilted)
Johnstown, Clwyd	-	St George
Keevil, Wiltshire	-	Crucifix
Keith,(Gordon Highlanders)	AG Walker	Soldier
Keyingham, E.Yorks	-	Soldier (mourning)
Kilburn, N.Yorks	-	Soldier (bust)
Kilkeel, Co Down	-	Soldier (mourning)
Kingscote, Glos	-	Cross + Face of Christ
Kingswood, Avon	-	Market Cross with Saint
Kippax, W.Yorks	-	Angel + Servicemen(R)
Kirkburton, W.Yorks	-	Crucifix + St George
Kirkconnel, Galloway	-	Soldier
Kirkfieldbank, Strathclyde	-	Soldier (mourning)
Kirkwall, Orkney	W G Storr-Barber (M)	Winged figure
Kirriemuir, Tayside	-	Soldier
Knockholt, Kent	-	Mourning soldier (R)
Langham, Norfolk	-	Crucifix
Lees, Gt Manchester	-	Soldier
Lezayre, Churchtown, Isle of Man	E Crellin (A)	Cross + Soldier
Liddesdale, Borders	-	Soldier
Little Bredy, Dorset	-	Cross + Christ with Lamb
Little Ness, Shropshire	Farmer & Brindley (M)	Crucifix
Liverpool,(Cathedral -55th Div)	W Gilbert	Angel + soldier
Llanfechell, Gwynedd	-	Clocktower + Soldier (mourning)
Llanfihangel Nantmelan, Powys	-	Soldier
Lochinver, Highland	-	Soldier
Longhope, Glos	-	Lion
Lostock Hall, Lancs	-	Crucifixion+ mourning figure & angel
Lostock Hall, Lancs	-	Victory (or Peace)
Louth, Lincs	R W Ray	Soldier
Lower Cam, Glos	-	Crucifix
Lower Crumpsall, Gt Manchester		Obelisk +Saints(R)
Lower Darwen, Lancs	-	Soldier (mourning)

Location	Sculptor/Maker	Subject
Lythe, N.Yorks	-	Market Cross with Crucifixion
Maerdy, Mid Glamorgan	-	Robed female
Magor, Gwent	-	Cross + portrait (R)
Maidstone, Kent	-	Knight, virgin, child, king, warrior (LC)
Malton, N.Yorks	-	Cross + Lions
Marple, Gt Manchester	-	Draped Female
Masham, N.Yorks	-	Crucifix
Medlar with Wesham, Lancs	-	Soldier (mourning)
Meriden, W.Midlands	-	Crucifix
Milborne Port, Somerset	-	Crucifix
Mildenhall, Suffolk	-	Soldier
Minto, Borders	-	Soldier
Monifieth, Tayside	JH Cawthra	Female
Montrose, Tayside	-	Victory
Moor Crichel & Witchampton, Dorset		Angel
Morecambe & Heysham, Lancs	-	Lion
Moxley, W.Midlands	-	Crucifix
Moy, Tyrone	Purdy & Millard (B)	Bugler
New Bradwell, Bucks	McArthur Gurney (M)	Soldier
New Ferry, Merseyside	-	Crucifix
New Radnor, Powys	-	Soldier (mourning)
New Silksworth, Tyne & Wear	-	Soldier
Newmilns, Strathclyde	-	Soldier
North Collingham, Notts	-	Crucifix
North Ormesby, N.Yorks	-	Soldier (mourning)
North Skelton, N.Yorks	-	Soldier (mourning)
North Tuddenham, Norfolk	-	Crucifix
Northam, Devon	-	Draped female
Northiam, E.Sussex	-	St George
Norton-on-Tees, Co Durham	-	Crucifix
Nympsfield, Glos	-	Crucifix
Oakley, Bucks	-	Crucifix
Old Gore, Herefordshire	-	Crucifix
Oldmeldrum, Aberdeen	-	Soldier (mourning)
Ossett, W.Yorks	-	Soldier
Oughtrington, Cheshire	-	Crucifix
Oxenhall, Glos	G Maile & Sons (Man)	Crucifix
Paddock Wood, Kent	-	Soldier
Palmers Green, W.London	J Angel	Christ + Dead Soldier
Paulerspury, Northants	-	Crucifix
Penn Fields, Bradmore & Merry Hill, W.Midlands		Soldier
Pen-y-Cae, Clwyd		Soldier (mourning)
Pitsea, Essex	R R Goulden	Figure with torch
Plockton, Highlands	-	Obelisk with Lion(R)
Plymouth, (Royal Marines)	W G Storr-Barber (M)	Nude male + Eagle
Port Sunlight(Hesketh Hall Cheshire Rgt)	C & S Co. (Man)	Soldier
Porthill, Staffordshire	-	Crucifix
Portknockie, Grampian	-	Kneeling female
Prestbury, Glos	-	Cross + figures including Christ
Prestonpans, Lothian	Birnie Rhind	Soldier
Princethorpe, Warwicks	-	Crucifix
Probus, Cornwall	-	Crucifix
Putley, Herefordshire	-	Crucifix
Quedgeley, Glos	S Gambler-Parry (D)	Crucifix
Ranby, Notts		Crucifix

Richmond, N.Yorks	-	Cross + relief (Ship)
Richmond, Surrey	-	Column + allegorical figure
Ripponden, W. Yorks	-	Soldier
Rothwell, Northants	-	Market Cross with St George
Rowley Regis, W.Midlands	-	Soldier
Rushden, Northants	-	St George/Fortitude/Sympathy
Rutherglen, Glasgow,	-	Nude male
St. Bees, Cumbria	-	St George
St. Blazey, Cornwall	-	Crucifix
Saintbury, Glos	Alec Miller -	Crucifix
Saltcoats, Strathclyde	-	Soldier
Sandhurst,(British Army)	F Gleichen	3 Soldiers
Sauchie, Tayside	-	Cross + 2 Angels
Scaynes Hill, W.Sussex	-	Crucifix
Sedgebarrow, Worcs	-	Crucifix
Sefton, Merseyside	-	Crucifix
Seghill, Northumberland	-	Soldier (mourning)
Shadwell, Gt London		Crucifix
Shaftesbury, Dorset	-	Cross + Angels
Shepley, W.Yorks	J Swift	Soldier (mourning)
Shepton Beauchamp, Somerset	-	Crucifix
Shirebrook, Derbyshire	-	Crucifix
Shobnall (St Paul's Parish) Burton-upon-Trent, Staffs		Christ
Skelmersdale, Lancs	-	Soldier
Skendlebury, Lincs	-	Crucifix
Soham, Cambs	- -	Soldier (mourning)
Somerton, Somerset	-	Soldier (mourning)
South Bank, N.Yorks	-	Draped female with trumpet
South Weald, Essex	-	Crucifix
Southampton,(Belgian Patriots)	Messrs. Garret & Haysom (B)	Crucifix
Sowton, Devon	-	Cross + Angel
Sparsholt, Oxfordshire	-	Medieval Cross with Christ
Stainforth, S.Yorks	Messrs. Tyas & Guest (M)	Soldier
Stamford Bridge, E.Yorks	-	Crucifix
Stanley, W.Yorks	-	Soldier
Stansted, Kent	-	Nude youth
Stanton, Glos		St George/crucifix/virgin & child
Stanway, Glos	A Fisher (lettering by E Gill)	Cross + St George
Staveley, Derbyshire	-	Soldier
Stonnall, Staffs	-	Soldier
Stranraer, Galloway	-	Soldier
Strathspey, Highland		Soldier (kilted)
Strelley, Notts	-	Crucifix
Stromness, Orkney	-	Mourning female
Sundridge, Kent	-	Crucifix
Sutton Benger, Wiltshire	-	Crucifix(LC)
Sutton-on-the-Forest, N.Yorks	-	Cavalryman/sailors/airplane(R)
Swanley, Kent	-	Victory
Swanwick, Derbyshire	-	Crucifix
Swinefleet, Humberside	-	Soldier
Swineshead, Lincs	-	Crucifix
Swynnerton, Staffs	-	Crucifix + 2 Marys
Taplow, Bucks	-	Crucifix
Taynton, Glos	-	Crucifix
Thornbury, Avon	-	Crucifix

Thurnscoe, S.Yorks	-	Soldier
Thrumpton, Notts	-	Soldier (dead)
Tilbury Juxta Clare, Essex	-	Crucifix
Tong, W.Yorks	-	Soldier (mourning)
Tough, Grampian	RW Morrison (M)	Soldier (mourning)
Tranmere, Merseyside	-	Crucifix
Tutbury, Staffs	-	Angel /Sts George & Michael
Tweedmouth, Northumberland	-	Kneeling angel
Teigworth, Glos	-	Crucifix
Udny, Grampian	D Morren & Co (M)	Soldier
Uffington, Lincs	-	St George
Ullapool, Highland	-	Seated woman
Upper Tean, Staffs	F D Howard (A)	Crucifix + 2 Figures
Upwell, Norfolk	-	Angel
Utkinton, Cheshire	-	Crucifix
Verwood, Dorset	-	Crucifix
Walker, Tyne & Wear	-	Victory
Wallasey, Merseyside	-	Crucifix
Walsall, W.Midlands	-	Crucifix
Walsoken, Cambs	-	Soldier
Walsworth, Hertfordshire	-	Crucifix
Warminster, Wiltshire	T Falconer, H Baker & F Bligh Bond(A)	Cross + Lamb / St George
Weeford, Staffs	- -	Crucifix
West Allotment, Tyne & Wear	A Scoular (D)	Angel
West Ashby, Lincs	-	Crucifix
West Ilsley, Berkshire	-	Crucifix
West Willoughby, Lincs	-	Crucifix
Westbury, Bucks	-	Crucifix
Westbury on Severn, Glos	-	Crucifix
Wheelock, Cheshire		Soldier
Whitburn, Lothian	-	Soldier
Whitefield, Gt Manchester	S March	Winged female
Whitehaven, Cumbria	F Derwent Wood	Draped female (R)
Whyteleafe, Surrey	-	Crucifix
Wigmore, Herefordshire	-	Soldier (mourning)
Wilbarston, Northants	-	Crucifix
Windsor, Berkshire	-	Crucifix
Winforton, Herefordshire	-	Crucifix
Winlaton, Tyne & Wear	G Maile & Son Ltd (Man)	Crucifix
Witchampton, Dorset	-	Winged female
Witham, Lincs	-	Crucifix
Woodford, Northants	-	Crucifix
Worcester Park, Gt London	-	Crucifix
Worfield, Shropshire	-	Crucifix
Wotton under Edge, Glos	-	Crucifix
Wychnor, Staffs	-	Crucifix
Wyre Piddle, Worcs	-	Obelisk + Lion
Yaxham, Norfolk	-	Crucifix
Yeadon, W.Yorks	-	Crucifix
Ynysybwl, Mid Glamorgan	-	Cenotaph + soldiers(R)
York,(Minster - 6th. Battn. King's Own Yorkshire Light Infantry)		Victory

APPENDIX II

SCULPTORS OF FIGURATIVE FIRST WORLD WAR MEMORIALS IN THE UNITED KINGDOM

War memorials for churches, clubs, workplace etc. and memorials to individuals - all of which are excluded from Appendix I - are included here. Non-figurative memorials by listed sculptors have however been excluded.

    This list also excludes those identified as architects, builders, masons, manufacturers and specialist craftsmen (such as wood carvers). To include all of these would produce a much longer list. This is undoubtedly unfair to some. Larger companies of stonemasons employed art school trained sculptors and 'untrained' masons were capable of producing impressive monuments. Nonetheless, for the sake of consistency, masons have been excluded.

B = Bronze ; S = Stone / Marble ; W = Wood

George Alexander
1923	Sheffield, South Yorks	Soldiers (mourning) (B)

Charles John Allen (1862-1956)
1923	Bootle, Merseyside (Liverpool Gas Co)	Soldier holding injured comrade (B)
1924	Eastham, Merseyside	Christ (B)+ relief (soldier/dying soldier) (S)
-	Liverpool (St Catherine's) - lost	Soldier holding injured comrade (B)
-	Liverpool University	Relief (Putti with palm leaves) (S)

John Angel (1881-1960)
1923	Exeter, Devon	Victory/soldier/sailor/prisoner of war/nurse (B)
1925	Bridgwater, Somerset	Female (Civilisation) /angels / male figures (B)
-	Palmers Gn, London (Frank Salisbury -design)	Christ/dead soldier (B)

William Aumonier (b.1870)
1920	Albrighton, Shropshire	Crucifixion (W)
1927	Alfreton, Derbyshire	Soldier / girl (B)
-	Hull, S.Yorks (Reckitt & Sons)	Fountain + female (Sacrifice)/dead youth /cherubs with dolphins

Stanley Nicholson Babb (1874 - 1957)
1921	Bridlington, S.Yorks	Cenotaph + reliefs (Victory /sailor) (B)
1921	London (Coutts Bank)	Relief (2 Allegorical female figures) (B)
1922	Tunbridge Wells, Kent	Soldier (B)

Gilbert Bayes (1872-1953)
1919	Aldeburgh, Suffolk	Relief (soldier (dying) /allegorical figures) (S)
1920	Broadstone, Dorset	Allegorical Female (Memory) + reliefs (Soldiers)
1920	Ramsgate, Kent	Draped, semi-nude female (Destiny) (S)
1921	Hythe, Kent	Victory (B)+ reliefs (servicemen / lions) (S)
1921	London (Law Society)	Relief (children) (S)

1921	London (Queen's Chapel of the Savoy)	Relief (St George) (B)
1922	Orpington, Kent (St. Olaves School - W. Reynolds-Stephens, design)	St Olaf (B)
1923	Broughton, Lincs	Soldier (seated) (S)
1924	Duffryn, Graig & Rogerstone, Gwent	Lych gate + St George (B)
1924	Todmorden, W. Yorks	Fountain + St George / children (mourners) (S)

Thomas Beattie
1925	Carnoustie, Tayside	Soldier with battlefield cross (S)

Percy George Bentham (1883-1936)
1920	Audenshaw, Lancashire	Soldier (B)
1920	Carnforth, Lancashire	Soldier + relief (marching soldiers) (B)
1920	Emsworth (St. James' Ch), Hants	Reredos (Christ / James / John) (W)
1921	Haydon Bridge, Northumberland	Soldier (B)
1921	Trowbridge, Wiltshire	Soldier (B)
1922	Dukinfield, Manchester	Soldier (B)
1922	Ballywalter, Down	Soldier (B)

William Bloye (1890-1975)
1921	Yardley (St Edburgha) Warwick	Relief (soldier/ woman & child) (B)
1925	Birmingham,	Reliefs (soldiers-enlisting/ in firing line/ returning) (S)
1925	Springfield,(St Christopher's) Warwick	Male figures (S)
1928	Dudley, W. Midlands	Clock tower with relief (St George) (B)

Ferdinand Victor Blundstone (1882-1951)
1921	London (Green Room Club)	Relief (allegorical female (B)(lost)
1921	Stalybridge, Gt Manchester	Winged angel holding soldier/ winged angel+ sailor(B)
1922	Folkestone, Kent	Female (Motherhood),cross+ relief(marching soldiers)(B)
1922	London (Prudential Assurance)	2 angels holding dead soldier (B)
1926	Manchester (Belle Vue Zoo)	Peace (B) stolen

Phyllis Bone
1927	Edinburgh,(Scottish Nat War Mem)	Unicorn/ lion/ animal heads/ animals (S)

Sir Thomas Brock (1847 - 1922)
1922	Gatcombe,Isle of Wight (Capt C.G Seely-St Olave's)	Soldier (recumbent) (S)
1924	Belfast, Antrim (Queen's University)	Victory / wounded youth (B)
	(Designer, with F. Arnold Wright, sculptor)	

Mary Pownall Bromet (d.1937)
1928	Watford, Hertfordshire	3 nude males (B)

Cecil Brown (1868-1926)
1920	London (Camel Corps)	Soldier (on camel) + reliefs (soldiers / camel) (B)

Kellock Brown (1856-1934)
1920	Kilmaurs, Ayrshire	Soldier (mourning) (B)
1920	Penpont, Dumfries	Soldier (mourning) (S)
1921	Largs, Strathclyde	Soldier / seated soldier / sailor (S)
1922	Inverary, Argyll	Soldier (kilted) (B)
1924	Johnstone, Strathclyde	Soldier (S)
1927	Dalry, Strathclyde	Angel (B)
-	Alyth, Tayside	Britannia (B)

Mortimer Brown (1874 - 1966)

| 1919 | Tean, Staffordshire | Christ (B) |
| 1921 | Twickenham,Gt London | Soldier (B)+ reliefs (Navy/Air Force/women's services)(B) |

Harold Brownsword (1885 - 1961)

1922	Allerton & Daisy Hill,Yorks	Hooded female(Death)/bare-chest soldier/naked youth(B)
1922	Eccleshill, W.Yorks	Draped female (B)
1922	Hanley, Staffordshire	Britannia (B)
1922	Thornton, W.Yorks	Draped female (B)

Frances Burlison, (c.1850-1920)

| 1920 | Bridport, Dorset (with Sir Giles Gilbert Scott - design) | Column+ St George (S) |

Alexander Carrick (1882-1966)

1920	Auchtermuchty, Fife	Soldier (mourning) (S)
1920	Killin, Highlands	Soldier (kilted) (S)
1920	Lochawe, Argyll & Bute	Soldier (S)
1921	Blairgowrie, Tayside	Soldier (mourning) (B)
1921	North Berwick, Lothian	Column + unicorn (S)
1921	St Margaret's Hope, Orkneys	Soldier (kilted (S)
1921	Walkerburn, Borders	Soldier (mourning)
1922	Dornoch, Highlands	Soldier (kilted) (B)
1922	Forres, Grampian	Soldier (kilted) (B)
1922	Newburgh, Fife	Soldier (kilted) (S)
1923	Berwick upon Tweed, Northumberland	Victory (B)
1923	Fraserburgh, Grampian	Female (Justice) + male (Valour) (B)
1923	Kinghorn, Fife	Soldier / sailor (S)
1923	Oban, Strathclyde	2 soldiers carrying wounded colleague (S)
1927	Edinburgh,(Royal Engineers, Scot Nat War Mem)	Relief (soldiers) (B)
1927	Edinburgh,(Royal Artillery, Scot Nat War Mem)	Relief (soldiers) (B)
1928	Workington, Cumbria (Design - Wm Reid Dick)	Reliefs
	(soldier carrying comrade/soldier + wife & child/ miners/ shipbuilders (S)	
-	Burnley (L & E.J Shuttleworth)	Relief Portraits (plaster)

John Cassidy (1860-1939)

1920	Clayton-le-Moors, Lancashire	Female / soldier (B)
1921	Heaton Moor, Gt Manchester	Soldier (B)
1922	Lower Peover, Cheshire	Crucifix(S)+ reliefs(soldier/ sailor/ battle) (B/S)
1922	Skipton, N.Yorks	Victory + nude warrior (breaking sword) (B)
1923	Colwyn Bay, Clwyd	Soldier + reliefs (soldiers march/on board ship/return (B)
1923	Stourbridge, Worcs	Female(Peace)+ flag + reliefs (soldiers/sailors) (B)
1925	Eccles, Gt Manchester	Victory + relief (soldier) (B)

Joseph Hermon Cawthra (1886-1973)

1920	Bury, Lancs	Cross+ reliefs (frontline figures/activity on the home front) (B)
1920	Shipley, W.Yorks	(Primitive Methodist Chapel)Peace
1921	Hackney, London	Column + female robed figure (B)
1922	Bootle, Merseyside	Mother & Child/ soldier/ sailor/ airman (B)
1923	Gwersyllt, Clywd	Figure with sword & wreath (B)
-	Monifieth, Tayside	Column + medieval knight (B)

Thomas John Clapperton (1879-1962)

| 1921 | Canonbie, Dumfries | Soldier (mourning) (B) |

1921	Minto, Borders	Soldier (B)
1922	St John Lee, Northumberland (Capt. S Newburn)	Soldier (reclining) (S)
1925	Galashiels, Borders	Border Reiver on horse(B)+ relief (female mourner)(S)
-	Selkirk, Borders	Female (B)

Philip Lindsey Clark (1889-1977)

1922	Southwark, Gt London	Soldier+ reliefs (battle(B)/St George/mourner (S)
1924	Glasgow, (Cameronians)	3 soldiers(one dead) (B)
1932	Kensal Green, W.London (Belgian Soldiers)	Pieta (S)

Robert Lindsey Clark

| 1926 | Smethwick, W.Midlands | Female(Peace)+ reliefs (army & navy)(B) |
| - | Highgate, N.London (All Saints) | Relief (soldiers marching) (B) |

Benjamin Clemens (1875-1957)

1921	Cheadle Hulme, Gt Manchester	Cross+ 2 Soldier & sailor (S)
1922	Royston, Hertfordshire	Soldier(B)+ relief(soldiers from the past) (S)
1922	Stockwell, London	Clock tower+ relief (female (Remembrance)) (S)

William Robert Colton (1867-1921)

| 1923 | Stafford (County Memorial-completed by LS Merrifield) | Angel / horse (B) |
| - | Portsmouth, (Cathedral - W T Wyllie memorial) | Soldier (recumbent) (B) |

C W Coombes

| 1921 | Kendal, Cumbria | Soldier (B) |
| - | Egremont, Cumbria | Soldier (B) |

Benjamin Creswick (1853-1946)

| 1920 | Sutton Coldfield, W.Midlands (Boldmere Swimming Club) | |
| | | Man teaching boy to swim (B) |

Jennifer Delahunt

| 1925 | Westfield Memorial Village, Lancaster, Lancashire | Soldier (kneeling) (B) |

Louis Reid Deuchars (1870-1927)

1920	Glenelg, Highland	Soldier (Peace)/2 females(Victory & Stricken Humanity) (B)
-	Cannongate, Lothian	Relief (soldier/ sailor-mourning) (B)
-	Newbattle, Lothian	Relief (2 angels) (B)
-	Windsor, Berks (Lt C.J Goodford)	Christ + angels (W)

Sir William Reid Dick (1879-1961)

1921	Rickmansworth, Hertfordshire	Lion & eagle/draped semi-nude female (S)
1922	Bushey, Hertfordshire	Draped female (morning) (S)
1923	London (RAF)	Eagle (B)
1926	London (Mercantile Marine Mem)	
1928	Workington, Cumbria (Designer with Alexander Carrick- sculptor)	
	Reliefs (soldier carrying comrade/soldier, wife & child/ miners/shipbuilders (B)	
-	Slough, Berks(Horlicks)	Female (mourning) (B)

Francis William Doyle-Jones (1873-1938)

1921	Jarrow, Tyne & Wear	Figure (Peace) (B)
1921	Teddington, Gt London	Sword, cap & wreath (S)
1921	Waterloo, Merseyside	Victory (B)
1921	Weymouth, Dorset	Christ/ angels (Ascension) (S)

1922	Brighouse, West Yorkshire	Victory (B)
1922	Cockermouth, Cumbria	Victory (B)
1922	Elland, West Yorkshire	Soldier (B)
1922	Gravesend, Kent	Victory (B)
1922	Sutton Coldfield, W.Midlands	Soldier (B)
1922	Woking, Surrey	Victory (B)
1924	Gillingham, Kent	Christ + angels (Ascension) (S)
1925	Houghton le Spring, Durham (St Michael & All Angels Ch)	Relief (soldiers) (S)
-	Northfleet, Kent (Bevans Cement Works)	Britannia (S)
-	Partick & Whiteinch, Strathclyde	Victory (B)

Edward Alfred Briscoe Drury (1856-1944)

1920	City of London (London Troops)	Soldiers (B)
1921	Hertford, Hertfordshire	White Hart (B)
1921	Pershore Abbey, Worcs	Victory(B)+relief(dead soldier/ widow & child/angel) (B)
1922	Malvern College, Worcs	St. George (B)
1922	Kidderminster, Worcs	Angel,child+relief(dead soldier/ widow & child/angel) (B)
1922	Weston-super-Mare, Somerset	Victory (B)
1923	Dinnington, North'ld (St Matthews Ch)	Relief(dead soldier/ widow & child/angel) (B)
1925	Denstone College, Staffs	St. George (B)

Arthur Sherwood Edwards (1897-1960)

1925	Sale and Ashton-upon-Mersey, Cheshire	St George (S)

Robert Jackson Emerson 1878-1944

1920	Walsall, Staffs (J.H Carless)	Portrait bust of Carless (B)
-	Wolverhampton, Staffs (D.M. Harris)	Pedestal with bust of Harris (B) + relief (of Harris at his post) (B)

David Evans (1893-1959)

1928	Liverpool(Anglican Cathedral-Women of WWI)	Relief (nurse/ wounded soldier) (S)

Henry Charles Fehr (1867-1940)

1920	Eastbourne, East Sussex	Victory (B)
1920	Grangetown, S.Glamorgan	Victory (B)
1921	Langholm, Dumfries	Victory (B)
1922	Burton-on-Trent, Staffs	Victory / St George / Peace (B)
1922	Hammersmith, W.London	Female (Peace) (B)
1922	Leeds, W.Yorks	Victory / St George / Peace (B)
1922	Lockerbie, Dumfries	Victory (B)
1923	Colchester, Essex	Victory / St George / Peace (B)
1923	Lisburn, Antrim	Victory (B)
1924	Keighley, W.Yorks	Victory / soldier / sailor (B)
1925	Portadown, Armagh	Victory, dying soldier (B)

Alexander Fisher (1864-1936)

-	Stanway, Gloucestershire	St George (B)

John Ashton Floyd

1921	Royton, Gt Manchester	Victory (B)
1922	Ashton-under-Lyne, Gt Manchester	Victory / soldier / lions (B)
1929	Manchester (Post Office)	Angel/ 2 children (B)

Stanhope Alexander Forbes (1857-1947)

-	Sancreed, Cornwall (W.A Forbes)	Relief portrait (B)

Sir George James Frampton (1860-1928)

1918	Birkenhead, Cheshire (Edith Cavell)	Bust of Cavell (S) (lost)
1919	Knowlton, Kent	Cross + 3 servicemen & nurse (S)
1920	London (Edith Cavell)	Female (Cavell) / woman & child (S)
1920	Ledsham, Cheshire (Phoenix Assurance Co)	2 reliefs (soldiers/allegorical females) (B)
1921	Fordham, Cambridgeshire	St George (B)
1921	Hove, West Sussex	St George (B)
1921	London (Pearl Assurance - now at Peterborough)	St. George (B)
1922	Maidstone, Kent	St. George (B)
1922	Portrush, Antrim (Design - with F Ransom, sculptor)	Victory/ relief(battleships) (B)

William Silver Frith (1850-1924)

1917	Smithfield, London (St Bartholomew the Great)	Crucifix (B)
1919	Muston, Leicestershire	Crucifix (S)
1920	Carlton Colville, Suffolk	Relief (Christ/ soldier/ sailor) (B)

Henry Snell Gamley (1865-1928)

1920	Montrose, Tayside	Victory (B)
1922	Cupar, Fife	Victory (B)

Walter Henry Gilbert (1872-1945) * with Louis Weingartner

1920	London (Women War Workers)	Relief (nurse) (B)
1921	*Birmingham, (Gas Dept.)	Britannia (B)
1921	*Eccleston, Cheshire	Soldier/ female+ reliefs(soldiers/airman/ naval scene) (B)
1924	Crewe, Cheshire	Britannia (B)
1924	Troon, Strathclyde	Britannia (B)
1926	*Burnley, Lancs	Cenotaph with servicemen (S)/2 women (B)
1927	Morley, W.Yorks	Britannia (B)
1931	Clydebank, Strathclyde	Female (Peace) (B)
-	Birmingham (Conservative Club)	
-	West Jesmond, Tyneside	Relief (Crucifixion/soldier with nurse/sailor with mother & child, St George/ St Michael/ angels) (B)
-	*Liverpool (Anglican Cathedral - 55th W.Lancs Div)	Angel / soldier (S)

Eric Gill (1882-1940)

1918	Briantspuddle, Dorset	Cross + Christ / Virgin & Child (S)
1919	Bisham, Berkshire	Crucifix (S)
1920	Chirk, Clwyd	Soldier (relief) (S)
1921	South Harting, W.Sussex	Cross + reliefs (Saints George, Patrick, Andrew, David) (S)
1921	Trumpington, Cambs	Cross+ St George/St Michael/Soldier/ Virgin & Child (S)
1923	Leeds, (University)	Relief(Christ driving moneylenders out of the temple) (S)
1927	Fleetwood, Lancs (Rossall School)	Relief (Crucifixion / Baptism / Beheading of John the Baptist) (W)

MacDonald Gill (1884-1947)

1920	Parkstone, Dorset (St. Osmund's Church)	Crucifix (S)

Ernest George Gillick (1874-1951)
1920	Forest Row, E.Sussex	Lantern cross + 2 children (S)
1922	Bishops Stortford, Hertfordshire	Military equipment (S)
1924	Glasgow	Lions / wreath (S)

Countess Feodora Gleichen (1861-1922)
-	Sandhurst, Berkshire (British Army)	3 soldiers (B)

Thomas Good
1922	Buckhaven, Fife	Soldier (kilted) (S)

Basil Gotto (1866 - 1954)
1920	Berriedale & Braemore, Highland	St. Andrew (B)
1924	London (Army & Navy Club)	Mars (B)

William D Gough
1920	East Malling, Kent (with Sir J Ninian Comper - design)	
	Lantern Cross with Crucifix+ Virgin & St John/Virgin & Child	
	St George/St Martin & Soldier (S)	
1920	Rogate, W.Sussex	Crucifix + 2 Marys / S George (S)
1920	Uppingham, Leics	Lantern Cross+ Sts George/Michael/Mother & Child/Crucifix (S)
1923	Burgess Hill, W.Sussex	St. George (B)
1927	Greenhill, Gt London (St. John the Baptist Ch)	Relief (angels) (S)

Richard Reginald Goulden (1877-1932)
1920	London (St Michael's Ch, Cornhill)	St Michael/children/wild beasts(B)
1920	Bromsgrove (St John's Ch)	Relief (allegorical female + marching soldiers) (B)
1921	Brightlingsea, Essex	Cenotaph + reliefs (soldiers/sailors) (B)
1921	London (Bank of England)	St Christopher/ Christ child (B)
1922	Gateshead, Tyne & Wear	Cenotaph + relief (Semi-nude warrior) (B)
1923	Crompton, Gt Manchester	Male warrior /children / wild beasts (B)
1923	Kingston-upon-Thames, Surrey	Man / child (B)
1923	Malvern, Hereford & Worcester	Winged male (Youth) (B)
1923	Reigate & Redhill, Surrey	Man / child (B)
1924	Dover, Kent	Boy (B)
1924	London (Middlesex County & Regt)	Soldier+reliefs(ruined Cathedral/ airman & plane/sailor & ship) (B)
1928	Hackney (St. John's Ch-Hackney Rifles)	St Michael/children B)
-	Crouch End, N.London (Old Hornseyans School)	St Michael/children (B)
-	Pitsea, Essex	Female with torch (B)

Edward Aveling Green (1842-1930)
1921	Eversholt, Bedfordshire	St. Michael (B)

Morris Harding (1874-1964)
1920	Eastergate, W.Sussex	Lion (S)

Charles Leonard Hartwell (1873-1951)
1921	Bushmills, Antrim	Soldier (B)
1921	Wimbledon, Gt London	Obelisk+ relief (winged female- Peace) (B)
1921	Wimbledon, Gt London (King's College School)(lost)	Nude youth (B)
1922	Denbigh, Clwyd	Victory(B)
1922	Sandwich, Kent (designed by Omar Ramsden)	Relief(St George) (B)
1923	Newcastle upon Tyne,	St George + reliefs (Peace / Justice (B) /lion (S)
1924	Clacton-on-Sea, Essex	Victory (B)

1926	Armagh, County Armagh	Female (Peace with Honour) (B)
1927	London (City of London School)	Relief (soldiers - mourning) (S)
1936	St. Mary-le-bone, London	St. George (B)
-	Ledsham, Cheshire (Sun Insurance)	Medieval knight (B)
-	Liverpool St. Station, London Field Marshall Sir H Wilson,	relief portrait (B)

Herbert Haseltine (1877-1962)
| - | London (Cavalry & Guards' Club) | Cavalry horse (B) |

Vincent Hill
| 1920 | Beverley, Yorkshire | Seated figures (army, navy, air force, medical servs) (S) |

Frederick Brook Hitch (1877-1957)
1919	St Mary's Ch, Shotley, Suffolk-(8 & 9th Submarine Flotillas)	Column + reliefs (Madonna / dolphins) (B)
1920	Pirbright, Surrey	Crucifix (W)
1922	London (Submarine Corps) Relief (submarine control rm/sea nymphs & females) (B)
1929	London (RSPCA)	Relief (Victory/ Army animals) (B)

Charles d'Orville Pilkington Jackson (1887-1973)
1920	Aberdeen (S Mary's Cathedral)	Crucifix (W)
1920	Markinch, Fife	St George (S)
1921	Dalbeattie, Galloway	Column + lion (B)
1921	Dumfries, (Dumfries Academy)	Relief (St. George) (B)
1921	Edinburgh, (St Giles' Cathedral-5th Royal Scots) Relief (female/2 mourning soldiers) (B)
1921	Kelso, Borders	Cross+ St. George (B)
1922	Rothesay, Bute	Victory (or angel) (B)
1923	Edinburgh, (Royal Bank of Scotland) Relief (figure (Sacrifice) & battle scene) (B)
1924	Alloa, Central Scotland	St Margaret + 3 soldiers (B)
1927	Edinburgh, (Scottish Nat War Mem)	Relief (portrait of Haig) (B)
1927	Edinburgh, (Scottish Nat War Mem- Reveille) Robed figure holding a sword (B)
-	Durham (Cathedral -Durham Light Inf) Reredos (St George/St Cuthbert/King Oswald)

Humphries Jackson
| 1923 | Shildon, Durham | Soldier (kneeling) (B) |

Charles Sargeant Jagger (1885-1934)
1921	Brimington, Derbyshire	Britannia (S)
1921	Manchester (S & J Watts)	Soldier (B)
1921	Portsmouth, Hampshire	Soldier & sailor with machine guns (S)
1922	Bedford	St George, or Justice (S)
1922	Hoylake & West Kirby, Lancs	Soldier / Hooded female (Humanity) (B)
1922	London (Gt Western Railway, Paddington)	Soldier (reading a letter) (B)
1925	London (Royal Artillery) Soldiers (B) + reliefs (battle scenes) (S)
1933	London (Thames House, Millbank)	St George / Britannia (S)

Francis Jahn
| 1923 | Sheffield, (York & Lancs Regt - with GN Morewood & R Smith) | Victory (B) |

Sir William Goscombe John (1860-1952)
1916	Liverpool (Marine Engine Room Heroes)	2 men (engineers) (S)
1917	Cardiff, (Lt Col Lord Ninian Crichton-Stuart)	Portrait of soldier (B)
1918	Heddon on the Wall (St Andrew's Ch- Capt. & Major Knott) Relief (equest knight) (S)
1921	Lampeter, Dyfed	Soldier (B)

1921	Port Sunlight,Cheshire Cross+ 11 figures(3 soldiers /2 women/6 children)+12 reliefs (B)
1923	Llanelli, Dyfed	Soldier (B)
1923	Newcastle,(Commercials) Enlisting men, women & children (B)+St George/soldiers (S)
1924	Carmarthen, Dyfed	Soldier (B)
1924	Llandaff, S.Glamorgan	Female/ man/ boy (B)
1924	Penarth, S.Glamorgan	Victory (B)
1924	Wrexham, Clwyd (Royal Welch) Soldiers (18C with flag / 20C) (B)
-	Hereford (Cathedral - Basil Webb) Altar + St Michael/St George/St Aethelbert (S)
-	Kilkhampton, Cornwall (Lt.Col Thynne) Obelisk with relief portrait (B)
-	Kilkhampton, Cornwall, Parish ch, Lt.Col Thynne - Equestrian + reliefs (B)

Adrian Jones (1845-1938)
1922   Bridgnorth, Shropshire   Soldier (B)
1922   Gloucester, Royal Glos Hussars Yeomanry   Cross+ reliefs(soldiers/ horses)(B)
1924   London (Cavalry Division)   St George+ relief(cavalry of the Empire)(B)
1924   Uxbridge, W.London   Victory (B)

Hazel Kennedy
1927   Edinburgh (Chaplains - Scottish Nat War Mem)   Relief (B)

Eric Henri Kennington (1888-1960)
1924   London (24th East Surrey Division)   3 soldiers (S)

William Charles Holland King (1884-1973)
1922   Dover, Kent (SE & Chatham Railway)   Victory/soldier/sailor/ bugler (B)
1922   Wolverhampton, Staffordshire   Obelisk+ figs of Servicemen/St George (S)

Gilbert Ledward (1888-1960)
1920   Cockfosters, Gt London (Heddon Court School)   Relief (bugler with flag) (B)
1920   Witham, Essex   Cross+ relief(kneeling soldier with lance/St George) (B)
1921   Abergavenny, Gwent (3rd Battn Monmouthshire Regt)   Soldier (B)
1921   Stonyhurst College, Lancs   Relief (Crucifixion / 4 servicemen) (S)
1923   Blackpool, Lancs   Obelisk+ reliefs(War/Justice, civilians/servicemen & Peace
                                with civilians/ servicemen + soldier/ sailor) (B)
1923   Harrogate, N.Yorks   Obelisk + reliefs (soldier w. bugle/ female (Peace)) (S)
1925   Stockport, Gt Manchester   Britannia / semi-naked warrior (S)
1926   London (Guards Division)   Cenotaph+ 5 soldiers(B)+ reliefs(battle /equipment)(B)

Alexander Leslie (1873-1930)
1921   Hawick, Borders   Victory (male) (B)

Benjamin Lloyd
1922   Llandrindod Wells, Powys   Soldier (mourning) (B)
1924   Rhayader, Powys   Clock Tower + Soldier / Peace / Welsh dragon
                                            defeating German eagle (S)

David McGill
1927   Kilmarnock, Strathclyde   Male nude (B)

Edgar Bertram MacKennal (1863-1932)
1919   Cliveden House, Bucks (Canadian Officers & men)   Victory (S)
1920   Taplow, Bucks (J.H & G.W Grenfell)   Relief (Apollo & chariot) (S)
1922   London (House of Commons)   Relief (angel / Faith / Fortitude) (S)

1923	London (Caledonian Club)	Mother & Son (Courage & sacrifice) (B)
1924	Blackburn, Lancashire	Female / dying man (B)
-	Eton, Berkshire	Male nude (B)

Robert Tait McKenzie (1867-1938)
| 1922 | Cambridge, | Soldier (B) |
| 1927 | Edinburgh,(Scottish-American Mem) | Soldier(B)+ relief (civilians/soldiers) (B) |

Thomas Eyre Macklin (1863-1943)
| 1927 | Bangor, Down | Female (Erin) / lion's head (B) |

William Macmillan (1887-1977)
| 1921 | Echt, Grampian | Soldier (Gordon Highlander) (B) |
| 1925 | Aberdeen, Grampian | Lion (S) |

Carlo Magnoni
| 1920 | Sledmere, Humberside (Waggoners) | Column + reliefs of war scenes (S) |

Sydney March (1875-1968)
1920	Lower Sydenham, S. London (South Suburban Gas Company)	Victory (B)
1921	Bromley(St Peter & St Paul Ch)	Lantern cross+ St George/ Victory/St Michael/ Peace (S)
1922	Bromley, Kent	Liberty/ Victory & Peace (B)
1922	Radcliffe, Gt Manchester	Liberty / Victory & Peace (B)
-	Whitefield, Gt Manchester	Victory (B)

Vernon March (1891-1930)
1922	Glossop, Derbyshire	Victory (B)
1922	Hadfield, Derbyshire	Victory (B)
1922	Lewes, E.Sussex	Victory / Peace/ Liberty (B)
1927	Londonderry	Victory / soldier/ sailor (B)

Walter Marsden (1882-1969)
1921	Fairhaven, Lancs (The White Church)	Pulpit, carved angel & soldier (W)
1923	Church, Lancs	Female (Peace) (S)
1923	Church, Lancs (Elmfield Hall)	Relief(2 females- Resurrection/ Peace) (B)
1924	St Anne's-on-Sea,Lancs	Female(Peace)/soldier/mother & child+ reliefs(soldiers) (B)
1925	Heywood, Lancs	Female (Peace) (B)
1928	Bolton, Lancs	Struggle & Sacrifice (woman & man / Pieta) (B)

Gertrude Alice Meredith-Williams (1878-1934)
1924	Paisley, Strathclyde	Mounted Crusader / 4 soldiers (B)
1925	Fleetwood, Lancs (Rossall School)	Pulpit w. carving of St John the Baptist (W)
1927	Edinburgh(S.Nat War Mem-Shrine)	St Michael(W)+ relief(servicemen & women)(B)
1927	Edinburgh, (S. Nat War Mem - Women's Services)	Relief (women) (B)
1927	Edinburgh,(S Nat War Mem- Nurses)	Relief(nurses/soldier on stretcher) (B)

Leonard Stanford Merrifield (1880-1943)
1920	Burnham, Bucks	Cross + Soldier (B)
1920	Newlyn, Cornwall	Cross + relief (Soldiers /Sailors) (B)
1922	Holywood, Down	Soldier (B)
1923	Comber, Down	Soldier (B)
1923	Stafford (County Mem-WR Colton, completed by Merrifield)	Angel & horse (B)
1923	Trawsfynydd, Gwynedd (Hedd Wynn-Pte E Humphrey)	Pte.Humphrey as shepherd (B)
1924	Bodmin, Cornwall (Duke of Cornwall Light Infantry)	Soldier (B)
1928	Lurgan, Armagh	Victory (B)
1931	Merthyr Tydfil, Mid Glamorgan	Female / miner / mother & child (B)

John Millard (1874-1957)
1921   Macclesfield, Cheshire   Dead soldier/ Brittania/ female mourner (B)

Alec Miller (1879 - 1961)
1920   Bampton, Oxfordshire   Market Cross + St George (S)
1921   Aberdeen, (St Mary's Cathedral)   Crucifix (W)
1921   Lockinge, Oxfordshire   Lantern Cross with Crucifixion (S)
1922   Chester   Cross+ Saints Werburgh, Maurice, David, Michael, Alban, George (S)
1925   Millom, Cumbria   St Michael+ reliefs(Soldier/Sailor/Airman) (S)
-     Cassington, Oxfordshire   Crucifix (S)
-     Saintbury, Gloucestershire   Crucifix (S)

Paul Raphael Montford (1868-1938)
1921   Croydon, Surrey   Cenotaph + Soldier / Woman & Child (B)

Joseph Herbert Morcom (1871-1942)
1919   Brampton, S.Yorks (Cortonwood Colliery)   Column+Soldier, Miner (B)
1919   Ellistown, Leics (St Christopher's Ch)   Plaque+ Crucifixion +St John(S)
1921   Quorn, Leics   Cenotaph + Relief (St George) (S)
-     Loughborough, Leics (All Saints Ch)   Plaque + 3 figs +
     Relief (9 figures - civilians and servicemen (S)

George N Morewood
1923   Sheffield, (Yorks. & Lancs Regt - with R Smith & F Lahn)   Soldier (B)

Sir Alfred Munnings (1878-1959)
1920   Mells, Somerset (St Andrew's Ch - E Horner mem)   Equestrian portrait (B)

Alex Murdoch
1922   Auchterderran, Fife   Cross+ 3 figures representing Army, Navy & Airforce (S)

George Noble (1879-1965)
1920   Leicester (Bridge Rd School)   Cenotaph+ relief (dead nude +2 boys) (B)

George Henry Paulin (1888-1962)
1917   Glendevon, Perth (Glendevon Ch- WN Russell)   Relief(Victory/bust of Russell) (B)
1920   Dollar Academy, Central Scotland   Male (Youth) (B)
1921   Denny & Dunnipace, Central Scotland   Female (seated) (B)
1921   Kirkcudbright, Galloway   Bare-chested warrior & child (B)
1922   Milngavie, Strathclyde   Female figure (kneeling) (B)
1924   Rutherglen, Lanarkshire   Semi-nude male with flag (B)

Henry Alfred Pegram (1862-1937)
1918   Norwich, (Edith Cavell)   bust of Cavell (B) + relief (soldier) (S)
1921   Liverpool, (Cunard)   Victory (male) (B)
1926   Preston, Lancs   Obelisk + relief (Victory) (S)
1928   Cardiff,(Welsh Nat War Mem)   Victory (male)/soldier/sailor/airman (B)

Joseph Phillips
1924   Liverpool,(Liverpool Newsroom)   Britannia /soldiers /sailor /nurse /girl (B)

W J Pickering
1921   Richmond, Surrey   Soldier / sailor (S)

Edward Maxwell Courtney Pollock (1877-1943)
1922   Ilfracombe, Devon   Winged figure (B)
1922   Newton Abbot, Devon   Freedom with broken chain (B)
1923   Broadstairs, Kent   Cross+ reliefs (soldiers/battle/Crucifixion) (B)

Frederick William Pomeroy (1856-1924)
1921   Ramsey, Cambs   St George (B)
1922   Coleraine, Londonderry   Cenotaph + Soldier/ Female (Daughter of Erin) (B)
1922   Dungannon, Tyrone   Soldier (B)
1922   Kensington, London   Column + relief (female / Remembrance) (S)
1922   Larne, Antrim   Cenotaph + Soldier / Sailor (B)
-       Banbridge, Down   Soldier (B)

Henry Poole (1873-1928)
1921   Evesham, Worcestershire   Soldier (B)
1921   Nottingham, (Capt. A Ball)   Portrait figure / female (B) + reliefs (bi-planes) (B)
1922   Nottingham, (Nottingham High School for Boys)   Soldier (officer) (B)
1922   Pudsey, W.Yorkshire   Soldier (B)
1924   Chatham, Kent (Royal Navy)   Obelisk + lions (S)
1924   Plymouth, Devon (Royal Navy)   Obelisk + lions (S)
1924   Portsmouth, Hants (Royal Navy)   Obelisk + lions (S)
         London (County Council Staff)

Percy Herbert Portsmouth (1874-1953)
1921   Elgin, Grampian   Draped female (Victory) (B)
1922   Lossiemouth, Grampian   Male (Victory & Peace) (B)
1923   Thurso, Caithness   Victory / child (B)
1923   Wick, Caithness   Victory (B)
1925   Olrig, Caithness   Allegorical male (B)
1927   Edinburgh(S.Nat War Mem)   Survival of the Spirit/ Freedom & Charity (S)

Sophie Rosamund Praeger (1867-1954)
1923   Belfast, (Campbell College)   4 figs (Courage/ Life/ Death/ Endurance) (S)
1927   Omagh,Tyrone (County Memorial)   Cenotaph+ Angels w. dead soldiers (S)
-       Belfast, (Belfast Royal Academy)   Angels (S)
-       Belfast, (Rosemary Street Presbyterian Church)

Henry Price
1921   Annan, Dumfries   Soldier (B)
1921   Maxwelltown & Troqueer, Dumfries   Soldier (B)

Alexander Proudfoot (1878-1957)
1922   Chatham, Kent (Royal Engineers)   Obelisk + reliefs (Victory / Soldiers / Britannia
                          + male & female/ Youth with 'Resignation' & 'Hope') (S)
1924   Bearsden, Strathclyde   Angel / wounded soldier (B)
1924   Greenock, Strathclyde   Victory (B)
1924   Stanley, Perth   Soldier (kilted) (B)
-       Cambuslang, Lanarkshire   Soldier (kilted) (B)

Omar Ramsden (1873-1939)
1922   Sandwich, Kent   (Designer - sculptor: CL Hartwell) Relief (St George (B)

Frank Ransom (b.1874)
1922   Portrush, Antrim (w. Sir G Frampton, designer)   Victory (B) + relief (battleships) (B)

Richard Ray (1884-1968)
1922   Sunderland, Tyne & Wear   Victory (B)

John Reid (born c1890)
1920   Newcastle upon Tyne, (Newcastle Exchange)   Victory (B)
1921   West Pelton, Durham (St. Paul's Ch)   Relief (saints/soldier/sailor/St George) (S)
1923   North Shields   Relief (Angel / marching servicemen) (B)
1924   Newcastle (6th Northumberland Fusiliers)   St George (B)

William Reynolds-Stephens (1862-1943)
1920   Great Warley, Essex (St Mary the Virgin Ch)   Relief (dead Christ /angels) (S)
1920   Saltburn by the Sea, N. Yorks   Cross + relief (dead Christ / angels) (B)
1920   London (St Marylebone Ch - G. V Pearce)   Relief (St George and dragon
1921   London (Atlas Insurance - now at Lytham, Lancs)   St. George (B)
1921   Hampstead, London (Lyndhurst Road Church)   Relief (St George) (S)
1922   Caterham, Surrey (Caterham School)   St. George (B)
1922   Orpington, (St Olave's & St Saviour's Sch) (designer, G Bayes, sculptor)   St Olaf (B)
-       Wargrave, Berkshire (St Mary's - RA Chancellor)   Relief (St George + portrait)

William Birnie Rhind (1853-1933)
1921   Edinburgh, (Fettes School)   Soldier (wounded officer) (B)
1921   Kelty, Fife   Soldier (S)
1921   Wallasey, Merseyside   Soldier/ kneeling sailor/ colonial soldier (S)
1923   Plymouth, Devon   Victory (B)
1925   Buckie, Grampian   Soldier / sailor (B)
-       Prestonpans, Lothian   Soldier (S)

Dorothy Anne Aldrich Rope
1919   Leiston, Suffolk   Crucifix (B)
1920   Little Glemham, Suffolk   Relief (Christ / man & child) (S)

Ellen Mary Rope (1855-1934)
1921   Eversholt, Berkshire (St John the Baptist)   Relief (Christ + dead soldier (B)
-       Blaxhall, Suffolk   Relief (Christ / dead soldier) (B)
-       Broadstairs, Kent (St Peter's Ch- WM Churchill)   Relief (angel) (B)
-       Broadstairs, (Stone House Sch - now in W.Calder, Lothian)   Relief (angel) (S)

Harild Rosenkrantz (1870-1964)
1918   Camberwell (St George's Church)   Christ (B)

Louis Frederick Roslyn (1878-1940)
1920   Bexhill, East Sussex   Victory (B)
1920   Buxton, Derbyshire   Victory (B)
1920   Swanley, Kent   Victory (B)
1921   Blackley, Lancs   Victory(+ figs of Army/Navy Airforce & Nursing -stolen) (B)
1921   Darwen, Lancs   Victory + reliefs (soldier / sailor / nurse) (B)
1921   Greengates, W. Yorks   Victory (B)
1921   Ipswich (Ipswich District of Oddfellows - lost)
1922   Calverley, W.Yorks   Draped female (Patriotism) (B)
1922   Denholme, W.Yorks   Soldier (mourning) (B)
1922   Oswaldtwistle, Lancs   Victory + 2 Soldiers (1 wounded) (B)
1922   Wetherby, W.Yorks   Victory + 2 lions (B)
1923   Basingstoke, Hampshire   Victory (B)
1923   Clitheroe, Lancashire   Soldier (mourning) (B)
1923   Holyhead, Anglesey   Cenotaph + reliefs (soldier / sailor) (B)
1923   Morriston, W.Glamorgan   Female (Peace) (B)
1923   Slaidburn, Lancashire   Soldier (mourning) (B)
1923   Tottenham, London   Victory (B)

1924	Haslingden, Lancashire	2 Soldiers (1 wounded) (B)
1924	Portstewart, Londonderry	Soldier (B)
1925	Kenfig Hill & Pyle, Mid Glamorgan	Victory (B)
1925	Port Talbot, W.Glamorgan	Victory + reliefs (nude male & battle scene / female with child & lamb/ female / marching soldiers) (B)
1926	Maesteg, Mid Glamorgan	2 soldiers (1 wounded) (B)
1929	Rawtenstall, Lancs	Obelisk+ reliefs (soldiers/sailor/airman/civilians) (B)
-	Dromore, Down	Soldier (B)
-	Edinburgh (St. Giles Cathedral - Scottish Nurses)	Relief 2 female figures (B)

Thomas Rudge
| 1921 | Finsbury, London | Victory + reliefs (battles) (B) |

Mario Rutelli (1859-1941)
| 1921 | Aberystwyth, Dyfed (Welsh Presbyterian Tabernacle) | Victory (B) |
| 1923 | Aberystwyth, Dyfed | Victory + female nude (Humanity) (B) |

George Salvesen
| 1927 | Edinburgh, (Scottish Nat War Mem) | Peace / Mercury (S) |

Francis William Sargant (1870-1960)
| 1924 | Oakham, Leics(Oakham School) | Relief(Biblical scenes/grief-stricken people)(B) |

Kathleen Scott (1878-1948)
1922	Oundle, Northants (Oundle School)	Nude boy (arm raised) (B)
1923	Huntingdon, Cambs	Soldier (seated) (B)
-	Slimbridge,(Wildfowl Trust - Winchester Coll boys)	Nude boy (arm raised) (B)

Anthony Smith
| 1920 | Earl Shilton, Leics | Female (Peace)+ reliefs (St George / St Michael / woman & child)(S) |
| 1921 | Whetstone, Leics | Crucifix (W) |

George Herbert Tyson Smith (1883-1972)
1915	Mossley Hill,Lancs (St Matthew's Ch- GL Harford)	Relief (medallion portrait) (B)
1920	Hightown, Lancs	Kneeling female (angel) (S)
1922	Accrington, Lancs	Draped female (Grief) (S)
1924	Liverpool, (Post Office)	Brittania (seated) (S)
1925	Bangor-Is-Y-Coed, Clwyd	Female (mourning) (S)
1925	Birkenhead, Merseyside	2 females (mourners) (S)
1927	Fleetwood, Lancs	Male 'warrior' (S)
1927	Southport, Lancs	Reliefs (Brittania / Brittania mourning) (S)
1928	Durham (Cathedral)	Cross + relief (military artifacts) (S)
1930	Liverpool	Reliefs (marching soldiers / mourners) (B)
-	Bootle, Lancs (Christ Church)	Relief (lion) (S)
-	Liverpool (Scottish War Memorial)	Relief Soldiers mourning (B)
-	Liverpool (St. Andrew's Ch - Scottish War Memorial)	
-	Wavertree, Merseyside	2 females(mourners)(S)

Roy Smith
| 1923 | Sheffield, (York & Lancs Regt) (with F Jahn & G. Morewood) | Soldier (B) |

Phoebe Stabler (1879-1955)
| 1925 | London (Underground Electric Railway Co of London) | St George (B) |

James Alexander Stevenson (1881-1937)
| 1922 | Dingwall, Highland | Soldier (kilted) (B) |

J Swift

| 1923 | Cinderford, Gloucestershire | Soldier (B) |
| - | Shepley, West Yorkshire | Soldier (mourning) (B) |

John Edward Taylerson

| 1921 | Warlingham, Surrey | Soldier / woman & child (S) |

George Havard Thomas (1893-1933)

1920	Frilford, Garford & Marcham, Oxfordshire	Crucifix (S)
1920	Waterhead, Gt Manchester	Soldier (helmet aloft) (B)
1922	Mountain Ash, S Wales (with J Havard Thomas)	robed female/slain male nude + reliefs (soldier/sailor/nurse) (B)
1924	Milnrow, Gt Manchester	Soldier (B)
1926	Abertillery, Gwent	Soldier (B)
1927	Merthyr Vale & Aberfan, Mid Glamorgan	Soldier (helmet aloft) (B)

James Havard Thomas (1854-1921)

| 1922 | Mountain Ash (completed by GH Thomas) | robed female/slain male nude + reliefs (soldier/sailor/nurse)(B) |

Sir William Thornycroft (1850-1925)

1920	Moulton, Cheshire	Soldier (S)
1922	Knutsford, Cheshire (H Baronian)	Soldier (B)
1922	Luton, Bedfordshire	Female (Courage bringing Victory) (B)

Albert Toft (1862-1949)

1921	Chadderton, Lancashire	Soldier (B)
1921	London (Joint City & Midland Bank)	Relief (St George / angel) (B)
1921	Sandon, Staffordshire	Soldier (B)
1921	Stone, Staffordshire	Soldier (mourning) (B)
1922	Leamington Spa, Warwickshire	Soldier (mourning) (B)
1922	Oldham, Lancashire	5 Soldiers on mound (B)
1922	Streatham, London	Soldier (mourning) (B)
1923	Benenden, Kent	female (seated) (B)
1923	Thornton Clevelys, Lancashire	Soldier (mourning) (B)
1924	London (Royal Fusiliers)	Soldier (B)
1924	Smethwick, Staffs (Guest, Keen & Nettlefolds Ltd)	Soldier (mourning) (B)
1925	Birmingham,	3 semi-nude males(soldier/sailor/airman)/female(nursing) (B)

Newbury Abbott Trent (1885-1953)

1921	Beckenham, Kent	Column + reliefs (St. George / phoenix) (S)
1921	East Barnet Valley, London	Victory (B) + relief (lion & eagle) (S)
1922	Ilford, Essex	Cross + Soldier (B)
1922	Wanstead, London	Victory (B)
1924	Tredegar, Gwent	Cross + soldier (B)
1925	Wallsend, Northumberland	Victory (B)
-	North Berwick, Lothian (St Baldred's - A.B Porter	Portrait relief (B)

Alfred Turner (1874-1940)

| 1920 | Fulham, London | Female (Peace) / cherub (B) |
| 1921 | Kingsthorpe, Northants | St George (B) |

1921	Northampton,(ER Mobbs) Female (Fame)+ reliefs(bust of Mobbs/rugby game/battle) (B)
1921	Radyr, South Glamorgan	Female (Peace) / cherub (B)
1924	St. Helier, Jersey (Victoria College)	Sir Galahad (B)
1924	Winchester, Hampshire (Winchester College)	2 Crusaders (S)

John Tweed (1869-1933)

1920	Bodfari, Clwyd	Soldier (B)
1921	East Wemyss, Fife	Soldier (B)
1922	Winchester, Hampshire (King's Royal Rifle Corps)	Soldier (B)
1924	London (Rifle Brigade)	Soldier / two 19th century soldiers (B)
1925	Barnsley, S. Yorks	Soldier + relief (Victory) (B)
1926	London (Earl Kitchener)	Portrait figure (B)
1932	London (House of Lords)	Female / youth (B)

George Wade (1853-1933)

| 1931 | Quarry Bank, Staffordshire | Christ (B) |

Arthur George Walker (1861-1939)

1918	Heston, Gt London	Soldier+ reliefs (naval gun crew/ bi-plane & airmen) (S)
1920	Heath Town, W.Midlands	Soldier+ reliefs(naval gun crew/ bi-plane & airmen) (B)
1920	Sevenoaks, Kent	Soldier+ reliefs (naval gun crew/ bi-plane & airmen) (B)
1921	Chesham, Bucks	Soldier (B)
1921	Limehouse, London	Christ + relief (battle scene) (B)
1922	Dartford, Kent	Soldier + reliefs (naval gun crew/ bi-plane & airmen) (B)
1923	Ironbridge, Shropshire	Soldier (B)
1923	Shrewsbury, (Old Salopians)	Sir P Sydney+ reliefs(battle/death of Sydney) (B)
1924	Derby	Mother & child (B)
-	Derby, (St. Werburgh's Church)	Christ (B)
-	Keith, Grampian (6th Battn, Gordon Highlanders)	Soldier (kilted) (B)

Clifford Wallett

| 1921 | Burslem, Staffs | Cenotaph + relief (soldier (mourning)) (S) |

Josef Walter

| - | Fordington, Dorset (St George's) - German Prisoners of War) Relief (German soldier (kneeling)) (S) |

Louis Weingartner (c1864-1936)

All with Walter Gilbert

1921	Birmingham (Gas Dept.)	Britannia (B)
1922	Eccleston, Cheshire	Soldier/ female+ reliefs-of servicemen (B)
1926	Burnley, Lancashire	Cenotaph with servicemen (S) /2 women (B)
-	Liverpool (Anglican Cathedral- 55th W.Lancs Div)	Angel / soldier (S)

Charles E Whiffen

| 1920 | Bury St Edmunds, Suffolk (Suffolk Regt) | Cenotaph with angels (S) |
| 1922 | London (Waterloo Station - LSWR. & Southern Railway) Britannia with Bellona & Victory / mourners / Peace & Victory (S) |

Frederick John Wilcoxson (1888-1974)

| 1921 | Ripon, N.Yorks | Column + bust of soldier (B) |
| 1922 | Hale, Gt Manchester | Soldier (B) |

Margaret Winser
1921	Wakefield, W. Yorks (Grammar School)	Soldier (officer with bugle) (B)
1922	Hastings & St Leonards, E.Sussex	
		Victory+ reliefs (soldiers/ pilot in cockpit/ sailors laying mines) (B)

Francis Derwent Wood (1871-1926)
1920	Ditchingham, Norfolk	Soldier (dead) (B)
1922	Keswick, Cumbria	Relief (female (Britannia) (S)
1922	Liverpool, (Cotton Exchange)	Soldier (B)
1925	London (Machine Gun Corps)	David (nude) (B)
-	Whitehaven, Cumbria	Relief (Victory) (S)

Frank Arnold Wright (1874-1930)
1924	Belfast (Queen's University)	Victory / wounded youth (B)
	(Designer, Sir Thomas Brock)	

Allan Gairdner Wyon (1882 - 1962)
1921	Doncaster, S.Yorks (Inst of Mining Engineers)	Female (with flag) (B)
1922	Hinckley, Leics	Robed female (arms outstretched) (B)
1922	Shrewsbury, (County Memorial)	St Michael (in a round 'temple') (B)
1924	Oswestry, Shropshire (Cambrian Railways)	Robed female(arms outstretched) (B)

Alexander Young
1922	New Stevenston, Strathclyde	Soldier (mourning) (S)

James Young
1922	Renfrew, Strathclyde	Column + Lion (S)
1923	Ardrossan, Strathclyde	Cross + reliefs (St Colomba / Robert Bruce & Admiral Sir A Wood/ David Livingstone, Robert Burns & James Watt) (B)
1923	Belfast, (Campbell College)	4 figures (Courage / Life / Death / Endurance) (S)
	(Designer: R. Praeger - sculptor)	

ACKNOWLEDGEMENTS

All photographs of war memorials are by the author with the exceptions of Pls.3, 105 and 108, courtesy of Birmingham City Council. The photos of Alexander Carrick's clay models for the Royal Artillery and Royal Engineer memorials (Pls.160 & 161) were kindly provided by Alexander's grandson, John Scott. (Jim McGinlay's help here was also much appreciated).

The author and publishers also wish to express their thanks to the following sources for their permission to reproduce additional related images: National Army Museum - Pl.21; Imperial War Museum - Pls.50, 59, 61, 90, 116, 117, 171, 172, 246, 256, 265, 266; National Galleries of Scotland - Pl.135; Daily Mirror - Pl.224; British Library - Pl.245. The photo of Goscombe John's 'Guardian Angel' (Pl.62) is courtesy of Peter Nahum at the Leicester Galleries. The Christmas card (Pl.63) is from the collection of Roy Slaymaker and was generously made available with the help of Stephanie Jenkins of All Saints Church, Headington. The photo of the unveiling ceremony at Macclesfield (Pl.214) was kindly provided by Doug Pickford. Pls.25, 68 & 103 are from 'Punch', Pls.127 & 205 from 'Illustrated London News' and Pls.121 & 137 from 'The Graphic'. Thanks also to Stockport Metropolitan Borough Council for their permission to use photos of the Stockport memorial and maquette (Pls.30 & 221) and similarly to Stonyhurst College (Pls.131 & 132), Reverend Malcolm Shaw at St Michael & All Angels Church, Brimington (Pl.23). and Ian Bartlett at St Columb's Cathedral, Londonderry, (Pl.227).

Acknowledgements must also be made, and thanks given, to the numerous people who have helped with the research, writing and publication of this book. The always helpful staff of Macclesfield Library, whose assistance was repeatedly called upon, must be singled out, as must the invaluable assistance provided by the staff of the UK National Inventory of War Memorials at the Imperial War Museum. Trevor Temple and Eamon Baker were generous with their time and information, for which I thank them. I would also like to thank Dr David Lomas for his encouragement and perceptive comments when this project was at its embryonic stage as a Master's dissertation. Most importantly I must acknowledge the hard work and unfailing enthusiasm of my editor and publisher Richard Barnes, who also provided the excellent cover photo. His remarkable patience and sensible suggestions have been greatly appreciated. Finally thanks to Pat Havis, whose enthusiasm and interest in this subject sparked my own and whose intelligent and incisive comments I have always valued.

In publishing this book, Frontier Publishing acknowledge gratefully the support of The Paul Mellon Centre for Studies in British Art.

Frontier Publishing Subscription Service gratefully acknowledge
the support of initial subscribers to this publication:

Neil Lanham ~ John W.Mills ~ John Jennings FRBS ~ Philip Blacker ~
Diana Thompson ~ Philip Jackson ~ Caroline Scott, Andy Scott Public Art ~
Ri Streeter ~ ES Morris~ Kath Taylor ~ Michael Gaskin ~ Gerald Laing ~
Robert Freidus ~ Viv Astling ~ Chloe Cockerill ~ Professor James Stevens Curl~
J.A.T Corke ~ Ann Sproat, H Moore Institute Library ~ Jo Darke ~ Charles Gurrey~
John Agnew ~ Terence Game ~ J Moir-Shepherd ~ Mrs Louise Boreham ~
Dr Pauline Rose ~ Percy Hood ~ Dr Julian W.S Litten FSA ~ P.T Higgins ~
Dr William Marshall ~ Mrs J.R Owen ~ Mrs JR Owen~ Peter Faulkner ~
Major Mark L Perkins T.D ~Carol Measures ~Richard Thackerah ~ Joyce Millard~
Michael Brookes ~ Anthony Bradbury ~ A.L Stubbs~Mr B.J Barrett ~Peter Hirschmann~
A.D Smith ~ M Mabett ~ Peter Kent-Baguley~ Rev.Canon G Greenwood ~
David A Ashley Hall~ Jill Tweed ~ H. Spry-Leverton~ Mr D.S Humberton ~
David Challen ~ Derek Boorman ~Mr TJ Bunting ~David Marlow~RD Pankhurst~
LJ Byrnes~ RG Coleman ~ Simon Heffer ~David Ware~ P Ward Jackson ~ Jeremy
Warren ~ Fr Derek West ~ DM Barnes~ TR Peacock ~ Mrs M Muraszko ~ DW
DW Routledge ~NW Hide ~ Richard Boden~ Rod Richard ~ MJ. O'Dell~ M Dales~
Richard & Sarah Cocke~ Michael Creese ~ Helen E Beale ~ AG McCue~Andrew McIntosh
Patrick ~ Jenny Freeman~PN Buckingham~James Butler RA~ Steve & Sylva Allen~
Timothy Stevens~ Peter & Jennifer Jones~ Bronze Restorations Ltd, Surbiton~
Mrs R Wakefield~Mrs J Morgan~Sophie Richard, Daniel Katz Ltd~ Guy Sinclair~
TimothyLees~ Humphrey Ocean R.A~ Mary Baker ~ J St Brioc Hooper ~
Viscount Ridley ~ David Hill ~ Library, Royal Academy of Arts ~ Dr Alan Clark
Marcia Pirie ~ Richard Graham ~ Mr D.A Hanlon ~ Brian Davis ~ L. Peter Cooper ~
Duncan Hayes ~ Dr Jonathan Hicks ~ Maria Ions ~ Ray McKenzie ~ James Brazier ~
Cecil Ballantine~Roland Buggey~Elizabeth Jackson~David Willey~Jean Nicholls ~
Terry Harrison~P Blackburn~PS Mason~Christopher Read~David Singleton
M.W Daniell ~ Gp Captain L.E Robins CBE ~ R.J Keatley ~ Mr C.A Hewson ~
Dr Eric Webb ~ Guy Powell ~ Paul Atterbury~ Keith Harris~ AL Stubbs~
Brennan Hiorns~ Brian Ash~ Greg Hughes~ Hilary Rosser~ Thomas Long~
Alan Seymour ~ Edward Dixon ~ PS McMillan~ Jo Stockdale ~ Steven J. Spear~
John Barker ~ Mrs Gail White ~ Mavis Sellers ~ E Turner ~ A Cashmore~ Ian
Rank-Broadley ~ Mr V.N Creek, RAF Museum ~ JE Hodgson~ S.G Kinsella ~ Robert
Harrison ~ Shirley Thatcher ~ Martin Passande~ Edward D Hancock Mrs
Jenny King ~ David Nash ~ Jeff Munroe ~ John Amos~ Mrs E.J Fairman ~ Gerard
F Rawson ~ Mrs Jenny Beyer ~ Major RF Hanbury ~ DH Flude ~ Robin
Sharp~CL Boothman~JA Bolton~ David L Bright ~William Gorvall- King~
Richard Harman~Gordon Wellham ~Andrew Polkey ~ MG Felton ~ Eric Webb ~
E Dixon ~ JC Watson Smith ~ R.J Marsh ~D Houghton ~ Sue Steer~CD Biggart~
J.C Hulme ~ Philip Davies, English Heritage ~ Keith Mackness ~ LR Corner ~
RR Jammes ~Frances Speakman ~ Mark Smith ~ Tom Tuerlinckx ~ P Hilferink ~
H.S Blagg ~ Tracy Bentley ~ Peter & Sarah Miles ~ Andrew Mann~ PD Farman~
P Corke ~RT Green~HH Judge Nicholas Philpott ~Glenn McKeown~John Vigar FSA~
Ronald Bubb ~ Malcolm Goode ~ The Library, National Museum of Wales ~
Alison Saville ~ Giles Quarme ~ Mr & Mrs D Wyatt ~ Brigadier Clive Elderton CBE~
Tim Dunce~ Matthew Saunders ~ Barry Friend ~ Bart Bryerton~ Matthew Hyde~
Roger Bowdler ~ Lucy Churchill ~ Dr Michael Turner ~ Paul Blumsom ~
Hilary Wheeler~ Robin Harries~ WW Hanna ~ Russell Taylor ~ Gavin Stamp~
Alan Buckley ~ Richard MA Marshall ~ M Lainchbury ~ Correlli Barnett CBE~
R Moore~Gareth Luke~ P Mason ~Robin Davies~Paul T Hornby~Michael Brown~
RE Stillman ~ Clifford Livens ~ Peter Cormack MBE, FSA ~ Denis Kenyon ~
PM Gant ~ Mrs O Aylmer

LIST OF PLATES

1. Macclesfield. John Millard, 1921
2. Macclesfield. John Millard, 1921
3. Birmingham (relief detail 1). William Bloye, 1925
4. Nelson Scouts. J. Davies, 1919
5. Bury 1 - detail. Hermon Cawthra, 1920
6. Llandaff. William Goscombe John, 1924
7. Port Sunlight (detail 1). William Goscombe John, 1924
8. Manchester Regiment. William Thornycroft, 1908
9. Haslingden. L.F Roslyn, 1924
10. Fettes school. William Birnie Rhind, 1921
11. Cavalry Division. Adrian Jones, 1924
12. St Marylebone. Charles Hartwell, 1907 / 1936
13. Sandwich. Charles Hartwell, 1922
14. 6th Northumberland Fusiliers. John Reid, 1924
15. Burton-upon-Trent. H.C Fehr, 1922
16. Leeds. H.C Fehr, 1922
17. St George. H.C Fehr, exhibited 1898
18. Maidstone. Sir George Frampton, 1922
19. Trumpington. Eric Gill, 1921
20. Liverpool Newsroom, Joseph Phillips, 1924
21. The Freeman's Oath. W.N Gardiner, 1803
22. Morley. Walter Gilbert, 1927
23. Troon. Walter Gilbert, 1924
24. Brimington. C.S Jagger
25. Keswick. F. Derwent Wood, 1922
26. Hanley. Harold Brownsword, 1922
27. The Shrine of Honour.J.B Partridge, Punch 10:11:1920
28. Macclesfield. J. Millard, 1921
29. Liverpool Newsroom. Joseph Phillips, 1924
30. Southport. G.H Tyson Smith, 1927
31. Stockport. Gilbert Ledward, 1925
32. Liverpool post Office. G.H Tyson Smith, 1927
33. Royal Welch Fusiliers, Wrexham. Sir William Goscombe John, 1924
34. Royston. Benjamin Clemens, 1922
35. Paisley. Alice Meredith Williams, 1924
36. Strathspey & District
37. Royal Fusiliers, Holborn. Albert Toft, 1924
38. Hale. Frederick Wilcoxson, 1922
39. Buckie. William Birnie Rhind, 1925
40. Twickenham. Mortimer Brown, 1921
41. Londonderry. Vernon March 1927
42. Llandaff. Sir William Goscombe John, 1924
43. Waggoners Memorial. Sir Mark Sykes & Carlo Magnoni, 1919
44. Waggoners Memorial. (detail 1). Sir M. Sykes & Carlo Magnoni, 1919
45. Liverpool. G.H Tyson Smith, 1930
46. Bolton. Walter Marsden, 1932
47. Bolton. Walter Marsden, 1932
48. Scottish American Memorial, Edinburgh. R.T McKenzie, 1927
49. Scottish American Memorial, Edinburgh (detail). R.T McKenzie, 1927
50. Step into Your Place. 1915 poster
51. The Commercials' War Memorial, Newcastle. Sir W Goscombe John, 1923
52. The Commercials', Newcastle (detail 1). Sir W Goscombe John, 1923
53. The Departure, Arc de Triomphe, Paris. Francois Rude, 1833-36
54. Workington (detail 1). Alexander Carrick, 1928
55. St Anne's-on-Sea (detail 1). Walter Marsden, 1924
56. Bury (detail 2). Hermon Cawthra, 1920
57. The Commercials, Newcastle (detail 2). Sir W Goscombe John, 1923

58. 'The Commercials', Newcastle (detail 3). Sir William Goscombe John, 1923
59. Wartime Poster 'Women of Britain say Go!' E.V Kealey, 1915
60. Clayton-le-Moors. John Cassidy, 1920
61. Wartime Poster 'Go! It's your duty lad', 1915
62. Wartime Christmas card
63. 'The Guardian Angel'. William Goscombe John, c1888
64. Bradford. H.H Martyn Ltd, 1922
65. Londonderry. Vernon March, 1927
66. Dingwall. James Alexander Stevenson, 1922
67. Cameronians War Memorial, Glasgow. Philip Lindsey Clark, 1924
68. The Recruit who Took to it Kindly'. H.M Bateman, Punch, 17:1:1917
69. Waggoners' Memorial (detail 2). Sir M. Sykes & Carlo Magnoni, 1919
70. Renfrew. James Young, 1922
71. Kingston-upon-Thames. Richard Goulden, 1923
72. Alfreton. William Aumonier, 1927
73. St Michael's, Cornhill, London. Richard Goulden, 1920
74. Crompton. Richard Goulden, 1923
75. Kirkcudbright. George Henry Paulin, 1921
76. Port Sunlight. Sir William Goscombe John, 1921
77. Croydon (detail 1). Paul Montford, 1921
78. St Anne's-on-Sea (detail 2). Walter Marsden, 1924
79. Derby. Arthur George Walker, 1924
80. Port Sunlight (detail 2). Sir William Goscombe John, 1921
81. Port Sunlight (detail 3). Sir William Goscombe John, 1921
82. Port Sunlight (detail 4). Sir William Goscombe John, 1921
83. Port Sunlight (detail 5). Sir William Goscombe John, 1921
84. Cavell Monument, London. Sir George Frampton, 1920
85. Nurse Cavell, Sir George Frampton, 1920
86. 'Miss Edith Cavell murdered. Remember!' postcard, c1915
87. Exeter. John Angel, 1923
88. Rawtenstall. L.F Roslyn, 1929
89. Rawtenstall (detail 1) L.F Roslyn, 1929
90. Darwen. L.F Roslyn, 1921
91. 'The Greatest Mother in the World' by A.E Foringer. Poster 1918
92. Bury (detail 2). Hermon Cawthra, 1920
93. Twickenham. Mortimer Brown. 1921
94. Birmingham. Albert Toft, 1925
95. Birmingham Hall of Memory, Arch; S.Cooke & W.Twist, 1925
96. Women's Memorial, Scottish Nat War Mem. A. Meredith Williams, 1927
97. Bury (detail 3). Hermon Cawthra, 1920
98. Bury (detail 4). Hermon Cawthra, 1920
99. Bury (detail 5). Hermon Cawthra, 1920
100. Rawtenstall (detail 2) L.F Roslyn, 1929
101. Rawtenstall (detail 3) L.F Roslyn, 1929
102. Workington (detail 2). Alexander Carrick, 1928
103. Croydon (detail 2) Paul Montford, 1921
104. 'Well done the New Army', F.H Townsend, Punch, July 1916
105. Port Sunlight (detail 6). Sir William Goscombe John, 1921
106. Birmingham (detail 2). William Bloye, 1925
107. St Anne's-on-Sea(detail 3). Walter Marsden, 1924
108. Huntingdon. Kathleen Scott, 1923
109. Abergavenny. Gilbert Ledward, 1921
110. Broughton. Gilbert Bayes, 1923
111. Trumpington. Eric Gill, 1921
112. Chirk. Eric Gill, 1920
113. St Anne's-on-Sea (detail 4). Walter Marsden, 1924
114. Blackburn. Bertram MacKennal, 1924
115. Portadown. H.C Fehr, 1925
116. Prudential Assurance Co, London. Ferdinand Blundstone, 1922
117. A frame from the film: 'The Battle of the Somme', 1916
118. Painting: 'Paths of Glory'.Christopher Nevinson, 1918, Imp War Museum

119. Birmingham (detail 3). William Bloye, 1925
120. Alloa. Charles Pilkington Jackson, 1924
121. Illustration: The Great Sacrifice, James Clark, The Graphic 25/12/1914
122. Red Cross Notice. The Times 25/5/1915
123. Liverpool Newsroom. Joseph Philips, 1924
124. Longridge. Messrs Alberti, 1920
125. Tredegar. Newbury Trent, 1924
126. Strensall. George Milburn & Son, 1922
127. Eastham. C.J Allen, 1924
128. Illustration: 'The White Comrade', G.H Swinstead, Illus' London News 1915
129. Limehouse, London. A.G Walker, 1921
130. Limehouse, London (relief detail). A.G Walker, 1921
131. Lower Peover. John Cassidy, 1922
132. Stonyhurst. Gilbert Ledward, 1920
133. Stonyhurst (relief detail). Gilbert Ledward, 1920
134. Bisham. Eric Gill, 1919
135. Briantspuddle. Eric Gill, 1918
136. The Risen Christ, Jacob Epstein, 1919
137. Briantspuddle (detail). Eric Gill, 1918
138. Proposed memorial for the dead of overseas contingents. Eric Gill, 1916
139. Leeds University war memorial. Eric Gill, 1923
140. Saltburn by the Sea, William Reynolds-Stephens, 1920
141. Great Warley. William Reynolds-Stephens, 1920
142. Kidderminster. Alfred Drury, 1922
143. Kidderminster (detail 1). Alfred Drury, 1922
144. Workington (detail 3). Alexander Carrick, 1928
145. The Cross of Sacrifice. Sir Reginald Blomfield
146. The Great War Stone. Sir Edwin Lutyens
147. Ditchingham. Francis Derwent Wood, 1920
148. Liverpool. Lionel Budden, Arch & G.H Tyson Smith, Sc
149. The Cenotaph. Sir Edwin Lutyens
150. Manchester -1. Sir Edwin Lutyens. 1924
151. Manchester -2. Sir Edwin Lutyens. 1924
152. Thrumpton
153. Royal Artillery Memorial (detail 1). C.S Jagger, 1925
154. Royal Artillery Memorial (detail 2). C.S Jagger, 1925
155. Royal Artillery Memorial (detail 3). C.S Jagger, 1925
156. Royal Artillery Memorial (detail 4). C.S Jagger, 1925
157. Royal Artillery Memorial (detail 5). C.S Jagger, 1925
158. Blackpool (detail 1). Gilbert Ledward, 1923
159. Stourbridge, John Cassidy, 1923
160. Hastings. Margaret Winser, 1922
161. Southwark. Philip Lindsey Clark, 1922
162. Dartford. A.G walker, 1922
163. Royal Engineers .Scottish Nat War Memorial, clay model. A Carrick, 1927
164. Royal Engineers .Scottish Nat War Memorial, clay model. A Carrick, 1927
165. Port Sunlight (detail 7). Sir William Goscombe John, 1921
166. Submarine Corps Memorial, London. Frederick Brook Hitch, 1922
167. Submarine Corps Memorial, London (detail).Frederick Brook Hitch, 1922
168. Guards Division Memorial. Gilbert Ledward and H.Bradshaw, 1926
169. Guards Division Memorial (detail 1). Gilbert Ledward, 1926
170. Royal Artillery Memorial (detail 6). C.S Jagger, 1925
171. Royal Artillery Memorial (detail 7). C.S Jagger, 1925
172. RSPCA Memorial Dispensary, Kilburn. Frederick Brook Hitch, 1929
173. Imperial Camel Corps Memorial, London. Cecil Brown, 1920
174. The First Battle of Ypres 1914 C.S Jagger, 1918-19. Imp War Museum
175. 'No Man's Land' .C.S Jagger, 1919-20. Imperial War Museum
176. Cambrai Tank Memorial. Louverval, France. C.S Jagger, 1928
177. Blackpool War Memorial. E. Prestwich & Gilbert Ledward, 1923
178. Blackpool (detail 2). Gilbert Ledward, 1923
179. Blackpool (detail 3). Gilbert Ledward, 1923

180. St Anne's-on-Sea. Walter Marsden, 1924
181. North Shields. John Reid, 1923
182. Ashton-under-Lyne. John Ashton Floyd, 1922
183. Berwick-upon-Tweed. Alexander Carrick, 1923
184. Bridgwater. John Angel, 1925
185. Bridgwater (detail 1). John Angel, 1925
186. Trumpington. Eric Gill, 1921
187. Shrewsbury. A.G Wyon, 1922
188. Bexhill-on-Sea. L.F Roslyn, 1923
189. Leeds. H.C Fehr, 1922
190. Hoylake & West Kirby. C.S Jagger, 1922
191. Denbigh. Charles Hartwell, 1922
192. Lockerbie. H.C Fehr, 1922
193. Thornton. Harold Brownsword, 1922
194. Whitefield. Sydney March, 1922
195. Lewes. Vernon March, 1922
196. Lewes (detail 1). Vernon March, 1922
197. Radcliffe. Sydney March, 1922
198. Skipton. John Cassidy, 1922
199. Maxwelltown & Troqueer. Henry Price, 1921
200. Stafford. Joseph Whiteread & Sons, manufacturers
201. Twickenham. Mortimer Brown, 1921
202. Bridgenorth. Adrian Jones, 1922
203. Cambridge. R.T MacKenzie, 1922
204. Lt. Haron Baronian. Knutsford, Sir William Thornycroft, 1918
205. Guards Crimean Memorial. John Bell, 1860
206. Winsford Boer War Memorial. Herbert Chatham, 1906
207. Ipswich Boer War Memorial. Albert Toft, 1906
208. Streatham. Albert Toft, 1922
209. The Queen in the East End. Illustrated London News, 19:8:1916
210. Westfield Memorial Village. Jennie Delahunt, 1924
211. Stockport Memorial Hall, 1925
212. Oban. Alexander Carrick, 1923
213. Fraserburgh. Alexander Carrick, 1923
214. Portsmouth. C.S Jagger, 1921
215. Gateshead. Richard Goulden, 1922
216. Hinckley. J.A Gotch & Allan Wyon, 1922
217. Hinckley (detail 1). Allan Wyon, 1922
218. Macclesfield Unveiling Ceremony, 1921
219. Beverley. R.H Whiteing & Vincent Hill, 1920
220. Beverley (detail 1). Vincent Hill, 1920
221. Mells. Sir Edwin Lutyens, architect & Sir George Frampton Sc, 1921
222. Hove Sir Edwin Lutyens and Sir George Frampton, 1921
223. Fordham. Sir Edwin Lutyens and Sir George Frampton, 1921
224. Horner Memorial, Mells. Sir E Lutyens and Sir Alfred Munnings, 1920
225. Horner Memorial (detail 1), Sir Alfred Munnings, 1920
226. Model for Stockport memorial. Gilbert Ledward
227. Model for Londonderry memorial. Vernon March, 1923
228. York & Lancaster Regt, Sheffield. G Morwood, F Jahn & Roy Smith, 1923
229. 'The War Memorial: Will it be like this?' W.K Haselden, Daily Mirror 1916
230. Liverpool (detail 1). G.H Tyson Smith, 1930
231. LNWR memorial, Euston Station. R Wynn Owen, 1921
232. Stourbridge. John Cassidy, 1923
233. Burnley. Walter Gilbert, 1926
234. Macclesfield. John Millard, 1921
235. Southwark. Philip Lindsey Clark, 1922
236. Rickmansworth. William Reid Dick, 1921
237. Bushey. William Reid Dick, 1922
238. Church. Walter Marsden, 1923
239. Todmorden (detail). Gilbert Bayes, 1924
240. Todmorden. Gilbert Bayes, 1924

INDEX

E

F